Maya Calendar Origins

THE WILLIAM & BETTYE NOWLIN SERIES
in Art, History, and Culture of the Western Hemisphere

MAYA CALENDAR ORIGINS

Monuments, Mythistory, and the Materialization of Time

PRUDENCE M. RICE

UNIVERSITY OF TEXAS PRESS, AUSTIN

Requests for permission to reproduce material

from this work should be sent to:

    Permissions

    University of Texas Press

    P.O. Box 7819

    Austin, TX 78713-7819

    www.utexas.edu/utpress/about/bpermission.html

♾ The paper used in this book meets the minimum requirements of
ANSI/NISO Z39.48-1992 (R1997) (Permanence of Paper).

Library of Congress Cataloging-in-Publication Data

Rice, Prudence M.

   Maya calendar origins : monuments, mythistory, and the materialization
of time / Prudence M. Rice. — 1st ed.

     p. cm. — (William and Bettye Nowlin series)

   Includes bibliographical references and index.

   ISBN 978-0-292-71688-9 (cloth : alk. paper) — ISBN 978-0-292-71692-6
(pbk. : alk. paper)

1. Maya calendar.   2. Maya chronology.   3. Maya cosmology.   I. Title.

   F1435.3.C14R53 2007

   529´.32978427—dc22

                        2007001064

Dedicated to my happy, helpful, quadripartite band of were-jaguar wannabes: Poodie, Binz, Ted, and especially Harley

Authority over the annual calendar . . . , or of other chronological instruments like clock time, not only controls aspects of the everyday lives of persons but also connects this level of control to a more comprehensive universe that entails critical values and potencies in which governance is grounded. Controlling these temporal media variously implies control over this more comprehensive order and its definition, as well as over the capacity to mediate this wider order into the fundamental social being. . . . Hence the importance of calendric and related time shifts connected with sociopolitical changes is more than political in the narrow pragmatic sense. It has to do with the construction of cultural governance through reaching into the body time of persons and coordinating it with values embedded in the "world time" of a wider constructed universe of power.

—Nancy Munn, "The Cultural Anthropology of Time: A Critical Essay"

Contents

List of Figures and Tables

TABLES

Note on Orthography and Dates

or nonlinguists and nonepigraphers, determining proper orthography and adhering to it can be a nightmare, particularly in dealing with the long time spans and the many languages, Mayan and non-Mayan, covered here. In general, I attempt to follow the orthographic conventions for Mayan words that have been accepted by the Academia de Lenguas Mayas in Guatemala, because I am most familiar with them. The use of Spanish diacritical marks on place names or cultural phases drawn from Maya or other indigenous languages often differs between Mexico and Guatemala, however, and in some cases Maya names themselves have changed recently (e.g., the site formerly known as Abaj Takalik is now Tak'alik Ab'aj). This makes it difficult to provide a concise explanation of my decisions, but in the end I have striven for internal consistency.

Dealing with time and the ancient Maya poses some twenty-first-century challenges, a major one being how to report radiocarbon dates. New and recently published dates typically note that they have been calibrated (to the bristlecone-pine curve) and are distinguished by capitalization, for example, as "B.C." dates, with older dates in radiocarbon years presented as lowercase "b.c." But in older publications, heavily cited herein, few dates have been calibrated and virtually all are capitalized as B.C. or A.D. How to distinguish the two? I elected generally to present all dates capitalized as B.C. or A.D.; calibrated dates are specifically designated, as, for example, "753 cal. B.C." (or cal. A.D.); where it is specifically indicated that dates are not calibrated or when calibrated and noncalibrated dates appear together, I use "b.c." or "a.d." to distinguish the latter.

Another important issue about Maya calendrics still remains, although the arguments have expired to the merest murmur: how to correlate the Maya and modern calendars (see Sharer 1994:755–762, for discussion). At least a dozen possibilities have been proposed and evidence can be adduced to support each one. One question concerns which Western calendar to compare to, the Julian or the Gregorian; another concerns specific correlation factors, the most popular being versions of the Goodman-Martínez-Thompson (GMT) correlation, named after its promulgators. Variations in dating resulting from the different correlations can be seen in an important date referred to repeatedly in this text, the beginning of Creation for the Maya and the point from which they (and the Epi-Olmec) calculated time in the Long Count. This date is August 11, 3114 B.C. in the Gregorian calendar using the GMT 584,283 correlation factor. The Thompson correlation of 584,285 days places the date at August 13, 3114 B.C.; using these factors with the Julian calendar instead of the Gregorian, the dates are September 6 and 8, respectively. I have elected to use the Gregorian calendar with the GMT correlation factor of 584,283 days (as I do in *Maya Political Science*), thus placing the creation date on August 11, 3114 B.C. It is important for me to state this choice, as several elements in my discussion concern this date as it approximates the fall solar zenith in southern Mesoamerica, although August 13 is not unacceptable.

Preface

n *Maya Political Science: Time, Astronomy, and the Cosmos* (2004), I explore a suggestion by the late ethnohistorian Munro S. Edmonson (1979) that Classic-period Maya geopolitics might have been based on the same structural principles that operated in the Postclassic and Colonial periods. The core structuring principle was the rotation of divinely sanctioned geopolitical capitals on a roughly 256-year cycle known as the *may*. Edmonson also suggested the possibility that Preclassic (or Formative) Mesoamerican societies might have observed *may* cycles, a possibility that I explore briefly in my text.

The present volume is both an outgrowth of *Maya Political Science* (*MPS*) and a "prequel" to it: an exploration of Maya Time with a capital T. While writing *MPS* I became fascinated with Maya calendars, particularly their beginnings. It is widely known that the Maya possessed astonishingly accurate systems of recording time (Time) in a series of intermeshing cycles. Today's archaeologists, however, not only take these achievements for granted, they consistently fail to incorporate the role of the calendar and calendrical celebrations into their interpretations of Maya history. Certainly, early twentieth century–style Maya calendrical studies have long been out of fashion: calendrical glyphs are now deciphered, the chronological position of the Maya civilization is no longer a significant archaeological problem, correlation issues are largely settled, and radiometric methods are available to date deposits not otherwise datable by inscriptions. But, perplexingly, examination of the calendars as expressions of deep-seated structural, cultural, and historical identities seems to hold little intrinsic interest for Mayanists (see P. Rice N.d.b). Questions about when, why, where, and how these instruments developed and what deeper meanings might be embedded are rarely if ever asked—not because the answers are transparently evident but because the questions themselves somehow do not seem to have been deemed pertinent. As I note in the preface to *MPS* (Rice 2004:xvii), scholars commonly pay lip service to the concept of Maya kings as "lords of time," but they have not examined what this might mean in an evidentiary or hypothetico-deductive sense: *if* Maya kings were indeed lords of time, *then* how does that structure our expectations about how this role might be manifest in the material record? Similarly, archaeologists, art historians, and epigraphers generally regard Maya rulers as embodiments of the sun—sun-god-kings—but how and when did such solar personification occur?

Such questions increasingly engaged me. Relevant information, speculation, and theorizing is scattered in a multitude of sources dating throughout the last century, but no effective synthesis exists. So as I worked on *MPS*, the masses of calendrical data and arguments that I was unable to include in that volume emerged as chapters for this one.

I was also intrigued by issues of early interactions between the lowland Maya and the cultures of the Isthmus of Tehuantepec, which also are rarely addressed directly by Maya archaeologists and, until recently, rather unsystematically by art historians. Postulated relations between the Maya and the Olmec, and between the Maya and Izapa, have been debated, swinging from direct contact to no contact, and "influence" has generally been shown to lie in the area of language and kingly symbolism evident in iconography and art styles (see, e.g., most recently, Fields and Reents-Budet 2005a). For my part, I believe language and royal symbolism are profound structural components of key cultural transmissions and that they, plus calendrical knowledge, signify long and deep-seated relations between the Maya and the societies of the Isthmian region. And I argue that both shared in an early rotational geopolitical system based on the *may*.

I began writing *Maya Calendar Origins* at the same time I was working on *MPS*, envisioning the present book as setting forth the underlying story of the earlier one, that is, the changing relations of very early Mesoamericans with their environment and their development of a broadly shared worldview and calendars. In fact, many elements of this worldview (such as quadripartition) are widespread not only in Mesoamerica but throughout much of the New World, and some can be recognized in the Old World in Greco-Roman and Indo-European civilizations. This has led at least one author (Kelley 1974) to suggest that Mesoamerican calendars originated in the Old World around the time of Aristotle.

Such suggestions aside, my perspective in this endeavor is something like that of Rosemary Joyce in an article exploring the unintended consequences of the beginnings of monumental construction in Formative Mesoamerica: "People engaged in making these monuments and those simply witnessing the events would have experienced profound changes in spatiality, connection to place, and materialization of time at multiple scales as a result of the new constructions," she writes. "But these changes cannot automatically be taken as the intended consequences of these projects" (Joyce 2003:8). Similarly, but millennia earlier, I contend, people making the observations that eventually led to calendars, and those whose daily lives would have been guided by the mysterious machinations of celestial bodies, would neither have known nor intended that the Long Count and *may*-dominated political organization would be end-products of their efforts. But, it is undeniable that the course of Mesoamerican cosmology and epistemology was predicated on the early observations that led to the development of systematic timekeeping. Time was *materialized*—that is, transformed into various kinds of physical reality—as well as politicized, and these processes stand at the core of *Maya Calendar Origins*.

In this volume, I propose that some key elements of ancient Mesoamerican cultures, particularly those relating to time and calendrical celebrations, have histories of as much as a millennium before full dependence on agriculture, permanent settlements, and the appearance of carved monuments. This may strike some readers as wildly improbable if not impossible. But I believe that rejection of such a proposition is rooted in an ethnocentrism that makes it difficult for those of us in the technology-rich twenty-first-century world to believe that hunters and gatherers could have possessed a "scientific" curiosity and a rich intellectual culture. Moreover, for many of us in the United States—a nation-state with a formal history of little more than two centuries, an enthusiasm for change, and a mobile culture that has rendered extended-family living nearly extinct—it is also difficult to comprehend the existence of deep cultural traditions that choreographed family, community, and all of life for thousands of generations. A compelling example of such tradition, however, was most recently evident in the April 2005 election and installation of Pope Benedict XVI as head of the Roman Catholic Church, which followed rituals and displayed symbols that have endured without change over centuries.

To understand the role of time and calendars in ancient Mesoamerica and among the Maya in particular, therefore, it is necessary to set aside such ethnocentrism and shortsightedness and suspend disbelief while reading the following pages. I ask that readers be willing to "imagine something different," in the thought-provoking words of Shirley Malcom, winner of the National Academy of Sciences 2003 Public Welfare Medal.

Maya Calendar Origins begins with the premise that the origin of the Mesoamerican calendars is a topic worthy of, and amenable to, investigation. Even though calendrical origins lie in the very distant past, I believe it is more useful to admit the how and why of this matter to scrutiny than to dismiss these difficult questions as unapproachable. Further, I am convinced that it is possible to amass a corpus of scientifically *plausible* (admittedly not airtight) data about how and why the process of calendrical development might have occurred, and to use principles of parsimony to evaluate these data. This exercise is admittedly largely inductive, but the alternative to informed speculation and induction in this case is to ignore a truly interesting core issue in ancient Maya culture history.

In investigating calendrical origins, then, I find myself situated amid a lively debate among philosophers and historians of science about hypothesis "testing": what is the relative value of a posteriori hypotheses that *accommodate data* versus those a priori hypotheses that *predict outcomes* (Lipton 2005; see also S. Brush 2005; Rothchild 2006; Stanger-Hall 2005)? My position here, as in *MPS*, is that to begin investigation of such issues it is necessary to accumulate data from multiple sources in order to bolster a position or emerging hypothesis. Prediction comes later. Questions of Maya calendrical origins and their cultural value or "meaning" have been disregarded for the last half century; the salient issue for me, therefore, is not the technicalities of addressing them via a strict hypothetico-deductive method but, rather, simply to reopen them to meaningful investigation. Nonetheless, I have crafted an if/then proposition that I examine in the text:

Given that my thesis is that the political power of early leaders was based on astro-calendrics, recording time, and demonstrating "control" over supernatural cosmic forces—"cosmo-political" power in Nancy Munn's (1992:109) terms—I propose that, *if* this is so, *then* we would expect that early objects of status and power should reflect calendrical and temporal concerns.

I should also comment here on my references to the *Popol Vuh*, the highland K'iche' Maya creation myth. As outlined in the chapters in this volume, I believe that this myth encodes the history of development of Mesoamerican calendars, and that the myth that we know today (Christenson 2003; D. Tedlock 1996) is the culmination of thousands of generations of reciting, rewriting, and performing this epic myth in song and dance. Some readers of early versions of this manuscript complained that the *Popol Vuh* is assuming an exaggerated role in interpreting the Classic lowland Maya cultural achievements, while others felt that I was distorting evidence to accommodate the *Popol Vuh* model. I cannot ignore the possibility that a kernel of truth might reside in both positions, but . . . let us "imagine something different": what *if* the *Popol Vuh* were the extant version of a very ancient myth, *then* what might we expect to recover archaeologically or iconographically?

Readers will note that my discussions address similar topics and reference the inspiring contributions of Linda Schele and David Freidel (most notably, Freidel and Schele 1988a, 1988b; Freidel, Schele, and Parker 1993; Schele and Freidel 1990), but I try to approach things from a slightly different angle. That is, I see those authors writing about the Classic Maya cosmos, creation, ritual, and rulership from an explicitly astronomical viewpoint, noting the relations between positions of planets, stars (especially Venus), constellations, the Milky Way, and so on, as they relate to rituals of creation and as the Maya would have experienced them in the night sky. I am less preoccupied with the explicit animation or personification of celestial bodies and their relation to Classic gods (à la Milbrath 1999) and more interested in the development of the calendars and their role in framing the legitimization, and rituals of legitimization, of kings and cosmic order.

Finally, I confess that in this book I am violating strong personal and professional convictions concerning the academic use of looted archaeological materials. As a former president of the Society for American Archaeology (1991–1993), founding editor of the SAA's journal *Latin American Antiquity* (1991–1994), and presidentially (William J. Clinton) appointed member of the U.S. Cultural Property Advisory Committee from 1994 to 2002, I fought vigorously in favor of legal action that would stop the importation of artifacts acquired without permits from their country of origin and opposed publication of articles about such artifacts in professional journals and other legitimizing venues. I have personally experienced the dire— even deadly—consequences of illicit excavations in the Maya area, and I abhor any and all activities that contribute to the desecration of the cultural patrimony of nation-states worldwide. I have taken considerable pride in my advocacy for protecting cultural heritage, but now I find myself in the awkwardly compromising position of needing to illustrate certain points about early Mesoamerican calendrics via unprovenienced Olmec and other materials. This was a personally difficult decision for me and I keep such illustrations to a minimum. I can only hope that my references to these artifacts constitute recognition of their singular contributions to understanding key aspects of Mesoamerican prehistory rather than being merely a shallow acknowledgment of their desirability as "collectibles."

Acknowledgments

umerous colleagues granted me the enormous favor of reading earlier versions of this manuscript and giving me the benefit of their greater experience with many issues; I am profoundly grateful to them for their suggestions and critiques. As with *Maya Political Science*, I particularly want to thank C. Andrew Hofling, who has cheerfully responded to my persistent questions about historical linguistics and orthography over the past few years. He also has allowed me his copy of Edmonson's *The Book of the Year* (1988) on semipermanent loan for about five years.

The present book benefited greatly from the critical comments of John E. Clark, who kindly sent me copies of many of his publications and generously allowed me to use the illustrations of Izapa monuments. I also appreciate the comments and suggestions of David A. Freidel, whose familiarity with early iconography and termination ritual, and the importance of "numeracy," prompted my closer attention to some of these matters. As usual, I was privileged to be able to exploit Don S. Rice's skills with computer illustration programs, and I am grateful to him for spending countless hours, and weekends away from sporting clays, to transform my often messy inked drafts into camera-ready form.

Finally, I acknowledge with many thanks the skills and assistance of Theresa May of the University of Texas Press and Kathy Bork.

Maya Calendar Origins

Introduction

 For Mesoamerican peoples and especially the Maya, time and cosmic order were inextricably fused. But when and how were the ideas and structures relating to time, the cosmos, and social order developed and integrated? Those questions lie at the heart of this book. My answer, in brief, is that their development began thousands of years ago through observations of cyclically occurring earthly and celestial phenomena. Such observations culminated in a complex set of calendrical principles and associated mytho-ritual practice that established the context for rulership and power in Mesoamerica . . . and this ordered context endured for millennia. My arguments are situated in the general area of the "anthropology of time" (Munn 1992), with more specific reference to three quasi-theoretical, cross-cultural frameworks. One is the "materialization of ideology" (DeMarrais, Castillo, and Earle 1996) and its politicization, specifically, the interrelated concepts and ideology(~ies) of time, calendrics, and the cosmos. Second, I am interested in how the materialization and politicization of these ideological constructs were harnessed into principles of order, legitimization, and wealth (Baines and Yoffee 1998, 2000). Third, I am concerned with the ways in which principles of order, legitimization/power, and wealth were combined with concepts of geotemporal space, distance, and the crafting and trade of exotic goods (Helms 1988, 1993).

My arguments are also situated in several contextual themes. For example, some thirty years ago Michael Coe (1973, 1978) began arguing that Maya myths, such as the *Popol Vuh* epic (Christenson 2003; D. Tedlock 1985, 1996), provide significant insights into the colorful scenes painted on Classic lowland Maya funerary pottery. Other sources illuminate places and events of the Mesoamerican Classic period, including the late Yucatecan "prophetic histories" (Edmonson 1982, 1986a; Schele, Grube, and Boot 1995), Aztec origin myths (Boone 1991; Schele and Guernsey Kappelman 2001), and Colonial-period documents. Additionally, the roles of astronomy and, to some degree, calendrics in geopolitical organization and ideology among the pre-Hispanic Maya are gaining more attention among scholars (Aveni 2001, 2002a; Edmonson 1988; Lamb 2002; Marcus 1992a; Milbrath 1999). Although considerable interest exists in the physical orientations of buildings to celestial phenomena

Historical memory in Mesoamerica transcended the rise and fall of individual civilizations and reproduced the beliefs and icons of an enduring world vision founded more than thirty centuries ago.

—David Freidel, *Landscape and Power in Ancient Mesoamerica* (see, e.g., Aveni and Hartung 1986), a deeper structurational role of astro-calendrical observations and ritual was until recently relatively ignored. But Munro Edmonson's (1988:x) exhaustive study of the "unitary calendrical system" of Mesoamerica—"the focal feature, greatest achievement, and almost the defining atribute [*sic*] of native America's most advanced civilization"—traces it back to the eighth century B.C.

Thirty years ago, Edmonson (1979) posed a series of intriguing "Postclassic questions about the Classic Maya" arising from his efforts to translate and annotate two of the Yucatecan indigenous histories known as the books of the *chilam b'alam* (speaker [*chilam*] of the jaguar priest [*b'alam*]). His studies prompted him to wonder if some of the features of Late Postclassic and early Colonial northern lowland Maya political organization might have relevance for understanding the Classic period. One of his interests was the possibility that the ca. 256-year calendrical cycle of the *may*, which structured the political geography of Late Postclassic Yucatán, also might have operated in the Classic-period southern lowlands. Despite archaeologists' awareness of long- and short-term calendrical cycling in the Maya area (A. Chase 1991; C. Jones 1991; Puleston 1979), such as celebration of the endings of twenty-year periods of time called *k'atuns*, no one had given serious attention to the applicability of the *may* model to the Classic Maya.

Recently, I (Rice 2004) pursued Edmonson's suggestions and used arguments based on direct historical analogy to retrodict the role of the *may* in the southern Maya lowlands. My investigation suggests that evidence can be adduced for the operation of the *may* beginning in the Preclassic period at sites around Tikal in central Petén, a possibility also suggested by Edmonson. But this prompted me to wonder why the Maya Long Count referenced a date in August of 3114 B.C. and, considered more broadly, when did the Mesoamerican calendars develop and where do the origins of calendrically based political ritual and power lie? The seemingly obvious answers to the last question are the Oaxaca area and the Gulf coastal Olmec region of Veracruz and Tabasco in the Formative period, where evidence for early writing is found. And, of course, Gulf coast origins

were a tantalizing possibility that Edmonson had sketched earlier in his musings.

But thirty years ago, relatively little was securely known about the Formative (or Preclassic) period in the Gulf coast region, or anywhere else in Mesoamerica, for that matter. In the decades since Edmonson proposed a series of ~256-year cycles based on repetitive occurrences of K'atuns 8 Ajaw, so important to the Maya, there have been numerous important developments in Mesoamerican studies that make this an opportune time to pursue new questions and lines of investigation into Formative sociopolitical organization and political ritual in the Maya lowlands. For example, there has been considerable new archaeological work on Archaic through Middle Formative sites throughout Mesoamerica, including in Oaxaca (e.g., Flannery 1986a; Flannery and Marcus 1983, 2005), the Olmec region (e.g., Coe 1989a; Coe and Diehl 1980; Coe and Grove 1981; Cyphers 1996, 1997, 1999; Diehl 2004; González Lauck 1996; Grove 1993, 1997, 1999; Rust 1992; Rust and Sharer 1988; Sharer 1989a; Sharer and Grove 1989; Stark and Arnold 1997; Symonds 1995; Wendt 2005a, 2005b), and the Pacific coast of Mexico (e.g., Blake et al. 1995; Ceja Tenorio 1985; Clark 1991, 2001, 2004; Clark and Blake 1994; Clark and Cheetham 2002; Hill, Blake, and Clark 1998; Voorhies 1989a, 2004; Voorhies et al. 2002).

Olmec site layout and iconography have been pursued anew (Reilly 1999, 2000; Tate 2001) and the post-Olmec period has been investigated archaeologically at Tres Zapotes (Pool 2000, 2003) and Cerro de las Mesas (Stark 1991), and by means of analysis of Epi-Olmec writing on the recently discovered La Mojarra stela (Houston and Coe 2003; Justeson and Kaufman 1993, 2004; Kaufman and Justeson 2001). In addition, excavations and new iconographic analyses at the Late Preclassic site of Izapa have been studied (Guernsey Kappelman 2001, 2002, 2003; Laughton 1997; Lowe, Lee, and Martínez 1982).

New archaeological research and epigraphic studies also have been undertaken at Kaminaljuyú (Hatch et al. 2001; Kaplan 1996; Mora-Marín 2005; Valdés 1997). In the Maya lowlands, a host of sites with Preclassic architecture have been excavated, including, in Petén—Nakbe and El Mirador (Hansen 1990, 1991b, 1998, 2000; Matheny 1986) and, most recently and spectacularly, San Bartolo (Saturno 2006; Saturno, Stuart, and Beltrán 2006; Saturno, Taube, and Stuart 2005); in Belize—Cerros (Freidel 1982, 2001b), Cuello (Hammond 1986, 1992, 1995), K'axob (McAnany 2004a), and Blackman Eddy (M. Brown 1997); and in Yucatán—Dzibilchaltun and Komchen (E. Andrews V 1986; Andrews and Andrews 1980) and Yaxuná (Stanton and Ardren 2005). New insights into early cultivators have emerged (Hansen et al. 2002; Pohl et al. 1996), and several syntheses or compendia of Preclassic or Formative research have appeared (e.g., Powis 2005a), including works on social patterns (Grove and Joyce 1999) and Maya art (Fields and Reents-Budet 2005a).

Moreover, new, well-annotated, and highly approachable translations of the highland Maya creation myth, *Popol Vuh*, have appeared (Christenson 2003; D. Tedlock 1985, 1996), making it far easier to investigate the complex correspondences that Coe noticed thirty years ago. Similarly, new annotated translations of the *Chilam Balam of Chumayel* (Edmonson 1986a) and the *Chilam Balam of Tizimin* (Edmonson 1982) permit fresh reflections on the relations between history and myth among the Postclassic lowland Maya.

POPOL VUH, A MAYA CREATION MYTH

Many of the interpretations developed herein are closely tied to the *Popol Vuh*, so it is appropriate to give a brief overview of this text. In its extant version, the *Popol Vuh* (book of counsel, book of the mat council) is seen as the creation myth of the K'iche' (Quiché) Maya in the north-central Guatemalan highlands, explaining cosmogenesis and the origins of humans, animals, and celestial bodies. It is thought to have been committed to writing by three lineage leaders in their own language using Latin orthography sometime between 1554 and 1558 (D. Tedlock 1992, 1996:56). Although it incorporates references to Christianity, the book is clearly an indigenous Maya document, and new clues relate it to the Maya lowlands: Dennis Tedlock (1992:230, 1996:16, 46, 51, 211n30) claims that K'iche' ancestors acquired a hieroglyphic *Popol Vuh* manuscript

while on a pilgrimage to the east coast of the Yucatán peninsula, and that the lowland site of Copán is referenced in the text. If true, this gives the *Popol Vuh* heightened significance for interpreting Classic lowland Maya history, ritual, iconography, and calendrics. Similarly, Allen Christenson (2003:33, 65n34, 97n178, 133n290, 196n479, 480) suggests that the extant *Popol Vuh* had its origins as a hieroglyphic manuscript from the lowlands and that the names of many characters and elements in it are derived from the lowlands and Yukateko Mayan. The origins of the specific incidents in this mythistory extend much farther back in time, however, and many, as we shall see in Chapter 6, can be recognized on the carved monuments at the Late Preclassic site of Izapa on the Pacific coast of Chiapas, Mexico (Kerr 1992; Laughton 1997).

The *Popol Vuh* can be read from the viewpoint of divination and narrative (D. Tedlock 1992) as well as poetry, given its couplet structure (Christenson 2003:42–52; Edmonson 1971). In fact, Michael Coe (1989b) has proposed that these stories were the Maya equivalent of the Greek *Iliad* and *Odyssey*.[1] The creation story told in the *Popol Vuh* is complex, beginning in a primeval epoch when the universe was dark. The gods labored together to create life and light,[2] a process known as "the sowing and the dawning" (D. Tedlock 1996:30–31; unless otherwise indicated, my summary is from this translation, pp. 30–44). As will be seen in later chapters, it is particularly significant that the first events of creation began with spoken words, thoughts, and conversation: in the *Popol Vuh*, Heart of Sky "is the name of the god, as it is spoken. And then came his word, he came here to the Sovereign Plumed Serpent. . . . He spoke with the Sovereign Plumed Serpent, and they talked, then they thought, then they worried. They agreed with each other, they joined their words, their thoughts. Then it was clear" (ibid.:65). Together they created the animals, which were given explicit orders relating to the calendar—"speak, pray to us, keep our days"—but because they did not "keep the days," they were destroyed (ibid.:67). The gods' next effort to create humans out of mud was also unsuccessful, so they conferred again: "What is there for us to make that would turn out well, that would succeed in keeping our days and praying to us?" They consult a pair of daykeepers, Xpiyacoc and Xmucane,[3] seers or diviners who count the days and who advise the use of wood for the creation of speaking creatures. This too fails. At this point, the narrative turns to follow the adventures of the diviners' children and grandchildren in contexts that appear to alternate between the earth's surface and the Underworld.

Xpiyacoc and Xmucane have twin sons named One Hunahpu and Seven Hunahpu.[4] One Hunahpu marries Xb'aqiyalo,[5] and they have twin sons named Hun B'atz' (One Monkey) and Hun Chuwen (One Artisan). The two sets of twins sometimes play a ballgame in a ballcourt in the east, and a falcon messenger from the sky god Heart of Sky (also known as Huracan) often comes to watch them (ibid.:35).[6] However, their exuberant sport angers the lords of the Underworld, or Xib'alb'a (Place of Fear), residing below. The senior lords of Xib'alb'a, One Death and Seven Death, deploy huge owl emissaries as messengers to issue a challenge to the elder twins to a game in their ballcourt, on the western edge of the Underworld. During their journey to the Xib'alb'a ballcourt, One Hunahpu and Seven Hunahpu unsuccessfully face numerous trials, so the Underworld lords sacrifice them the next day. "Both of them are buried at the Place of Ball Game Sacrifice, except that the severed head of One Hunahpu is placed in the fork of a tree that stands by the road there" (ibid.:36), and this tree becomes a calabash tree.

Blood Moon (or Blood Woman, Xk'ik'), the maiden daughter of Blood Gatherer, another of the Xib'alb'an lords, goes out to look at the calabash tree, whereupon the head of One Hunahpu, "animated by both brothers," spits in her hand, making her pregnant (ibid.). Her father, infuriated by her pregnancy, orders the owl messengers to sacrifice her and return her heart to him, but she persuades the owls to spare her and present her father with a nodule of incense in place of her heart. The owls guide her to the earth's surface, whereupon she goes to Xmucane claiming to be her daughter-in-law. Xmucane doubts the claim but, after testing Blood Moon by demanding that she fetch corn from the garden, Xmucane is finally convinced that Blood Moon is truthful (ibid.:37).

Blood Moon bears a set of twins, Hunahpu and Xbalanque,[7] known as the Hero Twins. They enjoy hunting birds with blowguns and playing the ballgame, as did their fathers. However, the Twins are treated cruelly by their half-brothers Hun B'atz' and Hun Chuwen. One day the Hero Twins get revenge: they ask their older brothers to climb into the trees to retrieve the birds that did not fall when they shot them, but the Twins cause the trees to grow tall and maroon their mean half-brothers, who are turned into monkeys. B'atz' is the howler monkey (*Alouatta pigra*) and Chuwen is the spider monkey (*Ateles geoffroyi*); astronomically, One Monkey and One Artisan correspond to Mars (ibid.:38).

At some point in the story (the order of events is confusing), the Twins are called by Heart of Sky to deal with Seven Macaw (Vucub-Caquix), who claims to be the sun and the moon, and his two sons, all of whom are arrogant and boastful "pretenders to lordly power over the affairs of the earth." The Twins shoot Seven Macaw with their blowgun while he is sitting atop a nance tree (*Byrsonima crassifolia*) eating the fruit and then persuade two curers to pull out his teeth and remove the metal disks from around his eyes. Stripped of his finery, Seven Macaw ascends to become the Big Dipper (see ibid.:240n77, 242n78–79), with its seven principal stars, and his descendants are scarlet macaws (*Ara macao*).

Next, the Twins deal with the elder of Seven Macaw's sons, Zipacna (from Nawatl *cipactli* 'caiman, crocodile'). Zipacna is a large mountain-making saurian who survives a trap set for him by the Four Hundred Boys, the gods of alcoholic drink. Zipacna then kills the Boys, who rise to become the Pleiades. To avenge the death of the Four Hundred Boys, Hunahpu and Xbalanque set a trap—a crab wedged in a crevice in a mountain—and when Zipacna tries to eat it, the mountain collapses on him and he turns to stone (ibid.:35). Finally, they kill the younger of Seven Macaw's sons, Cabracan (Earthquake), by casting a spell on a bird they were cooking for him, and he is buried in the east. Thus "Seven Macaw, as the Big Dipper, is . . . near the pivot of the movement of the night sky, whereas his two sons [in the east and west] make the earth move" (ibid.).[8]

The Hero Twins eventually take possession of the ballgame equipment owned by their fathers, One Hunahpu and Seven Hunahpu, and go to the ballcourt where their fathers had played. As before, their noisy play disturbs the lords of the Underworld, who summon the Twins to play a game in Xib'alb'a (ibid.:38–39). Cleverer than their fathers, Hunahpu and Xbalanque survive the journey by sending a mosquito in advance to learn the names of the lords and by employing various tricks to pass the tests the Xib'alb'ans devise for them. The next day sees actual ball play, first using a Xib'alb'an ball, which breaks open to reveal an animated sacrificial knife that fails to kill the Twins. The Twins and lords agree to a wager on the next game, using the Twins' ball, and the Twins allow themselves to lose the game. Again they are imprisoned and employ various ruses to survive the night in Razor House and produce the bowls of flower petals that were the game stakes (ibid.:40). The Twins subsequently survive stays in Cold House, Jaguar House, and Bat House, except in the last a bat is able to remove Hunahpu's head. The head rolls into the ballcourt, and Xbalanque transplants a squash on Hunahpu's shoulders as a replacement.

At this point in the story, a momentous event takes place: "[T]he eastern sky reddens with the dawn, and an opossum, addressed in the story as 'old man,' makes four dark streaks along the horizon" (ibid.:40–41). This is the first time light appears on the earth, and "[i]n the future a new solar year will be brought in by the old man each 365 days; the four streaks signify that only four of the twenty [Maya] day names . . . will ever correspond to the first day of a solar year" (ibid.:41).

The story returns to the Hero Twins and another ballgame with the Underworld lords, who use Hunahpu's head as the ball. Xbalanque sends it out of the court and makes the lords think that a scurrying rabbit is the ball/head. He also contrives to introduce the squash into play as a ball, but the lords soon realize that they have been ignominiously duped and prepare to sacrifice the Twins. The Twins, invited to the large stone fire pit where the Xib'alb'ans are preparing an alcoholic beverage, accept a challenge to see who can safely leap across the pit, but instead they jump into the fire. Thinking themselves rid of the pesky youngsters forever, the Underworld lords grind the bones of the Twins into a powder and pour it into a river (ibid.:42).

After five days, however, the Hero Twins return briefly as catfish and then as human dancers

and illusionists, one of their acts being the sacrifice of an individual without actually killing him. The Xib'alb'an lords are entranced and invite the boys to entertain them, whereupon Xbalanque sacrifices Hunahpu and then revives him. Lords One Death and Seven Death demand that the Twins perform the same stunt on them, but this time the sacrifice is genuine. The Hero Twins then reveal themselves to all in Xib'alb'a and declare that from that moment forward the only offerings they will receive are incense and sacrificed animals (ibid.). They go back to the Place of Ball Game Sacrifice to try to revive the buried body of Seven Hunahpu but are unsuccessful (ibid.:43). The Hero Twins then ascend to the sky, where they become the sun and the moon. The first sunrise and full daylight appear over the earth for the first time.

Although this creation narrative can be and has been explored on many levels, I offer two interpretations based on the theoretical perspectives at the heart of my study. One comes from Mary Helms's (1988) discussion of the directionalities of time and distance from a center (axis mundi) or from the known world into the unknown, conceptualized as horizontal/spatial and vertical/temporal directions. The Maya Hero Twins' movements between the terrestrial surface and Xib'alb'a, as well as their and other creatures' movements from the earth into the sky, fit with what she (ibid.:45) refers to as the "creational primacy of the vertical axis," in which heroic characters of myth travel easily between earthly (known) to otherworldly (unknown) realms, acquiring new knowledge in the latter. Second, in the following chapters I argue that these characters and events of the *Popol Vuh* "dawn of life" creation narrative encode the history of major developments of Mesoamerican and, more specifically, Maya, calendars.

TIME AND PRECLASSIC MESOAMERICA

Defined geographically, the cultural region known as "Mesoamerica" extends from northern Mexico (roughly the Tropic of Cancer, 23° north latitude) southward through Guatemala and Belize into western Honduras and El Salvador (roughly 14° north latitude; Fig. 1.1). Within this environmentally diverse expanse, numerous societies developed, flourished, interacted, and declined over the millennia but came to share more in common with each other than with societies outside these boundaries. As a result, Mesoamerica is easily recognized as constituting a "culture area" (Kroeber 1939). The classic study by Paul Kirchoff (1943) refers to Mesoamerica as a "superarea of superior cultivators" and itemizes the characteristics shared with cultures to the north and south (e.g., mixed horticultural subsistence with corn, beans, and squash as the principal crops; technology based on stone rather than metal; and construction of pyramidal structures arranged around plazas) and those that were absent. More recent discussions of Mesoamerica have continued to employ the culture-area concept but greatly diminish this trait-list approach (e.g., Joyce 2000, 2004:3–9).

What is important to the thesis advanced here is not so much shared material culture as language and ideas. Mesoamerica is also a strongly defined linguistic area, with broad sharing of features such as word order, nominal possession, relational nouns, locatives, and loan translations (Campbell 1997:156–169; Campbell, Kaufman,

and Smith-Stark 1986). In addition, Mesoamerican peoples observe deeply rooted and widely shared ideological, philosophical, and religious beliefs and rituals, including origin myths, cyclical time, vigesimal numeration, quadripartite cosmovision, and complex calendrical and writing systems. Gary Gossen's (1986:5–8) reflections on "Mesoamerican ideas" led him to identify five "key themes" shaping Mesoamerican intellectual culture over the millennia:

1. The abiding theme of cyclical time as a sacred entity . . .
2. A consistent delimitation of sky, earth, and Underworld in the spatial layout of the cosmos, with mediation among these realms as a key intellectual, political, and religious activity . . .
3. Supernatural combat and secular conflict as creative and life-sustaining forces . . .
4. The principle of complementary dualism . . . and,

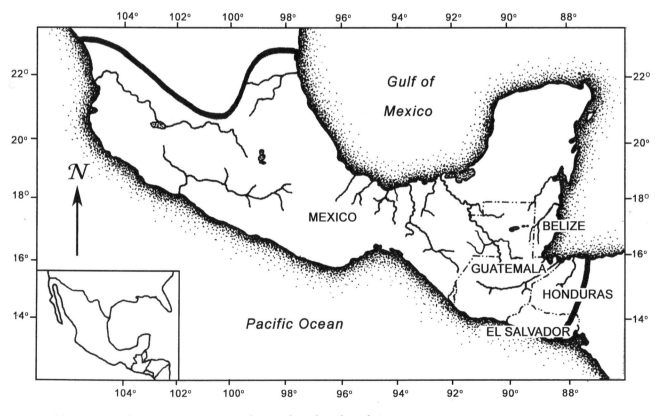

1.1. Mesoamerica, showing approximate northern and southern boundaries.

5. The extraordinary power of spoken and written language as a symbolic entity in itself, beyond its neutral role as a medium for routine communication."

The time depth of these themes is of particular interest here. As David Freidel (2001a:xiii–xix) elegantly phrases it in the epigraph, Mesoamerican historical memory resides in an enduring worldview some three thousand years old. My views are more liberal, and I agree with Joyce Marcus and Kent Flannery, who "do not find it at all surprising that certain basic cultural patterns should persist over a large area for 4000 years; in fact, we find it likely that certain patterns . . . persisted for more than 8000 years" (Marcus 1983a:9).

My focus is on time. When did Mesoamerican peoples begin thinking about time and recording its passage? Perhaps tens of thousands of years before they entered the region to become "Mesoamericans." Although the precise origins of calendrical, counting, writing, and cosmological systems throughout world prehistory are unclear (see Waugh 1999), certain principles underlying such record keeping can be taken as givens. Observation of celestial objects, particularly the sun and the moon, and the celebrated dualities of the natural world—day versus night, earth versus sky, rainy versus dry, hot versus cold, male versus female—have doubtless been fundamental to human cognition since *Homo sapiens* evolved (see Malinowski 1927; Nilsson 1920). Considerable research since the 1990s has made respectable the assertion that humans' "mental and cognitive capacities for symbolic behavior were already in place by the Middle Paleolithic" (ca. 100,000–40,000 B.C.) in the Old World (Hovers et al. 2003). Transmitted orally, early knowledge of the environment and the flow of cyclically occurring natural events might have begun to be formally recorded as early as 77,000 years ago, as indicated by engraved notations on red ochre from Blombos cave, South Africa (Bullington and Leigh 2002; Henshilwood et al. 2002). Later-dating carved bone artifacts from Upper Paleolithic Europe (ca. 40,000–10,000 B.C.) have been interpreted as tallies of lunar cycles (Marshack 1972) and likely relate to human gestation (Furst 1986:70).

The ancient art of astro-calendrics, based on observations of predictable regularities in movements of celestial bodies and their portents for human action, is nearly incomprehensible to people of the twenty-first-century Western world. Today we are scarcely able to appreciate the sky, day or night, because of smog and bright streetlights. In North America, time is merely a reflexive checking of our watches (or the Cesium[133]-based atomic clock at the National Institute of Standards and Technology, incorporated into our computers); weather changes mean tweaking the thermostat (after checking The Weather Channel™), and seasons are identified by lawn mowers, leaf blowers, and sports championships. Antedating the centuries of developments in predictive science and technology leading to these phenomena, however, prehistoric peoples around the globe relied on accumulating and orally transmitting knowledge of the cycling of the sun, moon, and other celestial bodies. As Anthony Aveni (2002a:298–299) comments,

> Time control began when somebody drove a stick into the ground and began to use the varying lengths of its shadow as a means of signifying the quiescent duration that separates one event from the next. Longer periods, like days and months of the year, could be marked out by timing the heliacal risings of bright stars or by notching the phases of the moon onto a piece of a bone. . . . These people were looking . . . for phenomena that repeat in a dependable way and occur in the right time at the right place.

Indeed, the human body itself—its twenty fingers and toes, the female menses, pregnancy—provided a basis for modeling time and its cycles that might have begun sometime in the Paleolithic era. The ability to correlate celestial movements with other time indications such as the cyclical onset and passage of the rains, migrations of animal herds and flocks of birds, and ripening of berries and grains—and, indeed, eventually to *predict* such correlations—would have been a mystical and advantageous skill commanding respect and awe, ultimately conferring power on certain sagacious individuals (see Helms 1988:11–19). Much of this understanding of natural rhythms, cycles, and periodicities would have been part of the intellectual toolkit of the earliest migrants into the Americas from Siberia.

While such knowledge might have been widespread, the early people in what later became Mesoamerica added a unique component: numeracy, the ability to reason and work effectively in quantitative terms, by manipulating numbers.[9] The importance of numeracy, alongside literacy, is most evident among the Maya, whose sophisticated vigesimal, or base-twenty, counting system and concept of zero or null permitted the systematization of their astronomical observations into complex, precise, and predictive calendars.

CHIEFDOMS AND CYCLES

I am interested here in things "temporal" in the word's time-specific meaning (of, relating to, or limited by time) but also in its other meanings: "of or relating to the material world . . . secular, lay, civil" (dictionary.com). These meanings assume importance when we consider the role of so-called middle-range societies—simple and complex chiefdoms—in the early stages of evolution of Mesoamerican civilizations. Although this book is not specifically "about" chiefdoms, rank and chiefly societies represent the sociopolitical context within which calendars and calendrical cycling emerged as key geopolitical devices in Mesoamerica and thus merit brief discussion.

As used here, the term *chiefdom* subsumes characteristics of sociopolitical organization intermediate between relatively simply organized societies (commonly called egalitarian, acephalous, or tribal), which lack permanent leadership positions, and those having highly complex and differentiated levels of information gathering and decision making (i.e., bureaucracies), commonly referred to as state-level societies (see, e.g., Cohen and Service 1978; T. Earle 1991; Feinman and Marcus 1998; Gregg 1991; Haas 1982, 2001a; Jones and Kautz 1981; Service 1975; Upham 1990; H. Wright 1984; Yoffee 1993). Between these extremes, chiefdoms exhibit considerable variability and have been defined in different ways. Some are characterized as simple: rank societies with two social strata, elites and commoners (Fried 1967:109, 116, 126).

Complex chiefdoms (H. Wright 1984), on the other hand, exist on a regional level, with a paramount chief and subsidiary local chiefs, and have at least two levels of decision making above the level of commoners.

Archaeologists and ethnographers have long noted the tendency of chiefdoms to fluctuate or cycle in their levels of sociopolitical complexity. David G. Anderson (1994:1), in his study of chiefdoms of the late prehistoric southeastern United States, describes chiefly cycling as long-term variations that occur when administrative or decision-making levels oscillate between one and two levels above that of the local community. The genealogical basis of leadership—descent from an apical ancestor—and competition for power between elites with different descent claims play major roles in the (in)stability of chiefdoms and result in cycling (ibid.:4, 6). As certain elite lines grow over generations, with chiefs able to attract an ever-larger retinue, including their own relatives and followers and lesser elites, complex chiefdoms may form. But chiefly leaders have no real authority or sanctions to enforce allegiance to themselves; they lead largely by example, persuasion, or some sort of ideoreligious power. Rules for political succession are nebulous at best. Some chiefs and their lines survive the challenges, but others succumb and, as Anderson (ibid.:50–52) explains, it is this instability that drives the cycling process over hundreds of years.

Another approach to prehistoric political cycling comes from the "dual-processual" model proposed by Richard Blanton and his colleagues (1996). This model, intended to strengthen neoevolutionary theory by focusing on processes rather than evolutionary stages, contrasts two types of political economies by using Mesoamerica as a case study: one is an open "network," or exclusionary, strategy centered on individuals and economic competition, particularly focused on prestige goods; the other is a "corporate," or group-oriented, strategy. The Early and Middle Formative periods in Mesoamerica,[10] for example, are characterized by the former: a network strategy emphasizing access to exotic trade goods available only in certain locations and to certain individuals or family lines at those locations (ibid.:8). One element of this widespread trade network was the spread of an artistic-symbolic tradition, generally dubbed

"Olmec," which the authors identify as an "international style." The subsequent Late and Terminal Formative periods saw a decline of this widespread tradition and the shift to a "strongly corporate [strategy], emphasizing social integration through communal ritual" (ibid.:9). This is evidenced by a new emphasis on creating special places for public ritual, such as pyramids and open plazas, and "cosmic-renewal ceremony" (ibid.:10). The Early Classic period in the Maya area, with its divine kings and stelae celebrating dynastic achievements, represents a return to a network strategy. Blanton and colleagues (ibid.:13) conclude that "Mesoamerican social history from the early Early Formative to the Spanish conquest consisted of cycles of long duration alternating between network and corporate emphases rather than a simple linear sequence. . . . These cycles were not strictly repetitive . . . and different areas had somewhat distinct cyclic histories."

At issue, of course, is why such cycling occurs. Why do some chiefdoms evolve into ever more complex formations and ultimately into states while others revert to simple chiefdoms? Why do some societies, through their evolutionary development, fluctuate between network and corporate strategies? What explains the operation of similar patterns in archaic states, Marcus's (1992b, 1993) "dynamic model," whose histories exhibit cycles of increasing complexity and centralization alternating with decentralization? The theoretical positions on this topic are too vast to review here, and the reasons why developing societies increase in complexity or fail to evolve are not the ultimate subject of this book. What *is* of interest is the role in that process, among early Mesoamerican chiefdom societies, of temporal cycling: cycles of time and cycles of geopolitical organization.

THE EARLY MAYA AND THE ISTHMIAN REGION

Mayanists' attention has long been captured by the peculiarities of the relations between the Classic Maya lowlands and the central Mexican city of Teotihuacan, and between Maya Chich'en Itza and Mexican Tula. Yet there has been comparatively less intensive exploration of the historical (or longitudinal) relations between Preclassic societies in the Isthmus of Tehuantepec, such as the Olmec or

Izapan, and the lowland Maya. Indeed, for a long time the prevailing view was that there was little interaction, if any, although more recent studies of architecture and iconography have emphasized that interactions among and between the Middle and Late Preclassic Gulf Coast, the Pacific piedmont area, and lowland Maya played an important part in early pre-Maya and Maya history (E. Andrews V 1986; Bove 2005; Clark and Hansen 2001; Fields 1989; Hansen 2005; Reilly 1991; Rust 1992).

Here, I define the Isthmian region (Fig. 1.2) more broadly than the Isthmus of Tehuantepec proper, as roughly the area between 92° and 96° longitude that encompasses eastern Veracruz, all of Tabasco, eastern Oaxaca, and western Chiapas, with a southeast extension along the Pacific piedmont of Guatemala. I propose that this region was long held sacred by Mesoamerican peoples, including the Maya, as a "cradle of civilization," at least with respect to the origins of shared cosmology, creation myth, calendrics, and the calendrical basis of political power. My focus is not so much on singling out the earliest examples of calendars, writing, or architectural forms, as these are consequences of the goals and intensities of past archaeological fieldwork and serendipity. Instead, I am more concerned with relations and continuities among the material and symbolic components—cultural, iconographic, glyphic, and especially astro-calendrical—as they relate to an "ideology of time" in the early Isthmian region (as defined herein) and the lowland Maya area of eastern Mesoamerica.

John Baines and Norman Yoffee (1998, 2000) emphasize the complex interrelations of three factors—order, legitimacy, and wealth (OLW)—in the "high cultures" of early states and civilizations. Order, legitimacy, and wealth are the foundations of politico-economic stability, and the expressions of these factors and their interrelations vary from civilization to civilization (Richards and Van Buren 2000). Briefly summarized, the Baines-Yoffee model posits that creating and maintaining social and cosmic order is the responsibility of the ruling elites. These derive their legitimacy through efficacious exercise of that duty, in part through interactions with the gods and ancestors. Wealth is an inextricable component of legitimacy and order because it is access to and conspicuous display of

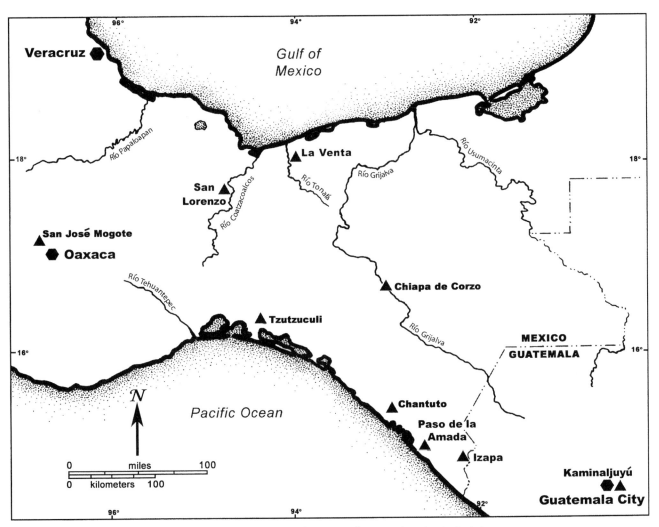

1.2. The Isthmian region, showing major sites (triangles), modern cities (hexagons), and principal rivers.

wealth—particularly wealth represented by exotic and therefore "expensive" goods (Helms 1993)—that sets elites apart from commoners, thus reinforcing the essential order of things.

And all this is based on an ideology which Baines and Yoffee (2000:14) define as "the ascribed set of meanings about social, political, and economic relations and events, and specifically about who has power and how it is got." Other valid definitions of ideology emphasize the way explanations of power relations serve to legitimize the social order (e.g., Godelier 1978; Knapp 1988; Santos Granero 1986:660). In their exegeses of their model, Baines and Yoffee explain that they are addressing neither the origins of these elements nor how they came to be important in the various civilizations under consideration.

The OLW model has already entered into at least two discussions of the Formative/Preclassic Maya (Joyce 2000; McAnany 2004b), and my goal here is not to undertake a rigorous analysis of all three elements and their interrelations among the Maya. Nor, for that matter, do I attempt a thorough application of the model to the other Formative cultures I overview here. Instead, and unlike Baines and Yoffee, I am concerned with the origins of these elements, and particularly with the ideology at their foundation. While the OLW model provides a rich context for exploring traditional causal factors addressed by Mayanists, such as trade and warfare, in the evolution of lowland civilization, I am interested specifically in the generally underplayed roles of time and the calendar in that process.

My central thesis is that a distinctive pattern of rotating geopolitico-ritual organization developed in the Isthmian region and the Maya area through the early development of calendrical precisioning. I propose that esoteric knowledge, such as numeracy, the recording of time, and the keeping of calendrical records, was the basis of political power—that is, legitimization—for early leaders (see Helms 1988:11–19). These chiefs or shamans demonstrated "control" of the supernatural forces of the cosmos through early calendrical observations and emerging predictive capabilities, thereby establishing social and cosmic order. *If* this proposition has any validity, *then* we would expect that early materializations of order, legitimacy, and wealth, both personal (elite) and public, would reflect such cosmogonic, astro-calendrical, and time-based ideologies. This should be exemplified in monumental architecture, for example, which structures the space experienced by humans and is the supreme earthly embodiment of cosmic order (Parker Pearson and Richards 1994a). Architecture and related materializations, such as sculpture, rituals, symbol-laden objects, exotic goods, and writing systems, constitute dramatic displays of elite wealth, through both control of labor expended in their manufacture and acquisition (Helms 1993) as well as by flaunting the exotic goods in ceremonial deposits and kingly costuming.[11] Altogether, I propose, early calendars and the materialization of time established the foundation of Maya rulers' intra- and intersite political power, order, legitimacy, and wealth.

The following chapters explore these complex relations of creation, cosmos, calendars, and cycling in chiefdom- and prechiefdom-level societies in eastern Mesoamerica. First, I briefly overview the very earliest periods of human occupation in Mesoamerica, the Paleoindian and Archaic periods, in order to establish the social, cultural, and technological foundations for, and earliest manifestations of, Mesoamerican cosmovision and ritual and the development of societal order and complexity. I argue that the scheduling of subsistence activities by seasonal changes, and particularly by settlement aggregations in what

those of us in temperate northern hemispheric climes identify as late summer and early autumn, was driven by observations of celestial (especially solar) phenomena that established the early foundations for calendrical development. Then I review ideational aspects of Mesoamerican culture and worldview manifest in calendrics and cosmology, including theories about the origins of the calendars and day and month names. I propose that the late K'iche' *Popol Vuh* myth of cosmogenesis and human origins is also an allegory of the history of calendrical developments.

These arguments are followed by chapters treating the Middle Formative Olmec and the Late Formative Izapan cultures in the Isthmian region. In these chapters I highlight themes of architecture, iconography, and ritual that reveal shared cosmovision and ideology, and also the growth and development of political power and rulership through manipulation of these symbols. The landscape of monuments at Izapa, in particular, can be seen as mapping out the course for ritual processions celebrating solar solstitial events as well as elements of the later *Popol Vuh* creation myth.

The next chapters focus on the lowland Maya in the Preclassic period, their early settlement and architecture and their "intellectual culture" of calendrical ritual and writing—many elements developing alongside those of the Isthmian region, which established the very foundations of kingly power and state-level organization. I suggest that a combination of factors, particularly a change from a north-south to an east-west primary architectural orientation, marks the beginning of a solar emphasis or "cult" underpinning kingly power.

Finally, I interweave the various strands of evidence to argue that most of the calendrical developments so distinctively tied to the lowland Classic Maya (and the Formative Olmec) occurred far earlier than generally supposed. Mesoamerican calendrical ceremony was from the beginning politicized to uphold a distinctive system of rotating geopolitical capitals, materialized in architecture and art and expressed most enduringly among the lowland Maya for at least two millennia.

In the Beginning
Early Mesoamerican Prehistory

Of the many debates that have engaged archaeologists and bioanthropologists working in the Western Hemisphere, one of the most enduring focuses on the hemisphere's earliest occupation by humans (see Fagan 1987). When European explorers discovered this previously unknown and hence "new" world they were compelled to explain the origin of its inhabitants, which they did via the only available treatise to explicate the natural world, the Bible. One question concerned whether or not the hemisphere's occupants were "human" (in a theological sense) and subject to baptism into the Holy Roman Catholic faith. A later question concerned the age of the known world itself: in the mid-seventeenth century, the head of the Anglican Church in Ireland, Archbishop James Usher, interpreted the events of the Book of Genesis to calculate that the world had been created at midday on October 23, 4004 B.C. His conclusion shaped the thinking of prehistorians, antiquarians, and geologists for the next two centuries, until a dedicated English cartographer, William Smith, mapped geological strata in Great Britain and proved that the world had to be much older than six millennia (Winchester 2001).

Similarly, early historians and antiquarians in the land that was to become the United States of America wrestled with questions concerning the indigenous occupants they discovered there and their relations to the abandoned earthworks newly discovered in the midwestern and southeastern parts of the country (see Willey and Sabloff 1980:20–43). Were the "savages" they encountered descendants of a mighty race of "Moundbuilders" who had earlier occupied the land (Thomas 1885)? Or were the mounds constructed by, or with the assistance of, a superior race of "Indians" in Mexico and Guatemala, who were literate and fabulously wealthy and built vast cities of stone? How and when did these Indians get to this part of the world, anyway?

Many fanciful answers to these questions have been proposed, and the origins of indigenous American populations have been hypothesized to include the Twelve Lost Tribes of Israel, Romans, Greeks, descendants of the lost continents of Atlantis or Mu, Egyptians, Vikings, Danes, ancient astronauts, Chinese, and so on (see Fagan 1987; Feder 1990; Wauchope 1962). A wealth of data marshaled from Pleistocene geology, biological anthropology, zoology,

There is a basic religious system common to all Mesoamerican peoples [which] took shape long before it was given monumental expression in Olmec art.

—Peter D. Joralemon,
"The Olmec Dragon: A Study in
Precolumbian Iconography"

and archaeology, among other fields, has led to several points of concurrence.

One is that the first people to arrive in the "New World" were the fully modern human species *Homo sapiens sapiens*, the same species as all humans today. Because *H. s. sapiens* is thus far known to have evolved only in the Old World, this means that there were no separate centers of evolution of humans in the Western Hemisphere. Indeed, no skeletal remains of earlier premodern humans have been found in this hemisphere; thus humans did not occupy the region until after *H. s. sapiens* evolved, no later than ca. 40,000 years ago.

Second, the first humans populating the Western Hemisphere moved across what is now the Bering Straits from Siberia (northeastern Asia) into Alaska. At times during the last forty thousand years this area of continental shelf, now under sixty-five to one hundred meters of water, was exposed by lowered sea levels, forming a broad "land bridge" joining the two continents. The notion of crossing a land bridge evokes images of bold Pleistocene pioneers striding purposefully across a perilously narrow path of dry soil, icy Arctic seas crashing on either side. But this "Beringia" region, perhaps as much as sixteen hundred kilometers wide at times, was a vast region of tundra supporting large herds of Pleistocene "megafauna" such as mastodons, mammoths, and woolly rhinoceros. Humans and animals could have spent many generations moving together as hunter and hunted, the humans unaware that they were initiating the colonization of a hitherto unoccupied continent.

EARLY OCCUPATION: THE PALEOINDIAN OR LITHIC STAGE

The still-unanswered question in this migration scenario concerns when this land bridge journey or journeys might have occurred, with arguments revolving around two hypotheses: early versus late entry (see Zeitlin and Zeitlin 2000:53–62). The early-entry hypothesis, which posits that humans might have entered the New World as early as twenty thousand to forty thousand years ago, is predicated on the early existence of the Beringia land bridge. Evidence consists of a handful of archaeological sites scattered from northern North America to southern South America that reveal associations, some genuine and some spurious, of human-made tools with Pleistocene geological strata and/or extinct faunal species. Many archaeologists remain highly skeptical of the evidence for such an early entrance of humans into the New World and criticize the reliability of the dates, the tools, the associations, and the contexts, although some support has been mustered through on-site peer-conference review of sites such as Monte Verde in southern Chile (Dillehay 1989, 1997; Meltzer 1997). Skeptics prefer to accept the far more abundant, widespread, and reliably dated evidence for a late entry of humans into this hemisphere, around twelve thousand years ago.

Further insights into the peopling of the New World come from linguistics, dental anthropology, and molecular biology. Linguistic studies suggest three or more migrations (A. Hofling, pers. com., August 30, 2004) and call attention to the diversity of native languages, particularly along the western coasts of North and Central America (Gruhn 1988). This diversity could indicate a long period of differentiation from a common ancestral tongue, perhaps beginning as much as forty thousand years ago (see also Greenberg 1987; Zeitlin and Zeitlin 2000). The morphology of teeth of early skeletal remains reveals shared traits ("sinodonty") between northern Asian and Native American peoples, indicating common genetic origin (Turner 1984). Research (ibid.) suggests the possibility of one early migration into the New World that distributed populations throughout the hemisphere, followed by two later migrations represented by groups settled only in North America: the Athabaskans and then the Eskimo-Aleuts (Nadene speakers). Comparison of mitochondrial DNA from different linguistic groups also indicates that Nadene speakers arrived separately and much later (Torroni et al. 1992).

Regardless of the time of entry, early hunters seem to have followed an ice-free corridor along the eastern flanks of the Rocky Mountains, which enabled them to move southward into the interior of the North American continent (Anderson and Gillam 2000). Some movement also might have been by boat along the western coast (Fladmark 1979). How long would it have taken people to travel the length of the hemisphere, whether trudging overland or furiously paddling canoes along the shoreline? Estimates range from a few generations to five thousand years or so (Anderson and Gillam 2000:54–59).

The earliest well-dated cultural stage in the New World is variously referred to as the Big-Game Hunting, Lithic, or Paleoindian stage;[1] it is roughly equivalent culturally to the late Upper Paleolithic in Eurasia. Materials recovered in early archaeological excavations consisted only of stone tools (spear points, knives, scrapers, butchering tools) and large animal bones, suggesting a subsistence reliance on hunting large Pleistocene game such as mastodons, mammoths, bison, camelids, and horses. These megafaunal species are now extinct as a result of climate changes and human hunting (Barnosky et al. 2004).

Relatively few Mesoamerican sites and data have played a role in arguments about the date of early humans in the New World, and relatively few sites in the region date to the Paleoindian stage, perhaps because heavy subsequent occupation, recurrent seismic activity, and sea-level rise destroyed evidence of such small and ephemeral sites. Most of the known early sites are in the highlands, particularly central and south-central Mexico, where locales such as Valsequillo in Puebla, Tlapacoya in the basin of Mexico, and Rancho la Amapola in San Luis Potosí support the early-entry hypothesis (Dixon 1999:91–97; Mirambell 1994; Zeitlin and Zeitlin 2000:56–62). Support for the late-entry hypothesis, including distinctive fluted points, is more widespread (Zeitlin and Zeitlin 2000) and includes sites in coastal Belize (Hester et al. 1982; MacNeish and Nelken-Terner 1983; Wilkerson 1985; Wilson, Iceland, and Hester 1998; Zeitlin 1984); highland Guatemala (Bray 1978; K. Brown 1980; Gruhn and Bryan 1977); the Tehuacán valley of Puebla; the site of Tequixquiac in Hidalgo (where a camelid sacrum was apparently carved to represent the face of a canid); Santa Isabel Iztapan in the basin of Mexico; and nearby Tepexpan. At this last, a burial of a woman, prone and flexed, was found with no associated artifacts. The fact that several Paleoindian sites have been identified in the basin of Mexico bears some note, because this valley, location of present-day Mexico City, was occupied by a large lake throughout pre-Columbian times until it began to be drained by the Spanish conquerors. This lake would have been attractive for

early human occupation because of the quantity and diversity of easily available plant and animal foods, terrestrial and aquatic.

The only well excavated Paleoindian site in the Maya lowlands is Loltún cave, in the Puuc hills of northwestern Yucatán, where chipped stone and bone tools were found, some in association with extinct Pleistocene megafauna, particularly the horse (*Equus conversidens*) (Velázquez 1980). No radiocarbon dates are associated with these early levels. A late Paleoindian lithic complex (Lowe-Ha) has been postulated, on the basis of stone tools recovered in survey, for the interior pine savanna regions of central Belize (Wilkerson 1985:278).

Excavations and painstaking recovery techniques have provided evidence for a far broader spectrum of subsistence activity than big-game hunting during the Paleoindian period throughout the hemisphere, including fishing, gathering vegetal foods, and trapping small game. People lived in small, mobile bands, judging from small sites found in caves or in the open, representing encampments or butchery activity. Settlement-subsistence patterns in the dry valleys of Oaxaca and Tehuacán (Marcus and Flannery 1996:45–48) are characterized by long-distance treks of small bands to capture herd animals, with a communal hunting mode (and pooling of the meat) of jackrabbits and antelopes (Flannery 1966), as well as deer, horses, and smaller animals such as ground squirrels and quail.

What kinds of beliefs and cosmologies might have accompanied the earliest settlers into the Western Hemisphere and have been a part of Paleoindian culture? Although these can only be inferred rather than empirically known, Anthony Aveni (pers. com., July 2005) observes that "hunter-gatherers would certainly have known of the Pole Star and the 'latitude effect' on sky orientation as they migrated north-south." Alexander Marshack (1985) proposes a tradition of shared beliefs, observations, and practices that still exist among the peoples of Siberia and Native Americans, a tradition probably carried into the Americas by the earliest immigrants. Regionally varying beliefs and practices include recognition of seasonal cycles, solstitial observations, and maintenance of a lunar year, along with the existence of specialists ("calendar keepers," "sky-watchers") who made these observations and recorded them as groups of marks on wood or bone ("calendar sticks"): "If it can be assumed that aspects of this tradition, carried non-artifactually in language and myth and as part of a generalized hunting-gathering adaptive lore and perhaps as part of the shamanistic tradition, came into the Americas with diverse groups of Asian migrants, it can probably also be assumed that these traditions formed part of the cultural preparation that helped to make the slow, seasonal, migratory movements of the dispersing hunter-gatherers possible" (ibid.:44).

THE ARCHAIC STAGE

The transition from the end of the Pleistocene to the beginning of the Holocene (modern) geological era in the New World occurred around eleven thousand to nine thousand years ago, depending on the particular locale under consideration and the kinds of indicators used. In high latitudes, the end is marked most dramatically by the melting and consequent northward "retreat" of glaciers, but everywhere there were changes: rising sea levels; faunal extinctions; climatic fluctuations (gradual warming and altered precipitation patterns); and varied patterns of vegetation redistribution. In highland central Mexico the transition was to a period of warmer and drier climate as compared with the closing millennia of the Pleistocene, whereas in the lowland Yucatán peninsula the climate became more moist.

Cultural transformations also were taking place, in different ways and at different times, in some places earlier and in others later, in some places dramatically and in others gradually. Everywhere, however, the impact was eventually the same: altered relationships between people and their environment, often on a highly regionalized scale. Throughout the world, cultures evolved and adapted to changing local environmental conditions that came to approximate those of the present, including modern weather patterns and floral and faunal distributions. Most important, subsistence transitions included what archaeologists often refer to as "incipient agriculture": changes in food-getting patterns—hunting, gathering, foraging, fishing—which, in certain

areas of the world, Mesoamerica among them, ultimately led to food production. These changes also established the foundation for many of the characteristics by which we define the Mesoamerican culture area.

The cultural stage following the Paleoindian in the New World is the Archaic (or sometimes Preceramic) stage (Table 2.1), culturally comparable to the Old World Mesolithic and early Neolithic. In Mesoamerica it lasted from about 9000/7000 to about 2400/1600 B.C. Throughout the Americas, Archaic occupation is found in caves or rockshelters, for example in Mesoamerica in Tehuacán (MacNeish 1967) and Oaxaca (Flannery and Marcus 1983), at El Gigante in Honduras (Scheffler 2002), and at the Santa Marta rockshelter in central Chiapas, where Richard S. MacNeish (1964:420) reported finding caches of rounded pebbles perhaps used in slingshots. In the K'iche' basin of the Guatemala highlands, Kenneth Brown (1980) found 117 sites dating to the Paleoindian and primarily Archaic periods, which he classified as chipping stations, base camps, and limited-resource camps. Archaeologists' reconstructions of subsistence activities during this critical interval (Flannery 1986b, 1986c; MacNeish 1964, 1967; MacNeish and Nelken-Terner 1983) indicate that hunting and gathering activities became increasingly focused on select resources and that settlement shifts accompanied these subsistence changes.

The best known of these reconstructions are based on data from the dry, interior highland valleys of Tehuacán and Oaxaca in south-central Mexico. Here, the end of the Pleistocene era was marked by decreasing rainfall, shrinking grasslands, and faunal extinctions, all contributing to a situation in which food was neither abundantly nor reliably available. Archaeological data suggest that, in response, slowly over the millennia, humans carefully scheduled their varied subsistence and settlement activities by the seasons to take advantage of foods that were available in different places at different times of the year (Table 2.2). Group sizes and movements shifted seasonally, with small, dispersed bands fanning out during the dry season, when foodstuffs were less widely available, and regrouping during periods of abundance, the rainy season. A variety of phenomena

TABLE 2.1. *Chronological intervals in preclassic Mesoamerica*

PERIOD OR STAGE*	GREGORIAN YEARS†	K'ATUN 8 AJAW Ending Date‡
Paleoindian/Lithic stage	pre-8000 B.C.	
Archaic stage	8000–2400 B.C.	
Late Archaic, or Archaic—Formative* transition	2400–1600 B.C.	1614 B.C.
Formative stage/Preclassic period		
Initial Early Formative/Preclassic	1600–1200 B.C.	1358 B.C.
		1102 B.C.
Late Early Formative/ Preclassic	1200–900/850 B.C.	846 B.C.
Middle Formative/Preclassic	900/850–400 B.C.	
Early		591 B.C.
Late		334 B.C.
Late Formative/Preclassic	400–100 B.C.	78 B.C.
Epi-Olmec	400/300 B.C.–200 A.D.	
Terminal Formative/ Preclassic	100 B.C.–A.D. 200	A.D. 179
Early Classic	A.D. 200–450	A.D. 435

Notes: *See Chapter 1 and Chapter 2, note 1, for explanation of the distinction.
†Slightly modified from Joyce (2004:fig. 1.4) and Lesure (2004). Dates are calibrated.
‡Based on a hypothesized *may* cycle of 256 years, ending in K'atuns 8 Ajaw (see P. Rice 2004).

TABLE 2.2. *Seasonality of plant foods in Mexico's dry highland valleys in the Archaic stage*

SEASON	PLANT FOOD
Dry	
December	Agave
January	Agave
February	Agave, organ cactus fruit
March	Agave, organ cactus fruit
April	Agave
May	Mesquite, hackberry
Rainy	
June	Mesquite, hackberry, prickly pear
July	Mesquite, hackberry, prickly pear, cherry
August	Mesquite, hackberry, prickly pear, cherry
September	Grasses, beans, hackberry, cherry
October	Grasses, beans, piñon, acorns
November	Agave, piñon, acorns

Source: After Flannery 1986a; Marcus and Flannery 1996:52–57.

could have triggered the seasonal movements: the call or migration of particular birds; the time of new growth, blossoming, or ripening of certain plants (fruits, grasses, nuts); the time of birthing of certain animals; the presence or absence of rains, winds, visibility of stars; and so on (Nilsson 1920:46–52). Similarly, it might have been recognized early on that certain flowers signaled that desirable pods or seeds would be available in the area in a later season (Flannery 1986b).

From the viewpoint of the later Mesoamerican diet, the most important early foods, especially various types of wild beans, grasses, and squashes (*Cucurbits* spp.), were found in a wide range of environments. Beans (*Phaseolus* spp.) produced edible pods and tubers in September or October. Grasses such as *Setaria* (foxtail grass) and especially *Zea* (including teosinte and corn or maize, *Zea mays* ssp. *mays*) yielded seeds that ripened from September to mid-October, respectively. Other cultigens included chile peppers (*Capsicum*), tomatoes (*Lycopersicum*), and avocadoes (*Persea*). These plants were accorded ever-increasing dietary importance through the Archaic stage, and human selection and other behaviors resulted in their eventual domestication.[2]

But even in arid regions of Mesoamerica, a variety of wild foods was available, particularly during the rainy season (Flannery 1986b:23–25; see also Kirkby, Whyte, and Flannery 1986). These include the roasted heart of the maguey cactus (*Agave* spp.), the pads (*nopales*) and fruits (*tunas*) of the prickly pear cactus (*Opuntia* spp.), picked with tongs. In addition, a variety of xeriphytic leguminous trees, including *Acacia* and *Leucaena*, had pods filled with seeds; the pods of mesquite (*Prosopis juliflora*) could be cooked into a jelly. A type of cherry (*Malphigia*) and seeds of hackberry (*Celtis*) were also consumed.

Food-procurement strategies are described as evolving from foraging in the early Archaic to later collecting (Binford 1980; Zeitlin and Zeitlin 2000:94), a distinction that is not merely semantic but has significant implications for decision making and decision makers. Foraging refers to opportunistic rather than planned pursuit of available foodstuffs by small mobile groups of two to eight related individuals (often called microbands) moving frequently from food source to food source. In the early Archaic period in Oaxaca, for example, foraging strategies seem to have deemphasized the preceding Paleoindian pattern of hunting in communal drives, and with the extinction of big game the hunt necessarily shifted toward other animals, especially small mammals (rabbits), birds (quail, doves), and reptiles, as well as deer and peccaries (Flannery 1966; MacNeish 1964; Marcus and Flannery 1996:49–52). Collecting, by contrast, refers to seasonally scheduled and prioritized food getting based on more intimate knowledge of the

environment. Larger groups of fifteen to twenty-five people (macrobands) resided at a base camp where food was available for a period, with small task groups deployed from time to time to hunt deer, gather acorns, collect ripe cactus fruit, and so on, and bring the foods (and other resources) back to camp.

Archaeologists theorize that, under certain favorable ecological circumstances, these larger settlement aggregations and specialized collecting strategies led, over many generations, to reduced mobility and a sedentary life. Many early cultigens may have been "commensals": edible weeds that grow in disturbed soils or organic refuse around human encampments, thriving in symbiotic relationships with humans. Patches of certain preferred plants, such as corn, beans, and squash, may have begun to be tended and protected, and their seeds collected, dried, and stored. Stored foodstuffs would have gradually permitted (and later necessitated) macroband settlements to be extended for longer and longer periods, as evidenced by the increasing size and thickness of Archaic-period archaeological deposits.[3] These processes ultimately culminated in sedentary, agricultural, pottery-producing villages by 2500–1500 B.C.[4]

Food-procurement strategies leading to even earlier sedentarization existed in the rich lacustrine and coastal wetland regions of Mesoamerica. In such high-energy (high-caloric-yield) environments there was a ready supply of fish, shellfish, reptiles, and waterfowl as well as various grasses, vegetal foods, and terrestrial fauna that were less seasonal in their availability, at least in the lowlands, compared with the arid highland valleys. In the basin of Mexico, permanent villages began to appear as early as ca. 5500–3500 B.C. at Zohapilco on the southern shore of the lake, which boasted freshwater springs and higher rainfall than the northern shore. Food storage pits and obsidian tools were also used in the region, but the area was covered by deposits from a volcanic eruption around 3000 B.C. and hence is poorly known archaeologically (Niederberger 1979, 1996).

Identification of Archaic-period sites in the lowlands is plagued by numerous difficulties, some of them problems of preservation in this humid environment (Zeitlin 1984) but also because sites are small, shallow, and tend not to have occupation continuing into later periods

(Clark and Cheetham 2002:283, 286). There is also the likelihood that sites in nutrient-rich coastal areas dating prior to 3000 B.C. were inundated by rising sea levels (see Voorhies et al. 2002). This process would have been most dramatic on the northern and western coasts of the Yucatán peninsula, where the continental shelf is exceptionally broad. Other environmental disturbance problems in the lowlands are caused by frequent hurricanes, bioturbation, and rivercourse meanders, which easily would have discomposed or erased small campsites.

In the Chantuto region of Pacific coastal Chiapas (see Fig. 6.17), amid estuaries, swamps, lagoons, and mangroves, the shellmound site of Cerro de las Conchas (Voorhies et al. 2002; see also Voorhies 1976) began to be formed during the Middle Archaic by 5500 cal. B.C. The lowest levels were composed principally of marsh clam shells (*Polymesoda radiata*), with vertebrate fauna primarily represented by salt- to brackish water fish species and a small proportion of reptiles; associated artifacts included cooking stones and scrapers and fishhooks of shell. Excavations in the nearby Tlacuachero shellmound site encountered clay floors with postholes indicating two oval structures dating to the Late Archaic, ca. 2700–1800 B.C. (Voorhies and Michaels 1989). A diverse hunting-fishing-collecting subsistence pattern seems to have obtained in this region, perhaps with seasonal (including macroband) settlement shifts: shell middens were occupied during the rainy season with inland base camps at other times of year (Kennett and Voorhies 1996). The diet may have incorporated cultivated maize as well (Blake et al. 1995:167; Neff et al. 2006), although its contribution here and at coastal sites in other regions seems to have been highly variable and may indicate experimentation (Pohl et al. 1996).

Research along the Gulf coast of central Veracruz has revealed evidence for Archaic population concentrations along the delta and estuarine portions of the region's rivers, particularly on islands (Wilkerson 1981, 1985:277). A campsite at La Conchita, northwest of the Río Tecolutla, has a radiocarbon date of ca. 5600 B.C.; the nearby site of Santa Luisa, with packed-earth floors, hearths, and middens, was apparently permanently occupied from 4100 to 2400 B.C., when it was covered with sediment from a major flood. The inhabitants' diet included shellfish, especially oysters cooked with heated stone cobbles. Farther to the east, at San Andrés, Tabasco, sediment cores yielded pollen from what is interpreted as cultivated maize (*Zea mays*) about 5100 cal. B.C. and domesticated maize pollen by 5000 cal. B.C.; domesticated manioc (*Manihot* spp.) pollen is dated around 4600 cal. B.C. (Pohl 2001).

In the Yucatán peninsula, the transition to the Holocene was marked by increasing moisture and the initial growth of the tropical deciduous forests that later blanketed the area. Archaic materials have been found in various areas of northern Belize, particularly near the coast (MacNeish and Nelken-Terner 1983; Wilkerson 1985; also Masson and Mock 2004:389). However, there has been considerable disagreement about the lithic typology used in the early work, and a restudy suggests that, except for one Clovis point, no projectile points have been found that reliably date before about 3000 B.C. (Kelly 1993). Fieldwork around Freshwater Creek, where bulldozing is common, identified numerous early sites characterized by patinated constricted uniface lithics in orange soil, frequently underlying Postclassic occupation (Rosenswig and Masson 2001). Also in northern Belize, the Colha Preceramic Project recovered evidence suggesting that wetland raised fields were used to cultivate maize and possibly manioc by 3500 cal. B.C., and chile peppers and cotton were grown later (J. Jones 1994; Pohl et al. 1996; Wilson, Iceland, and Hester 1998:348). In Cob Swamp, a maize pollen grain was found just below a radiocarbon date of 3360 cal. B.C., with other early maize pollen dating 2500 B.C., and domesticated manioc pollen is possible around ca. 3400 B.C. (Pohl et al. 1996:361–362).

THE ARCHAIC-TO-FORMATIVE TRANSITION

The interval following the Archaic is known variously as the Formative stage or the Preclassic period (see Chap. 1, note 10). Culturally, it is roughly comparable to the latter part of the Eurasian Neolithic and later stages, except that Mesoamerica lacked development of metal tools.

The transition from the Archaic to the Early Formative is poorly dated, ranging from ca. 2400 to ca. 1600 cal. B.C., depending on the Mesoamerican region under study. It is also rather poorly known archaeologically. At the beginning of this transitional period, sedentary, agricultural, pottery-making hamlets and villages began to appear in certain parts of Mesoamerica, while by the end of it, such small communities were widely scattered throughout the region. How this happened—the causes as well as the timing and sequence—is the subject of endless debate, and this period remains one of the most enigmatic yet pivotal for understanding the development of Mesoamerican civilizations.

A key focus of anthropological interest in the Archaic-to-Formative transition or Early Formative itself is the inception of nonegalitarian societies—those with nascent social statuses or rankings—accompanied by settlement hierarchies. Such statuses are critical characteristics of later Classic civilizations in Mesoamerica, and a vast literature is devoted to theories of and data on their emergence in several areas of both highlands and lowlands. To date, the most closely examined sequences are those of the dry highland valleys and basins of central Mexico (J. Parsons 1974), Tehuacán (MacNeish 1972), and especially Oaxaca (Flannery 1976a; Flannery and Marcus 1983, 2005) and the Isthmus of Tehuantepec. Leaving aside the literature on transitional sequences in central Mexico, I focus here on the greater Isthmian region, including the valley of Oaxaca on its western margin.

Oaxaca

The Archaic-to-Formative transition to village life on a regional level was thoroughly explored in a multiyear project directed by Kent Flannery in the valley of Oaxaca. As described in *The Early Mesoamerican Village* (Flannery 1976a) and *The Cloud People* (Flannery and Marcus 1983; see also Drennan 1983a, 1983b; Flannery and Marcus 2003, 2005), the nonsedentary, non-food-producing lifeways of the Archaic continued here until roughly 2000 B.C., but sometime within the next few centuries people began to adopt a sedentary lifestyle with gradually decreasing reliance on wild foods. The Espiridión complex,

ca. 1800–1500 B.C., yielded the earliest pottery, completely undecorated. The complex is virtually identical to that of the Purron complex of the Tehuacán valley to the north except that it lacks neckless jars (*tecomates*). Vessels may have been formed by press-molding, using gourds as forms (Marcus 1983b). A feline figurine head was found in one of the structures (Marcus 1989:163). Flannery and Marcus (2005:6) consider San José Mogote to have been a "small, egalitarian, politically autonomous hamlet whose economy was a mixture" of farming, collecting, and hunting.

During the succeeding Tierras Largas phase (1800–1350/1300 cal. B.C. [1500–1150 b.c.]; Flannery and Marcus 2005:459), a two-tiered settlement hierarchy emerged, with at least nineteen permanent hamlets or small villages in the valley (see Marcus 1989:158–159). San José Mogote was the largest of these, originally estimated at approximately twenty hectares (Flannery 1976b:59), with perhaps 170–340 or so residents (Flannery and Marcus 2005:7). The village boasted lime-plastered public buildings, and specialized architecture began to appear: Structure 6, measuring 4.4 x 5.4 meters and oriented 8° west of north, had a step or altar in the center of the south wall. Inside and north of the wall was a lime-filled cylindrical pit, approximately 40 centimeters in diameter, interpreted as storage for powdered lime to be mixed with narcotics such as tobacco (Drennan 1983b:47–48). Flannery and Marcus (2000:7; idem 2005:7) interpret this structure as a men's house, oriented roughly to "the point where the sun rises on the equinox." The floor of this building was resurfaced three to five times, and another contemporaneous construction, Structure 3, provides evidence of having been built and rebuilt eight times.

An open area at San José Mogote, roughly seven meters wide and also oriented slightly west of north, was set apart from the residential areas by a double line of staggered posts, reinforced at places by a row of heavy stone slabs set on edge (Drennan 1983b:47; Flannery and Marcus 1976:208). Flannery and Marcus (2005:114) interpret these postholes as evidence of a palisade that protected the western part of the site. An area near the eastern limits of the site provides evidence of production activities, with worked and unworked magnetite, mica, quartz, and marine shell (Flannery 1976b:60).

During the succeeding San José phase (1350/1300–1000/950 cal. B.C. [1150–850 b.c.]; Flannery and Marcus 2005:462), San José Mogote continued to grow in size (to approximately seventy hectares; ibid.:10) and complexity, with the "downtown" area of twenty hectares divided into four residential wards (Marcus 1989:168). The site also exhibited more varied architecture, evidence of ritual, and exotic goods, including household shrines (Drennan 1983b:49); carved monuments, one possibly a feline and the other a raptor (Marcus 1989:165); ritual objects such as magnetite mirrors, marine shell, and lowland turtle shell; pottery from various areas of Mexico and the Isthmian region (Flannery and Marcus 2005:10, 64); fragments of *Strombus* (conch) shell trumpets and turtle shell drums in debris around public buildings (Flannery 1976c:335–336); figurines, often of dancers, in household debris (ibid.:337); pottery masks (ibid.:338–339); macaw bones (ibid.:340); and marine fish spines, stingray spines, and a shark tooth (ibid.:342–343). The occupants of San José Mogote also made and used pottery with complex decoration, best known for its distinctive sky and earth motifs (see Chap. 5), which also have distinct spatial distributions at the site (Flannery and Marcus 1994; Pyne 1976).

The two-tiered settlement hierarchy that emerged in the Early Formative in the Oaxaca valley was maintained to the Middle Formative (ca. 500 B.C.), at which point a three-tiered settlement hierarchy is evident. During this time San José Mogote increased twenty times in area, while two other hamlet-sized sites, Fábrica San José and Tierras Largas, stayed essentially the same size (Winter 1976). Most of the growth in San José Mogote was in public buildings.

The Isthmian Region

In the Isthmian region, the Archaic-to-Preclassic transition has been investigated archaeologically for decades but, as elsewhere, much remains unsatisfactorily understood. Poor dating, stratigraphic discontinuities, gaps in the sequence, and a lack of evidence for pre-Olmec occupation along the Gulf coast long posed insuperable obstacles to understanding developmental and transitional processes, but recent work on both coasts and in the Pacific piedmont region has resolved some of these problems.

On the Pacific coast of Chiapas and Guatemala, a region known as Soconusco (after the Aztec province of the same name; Voorhies 1989a, 1989b, 2004), reevaluations of the early chronology using calibrated radiocarbon dates (Blake et al. 1995; Lesure 1998; Love 1999; also Clark 1991) have revised some long-standing difficulties and provided a much more detailed look at changes from the Archaic Chantuto phases A and B through the Early Formative, which is dated 1850–950 cal. B.C. (1550–850 b.c.) (see Table 2.3).

During the earliest phase in this sequence, the Barra phase, subsistence consisted of a variety of terrestrial and aquatic animals (fish, turtles, deer, dogs, rabbits, armadillos, squirrels, pocket gophers, opossums, birds, snakes, crocodiles, iguanas, crabs, shellfish; Clark 1991:16), suggesting a broad-spectrum hunting-fishing-collecting economy augmented by some horticulture (sweet potatoes, manioc, maize, beans, squash). Sedentary settlement begins in this phase (Love 1999:132).

TABLE 2.3. *Early Formative chronology in the Soconusco region*

FORMATIVE PHASE OR COMPLEX	CALIBRATED DATE (B.C.)	NONCALIBRATED DATE (B.C.)	INNOVATION
Barra	1850–1650	1550–1400	Sedentism, pottery
Locona	1650–1500	1400–1250	Two-tiered settlement hierarchy; ranking
Ocós	1500–1350	1250–1100	Figurines with mirrors; ballcourt
Cherla	1350–1100	1100–1000	"Olmec" material present

Pottery also appears during the Barra phase: most vessels of the Mokaya culture in the Mazatán zone of Chiapas have restricted orifices, and approximately 85 percent of the vessels are *tecomates* (Blake et al. 1995; compare with the undecorated pottery and lack of *tecomates* in early Oaxaca).

John Clark and Michael Blake (1994:24–25; see also Clark and Gosser 1995) argue that this pottery was introduced into the area by "aggrandizers," local individuals competing for status and power in an otherwise egalitarian system. These aspiring "big men" would have brought in nonlocal technology (either the ceramics themselves or the potters who could make them) to enhance their prestige by display at competitive feasts (see Hayden 1990, 1998; Rice 1999). These vessels—large jars, bowls, and *tecomates*—do appear better suited for display or serving purposes than for prosaic cooking functions by virtue of both their shape (flat bases) and their exquisite decoration. Their sophistication, certainly in decoration but also in the technically difficult sharp shoulder angles, raises the possibility that the pots were made by nonlocal artisans, unless the residents were already familiar with the characteristics of local clay resources. Perhaps the vessels were brought in as gifts for feasting ceremonies. They likely constituted "wealth," in the sense of the order-legitimacy-wealth model (Baines and Yoffee 1998, 2000): as products of skilled artisans and used in public events, they represent "power conceived as art" (Helms 1993:27), meaning that they also underwrote legitimacy.

The succeeding Locona phase is interpreted as marking the early development of rank society and chiefdom social organization in the Mazatán region. This is inferred from settlement size, which evidences a two-tiered hierarchy. Two sites, Chilo and San Carlos, are described as "large villages" of five hundred to one thousand or more people (Clark 1991:18). Paso de la Amada, with a site core of some 53 hectares (Ceja Tenorio 1985), is now thought to sprawl over 140 hectares with some fifty mounds and an estimated population of two thousand to three thousand in its realm (Clark 1997:228; idem 2004:54; Clark, Gibson, and Zeidler 2004). These sites are also the only ones with large, elevated, earthen platforms supporting structures that may be interpreted as chiefly residences or as public architecture, although the structures are not arranged in groups (Clark 1991:18; Lesure 1997). Pottery occurs in greater variety, with an increased number of shapes that may relate to functional differentiation. There may be evidence for village specialization in making obsidian tools and salt production (Bove 1989:4). Ranking is suggested by the presence of burials with differential distribution of goods, including jade beads, obsidian (from three sources), and mirrors of white mica. Only two mirrors have been recovered, one with the burial of a child (Clark 1991:20–21). The child's mirror was affixed to a sherd disk; otherwise, they may have been mounted on helmets or tied to a headband. These data on burial goods, mirrors, and specialization can be interpreted within the OLW model to support a more direct correlation between wealth and legitimacy; their role in social/cosmic order is less direct.

There is considerable continuity between Locona and the following Ocós phase (Blake et al. 1995:171). A study of obsidian distribution in the Ocós phase suggests that the region had a well-organized and stable political economy, exchange relations between autonomous polities, "economic managers," and some redistribution (Clark and Salcedo Romero 1989:24). One unusual feature is the presence of figurines of obese males seated on three-legged stools and wearing animal-skin chest covers. On their heads they display animal masks or helmets with mirrors in front; sometimes, however, the mirrors are chest ornaments. These figurines, which are very realistic, individualized, and portraitlike, might be interpreted as suggesting shaman-type leaders among the Mokaya.

Paso de la Amada is the largest and most complex site known in the region. Its largest structure, Mound 6, was rebuilt nine times to a height of 4 meters and supported a sequence of oval or apsidal structures, interpreted as domestic, measuring 20–22 x 10–12 meters in size (Clark 2004:56; Clark, Gibson, and Zeidler 2004). The site also features a ballcourt (Hill, Blake, and Clark 1998), apparently the earliest court construction in Mesoamerica with a date of 1400 B.C. Oriented northeast-southwest, the court has a playing alley measuring 78 x 7 meters, flanked by low benches backed by earthen mounds 1.5 meters high.

Warren Hill and John Clark (2001) have argued, using Paso de la Amada as a case study, that ballcourts and the ballgame were closely tied to the emergence of heritable political power in Early Formative Mesoamerica. Their argument about the relations of the ballgame to the beginnings of "government" in the region hinge on comparative data attesting to the role of gambling on games as part of redistribution of wealth in rank societies, and on the role of such ritualized games in creating and reinforcing individual and community identities. Gambling on the ballgame is attested in one of the Hero Twins' episodes in the Underworld in the *Popol Vuh*. Clearly, this kind of role for the ballgame also invokes imputations of "order."

Paso de la Amada Mound 6 is located south of the ballcourt, suggesting that its residents might have played a role in both the ballcourt's construction and use. These two structures form the northwestern and southwestern sides of a square plaza covering three hectares (Clark 2004). Clark (ibid.:57, 59) concludes, following Lowe (1977:211), that by 1650 cal. B.C. the site was a ceremonial center, and that it evinces a quadripartite plan and "cosmological notions of world directions and centering." Intriguingly, the site appears to have been planned and constructed using standard units of measurement of 1.666 meters (presumably an arm span?), with larger measurement modules of 21.66, 43.32, and 86.63 meters (Clark 2004:59; note that this is double the standard unit of Teotihuacan construction, 83 centimeters [Sugiyama 2004:103]). The ballcourt structure, Clark asserts, is 86.63 meters long, or fifty-two units of 1.666 meters; the length of Mound 6, the presumed chiefly residence, is one-fourth that of the ballcourt, 21.66 meters, or thirteen of the 1.666 meter units.[5] The significance of these units becomes apparent later.

The succeeding Cherla phase saw a "rapid and significant shift" in the Mokaya tradition and the first appearance of Olmec-like material (Blake et al. 1995:173). It is viewed as transitional between the Mokaya Ocós and the later Olmec-related Cuadros phase, which saw the "peak development of the Early Olmec tradition in the Pacific Coast region" ibid.:175). Paso de la Amada was abandoned about 1250 cal. B.C.

THE EARLY MESOAMERICAN TRADITION

The cultural processes leading to food production, sedentary settlement, and societal complexity were slow and highly variable from region to region within Mesoamerica, and the precise causes and events underlying these developments during the five millennia from roughly nine thousand to four thousand years ago cannot yet be specified. Nonetheless, certain critical elements of the distinctive Mesoamerican culture pattern were established during the Archaic stage (see Clark 1991:22; Drennan 1983a; Marcus, Flannery, and Spores 1983) and were greatly elaborated in the transition to the Formative and during the Early Formative itself.

Cuisine

Diet and cuisine are defining elements of a culture and are highly resistant to change, as are the fundamental tools—ceramic and stone—of food preparation. It is not surprising, then, that the basic Mesoamerican diet emerged early, with first wild then domesticated plants, including varieties of squash and beans, maize, chile peppers, avocadoes, and tomatoes (Flannery 1986b; MacNeish 1967).[6] Archaic peoples also developed several "industrial" domesticates, including gourds for containers and cotton for textiles. The size and nutritional yield of the preferred plant foods increased through the Archaic period by means of selection, tending, and natural hybridization and genetic mutation. Modes of consumption changed too, as evidenced by analysis of coprolites: "Pumpkins and squashes were at one time gathered for their seeds (often roasted), later for their flesh (often crushed). Beans in early times were eaten green (in or out of their pods), later eaten mature (after being soaked). Corncobs (perhaps green) were once masticated whole and then expectorated after the juice was sucked out; later, kernels were eaten off the cob, ground to flour, or made into leached dough" (MacNeish 1964:421).

The domestication of corn (maize) is particularly interesting, having been the subject of debate among botanists and other scientists for decades. Molecular analyses have confirmed the long-held belief that the earliest ancestor of modern corn is a wild grass, teosinte (*Zea mays* spp. *parviglumis;* Doebley, Stec, and Hubbard 1997). This grass bears tiny "ears" or seed heads (perhaps only two centimeters long) with several indigestible grains on them, each ear enclosed in a separate husk, or glume, that readily breaks free of the stalk, thus rendering it difficult to harvest efficiently. Further genetic analyses (Wright et al. 2005) indicate that 2 to 4 percent of genes in the maize genome, or some twelve hundred genes, have been affected by artificial selection. Researchers note that the dramatic structural transformations that made maize much more nutritious than teosinte were the result of mutations in only three genes, and that ancient farmers were consciously selecting plants that exhibited the desired traits of larger kernels and cobs (Fedoroff 2003; Jaenicke-Després et al. 2003). One of the altered genes affects the starchiness of the grain, which in turn affects the texture of dough made from the grain, and this might have been selected in the process of domestication (Jaenicke-Després et al. 2003). Other researchers (Smalley and Blake 2003) suggest that *Zea* may have been domesticated for the sugar content of its stalk rather than for its grain, which would have been important as a sweetener and perhaps in making fermented beverages such as *chicha* (maize beer).

It appears that maize probably evolved from a "single domestication event" of teosinte in the Río Balsas basin of southwestern Mexico around nine thousand years ago (Fedoroff 2003), where teosinte ripens in October (Flannery 1986b:25). Apparently, a rather sudden transformation in the structure of *Zea*, perhaps as a result of some "abnormal conditions (such as accidental irrigation during the winter dry season)," produced plants over a few generations that bore cobs with multiple rows of "naked" kernels (i.e., lacking individual glumes) that did not disarticulate naturally (Iltis 1983: 890–891). New accelerator mass spectrometry (AMS) radiocarbon dates on the earliest samples of *Zea mays* from Tehuacán, Guilá Naquitz, and other caves suggest that these changes were well established by forty-four hundred years ago (Benz and Iltis 1990:506; Fedoroff 2003; also Benz 2001). Genetic evidence indicates that this early maize was already fully domesticated rather than wild.

This is the kind of corn that was found in the Tehuacán caves: it "required planting," and "only

human intervention could have fostered its growth and reproduction" (Benz and Iltis 1990:507). Thus the "accidental irrigation" referred to above might have been the intentional processes of tending. Estimated yields of grain from hypothetical plots of early corn are on the order of sixty to eighty kilograms per hectare (Flannery 1986b:26). Continued selection and cultivation over the next few millennia led to increased yields of maize, estimated for arid highland conditions at roughly two hundred kilograms per hectare around 2000 B.C. and probably three hundred kilograms per hectare by 1000 B.C. (see note 4 here; Flannery 1986a:26).

Material Culture

Marcus, Flannery, and Spores (1983:39) call attention to the complex technology for plant and animal hunting, collecting, and use that developed during the Archaic period, including the *atlatl* (throwing stick), lance, net, basket, snare, and roasting pit. Much of this early technology was made of perishable materials such as wood and plant fibers, and thus is rarely recovered except in unusual environmental conditions. Such conditions are typical of caves in arid regions, as in Oaxaca and Tehuacán, where samples were abundant. Mats woven from strips of palm, agave, or yucca were used as sleeping pads, seats, and bags and were so common that archaeologists referred to the people as "mat-makers" (MacNeish 1964:422).

Pottery began to be used, accompanying sedentary settlement, about 2300 B.C. in the Mexican highlands (see, e.g., C. Brush 1965; cf. Clark and Cheetham 2002:316, who prefer a date of 1500 B.C. because of the pottery's resemblance to Tierras Largas materials from Oaxaca) and around 1550 or so on the Pacific coast (Blake et al. 1995:167; Clark and Gosser 1995). The advent of pottery roughly corresponds to the Archaic-Formative transition in these areas. Throughout Mesoamerica, as in many other areas of the world, this early pottery frequently mimics the shapes of gourds (*Lagenaria* spp.) (Joesink-Mandeville 1973), which were among the earliest domesticates, around 7000 B.C. It is of interest, however, that the early ceramic industries on the Pacific coast differ considerably from those in Oaxaca both in form and in the presence or absence of decoration, suggesting different inspiration, functions, or both.

Stone grinding or milling stones, known as *manos* and *metates* in Spanish, continue to be used to grind corn into coarse flour, or *masa*, for gruel or toasted cakes. Their development seems to coincide with increased yields of maize in the Early Formative period, as they are known at Gulf coastal sites beginning around 1500–1350 B.C. but are not common on the Pacific coast until around 1150 B.C. (Grove 1981a:389). Although botanists specializing in maize suggest that early selection processes leading to domestication might have been influenced by the texture of tortillas, there could have been greater early emphasis on boiling the stalks (Smalley and Blake 2003). It is not known when tortillas became an important part of the Mesoamerican diet. Archaeologically, the making of tortillas is attested primarily by the presence of flattish, round pottery griddles, or *comales*. However, tortilla-like breads could have been made for millennia by toasting patties of moistened corn flour on heated rocks absent specialized griddles for their cooking. In the Maya lowlands, pottery *comales* for toasting tortillas are a relatively late component of the *batterie de cuisine* and do not begin to be recovered archaeologically until the Terminal Classic period, after ca. A.D. 900. Similarly, it seems that griddles were not made in Chiapas until about A.D. 1000 (Clark and Blake 1994:30n2).

Obsidian was used for several classes of stone tools and preciosities, and it appears that obsidian trade began sometime during the Late Archaic period (ca. 3000–1800 B.C.) (Blake et al. 1995:165–166). Obsidian from the Tajumulco source was most common in the Soconusco region of the Pacific coast from the Late Archaic period through about 1150 B.C., after which time the El Chayal source was more widespread (Clark and Salcedo Romero 1989). Mirrors made of iron ore or mica were worn by important males as headdress or chest ornaments by the Early Formative. One activity area at the campsite of Gheo-Shih in the Oaxaca valley yielded a number of ornaments, mostly pendants, of drilled flat river pebbles (Flannery and Spores 1983:23–24). Jade, one of the quintessentially precious materials of later Mesoamerican societies, did not attain that role until the Middle Formative period.

Sedentary Settlement and Public Architecture

By around 1500–1400 B.C., sedentary communities with increasing subsistence dependence on horticulture were fairly widespread in Mesoamerica. A variety of late Early Formative settlement types are known, including regional centers (occupying up to approximately fifty hectares, with public architecture and populations of one thousand to two thousand), nucleated villages, dispersed villages, hamlets (covering one to three hectares with fewer than one hundred residents), isolated residences, and camps, plus various functionally specialized sites such as stone-chipping stations, kill or butchering stations, salt-making sites, maguey-roasting camps, fishing or shell-fishing camps, and so on (Flannery 1976d:163–164).

The Archaic period saw the beginning of what might be called "public architecture" (Flannery and Marcus 1976). The site of Gheo-Shih in the Oaxaca valley is a seasonal macroband encampment occupied during the early rainy season (June through August) ca. 5000–4000 B.C. One feature of the site is a linear open area of 20 meters x 7 meters (long axis oriented to azimuth 110°, not quite reaching the winter solstice sunrise angle of 115–116°), bounded by two parallel rows of boulders, which was devoid of artifacts (Drennan 1976:353, citing a mimeographed report; Flannery and Spores 1983). In addition, in the Chantuto region on the Pacific coast of Chiapas, a structure, a possible shrine feature, and prepared clay floors lacking artifacts, all dating around 2700–1300 B.C., might also be representative of such early "public architecture" (Voorhies and Michaels 1989).

These open areas have been suggested to be dance grounds, an interpretation derived from ethnographic analogy to similar areas at hunter-gatherer macroband camps in the Great Basin of the southwestern United States (Steward 1938). The importance of dance in community rituals during a time of increasing dependence on agriculture and growing evidence of social ranking has been highlighted in a study combining cross-cultural ethnographic data with depictions of dance on Neolithic pottery. The study concludes that early dancing was primarily circle dancing, usually performed in a counterclockwise direction and at night, and might involve masks, body painting, and distinctive dress (Garfinkel 2003). These public dances promoted "the bonding of individuals into communities, and of individual households into villages" and were "probably calendrical rituals celebrated during the crucial points of the agricultural cycle. . . . Dancing together creates unity, provides education, and transmits cultural messages from one generation to the next" (ibid.:100). Moreover, to judge from cross-cultural ethnographic data, it is likely that dances would have been held particularly to celebrate the occasion of the new moon's appearance, or the rise of the full moon (Malinowski 1927; Nilsson 1920:151–154). Dance was clearly significant, in Oaxaca, at least, as evidenced by the recovery of musical instruments and figurines of dancers.

Although there is considerable likelihood that such features were dance grounds, their size and linear footprint suggest another interpretation: a playing court for some type of game, such as a prototype of the well-known Mesoamerican ballgame (Flannery and Marcus 2000:8; Marcus and Flannery 1996:58–59). As noted, the earliest formally constructed ballcourt thus far known in Mesoamerica, at Paso de la Amada, dates around 1400 B.C. (Hill, Blake, and Clark 1998); the width of the cleared space (seven meters) is roughly similar to the "dance floor" of Gheo-Shih, but the orientation is northeast-southwest, perhaps relating to winter-solstice sunset or summer-solstice sunrise. Whether dance grounds, ballcourts, or sites for other public performances, these constructions represent ideological materializations that, while long invisible archaeologically, begin to accrue greater significance at the time of the Early–Middle Formative transition, reflecting the many transformations and formalizations occurring at the same time.

Periods of seasonal settlement aggregation provided regular opportunities for social contacts and exchange of seeds, foodstuffs, and artifacts among widespread groups. Ethnographic analogy suggests that various kinds of integrative activities and rituals would have been carried out, including partnering or "marriage," mourning rituals, curing ceremonies, dances, games, feasting, propitiatory rites (perhaps directed toward some ancestor or deity), and so on, many of them probably officiated over by a shaman. The discovery of a "small bag with herbs, an awl, some flint knives, string, and polished pebbles" in Romero's cave in southwest

Tamaulipas, northeastern Mexico, suggests just such a shaman's or curer's kit (MacNeish 1964:425). In Michoacán, in west-central Mexico, a young adult male in a burial dating 2570–2322 B.C. had distinctive filed upper teeth in order to accommodate a "ceremonial denture, perhaps the palate of a jaguar or wolf" (Roach 2006). This interment was placed "below a cliff wall emblazoned with elaborate paintings of people dancing and hunting" (ibid.), suggesting that it was a shamanlike individual buried at a macroband location.

With increasing dependence on stored cultigens and lengthened periods of macroband settlement, it is not unlikely that these kinds of seasonal festivals became more formalized. It is also not unreasonable to suggest that they came to include rituals and exchange of information about celestial observations concerning the positions of the sun, moon, fixed stars (especially the Pleiades [Nilsson 1920:129–146] or the three stars we know as Orion's Belt), and planets (especially the highly visible and mobile Venus) and their correlations with availability of food, seasonal rainfall, and planting/harvest times.

Perhaps the most important specialized architectural forms, at least in archaeological hindsight, are raised platforms supporting structures on top and incorporating burials. These are such widespread distinguishing characteristics of Mesoamerica that we tend to think of them as having been intentionally created for those purposes at the very outset. Rosemary Joyce (2003), however, has argued that early monumental platforms might instead have been created with an emphasis on outward rather than upward expansion, in part by repeated refurbishment, in order to enlarge and raise areas of public activities for increased participation and visibility. In any case, by the Middle Formative, the Maya and other Mesoamericans were raising platforms and pyramids tens of meters in height as material references to an ideology of cosmic landscapes of sacred mountains. Their use as ancestral mortuary shrines—mountains enclosing sacred caves as places of birth and rebirth—seems to have been a later development (McAnany 2004b:151).

Besides pyramidal structures and ballcourts, additional specialized architectural forms appear to have developed by or during the Early Formative, including men's houses. Other patterns and behaviors characteristic of later Mesoamerican civilizations also are manifested, such as the creation of open plazas, consistent structural orientations to north, and division of villages into quarters. Clark (2004:45) considers rank society to have emerged at Paso de la Amada by about 1600 cal. B.C., "partly as a consequence of creating formal, public space."

Death, Sacrifice, and Mortuary Ritual

Ritual sacrifice of adults and children is a distinctive feature of Mesoamerican cultures, and evidence for this practice has been found in the early Archaic period. Excavations in Coxcatlán cave in the Tehuacán valley, in a deposit dated to the El Riego phase (ca. 5500–5000/3400 B.C.), revealed three extended burials in a pit. A child lay underneath an adult male, who was beside an adult female. The burial pit was lined with grass, the bodies were wrapped with net and cloth, and baskets were placed with each body. In addition, the female, possibly beheaded, had been sprinkled with red pigment, a widespread practice known as far back as the Old World Paleolithic (see Hovers et al. 2003), and the upper body of the male was partially burned (MacNeish 1961:8–9). That three individuals (a family?) would die at the same time of natural causes seems unlikely, and MacNeish (1981:34) proposes the existence of "mechanisms for population control via the ceremonial use of infanticide and (female) human sacrifice." The preparation of the bodies and their interment in a cave, however, appears to indicate some social or ritual significance attached to the people and their deaths.

In the same cave, infanticide may be a more viable explanation for another deposit of the same general date. Two burials of decapitated children were found, one above the other in a pit. The bodies were separately wrapped in blankets and nets and placed with various baskets, including ones holding their skulls. Their skulls had previously been defleshed, the occipital region broken, and the skull burned or roasted, perhaps prior to consumption of the brains (MacNeish 1964:425). Both sets of burials in Coxcatlán cave were found in the cave's eastern end, and, in both, the plant and animal remains reflect the "late 'wet' or early 'dry'

season, August–October" (Drennan 1976:351, citing Flannery pers. com.).

Language

Language is a critical element of ethnosocial identity and worldview, and, even though linguistic data cannot be excavated, it is possible, through the comparative method and techniques known as glottochronology and lexicostatistics, to provisionally reconstruct part of the history of language families. Similarly, cosmology and worldview are expressions of identity and cultural cohesiveness that, while not recorded exegetically, can be cautiously reconstructed through linguistic, historical, ethnographic, epigraphic, and iconographic data and comparisons spanning the millennia. Combining this information with archaeological data (structures, portable objects, dates, contexts, associations, etc.) yields further insights into the early development of the intangible but nonetheless core features of ancient Mesoamerican civilizations played out in the first millennium of the Common Era.

As mentioned in Chapter 1, Mesoamerica is a discrete linguistic area because its languages share features largely coterminous with the geographic boundaries of the culture area (Campbell 1997:156–169; Campbell, Kaufman, and Smith-Stark 1986). The origins of specific Mesoamerican languages are impossible to pinpoint in the absence of written systems; most are reported as "proto" languages reconstructed through the comparative method and interpreted as "real-life" early languages (see Wichmann 2002). Although previous reconstructions postulated a single early language, dubbed Amerind, in the Western Hemisphere, this idea is no longer accepted by most linguists (A. Hofling, pers. com., May 27, 2004).

In central and south-central Mexico, the earliest major language family is referred to as Proto-Otomanguean, believed to have emerged sometime between 8000 and 5000 B.C. (Marcus 1983a:6); it began diverging into its constituent languages about 4400 B.C. (Campbell 1997:159). Proto-Otomanguean included words for maize, beans, squash, chile pepper, avocado, cotton, tobacco, and cacao (ibid.), the major cultigens of early Mesoamerica. Its specific homeland is unclear and a matter of some debate. Three other major language families of Mesoamerica are Uto-Aztecan, Mixe-Zoquean, and Mayan, but it is not known when any of these developed. Jared Diamond and Peter Bellwood (2003:600) suggest that all four Mesoamerican language families diversified between 3000 and 1500 B.C., accompanying the spread of cultivation and sedentary settlement. Jane Hill (2001; cf. Campbell 2002) uses reconstructions of the vocabulary associated with maize cultivation to suggest that Proto-Uto-Aztecan was spoken by early farmers in central Mexico, and the protolanguage began to separate into northern and southern groups about 2500 B.C. These dates situate the process of diversification of major Mesoamerican language families squarely in the Archaic-to-Formative transition.

The modern family of Mayan languages is thought to have originated in a hypothetical or reconstructed language that linguists call Proto-Mayan. Proto-Mayan might be related to ancestral Mixe-Zoquean, spoken in the Isthmian region, but this too is a matter of argument. It is generally thought that the Preclassic Olmec peoples spoke some form of a (Proto-) Mixe-Zoquean language, as the modern distribution of Mixe-Zoquean closely tracks the spatial distribution of Olmec sites (Campbell 1997:161–162; Kaufman 1976; Kaufman and Justeson 2004).

In this context of early language differentiation, it is of interest that Flannery and Marcus (2000:9–11, fig. 3) propose a boundary across the Isthmus separating two style zones of material culture: the Isthmian, Gulf coast Olmec, and Maya areas in the east; and the Oaxaca and central Mexican areas to the west (see Fig. 8.2). This boundary was in place by 1400–1150 B.C. (Clark 1991). Their map significantly resembles a map of language distributions of old writing systems (Schele 1992:fig. 1, crediting Mathews and Justeson): Proto-Mixe-Zoquean and Proto-Mayan in the east, and Proto-Otomanguean and Proto-Uto-Aztecan to the west, a consequence of the diversification that Diamond and Bellwood (2003) note. A later boundary crosscutting the Isthmus relates to utilitarian pottery (Lowe 1989a:364–365): Middle Preclassic Olmec/Chiapas assemblages in the west were dominated by *tecomates*,

whereas jars with handles were more common to the east. Lowe relates the traditions to Mixe-Zoque versus Maya language speakers, respectively.[7] These various east-west distinctions were further strengthened by later calendrical developments, as discussed in Chapters 3 and 4.

Status Objects, Ranking, and Ritual

The differentiation in architecture and distribution of exotics in Early Formative Mesoamerica strongly reflects related processes of social differentiation, that is, the beginnings of rank society. Such exotic wealth goods include obsidian, marine shell, jade beads, and other items. Mirrors of iron ore (magnetite, ilmenite, pyrite) or mica, in particular, seem to have been possessed and displayed as symbols of rank and authority in these Preclassic societies as well as among the later Olmec. They were perhaps also instruments of divination and continued to be powerful symbols of wealth and legitimation into the Postclassic period (Miller and Taube 1993:114–115).

There is also the development and differential distribution of a variety of items that might have been used in ritual—dancing, feasting, celebrations of calendrical events—at either the community or the household level, including musical instruments, masks, figurines, and certain kinds of pottery. We can only guess at the degree to which perishable materials, such as feathers, fur, animal skins or parts, basketry, mats, cordage, pigments, wood, and grasses, must have been incorporated into such activities but failed to survive the succeeding millennia. Other elements of ritual, similarly perishable, are wild or domesticated narcotic substances such as jimson weed (*Datura*), hallucinogenic mushrooms (*Psilocybe*), wild tobacco (*Nicotiana*), and pulque, the fermented sap of the *Agave* cactus (Marcus and Flannery 1996:15).

Competitive-feasting models have been useful in some areas of the world to explain the origins of ranking and political relations. These would suggest that early rank societies in Mesoamerica witnessed competitive displays of wealth among aggrandizers, or "big men," who sought technological innovations (pottery, mirrors, etc.) to gain more followers and enhance their prestige and standing in the community (Hayden 1990, 1998).

There also might have been an element of competitive gift giving—perhaps in the style of the potlatch on the northwestern U.S. coast—among chiefs of adjacent regions to further augment their stature (see also Flannery and Marcus 2000:3).

DISCUSSION

It is apparent that many key components of the Mesoamerican culture area came into existence and were widely shared during the Archaic period. Some (e.g., dietary cultigens) developed fairly early while others, such as pottery, accompanied later transitions to sedentary settlement and the beginnings of social-status differentiation that indicate a change from egalitarian to rank society. In this regard, Clark (1997:215) opines that "Mesoamerica as a cultural area began in the twelfth century B.C. with the development of complex sociopolitical formations based on social stratification." Most of the components discussed thus far left clear indicators in the archaeological record as material objects and features, including spatial relations and associations indicative of human behavior.

But what of other aspects of the Mesoamerican culture area, equally if not more distinctive of its ancient civilizations, such as cosmology, calendrics, counting, writing, ritual knowledge and practices, ideology, and related arcana and esoterica? These are the ideological foundations underpinning expressions of order, legitimacy, and wealth in later Isthmian and lowland Maya societies. We are aware of—although we do not fully comprehend—these often-flamboyant practices in the Late Preclassic, Classic, and Postclassic periods, when they were recorded for posterity on monuments and buildings of stone and in painted artworks. But, clearly, these ideas and beliefs did not suddenly emerge in response to the creation of new, permanent media of expression. Instead, they would have had centuries if not millennia of elaboration and practical testing, as Peter David Joralemon (1976:58–59) observes in the epigraph opening this chapter. Given the growing illumination of the deep roots of "Mesoamericanness" in the Archaic stage, as just discussed, it is likely that some of these elements also should be traceable back to the Archaic-to-Formative transition.

Research into the early prehistory of the Oaxaca valley, for example, has addressed the beginnings of certain aspects of Mesoamerican (or at least Zapotec and Mixtec) ideology, a cosmovision that may have Archaic origins. One such element is the concept of color-related world quarters, which "is so widespread among the Indians of North, Middle, and South America, as well as vast areas of Asia . . . as to suggest that it may have been part of the cultural baggage of the first immigrants to cross the Bering Straits" (Marcus, Flannery, and Spores 1983:38–39; also Coe 1981a:161–162; Grove 1989:12; Lathrap 1974; see also Hovers et al. 2003:492–493 for earlier Old World color symbolism). In addition, figures and notations dating from the late Middle Paleolithic in Africa and the Upper Paleolithic in Europe—on stone, bone, cave paintings, and so on—have been interpreted as recognition of seasonal cycles and cyclical renewal (Henshilwood et al. 2002; Marshack 1972, 1985). While such broad cognitive awareness (including a mathematical/geometric sense "hardwired" into human brains; Dehaene et al. 2006) might be traced even earlier to the Early Paleolithic, it seems certain that it too was part of the "cultural baggage" of the earliest New World settlers.

In Chapter 1 I proposed that the basis of political power in Mesoamerica was related to an ideology or ideologies of time, calendars, and knowledge of cycles of nature and the skies. I suggested that, if this were valid, then early materializations of order, legitimacy, and wealth, in the Baines-Yoffee (1998, 2000) OLW model, should reflect such ideology(~ies) in both individual elite items and community constructions. Can this be seen as early as the Archaic stage or the Archaic-Formative transition?

Given that Archaic cultures lacked ranking or permanent status positions, it is not surprising that personal items of "wealth" are rarely present. One relevant item is the mat.[8] Among the later Maya, mat is a term for "seat of authority" that survived into historical times. It is not difficult to imagine that special kinds of early mats—woven from a rare or valued fiber, perhaps in a certain pattern, or with dyed colors or attached feathers, fur, or whatnot—were created for elders or shamans and came to be recognized as symbols of authority and legitimacy. The fixed woven patterns, like those of modern nets (Christenson 2003:136n304), could have been symbolic of cosmic and social order and the "regularity of the seasons in the fabric of time" (ibid.).

Later, as ranking and hierarchies came to exist during the Archaic-Formative transition and the Initial Early Formative, exotic goods, such as obsidian, iron-ore/mica mirrors, and marine shells began to be widely moved throughout Mesoamerica. These goods represent wealth in the OLW model, and their early circulation supports the position that the basic material manifestation of the legitimization of elites is trade in prestige goods (see Helms 1988, 1993). Concave iron-ore mirrors are of particular interest. Worn as pectorals or as part of headdresses, as indicated by Early Formative figurines, these impeccably crafted objects may stand as "the root of a general Mesoamerican mirror tradition associated with a Smoking Mirror deity [Classic Maya God K and Aztec Tezcatlipoca] and a system of deified royal lineage and rulership" (Carlson 1981:125). It is not easy, however, to ascertain a function for these mirrors that relates them to time and calendars. John Carlson (ibid.) sees an "obvious" connection between mirrors and the sun, largely based on analogies to the later Classic period, but at this early date such a connection might relate to solar movement observations. Experiments suggest the possibility that mirrors were used to flash the rays of the sun toward an audience or to start fires (Heizer and Gullberg 1981) as part of calendrical rituals.

There are also hints of communal structures that might reflect ideological or astro-calendrical concerns. The Archaic campsite of Gheo-Shih in Oaxaca features an early example of public architecture: a large, cleared, linear area oriented roughly toward the southeast and winter-solstice sunrise, which may have been a ballcourt feature (recall the importance of the ballgame in the *Popol Vuh*) or a dance ground. Some millennia later, the site of Paso de la Amada in southern Chiapas boasted a formally constructed ballcourt, oriented northeast-southwest (summer-solstice sunrise? winter-solstice sunset?). Regardless of their azimuth orientations, these structures would have been locations of public gatherings and ritual activities (dance or ball play) that served to unite participants in service to a shared ideology. Cross-cultural data suggest the likelihood that some of these activities would have transpired in accordance with celestial or seasonal phenomena, such as solar or lunar positions (solstices; new or full moon) or agricultural activities (planting or harvest). Clark (2004:67) describes the architectural layout of Paso de la Amada as "a device for capturing and centering cosmic and social power"; Martin Nilsson (1920:336) comments that "festivals and time-reckoning are from the beginning inseparably bound." It is evident that, by the beginning of the Formative or Preclassic, the foundations were laid for both of these long-lived Mesoamerican traditions relating to social and cosmic order.

A summary of the Archaic (or Proto-Otomanguean) contributions to the enduring Mesoamerican nonmaterial cultural legacy—one that acknowledges the important role of astro-calendrical phenomena—recognizes the following (Marcus, Flannery, and Spores 1983:39; also Marcus 1989:153; see also Gossen 1986:5–8):

1. A view of the world as divided into four quarters, each associated with a color and other attributes;
2. A set of directional terms based on the east-west path of the sun;
3. A concept of a breathlike "vital force," perhaps related to wind (Taube 2001:121);
4. A set of great supernatural forces, including earth (earthquake), sky-lightning (or lightning-rain-storm), clouds, thunder, fire, and also wind;
5. A single word for "day," "time," and "sun"; and
6. A concept permitting ancestors, especially royal ancestors, to participate in contemporary affairs.

These ancient concepts provide the underpinnings for ideology, cosmology, and calendars as the basis for the later key features of Mesoamerican civilizations, including order, legitimacy, and wealth. Thus, before returning to culture histories in the Isthmian region, specifically, the Formative societies of the Gulf coast Olmec and the Pacific piedmont Izapa, I turn to the subject of calendrics.

Mesoamerican Calendrics
Time and Its Recording

3 One of the most distinctive features of Mesoamerican civilizations is their extraordinarily
complex and precise calendrical systems. Mesoamerican peoples from Mexico through Honduras,
comprising nearly one hundred ethnolinguistic
groups, developed at least sixty variant calendars
that were based on a shared structure and may have had a single origin (Edmonson 1988:4, fig. 3; cf. Kelley 1974; Marcus 1992a:127). As
late as the middle twentieth century, fifty-six indigenous communities in Mesoamerica still retained one or both of the major calendars
from pre-Columbian times (Gossen 1974a:217).

Ancient and modern non-Western peoples throughout the world
are able to order past events in time through reference to "time-
indications." Time-indications are events, including phenomena of
the natural world and the skies, that are often unpredictable or of
fluctuating duration but that are culturally significant, for example,
a volcanic eruption, an earthquake, a flood, an eclipse, a war, or the
construction of a building (Nilsson 1920:9). The passage of time is
understood as the number of nights (sleeps), dawns, moons, snows,
rains, and so on, since that indicator event. In Mesoamerica, however, time was counted and reckoned far more precisely by calendars,
but before describing these calendars in detail and reviewing theories
of their origins, three key points must be made.

First, Mesoamerican peoples recorded time's passage by counting days. Days were named and numbered and boasted patron
deities; they "were animate; they moved and behaved in known and
predictable ways" (Marcus 1992a:136). Days held complex positive
and negative auguries (B. Tedlock 1992a:98–99), which could be com-
prehended only by specialists in such affairs; these auguries influenced both the personalities and the careers of children born on a
particular day and the outcomes of events occurring on that day.
Units of time, be they days or years or larger units of multiple days
and years, were conceived by the Maya as bearing a sacred burden: a
portion, albeit miniscule, of the cosmos.

Second, Mesoamerican cultures were "numerate"; that is, they
were skilled at using numbers, which is particularly evident in
their calendrics. Their counting system (Lounsbury 1978) was
vigesimal, or base twenty (as distinct from the Western decimal, or
base-ten, system), frequently interpreted as derived from counting

If there is one topic that is calculated
to make most Mesoamericanists run
screaming into the night, it is the
calendar.

—Ross Hassig, *Time, History, and Belief*
in Aztec and Colonial Mexico

by ten fingers and ten toes. Consequently, dates were calculated by units of time that were primarily multiples of twenty. In addition, dates were registered by means of two main calendars: one of these comprised 260 days, while the other encompassed 365 days and approximated the solar year. As explained below, any given date was specified by its unique number and day or month in *both* calendars simultaneously. A total of 37,960 days, or fifty-two years, must elapse before the same day names and numbers in both calendars again coincide; this interval is known as the Calendar Round.

Third, for Mesoamerican peoples the most salient aspect of time was its cyclicity. The concept of cyclical time—and its spatial translations—was a fundamental component of ancient Mesoamerican cosmology, ritual, and administrative life that continued into the twentieth century in many areas, particularly in remote parts of the Maya highlands (Gossen and Leventhal 1993; B. Tedlock 1992a).

THE 260-DAY CALENDAR

One of the most widespread characteristics of the Mesoamerican culture area is its calendar of 260 days. This calendar had two components: a succession of twenty day names (often called the *veintena*, from Spanish *veinte* 'twenty') preceded by a count of numerals from 1 to 13 (*trecena*, from *trece* 'thirteen'). The result—20 x 13 days—is a permutative calendar that proceeds for 260 days before the same number/day-name combination recurs. The day names in the colonial Yukatekan calendar are given in Table 3.1; their glyphic signs appear in Figure 3.1.

The "yearbearers" referred to in the right-hand column of Table 3.1 allude to the animate character of the days. That is, because of the complex calculations involved in the cycling of the two Mesoamerican calendars, only four of the 20 day

Imix Kimi Chuwen Kib'

Ik' Manik' Eb' Kab'an

Ak'b'al Lamat B'en Etz'nab'

K'an Muluk Ix Kawak

Chikchan Ok Men Ajaw

3.1. Classic Maya day-name glyphs (drawing by John Montgomery, © Foundation for the Advancement of Mesoamerican Studies, Inc., www.famsi.org).

TABLE 3.1.

The day names in the Colonial Yukatekan calendar

DAY NAMES				YEARBEARER
Imix	Kimi	Chuwen	Kib'	?
Ik'	Manik'	Eb'	Kab'an	Tikal calendar
Ak'b'al	Lamat	B'en	Etz'nab'	Campeche calendar
K'an	Muluk	Ix	Kawak	Mayapán calendar
Chikchan	Ok	Men	Ajaw	"Burner days"

Note: Read from top to bottom, left to right.

names of the 260-day calendar could ever occur with the first day of the 365-day calendar to begin or carry the year. As a result, these four days were called year "bearers." Through time, as existing calendars were modified and new calendars were promulgated, the four yearbearers changed. For example, reading across in Table 3.1, we see that those day names associated with the "Tikal calendar" (Ik', Manik', Eb', Kab'an) were yearbearers in the Classic period;[1] the Campeche calendar came into use in the Terminal Classic and had the yearbearers beginning with Ak'b'al, while the Mayapán calendar (K'an, etc.) was common in the Postclassic. "Burner days," celebrated by the Yucatán Maya, may be vestiges of Olmec yearbearers (Edmonson 1988:21, 231).

The 260-day calendar had an ancient geographical distribution from as far north as Hidalgo, Mexico, south- and eastward into Honduras (Marcus 1992a:33). Among the Aztecs (Nawatl speakers) it was known as the *tonalpohualli* (count of days), but its name among the Maya is unknown. Mayanist scholars call it the *tzolk'in* 'ordering of days', a term that derives from Yukatekan *tzol* (row, order, succession) plus *k'in* (day, sun) (compare K'iche' *ch'ol k'ij*; B. Tedlock [1992a:254n2, citing W. Gates in 1921]). Referred to as the "sacred almanac" or "divinatory almanac," the Maya 260-day calendar is commonly believed to have had primary importance in prognostication and in tracking mytho-ritual time.

The Maya *Book of Chilam Balam of Chumayel*, which dates to the post–Spanish contact period in Yucatán, has a chapter titled "The Creation of the Winal." It is a recitation of the days and numbers of the *tzolk'in* proceeding from day 12/13 Ok through 13 Ak'b'al to 6 Muluk, for a total of twenty days (a *winal*). This narrative, framed as the accomplishments of the first sage (prophet, priest; likely a daykeeper), recapitulates the creation of month and day names, of sky and earth, of land and sea, the first humans, and the first speech, all embodied in the notion of time as a journey. In capsule form, it reads as follows (Edmonson 1986a:120–126; Roys 1967:117–118):

12/13 Ok—he was born
1   Chuwen—he raised himself up to divinity

2   Eb'—he made the first pyramid/ stairway, descending from the heavens
3   B'en—he made all things of the sky, sea, and earth
4   Ix—sky and earth were separated
5   Men—he made everything else
6   Kib'—the first candle was made and gave light before the sun and moon
7   Kab'an—the earth was first born/ honey was first created
8   Etz'nab'—Edmonson: "he planted his hands and feet and made birds upon the earth"; Roys: "his hand and foot were firmly set, then he picked up small things on the ground"
9   Kawak—hell was first tasted/ considered
10   Ajaw—wicked men went to hell
11   Imix—rocks and trees were formed
12   Ik'—the breath of life was created
13   Ak'b'al—he watered the soil, shaped it, and it became man
1   K'an—Edmonson: "he was first disturbed at heart by the evil that had been created"; Roys: "he created anger because of the evil he had created"
2   Chikchan—he discovered evil within the town
3   Kimi—he invented death
[4   Manik' is missing in the manuscript, perhaps a copying error (A. Hofling, pers. com., March 21, 2002)]
5   Lamat—Edmondson: "there was the invention of the seven floods of rain, water, and sea"; Roys: "he established the seven great waters of the sea"
6   Muluk—all caves/valleys were submerged, when the world was not yet created.

The text contains numerous apparent references to the biblical stories of creation and flood, and Edmonson (1986a:125n2169) dates its writing to A.D. 1562. Nonetheless, the activities and events reported for many of the days closely match the senses of the Yukatekan day names.

For several reasons, the 260-day almanac is believed to be older than the 365-day calendar. In particular, the *veintena*, the twenty day names of this calendar, is a striking feature shared throughout Mesoamerica. Drawn from the natural world of earth and sky, animals and plants, these day names maintained a remarkable oral and written conservatism: they occurred in the same sequence, and eleven had "substantially the same meanings in all calendars from Olmec times onward" (Edmonson 1988:169), despite the language of the speakers (Table 3.2). These eleven day-name senses are wind, snake, death, deer, water, monkey, jaguar, eagle, quake, flint, and rain. Perhaps cane should also be added to Edmonson's list. Two other day names, sun and star, are shared between the Olmec and the Zapotec of Oaxaca, the Zapotec calendar having as good a claim as the Olmec to being the earliest, given the exiguous evidence. This broad dissemination suggests that the day names originated long ago, prior to the major Archaic-to-Formative language separations—that is, perhaps as early as 3500 B.C., and before ca. 2000/1600 B.C. at the latest—which roughly coincide with dated archaeological evidence for more sedentary populations.

In addition, with respect to the Classic Maya calendar specifically, the written day glyphs are much simpler than are the glyphs for the months in the 365-day calendar. Day signs are not written phonetically (see B. Tedlock 1992a:107); instead, they are logographs independent of any particular language (A. Hofling, pers. com., August 27, 2001). The day glyphs (Fig. 3.1) always appear in a cartouche, perhaps a glyph for 20 (Houston 1989:35) or a container such as a jar or gourd or bag, and some of these cartouches have small, curled, foot-like pedestals. One possibility is that the day signs are depicted in a protective nest or cave, where they are formally "seated," or enthroned, on a legged stool.

The 260-day *tzolk'in*, then, is deeply rooted in Mesoamerican history, but what accounts for the selection of such a seemingly (to the Western world) odd period of time? Modern efforts

at explanation are premised on ancient observations of celestial bodies, including the sun, the moon, and Venus, and agricultural cycles.

Solar Observations

As many scholars have noted, the day, or *k'in*, and, more specifically, the sun's diurnal movement through the sky and the Underworld are apt metaphors for time, space, and cosmic order in Mesoamerica (Earle 1986:156; Gossen 1974a; Graulich 1981; León-Portilla 1988; Watanabe 1983). The Maya *k'in* refers in a singularly metaphorical way to the sun, to the day, to time itself, and to the inherent sacrality of all of these. Each day is defined by the sun's traverse of the sky from east to west, where it descends into and travels through the Underworld to rise again in the east, beginning a new day. The sun's journey establishes spatial order—the cardinal and intercardinal directions—as its positions of rising and setting glide smoothly north and south along the horizons from solstice to solstice;[2] it also establishes temporal order by these same movements and by bearing the cycle of the seasons. The sun is a god, both young and old, with distinct daytime and nighttime aspects. Postclassic Maya priests were referred to as *aj k'in*, denoting their calendrical responsibilities; Classic kings were often given the epithet *k'inich* 'sun-faced'. The concept of *k'in*, then, as "sun-day-time—was not an abstract entity but a reality enmeshed in the world of myths, a divine being, origin of the cycles which govern all existing things" (León-Portilla 1988:33).

It has long been argued (by, e.g., Apenes 1936; Aveni, Dowd, and Vining 2003; Malmström 1973; Merrill 1945; Nuttall 1928; Pío Pérez 2001:215; see also B. Tedlock 1992a:93; idem 1992b:219) that the 260-day calendar developed from observation of the solar zenith in southern Mesoamerica. Solar zenith refers to the time when the sun is directly overhead at noon and casts a minimal or no shadow. In Mesoamerica, situated in the tropics, there are two zeniths, one in early May (which heralds the approach of the rainy season and the time of planting) and a second in early August (Milbrath 1999:13), but the precise dates vary with latitude (Table 3.3). In the area around 15° north latitude, the latitude of the sites of Izapa and Copán, there

TABLE 3.2.

Senses or meanings of day names in several Maya calendars

OLMEC	MIXE	CH'OL	TZELTAL	YUKATEKAN*		ZAPOTEC	NAWATL		CLASSIC MAYA	
Sense	Sense	Name	Name	Name	Sense	Sense	Name	Sense	Glyph T-No.	Sign Source?[†]
Sun, day	Root	*Imux*	*Mox*	*Imix*	Water lily	Sun, day	*Cipactli*	Alligator	501/ 1031a, b	
Wind	**Wind**	*Ik*	*Yoh, Yigh*	*Ik'*	**Wind**	**Wind**	*Ehecatl*	**Wind**	503	"T" sign
Night	Palm	*Votan*	*Votan*	*Ak'b'al*	Darkness	Night	*Calli*	House	504	
Hard	Hard	*Canan*	*Chanan*	*K'an*	Yellow	Black	*Cuetzpallin*	Iguana	506	
Snake	**Snake**	*Chacchan*	*Abagh*	*Chikchan*	**Snake**	**Snake**	*Coatl*	**Snake**	508/764	Snake? head
Death	World	*Tox*	*Tox, Tog*	*Kimi*	**Death**	Head	*Miquiztli*	**Death**	509/1040	Death head?
Deer	Rabbit	*Cuc*	*Moxic*	*Manik'**	**Deer**	Deer	*Mazatl*	**Deer**	671	Hand
								* Not a Maya word; Oto-Manguean 'hand', 'to eat (meat)'		
Star	Deer	*Lambat*	*Lambat*	*Lamat**	Venus	Rabbit	*Tochtli*	Rabbit	510	Quincunx
								* Not a Maya word; Zapotec		
Water	River	*Mulu'*	*Mulu*	*Muluk*	**Water**	**Water**	*Atl*	**Water**	513	
Foot	Vine	*Oc*	*Elab, Elah*	*Ok*	Foot	Dog	*Itzcuintli*	Dog	765	Animal head Oaxaca Mixe
Monkey	Ashes	*Batz'*	*Batz*	*Chuwen*	**Monkey**	**Monkey**	*Ozomatli*	**Monkey**	521	Mixe
Jaw	Tooth	*Eb*	*Enoh, Enob*	*Eb'*	Tooth	Sun	*Malinalli*	Grass		Animal head
Cane	**Cane**	*Bin*	*Been*	*B'en*	**Cane**	**Cane**	*Acatl*	**Cane, reed**	584	Zapotec
Jaguar	**Jaguar**	*Ix*	*Hix*	*Ix*	**Jaguar**	**Jaguar**	*Ocelotl*	**Jaguar**	524	Oaxaca Mixe
Eagle	Tobacco	*Men*	*Tsiquin*	*Men*	**Eagle**	**Eagle**	*Quauhtli*	**Eagle**	1017	Bird? head
Owl	Edge	*Chibin*	*Chabin*	*Kib'*	Buzzard	Crow	*Cozcaquauhtli*	Buzzard	525	
Quake	**Quake**	*Cabnal*	*Chix, Chige*	*Kab'an*	**Earth**	Quake	*Ollin*	**Movement**	526	
Flint	Soot	*Chaab*	*Chinax*	*Etz'nab'**	**Flint**	Cold	*Tecpatl*	**Flint**	527	X
								* If Yukateko, would be Tok'		
Rain	Grass	*Chac*	*Cabogh*	*Kawak*	**Rain**	Cloud	*Quiahuitl*	**Rain**	528	
Lord	Eye	*Ahau*	*Aghual*	*Ajaw*	Lord	Flower	*Xochitl*	Flower	533, 747, 1000d, e	Stylized head, human head, vulture head

Source: Edmonson 1988:6, 169, 174–175, 247, 220–221.

Notes: *Ethnographically known.

†Justeson et al. 1985:21–24.

Boldface: names nearly universal throughout Mesoamerica.

are 260 days between late-summer zenith and spring zenith. The zenithal sun positions are the "critical fixed points of the *tzolkin*," and the summer zenith correlates with the starting date of the Maya calendar in August 3114 B.C. (Malmström 1973:939).

This proposition has been rejected by some Mayanists, however, chief among them J. Eric Thompson (1966:99), who concludes rather lamely that the cycle developed in a "haphazard way from two counts, one of 20, the other of 13." The reason for the emphasis on twenty has already been discussed; the number 13, according to Thompson, comes from a general Mesoamerican belief in the existence of thirteen heavens ruled by thirteen gods (Table 3.4), which accompanies a notion of

TABLE 3.3. *Solar-zenith passage dates and elapsed days at different latitudes in Mesoamerica*

Latitude (°N)	Date		Elapsed Days	
			North-South	South-North
20	July 24	May 21	64	301
19.5	July 26	May 18	69	296
19	July 28	May 16	73	292
18.5	July 30	May 13	78	287
18	August 1	May 11	82	283
17.5	August 3	May 10	85	280
17	August 5	May 8	89	276
16.5	August 7	May 6	93	272
16	August 8	May 4	96	269
15.5	August 10	May 2	100	265
15	August 12	May 1	103	262
14.5	August 14	April 29	107	258
14	August 15	April 27	110	255

Source: Aveni 2001:67; Malmström 1997:50.

an Underworld with nine gods: "The nine gods of the underworld ruled the nights; the 13 sky gods presumably ruled the days. . . . This series of 13 gods of the days appears to have been of great antiquity [and because] the days [from Kab'an to Muluk; see below] represent the gods whose heads stand for the numbers 1 to 13, it would seem that the concept of the 13 gods was older than the 20 day signs. . . . Then the 13 days were increased to 20 to conform to the vigesimal system, by the addition of seven" (ibid.).

Marcus (1992a:137) disagrees with Thompson's notion that days were or had gods, believing instead "that the 20 day names were probably the names of supernaturals or revered ancestors—perhaps royal ancestors—rather than deities." The significance of the number 13, not addressed by Thompson, is discussed below. Nonetheless, his view that the sequence of day names beginning with Kab'an corresponded to the numbers 1 through 13 has been upheld by recent epigraphy, which shows both semantic and phonetic relations (Macri 2005).

Agriculture and Maize

A well-known techno-environmental suggestion, a variant of the solar theory, is that 260 days refers to an agrarian year. Indeed, an agrarian year running from February 5–8 (or early to mid-February in general) through late October (when wild grains like teosinte ripen) is known among the twentieth-century Ch'orti' Maya in the Guatemala highlands and the Mopan Maya in Belize (see Girard 1962:328–342; Milbrath 1999:13–14; Sprajc 2000; Thompson 1930:41; Tichy 1981:236–237).[3] A similar year exists in central Mexico (Broda 2000:409–417), beginning with a date of February 12, the first day of the 365-day year for the Aztecs. A variation states that "the year is divided into a planting and growing period of 105 days and a harvesting and devotional period of 260 days" (Fitchett 1974:543).

The 260-day agrarian year is based on five measurable solar events: spring equinox, spring zenith, summer solstice, summer zenith, and fall equinox, plus thirty-six days at the beginning and at the end. The remaining 100 days, November through February, plus the five unlucky Wayeb' days, are essentially the agricultural "off-season." This pattern, according to Franz Tichy (1981:237), can occur only around 15° north latitude—the piedmont and highland area of Chiapas and Guatemala—which has been interpreted as hinting at a possible area of invention of the calendar. As noted, at this latitude the period between summer zenith and spring zenith is 262 days; in addition, a variety of corn used in highland Guatemala is harvested 260 days after planting (B. Tedlock

TABLE 3.4.

Yukatekan Mayan day names, gods, and numbers

DAY NAME	GOD	NUMBER
Kab'an	Youthful earth, moon goddess	1
Etz'nab'	God of sacrifices	2
Kawak	Celestial dragon; Itzamna	3
Ajaw	Sun	4
Imix	Earth crocodile	5
Ik'	God B	6
Ak'b'al	Jaguar	7
K'an	Maize	8
Chikchan	Celestial snake	9
Kimi	Death	10
Manik'	Earth	11
Lamat	Venus	12
Muluk	Ah Xok (fish)	13
Ok	Dog of Underworld	
Chuwen	Ah Chuwen (monkey)	
Eb'	Destructive rain god	
B'en	Maize	
Ix	Jaguar	
Men	Old moon goddess	
Kib'	B'akab'-Tzitzimime?	

Source: Thompson 1966:table 4.

1992a:189–190; D. Tedlock 1985:232). This agrarian explanation is attractive because it could accommodate a very early date for the beginning of the concepts of the 260-day calendar in Mesoamerica accompanying early plant domestications, as well as account for how and why the additional 105 days were added to make the 365-day calendar fit with it.

A somewhat related explanation has been outlined on the basis of the life cycle of maize. Brian Stross (1994:29–31) notes that the modern Tzeltal Maya have names for a sequence of thirteen 20-day intervals that correspond to thirteen stages of growing maize, beginning with preparation of the milpa to soaking the dried kernels prior to grinding into meal. The names of these stages can be correlated closely with a sequence of thirteen of the twenty Yukatekan day names of the 260-day calendar. It commences (Table 3.5) with Kab'an (earth), which refers to preparing the milpa, and continues with Etz'nab' (flint, the chipped stone point on the digging stick used to plant the maize), Kawak

(rain), Ajaw (sun), and so on through Muluk (pot or water; the harvested, dried maize kernels are put in a pot with lime to soak and boil to soften them). This is the same sequence of day names that corresponds to the head variants for the numerals 1 through 13 (Table 3.4) and a portion of the sequence with nearly identical meanings in most Mesoamerican calendars (Edmonson 1988:169). The Tzeltal sequence is not the 260-day ritual calendar per se, but, rather, a 260-day interval within the 365-day calendar.

Stross's (1994) conclusions are proffered with reference to the maize agricultural cycle in a modern Maya culture. Given the universality of the *veintena* and the long history of maize cultivation in Mesoamerica, his explanation might reach much farther into the late Archaic period, when maize began to assume greater importance in the ritual and subsistence systems. As discussed below, it is increasingly evident that it was the 260-day calendar, not the one of 365 days, which governed ritual and agriculture.

TABLE 3.5.
Thirteen tzolk'in *day names and senses interpreted in the context of the maize cycle*

YUKATEKO DAY NAME	SENSE	MAIZE CYCLE SYMBOLISM*
Kab'an	Earth	Prepare milpa for planting
Etz'nab'	Flint	Point of digging stick to plant maize
Kawak	Rain	Moistens soil
Ajaw	Sun	Warms soil
Imix	Water lily	Roots and leaves appear
Ik'	Wind	Life enters maize
Ak'b'al	Darkness	Kernel inside "house" (husk), faces down toward Underworld darkness
K'an	Yellow	Edible ear of corn; yellow, ripe
Chikchan	Snake	First fruits
Kimi	Death	Maturity of maize
Manik'	Deer	Come to eat maize in field
Lamat	Rabbits	Come to eat maize in field
Muluk	Water (or pot)	Soaking harvested maize

Source: Stross 1994:29.
Note: Symbolism drawn from the Tzeltal Maya.

Venus Cycles

A more recent and intricate explanation for the origins of the 260-day almanac is based on cycles of visibility of the planet Venus (Aveni 2001:90–94, 184–196; D. Tedlock 1985:40, 233–34; cf. Justeson 1989:78). Venus, the third-brightest object in the sky after the sun and the moon, and known as Chak Ek' or Noh Ek' (great star) by the Maya, closely tracks the emergence and disappearance of the sun, appearing on the horizon either at dawn just before the sun rises or in the evening just after the sun has set. Over a mean period of approximately 584 days Venus goes through a cycle of morning star, superior conjunction (when it is obscured by passage behind the sun), evening star, and inferior conjunction (passing in front of the sun).[4] It is visible as morning star and evening star for a mean of 260 days each; the intervals range around 253–265 days (Aveni 1991:309–310). The periods between these apparitions, when Venus is not visible, total about sixty-four days. Five Venus "years" of 584 days, during which exact positions of the planet recur in the sky, correspond to a cycle of eight solar years, or 2,920 days (see Lounsbury 1978:777). Two Calendar Rounds, or approximately 104 years, are equivalent to sixty-five short (584-day) Venus cycles, or thirteen long (eight-year) cycles.

Venus plays several important roles in Mesoamerican mythology, being identified with the central Mexican deity Quetzalcoatl. In addition, one of the day names in the Olmec calendar means "star," perhaps referencing Venus. The movements of Venus also have been correlated with the agricultural cycle of maize, the rainy season, and the *Popol Vuh* (see Milbrath 1999: 159–160; Sprajc 1996). In particular, One Hunahpu has been identified with both Venus (see Aveni 2002b) and the Maya Tonsured Maize God (Taube 1986, 1992:48). Moreover, Venus as morning star may be linked to the planting of maize, while Venus as evening star relates the growth of maize through One Hunahpu's decapitation and his skull's fertilization of Blood Moon (Milbrath 1999:159).

The Maya Venus calendar appears to have been formally instituted, following centuries of corrections to achieve precision, in the tenth century A.D. (Lounsbury 1983), and the planet's peculiar movements are recorded in the Postclassic Dresden Codex (see Aveni 2002b).

Cycles of the Moon

The Mesoamerican 260-day calendar long has been interpreted in terms of lunar cycles, and records of lunar cycling may go back into Paleolithic times in Europe. The moon is the "first chronometer," writes Nilsson (1920:148): "The phases of the moon represent a gradual waxing and waning, a continuous development. The principle of continuous time-reckoning is therefore suggested by the moon, in opposition to the time-indications from natural phases and from the stars." Several Old World calendars are lunar based, including those of ancient Babylon and modern Islam (Nilsson 1920; Whitrow 1988). In coastal areas, the daily rhythms of high and low tides, and particularly the coincidence of especially high tides with new and full moons, might have prompted attention to these phenomena. Months are often distinguished in these kinds of systems by natural phenomena or human activities, as, for example, "moon of the ripe corn" or "rutting moon of bison" (Marshack 1985:28; also Nilsson 1920:215), thereby creating a "calendar" of sorts that encodes sequences of environmental phenomena. A petroglyph at Presa de Mula, located near Monterrey in northern Mexico and believed to date roughly 3000–2000 B.C., may represent lunar tallies (Aveni 2002a:62–63).

Etymologically, the English word *month* derives from *moon*, and the same is roughly true in Yukatekan Maya; indeed, this is a common practice cross-culturally (Nilsson 1920:148). The twenty-day *winal* (or *uinal*) comes from the Yukatekan word for moon, *u* or *uj* (Pío Pérez 2001:213), and the moon glyph is used as a sign for 20 in Maya writing. Lunar cycles, which we, unlike the Maya, know are a consequence of the position of the moon in relation to the earth and the sun, also provide a convincing explanation for the origin of symbolically important numbers among the Maya. According to Martha Macri (2005), these numbers—20, 13, 7, and 9—are based on average segments of lunations. The moon is visible for a period of twenty days: waxing for thirteen days (the *trecena*) from first visible crescent to full moon, then waning for seven days to the third quarter moon (cumulatively, the *veintena*). Then over the next nine days the moon becomes invisible before reappearing in the west as the thin crescent of the new cycle. This explanation accounts for the Maya belief in thirteen levels and gods of the celestial world and nine lords of the Underworld. Support comes from the *Motul Dictionary*, which gives the colonial Yukatekan Maya word for full moon as *oxlajun ka'an u* 'thirteen sky moon'.

Work by Helen Neuenswander (1981:126) among the Cubulco Achi, a group of K'iche'an Maya speakers, has revealed that "the Maya layman has retained, from earliest times, a high level of proficiency in the art of telling time and that the unit upon which his most exacting calculations are based is now, as then, the lunar cycle." The Cubulco Achi define the day "precisely in terms of what the moon looks like at night and where it appears at dark or at dawn. . . . [I]n addition, the position of the moon determines the rainy and dry seasons" (ibid.:130, 146–147): during the dry season, the crescent moon is "upright" and the "stomach" of the moon increases with water/rain, while in the rainy season the crescent moon is "lying on its side" so that water can pour out.

Doubtless, the coincidence of lunar and solar cycles every nineteen years did not go unnoticed, because a full moon occurring, say, on the summer solstice would be seen again on the solstice nineteen years later (Milbrath 1999:106), a phenomenon known as the Metonic cycle.[5] Similarly, the recording and tracking of eclipses and their correlation with lunar cycles might go back to the Late Preclassic period (Justeson 1989:87–88). The ability to keep track of such intervals and, more important, to use them to *predict*—predict times for seasonal camp movements, readiness of harvestable plants, coming of the rains, birth of babies—must have been a significant early source of power and legitimation for certain knowledgeable individuals.

Human Gestation

The 260-day calendar frequently has been considered to approximate the human gestational cycle from last menstruation (Bowditch 1910: Brotherston 1983; Earle and Snow 1985; Fields 1989:83–84; Furst 1986; Miller and Taube 1993:48; Paxton 2001:50–57; Schultze Jena 1986; B. Tedlock 1992a:93, 190; D. Tedlock 1985:232; Thompson 1966:98). One lasting indication of such a connection is the Mesoamerican practice of naming children by the day of their birth in the 260-day calendar. Ties between lunar cycles and pregnancy could be an ancient observation, as the apparent seven and a half lunar cycles recorded by marks on a bone dating to the Upper Paleolithic at La Marche, France (Marshack 1972:826) might record the duration of parturition.

Neuenswander's work with the Cubulco Achi is particularly significant in clarifying the associations among the 260-day calendar, lunations, and pregnancy. Pregnant women who claim to be unable to count and measure time in the Western manner are able to give precise accounts of the progress of their term of gestation by reference to the moon, which they call "our grandmother" (see also Watanabe 1983:724). The moon's journey in the night sky from its first appearance on the western horizon is conceptualized in terms of four periods of seven days each and described by hand gestures. During the first period the moon is a child; in the second it is becoming mature to the point of being directly overhead; in the third stage the moon is mature; the fourth involves the moon shrinking, followed by its "death" or burial in the Underworld (Neuenswander 1981:140–142).

THE 360- AND 365-DAY CALENDARS

The second major Mesoamerican calendar, an approximation of the 365-day solar year, comprises 360 plus 5 days. One explanation of its origins suggests that it began simply by multiples of 18 and 20, while another argues that it is a reduction from a calendar of 400 days, based on 20 times 20. For example, Edmonson (1985:262–263, also 1971:6; see also Miles 1965:272) argues that the 365-day calendar "almost certainly" originated as a period of 400 days from the propensity to count in twenties, with each month having a major god as its patron. But sometime early on, Mesoamerican daykeepers realized that a period more closely approximating the solar cycle would

be more useful, and they reduced the count from 400 days to 360 (Edmonson 1986a:8–9). The period of 360 days, known as the *tun* among the Maya, was ritually important to them and to the Epi-Olmec as the basis for the Long Count (see below) and it was also the structural foundation of the solar calendar.

But Mesoamerican daykeepers seem to have desired a calendar that even more precisely matched the true solar year, which modern scientists measure at 365.2422 days. The 365-day calendar, known as *ja'ab'* or *hab'* (year, time, season) among the Yukatekan-speaking Maya and as *meztlipohualli* among Nawatl speakers, groups the 360 days into eighteen *winals*, or "months," with each day numbered from 0 to 19 or 1 to 20 (numbering systems varied in different times and places throughout Mesoamerica). The year concluded with a period of five unlucky days, a "dangerous dead space" (Edmonson 1988:214), called Wayeb' (nameless days) by the Maya and *nemontemi* by the Aztecs. The month names in the modern Yukatekan calendar are listed in Table 3.6 (read top to bottom, left to right; see also Fig. 3.2). The process by which ancient daykeepers determined that five days needed to be added to 360 days would be fascinating to learn but remains opaque today. Edmonson (1988:114–115) suggests that the Olmec calendar initially might have overcorrected for what we observe as a leap year by adding six, rather than five, days.

Weldon Lamb (2002) has completed an exhaustive comparative linguistic analysis of month names across all Maya languages from the Early Classic period to modern times. One of his conclusions is that the meanings or senses of most of the ethnographically known names reflect those of the calendar of the Classic-period glyphs, that is, in

TABLE 3.6.

Month names in the modern Yukatekan calendar

Pop	Sek	Ch'en	Mak	K'ayab'
Wo	Xul	Yax	K'ank'in	Kumk'u
Sip	Yaxk'in	Sak	Muwan	Wayeb'
Sotz'	Mol	Kej	Pax	

Note: Read top to bottom, left to right.

 Pop

 Xul

 Zak

 Pax

 Wo

 Yaxk'in

 Kej

 K'ayab'

 Sip

 Mol

 Mak

 Kumk'u

 Sotz'

 Ch'en

 K'ank'in

Wayeb'

 Sek

Yax

Muwan

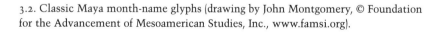

3.2. Classic Maya month-name glyphs (drawing by John Montgomery, © Foundation for the Advancement of Mesoamerican Studies, Inc., www.famsi.org).

the Ch'olan (or Yukatekan) languages (Table 3.7; ibid.). Another observation concerns spelling (ibid.:10–11): five names are exclusively phonetic, never logographic (Sek, Xul, Mol, Mak, Pax); three are logographs plus phonetic syllables (K'ayab', Uniw, Wayeb'); eight are only logographic, with optional phonetic complements (Pop, Wo, Sip, Yaxk'in, Ch'en, Yax, Sak, Kej); and three are variable (Sotz', Muwan, and Kumk'u/Ol). In considering the Yukatekan calendar, Lamb (ibid.:206) suggests that innovations include the month names K'ank'in, Wo, Pax, and Sek. Only the names

Yaxk'in and Muwan do not change at all during their long history; K'ank'in, Ch'en, and Pax are the most modified names (ibid.:36).

There is a "reasonable chance" that Maya month names go back to "the era in which the Maya hieroglyphic script was shared with or borrowed from Greater Izapan civilization" (Justeson and Campbell 1997:47). Linguists generally agree that most of the month names in the Classic-period inscriptions in the lowlands are of Ch'olan rather than Yukatekan (or technically more correct, Proto-Yukatekan) origin (ibid.:47–49; see also

TABLE 3.7. *Senses or meanings of month names in some Mesoamerican 365-day calendars*

YUKATEKAN*		CLASSIC MAYA			CH'OL*		TZELTAL		K'ICHE'	
Name	Sense	Phonetic	Direct Translation	Other Meaning**	Name	Sense	Name	Sense	Name	Sense
Pop	Mat	K'anjalab'			Ik' K'at	Mat	Huc winikil	7	Liqin Ka	Soft
Wo	Frog	Ek' K'at	Black k'at		Chak K'at		Uac winikil	6	U Kab Liqin Ka	Soft (2nd)
Sip	Stag	Chak K'at	Red k'at	Mars	Zotz'	Bat	Ho winikil	5	Nabe Pach	Moss (1st)
Sotz'	Bat			Leaf-nosed bat	Zek	Bat	Chan winikil	4	U Kab Pach	Moss (2nd)
Sek	Skull	Ka-se-wa			Kasew	Skull	Ox winikil	3	Ts'ikil Lakam	Shoots
Xul	End	Ts'ik'in			Chichin	Bird	Pom	Incense	Tz'ikin Q'ih	Bird
Yaxk'in	Green day		First sun		Yaxk'in	Green	Yaxk'in	Green	K'aqam	Red
Mol	Gather				Mol	Gather	Mux	Mud	Balam	Jaguar
Ch'en	Well	Ek' Ja'ab'	Black year		Ik' Zih	Black	Tz'un	Plant	Nabe Zih	Flower (1st)
Yax	Green	Yax Ja'ab'	Green year	Yax Zih	Batz'ul	Green	U Kab	Amaranth	Zih	Flower (2nd)
Sak	White	Sak Ja'ab'	White year		Zac Zih	White	Zacilab	White	R Ox Zih	Flower (3rd)
Kej	Deer	Chak ja'ab'	Red year		Chak Zih	Red	Ahel chac	Red	Chee	Tree
Mak	Cover	Ma-ja-ka			Mac	Cover	Mak	Cover	Tacaxepeual	Flay
K'ank'in	Yellow day	Unew			Oneu		Olalti		Tz'iba Pop	Mat
Muwan	Owl			Solar bird, owl	Muwan	Owl	Hulol	Arrive	Zaq	White
Pax	Drum				Canaazi		Oken Ahau	Lord	Ch'ab	Arrow
K'ayab'	Turtle	K'anasi			Ohl	Turtle	Uch	Possum	Nabe Mam	Lord (1st)
Kumk'u	Dark				Pop	Mat	Muc uch	Possum	U Kab Mam	Lord (2nd)
Wayeb'	Specter				Mahi I kaba	Nameless	Ch'ai k'in	Lost	Tz'api Q'ih	Extra

Source: *Edmonson 1988:216–217; **Lamb 2002.

Lamb 2002:9–10). Twelve, and possibly fifteen, of the modern Ch'olan month names are attested in the inscriptions, while only seven or eight of the modern Yukatekan month names are found in hieroglyphic form.

It is of interest, in this regard, to compare month names among the modern Yukatekan, Ch'ol, and Tzeltal calendars. One name (Wayeb') shares meaning (lost days or sleep) with Tzeltal. Two others (Yaxk'in and Mak) are found in Yukatekan, Ch'olan, and Tzeltal; another two months (of the four "color months"; see below) hold the color designations of white and red. These sharings seem to indicate that at least three Yukatekan month names (Wayeb', Yaxk'in, and Mak) and possibly as many as five are very old, dating back to before 1400–1000 B.C., when Proto-Yukatekan split from Late Proto-Mayan. These early month names include the extra five-day "month" required to accommodate the 365-day approximation to the solar year, suggesting that such an adjustment might have taken place during or by the Early Preclassic period. Two names in the Yukatekan calendar (Xul and K'ank'in) have no apparent connection, lexical or iconic, with equivalent month names in any other Mesoamerican calendar (Edmonson 1988:216– 217), suggesting that they were added after Proto-Yukatekan differentiation.

Apart from the months Yaxk'in, Mak, Wayeb', and the two color months, the remaining fourteen Tzeltal month names differ considerably from those of the Yukatekan and Ch'olan calendars. On the other hand, five month names are identical in the Yukatekan and Ch'olan calendars (Yaxk'in, Mol, Muwan, Pax, and Sotz') and another (Sek [Kasew in Ch'ol], both meaning "skull") is very close. All this supports the idea that Classic lowland Maya month naming was shared primarily between Yukatekan and Ch'olan, despite the fact that the Tzeltal and Ch'ol protolanguages do not appear to have separated until A.D. 100. However, linguists indicate that these similarities were not just shared but, rather, directionally borrowed, from Ch'olan into Yukatekan, because the Ch'olan month names are spelled out phonetically (Table 3.8) and the Yukatekan month names are not. This borrowing would have had to have occurred between roughly 1000 B.C. and

A.D. 600, most likely in the Late or Terminal Preclassic period.

Because the 365-day calendar closely approximates the solar or seasonal year, it seems particularly appropriate for it to have regulated agricultural and related secular events. Lamb's (2002:216) investigation of the linguistic history of the Maya month names identifies 572 senses or meanings, of which 161 (28 percent) come from agriculture, including 75 for seasons and weather and 69 for agriculture-related activities. He notes that the *ja'ab'* month names "recapitulate the fundamental realities of nature, agriculture and ritual. They articulate the round of ceremonies, festivals and myths to integrate culture with nature and unite all the levels of a society. The names relate man not to dates but to Time, not to the weather but to the natural world, not to literal interpretations but to complexes of meanings. The year does not track the rains or follow the sun; rather, it intimates the myths and distills the rituals" (ibid.:342–343)

At the time of European contact, the month names of the solar year in neither the Aztec (Graulich 1981) nor the Maya (Bricker 1982) calendars coincided with the appropriate seasons. In fact, they were four to five (of our Gregorian) months out of phase, hinting that the agricultural activities they originally might have marked were no longer the principal focus of the calendar. Thus Mesoamerican calendar priests apparently made no effort to adjust or intercalate their calendar to accommodate the imprecision of their five-day approximation to the true solar year. This imprecision led to the loss of one full day every 1,508 days (or thirty-one days every 128 years), which modern calendars accommodate through the addition of a "leap" day every four years. For Mesoamericans, however, as Michel Graulich (1981:58) has pointed out, any such intercalation efforts would have disastrously disrupted the far more critical concordance of the 260- and 365-day calendars in the 52-year Calendar Round, as well as their cycling with the Venus calendar of 584 days every 104 years. Consequently, calendar priests seem to have let well enough alone. However, this evidently tolerable but ever-widening disjunction between the month names and agricultural practices calls into question the

TABLE 3.8. *Linguistic characteristics of the month names in the Classic Maya 365-day calendar*

YUKATEKO MONTH	CLASSIC SIGN	PHONETIC (P)/ LOGOGRAPHIC (L)	VERY OLD?	CHANGE	SAME AS CH'OL	LATE YUKATEKO INNOVATION?
Pop	Braid + *k'an* (yellow)	L				
Wo	Crossed bands + black	L				Yes
Sip	Crossed bands + red	L				Yes
Sotz'	Leaf-nosed bat head	Varies			Yes	
Sek	Defleshed jaw	P				Yes
Xul	Animal head	P	Yes			Yes, unique
Yaxk'in	*Yax + k'in*	L	Yes	No	Yes	
Mol	Infixed *muluk*	P			Yes	
Ch'en	*Kawak* + black	L		High		
Yax	*Kawak* + green	L				
Zak	*Kawak*	L				
Kej	*Kawak* + ? + white	L				Yes
Mak	*Ajaw* + *Imix* infix	P	Yes		Yes	
K'ank'in	Tree + *wa* + *ni*	L+P	Yes	High		Yes, unique
Muwan	Bird head	Varies		No	Yes	
Pax	*Tun** + toad head	P		No		
K'ayab'	Turtle head (yellow) + *k'an*	L + P				
Kumk'u	*K'an* day sign	Varies				Yes
Wayeb'	*Tun** + hole glyph	L + P	Yes			

Source: Lamb 2002.

˙The *tun* sign is sometimes seen as depicting a log drum.

interpretation of this calendar as a tool of the agricultural enterprise over the long term.

Despite the wide concurrence that the 365-day calendar is solar based, there are at least two possible references to the moon among the names and/or patrons of months of the Yukatekan calendar. The god of Number 1 is the moon goddess (Thompson 1966:231), who is related to both the month of K'ayab' as the young moon goddess and the month of Ch'en as the aged and dying moon that descends into a well—*ch'en*, the opening to the Underworld—and disappears to complete the lunar cycle (Milbrath 1999:118, 119). In addition, the twenty-day months of the 365-day calendar parallel the twenty-day *winals*, etymologically linked to the moon, *uj*, of the 260-day calendar.

Edmonson (1988:214), who made extensive comparative studies of Mesoamerican calendrical systems, concluded that the 365-day calendar primarily governed public ritual, especially ceremonies occurring at the start of the new year. He (ibid.) interpreted the month names as referring to ritual symbols rather than to the phenomena of nature recorded in the day names of the 260-day calendar (cf. Lamb 2002:216, who identifies only 87, or 15 percent, of the Maya month names as having ritual or religious senses), and these names are both historically and calendrically unstable from culture to culture in Mesoamerica.

THE LONG COUNT AND THE *MAY*

The quintessential achievement of Mesoamerican numeracy is the Long Count, which was used by the Maya and the Epi-Olmec, but not by Mexican cultures.[6] The Long Count is a system of recording a date by means of a tally of elapsed days in both calendars since an arbitrary starting point. That starting date was a day 4 Ajaw 8 Kumk'u, corresponding to August 11 (or 13; see Note on Orthography and Dates) in 3114 B.C. in the Gregorian calendar.

To understand this system, it is necessary to know more about the vigesimal Mesoamerican counting system. Counts of units of one were recorded as dots (fingertips), but the Maya modified this system substantially, using dots for units of one through four and a bar (the thumb? the hand held flat?) for units of five; bars and dots were combined to represent numbers up to twenty. For units larger than twenty, they used a system of positional notation and, if there were no counts to register in one of the positions, they used an oval shell-like sign to symbolize zero, null, or completion. Linguistically, the Maya counting system was decimal: there are "separate roots" for each numeral from 1 through 11, and compounds (e.g., ten plus a numeral) represent numbers 12 through 19 (Edmonson 1986a:8). Etymologically, the Maya word for "month of twenty days" (*winal*) has the same root as the word for moon and also "man" (*winik*), perhaps in the sense of "whole" or "complete" (i.e., all fingers and toes). Modern Maya shamans who keep track of the days will sometimes count up to twenty on a single hand by using the three joints and tip of each finger and thumb (A. Hofling, pers. com., October 1, 2003).

Barbara Tedlock (1992a:107–108, also citing Ruth Bunzel) reports that, among modern calendrical specialists in the Maya highlands, the numbers used to identify days in the calendars have certain values. Low numbers (1, 2, 3) are "gentle" because they are young and new, while high numbers (11, 12, 13) are powerful or even "violent" because they are older and more mature; numbers in the middle (7, 8, 9) are "indifferent." Tedlock discusses the numbers specific to the 260-day calendar, and it is not clear whether or not these principles might also apply to the 365-day calendar. Similarly, we do not know whether the Classic Maya might have had similar interpretations.

The Long Count was a record of specific dates on carved monuments in a vertical hierarchy of "bundles" of elapsed days in their 360-day count that were mostly (though not always) multiples of 20, as follows: *b'ak'tun*—20 *k'atuns* or 400 *tuns*, or 144,000 days (approximately 396 Gregorian years); *k'atun*—20 *tuns*, or 7,200 days (nearly 20 Gregorian years); *tun*—18 *winals*, or 360 days; *winal*—20 days; *k'in*—1 day. The counts of each unit of time completed were indicated by bar-dot numbers followed by the day number and name in the 260-day calendar. As elaborated by the Classic Maya, the units themselves were indicated by glyphs following the number, and the columns tallying *b'ak'tuns*, *k'atuns*, and so on were followed by a series of other time-related glyphs, ending with the day number and month name in the 365-day calendar (Fig. 3.3). Mesoamerican civilizations, and we ourselves, live in a "Great Cycle" of thirteen *b'ak'tuns* that will end in A.D. 2012.

Among the Maya, the Long Count calendar and its manipulation not only provided a way to track time's passage since a specific starting date, but it also was a means of structuring geopolitical relations. I propose that from its inception, the Long Count was tied to the celebration of twenty-*tun k'atuns* (see Chap. 8), and these were expanded into a thirteen-*k'atun*, 260-*tun* (256 Gregorian years) cycle known as the *may* (cycle).[7] This *may*-based geopolitical system, the exegesis of which was an outgrowth of Edmonson's (1982, 1986a) translations of late Yukatekan Maya books of the *chilam b'alams*, played a significant role in Postclassic- and Colonial-period Maya political relations in Yucatán.

According to Edmonson (1979:11; idem 1982:xvi; idem 1986a:4–5), the *may* cycle was ritually "seated" in an important city that became the politico-religious "capital" of a region. Held to be sacred or holy and bearing the title "born of heaven" (*siyaj kan*), this city had a temple (*may k'u*, the "cycle seat" proper) housing the cycle and a sacred ceiba tree, grove, and well, or cenote (*ch'en*). Its plaza was the crossroads and religious center of the country and the navel of the world. The seat of the *may* held "dynastic and religious primacy over the whole country" for 260 *tuns*, or approximately 256 years, after which the city, its roads, and its idols were ritually destroyed and the city was "abandoned," although this might simply have been the symbolic departure of the ruling dynasty. Within the realm of any *may* seat were numerous subsidiary sites serving as seats of *k'atuns* (thirteen of them in an idealized model), each of which served as the administrative center for one of the thirteen constituent twenty-year *k'atuns* of the *may*.

ORIGINS OF THE MESOAMERICAN CALENDARS

When and where did these Mesoamerican calendars originate? Certainly, celestial movements, the changing seasons, and the dualities of day and night could not have passed unremarked by even the most ancient sapient humans. Those of us resigned to the twenty-first century's light-polluted nights can hardly imagine the awesome grandeur of starry night skies hundreds and thousands of years ago. Phenomena we identify today as the moon, the Milky Way, Venus, Mars, the Big Dipper, the Pleiades, and so on must have appeared as a majestic pageant of celestial beings promenading along overhead paths.

One study of the two major Mesoamerican calendrical systems and their historical development suggests that because they are so similar they probably had a common origin (Edmonson 1988:12, 119), but their precise beginnings are unknown. The earliest known carved day names or dates probably were inscribed in the mid-first millennium B.C. and were found in central and western Mexico (Cuicuilco, Chalcatzingo), Oaxaca (San José Mogote, Monte Albán), and the Gulf coastal lowlands (see Edmonson 1986b; idem 1988:20–21; Justeson 1986; idem 1989:79). Stelae 12 (594 B.C.) and 13 (563 B.C.) from Monte Albán (Marcus 1992a:38–41) are the first unequivocal evidence of use of both the 365- and 260-day calendars in Oaxaca. Edmonson (1988:20–21) believed objects—the Cuicuilco earspool and the Tapijulapa ax—might represent Calendar Round dates referencing the years 679 and 667 B.C., respectively, although the more conservative position is that they are just what is inscribed: day names and numbers in the 260-day count only.

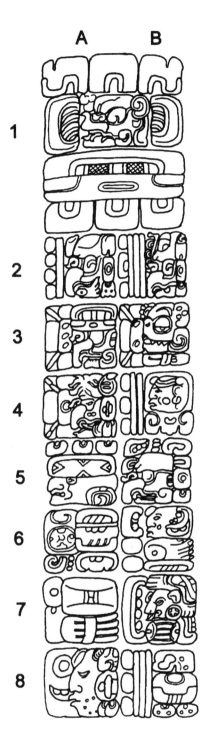

3.3. A Maya Long Count date, from the east side of Monument 6, Quiriguá (drawn from Sharer 1994:fig. 12.8). The inscription gives a period-ending date of 9 *b'ak'tuns* (A2), 17 *k'atuns* (B2), 0 *tuns* (A3), 0 *winals* (B3), 0 *k'ins* (A4), a day 13 Ajaw in the 260-day calendar (B4) and 18 Kumk'u in the 365-day calendar (B8). The large glyph at the top (AB1) is the Initial Series Introducing Glyph, the central element of which is the name of the patron deity of the month Kumk'u. Glyphs A5 and B5 represent the Lords of the Night, and A6 through A8 are the lunar series.

Regardless of the particulars, it is inconceivable that these late Middle Formative carved dates represent the earliest glimmers of calendrical record-keeping per se in Mesoamerica. Obviously, during the millennium or more between the beginning of the Formative and the early sixth century B.C., the two Mesoamerican calendars were developed, but considerable disagreement exists as to when and where they were created and how they are related.

Day and Month Names

One perspective on calendrical origins comes from consideration of the names of the days and months. Cross-culturally, these are typically drawn from natural phenomena or food or food-getting activities (Nilsson 1920:160–165, 174–215). In Mesoamerica, nearly all are drawn from environmental features such as plants, animals, and weather and can be viewed as ancient symbols and mnemonics for tracking annual cycles. Existing reconstructions of late Archaic subsistence and settlement patterns are primarily based on the well-preserved remains from arid highland environments of south-central Mexico, which emphasize pronounced seasonality in the scheduling of food procurement and settlement activities. Nonetheless, the rich lowland environments of the lakes, river mouths, and estuaries along the Gulf, Pacific, and Caribbean coasts would have been highly desirable settings for pre- and nonagricultural exploitation. As discussed in Chapter 2, occupations in such ecozones appear to have become semi- or fully sedentary earlier than in dry highland valleys, and to have benefited from less seasonal variability, thus perhaps calling forth different sets of symbols, gods, and events by which to track monthly and annual cycles.[8]

It is of interest to consider the ecological contexts of the plants, animals, and other natural phenomena constituting the names of the days and months in Mesoamerican calendars. Table 3.2 gives the day names of several Mesoamerican calendars translated into English. The translated senses of the month names range over many of the same natural-world subjects (Table 3.5), such as plants, animals, and colors, but some calendars also include references to prepared foods (tortillas, stew), rituals (flay, feast, flag), and even one obvious recent addition, mule (see Edmonson 1988:216–217).

The many day and month names referring to animals can be compared with a survey of the geographical distribution of Mesoamerican fauna (Stuart 1964). This survey highlights the zoogeographically transitional character of Mesoamerica, in which the southernmost distribution of Nearctic fauna of the central Mexican plateau and areas to the north overlaps the northernmost distribution of Neotropical fauna of the coastal lowlands and southern areas. Many animals referred to in the calendrical names are genera and species found widely throughout the region, including deer, dogs, snakes, turtles, various birds, opossums, bats, toads, rabbits, and various insects.

There are also certain animals from more restricted—specifically, tropical lowland[9]—habitats, such as monkeys (day name), iguanas (day), alligators (and/or water lilies; day), jaguars (day and month name), leaf-nosed bats (month), macaws/parrots (month), crabs (month), and vipers (month) (see Thompson 1965a:651). Monkey and jaguar are among the quasi-universal day names found in all Mesoamerican calendars, revealing great antiquity (and also suggesting lowland origins), while alligator and iguana are found in all but Zapotec (Edmonson 1988:169). Tropical species are less frequently used as month names and then only in calendars of Mayan speakers (Edmonson 1988:216–217), suggesting specifically lowland Maya modifications of the 365-day calendar.

Jaguar is a month name in only two calendars, those of the K'iche' and the Mixe (in the Yukatekan calendar it is an introduced non-Mayan day name). In the K'iche' calendar, jaguar is equivalent to the Yukatekan month Mol ("water"), which I propose originally fell between the spring equinox and zenith; in the Mixe calendar it is equivalent to the Yukatekan month of Muwan between the late-summer zenith and the equinox (ibid.:216). The jaguar is particularly appropriate as an icon for these months. Because jaguars make their dens in caves and their preferred habitat is heavy forest near water (Leopold 1959), the jaguar represents the sun entering and emerging from its cave entrance to the watery Underworld during these months of transition.

Isthmian Origins

The Isthmus of Tehuantepec has long been seen as an important zone of early calendrical elaboration and differentiation in Mesoamerica, although researchers differ as to which side of the Isthmus may claim precedence. Some scholars look to Olmec society on the northern side of the Isthmus in the states of Veracruz and Tabasco on the coast of the Gulf of Mexico. Others look farther south, at the vibrant cultures on the Pacific coast of Chiapas, Mexico, and adjacent Guatemala. And still others point westward, to Oaxaca.

With respect to Olmec origins, Edmonson (1986b:85) believed the Olmec calendar was ancestral to all other Mesoamerican calendars and that by 739 B.C. Olmec calendrical specialists had invented the 52-year Calendar Round correlating the two calendars (Edmonson 1988:20–21). Following a study of Olmec iconography, Marion Popenoe de Hatch (1971) proposed that many elements had celestial referents and that precise observation of the skies began to be made as early as 2000 B.C. Victoria Bricker (1982:103), noting the dates of "proper" seasonal alignment of the month names of the (Yukatekan) solar calendar, suggested a date of ca. 550 B.C. By 433 B.C., Edmonson (1988:117) claims, Mesoamerican astronomers "had attained the accuracy of modern astronomy in [their] estimate of the length of the tropical year" of 365.2422.

Other arguments about the Isthmian origins of Mesoamerican calendars focus on the Pacific coast. One suggestion (Malmström 1978; idem 1997:52–53, 77; Tichy 1981:237) is that the 260-day almanac began in 1359 B.C. in the Soconusco region, specifically at Izapa, an area known for its cultural precocity. Vincent Malmström bases this claim on the occurrence of a day 1 Imix, which is commonly regarded as the first day and month of that calendar, coinciding with August 13 in that year. He further suggests (Malmström 1997:63–64), on the basis of the occurrence of the first day of that calendar, 0 Pop, on the summer solstice, that the 365-day calendar began only a few decades thereafter, between roughly 1330 and 1320 B.C.

In considering the time of origin of the Mesoamerican calendars, the dimensions of the structures at Early Formative Paso de la Amada are suggestive. As noted in Chapter 2, Clark (2004:59)

found that constructions were based on standard measurement units of 1.66 meters: the ballcourt was 52 of these units long and 20 units wide; the elite residence measured 13 of these units; and other measurements were multiples of 260 and 365 units. The incorporation of the numbers 52, ~260, and 365 are highly suggestive, appearing to indicate that, by the time of construction of this site, 1650 cal. B.C., not only were the 260-day and the 365-day calendars developed and perfected, but also the 52-year Calendar Round had been invented.

The Long Count

Although the August 3114 B.C. starting day of the Long Count is known, the time of actual creation of this system by early daykeepers is a different question. As we have seen, August 3114 predates formal written recording systems, although notations on perishable media are not out of the question. No dates were recorded in Mesoamerica on permanent media such as stone until two and a half millennia later. There are two general views of why the 3114 B.C. date was selected as the beginning of the Long Count: (1) it was an arbitrary retrodiction from some more recent and important event; or (2) this date had some cultural and historical significance in its own right. The former position is dependent in part on determining when the Long Count was created by daykeeper-priests, which in turn depends on when the 260-day and the 360/365-day calendars (and the Calendar Round) were created.

Early proposals dated the creation of the Long Count to *k'atuns* ending in either 236 B.C. (Teeple 1926) or 256 B.C. (Thompson 1932:370). The date of 236 B.C. falls on September 12 on a *k'atun* ending that Mayanists record in conventional notation as 7.6.0.0.0 11 Ajaw 8 Kumk'u; that is, exactly seven *b'ak'tuns* and six *k'atuns* were completed, with no leftover *tuns*, *winals*, or *k'ins*, and it was a day 11 Ajaw and 8 Kumk'u in the 260-day and the 365-day calendars, respectively. It was thought that on this date, daykeepers, or calendar priests, might have attempted to standardize the calendars and extrapolate backwards to an "origin" point, thereby establishing the "beginnings of time" in 3114 B.C. on another day 8 Kumk'u. In addition, Ajaw is the last day name of the

Yukatekan 260-day calendar and Kumk'u might be the last month in the 365-day calendar. Thus this date would have marked the ending of the Third (or Fourth for the Maya) Creation and the beginning of the Fourth (or Fifth, and present for the Aztecs) Creation of the cosmos.

Edmonson (1988) suggests that the Olmec began using the Long Count earlier, in 355 B.C. He bases this on the coincidence of the start of a new Calendar Round with b'ak'tun completion that same year, an event that happens only every 937 years. Its occurrence on 6.19.19.0.0 1 Ajaw 3 Kej (June 8, 355 B.C.) represents, he surmised, the initiation of the Long Count as well as of other important intervals such as the *may* (thirteen *k'atuns*) and the *b'ak'tun* (twenty *k'atuns*); a cycle of thirteen *b'ak'tuns* is equivalent to twenty *mays* (ibid.:101, 118–119, 124; see also Justeson and Campbell 1997:52).

Edmonson (1988:120) further proposes that the development of the Long Count was "predictive," based on placing the *end* of the current creation in A.D. 2012, thus making its beginning (in August 3114 B.C.) simply an artifact of that calculation. In other words, he thinks astronomers determined that the present Great Cycle of thirteen *b'ak'tuns* should end on a winter solstice, fitting their calculations to "the numerological coincidence of the katun and haab cycles in 355 B.C.," his hypothetical inaugural date of the Long Count on 6.19.19.0.0 1 Ajaw 3 Kej. In fact, the current Great Cycle—the same one in which the Classic Maya flourished—is due to end on the astronomically correct winter solstice on December 21, 2012.

The idea that August 11/13, 3114 B.C., had some real and long-recognized significance to ancient Mesoamericans bears attention, however. Efforts at explaining this origin date for the Long Count have called attention to the positions of the Milky Way and the constellation we know as Orion in August of 3114 B.C. (Christie 1995:35; Freidel, Schele, and Parker 1993:75–107). In addition, there was a multiple conjunction—that is, proximate positions—of all the visible planets in the constellation of Aries on the night of February 17–18, 3100 B.C. (Aveni 2002a:115). It is not unreasonable to propose that over time early calendar priests might have conflated, intentionally or unintentionally through repeated calendrical adjustments, the events and the fourteen years

between 3100 and 3114. What I see as important here, however, is that our month of August—now, and presumably also five millennia ago—would have corresponded to the time of the "second solar zenith," which occurs between August 10 and 13 in southern Mesoamerica (Table 3.3).

More generally, we have already seen (Chap. 2) that late summer–early fall (August-September-October) was a time of harvest and relative abundance of food near the end of the rainy season in the late Archaic period in Mesoamerica.[10] Late summer was also a season of temporary settlement aggregation, in the highlands, at least, and perhaps also in the coastal lowlands, when previously dispersed groups came together in macroband camps for weeks or, by the late Archaic, months at a time. Ethnographic analogy suggests that this would have been a time of celebration and ceremony, including feasts, dances, games, rituals honoring ancestors, and exchange of goods and information. The start date of the Long Count in mid-August of 3114 appears to commemorate these seasonal gatherings at the time of food abundance at the solar zenith, celebratory gatherings that might have been continued within or among early villages and ultimately commemorated (materialized) in their calendrical systems.

RECORDING TIME

The development and maintenance of the Mesoamerican calendars would have required copious arithmetic computations, raising the question of how Archaic and Formative peoples, lacking a writing system, would have been able to accurately retain such knowledge generation after generation. Those of us in the modern world rely heavily on written texts and electronic devices, but in preliterate societies history was maintained by memorization and oral transmission (see Nilsson 1920:104–105; Sullivan 1986). Even so, the Mesoamerican calendars, especially their correlations, virtually demand concomitantly sophisticated counting and recording systems beyond merely notching a piece of wood.

Who Kept Records of Time?

From an anthropological perspective, it is important to consider who might have been keeping and recording these counts of time. In virtually all fields of human endeavor, some individuals are more talented than others, and the same is likely to have been true with respect to ancient celestial observers. As increasingly specific knowledge was accumulated, the responsibilities would have become more complex and might have been handed down in certain families in what Marshall Sahlins (1968:12) calls a "ceremonial division of labor among kin groups." Specialist occupations would have developed over time, and cross-cultural examples abound: Marshack (1985:28–29), for example, mentions specialized calendar keepers, or skywatchers, in various parts of the Americas as well as in Siberia who were "in charge of maintaining the schedule of practical and ritual activities" based on observation of lunar and solar phenomena, including solstices. Seasonal economic activities, such as hunting, would be based on these observations. Among the Kenyah of Borneo, "the determination of the time for sowing is so important that in every village the task is entrusted to a man whose sole occupation it is to observe the signs. He need not cultivate rice himself, for he will receive his supplies from the other inhabitants of the village" (Nilsson 1920:350). Among the Zuni in the American Southwest, the calendar was kept by a sun priest who took daily observations of the rising and setting of the sun, particularly with respect to where light fell and where the sun set with respect to mountains on the west side of the pueblo (ibid.:312–313, 351). On Simbu in the Solomon Islands, the "keeper of the calendar" was a member of the island's founding descent group (Munn 1992:109).

In the Maya area in the late twentieth century, in some highland communities in the K'iche' region, these kinds of ritual specialists were known as daykeepers and they still practice their craft. Daykeepers are "diviners who count the days of the 260-day calendar" using the hard red seeds of the coral tree (*Erythrina corallodendron*; D. Tedlock 1996:340, 341; also Earle 1986:161; B. Tedlock 1992c). These seeds are kept in small bundles or pouches with other objects, including crystals, jade objects from pre-Columbian times, coins, and so on. Until the late twentieth century, in Chamula, Chiapas, Tzotzil Maya daykeepers used a wooden calendar

board for performing part of their duties (Gossen 1974b; Marshack 1977). Daykeepers play an important role in the story told in the *Popol Vuh*, and in Classic and Postclassic times in the Maya lowlands such individuals—whether they were identified as diviners, shamans, shaman-priests, calendar priests, skywatchers, or daykeepers—probably consulted written books to aid them in their prognostications.

Barbara Tedlock (1992c:33) provides insights into the responsibilities of daykeepers (also known as "motherfathers") in traditional Momostenango, highland Guatemala. One duty is "greeting the Mam, or year bearer, at sunrise and sunset on each occurrence of his day name (once each 20 days), at one of four hilltop shrines located a short distance from the town center. . . . Their dawn and dusk visits involve not only ritual activities such as praying, burning copal incense, and setting off fireworks, but also the observation of the sun's position along the horizon. This is an important task, for . . . observations of sunrise and sunset positions at 20-day intervals helps [*sic*] in properly anticipating the zenith passages of the sun." They also play a role in New Year ceremonies: "The new Mam is received at midnight . . . on a series of local hilltops by the traditional religious and political leaders of the community, who carefully note which stars and constellations are directly overhead. Upon signal these leaders welcome the new Mam with prayers, special food, incense, bonfires, fireworks, drum-and-flute music, chanting, marimbas, and dancing" (ibid.:26).

Some equivalent to a daykeeper could have existed as early as Archaic times in Mesoamerica. In acephalous, or "egalitarian," societies lacking formal social rankings and statuses, individuals may be recognized for their special skills or knowledge and be called on to lead a raid on another community, plan a hunting expedition, cure an illness, or find a source of water. Individuals with special knowledge of rituals for communicating with ancestors and forces of the spirit world are often called "shamans" or "diviners," and such shamanic roles also could have been predecessors of the later Maya daykeepers: calendar priests of some sort, early "big men," or chiefly leaders who counted the days since, until, or between particular events. Keeping counts of the days in the cycles of the moon and counts of days between solar zeniths, equinoxes, and solstices may have been among the earliest duties and achievements of the ancient daykeepers. I propose that the role of daykeeper, an individual who counts the days, was fundamental to later Mesoamerican leadership positions that anthropologists and historians call "chief," "ruler," or "king."

Day-keeping Devices

Early daykeepers probably would have eventually needed and developed devices for making observations and for recording information, as well as emblems of their status. Tallying days or moons in earliest times might have been accomplished by simply putting seeds, nuts, or pebbles into a pouch or gourd (Nilsson 1920:320–321), a practice continued in more elaborate form by the twentieth-century motherfathers of Momostenango. Direct observation of most solar phenomena would have been possible only if the daykeepers employed something to protect their eyes, such as looking through obsidian (Peeler and Winter 1992:43), or perhaps the ore mirrors were somehow used. It is more likely, and safer, for the sun's position to be measured indirectly, by the shadow it casts. For example, the Kenyah, Borneo, daykeeper measures the shadow of the midday sun cast by a pole (a gnomon), using a stick with notches on it that match successive lengths: maximum extent (at solstice); length three days later; another three days later; and so on (Nilsson 1920:318).

It is likely that early preliterate Mesoamerican daykeepers would have relied on some mnemonic devices, perhaps of perishable materials, such as knots in cords (e.g., the Inka *khipu*; Urton 2003, 2005) or notches or charcoal marks on wood (Gossen 1974a; Marshack 1974), to track the days and make calendrical computations. These kinds of devices would have constituted early "specialized and elitist tools" (Marshack 1985:28–29), as well as personal materializations of astro-calendrical ideology and wealth (though not of exotic materials). Such artifacts, being perishable, are not commonly recovered in the archaeological record in Mesoamerica, although there are hints of various kinds of observing devices in Classic iconography and Postclassic codices.

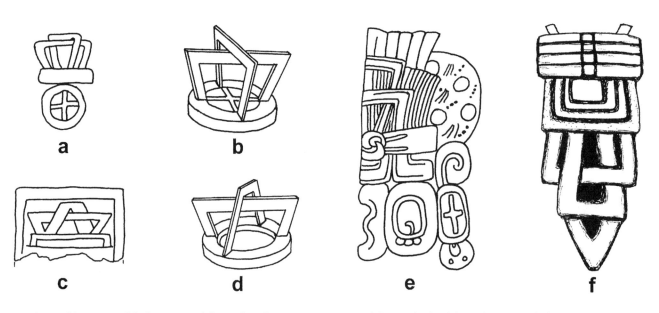

a **b** **c** **d** **e** **f**

3.4. A possible trapezoidal observational device based on Mexican trapezoidal year glyphs: (a) on the pyramid of the Plumed Serpent, Xochicalco; (b) perspective reconstruction (drawn from Digby 1974:fig. 2a, c); (c) on the Lápida at Tenango; (d) perspective reconstruction (drawn from ibid.:fig. 2 b, d); (e) worn as a headdress on figure on Yaxchilán Lintel 25 (drawn from Tokovinine N.d.:fig. 5c, left); (f) worn on back of Aztec figurine of Xiuhtecuhtli (drawn from Solís 2004:28).

Crossed Sticks

Crossed sticks and particularly pairs of crossed sticks—one used as foresight and the other as backsight—might have been useful for observing objects on the horizon from a vantage point on top of a temple (Aveni 2001:20). Such instruments are depicted with an eye in several pages of the Postclassic Mixtec codices (ibid.:21–25). A Tzeltal Maya word *ilab'* means "see-instrument" (Lamb 2002:183), perhaps some kind of device that aids in astronomical sightings.

The central Mexican "year sign" known from Classic iconography might be a representation of a portable crossed-trapeze "astronomical instrument" described by Adrian Digby (1974). Made of wood, such instruments would have consisted of a ring base with two trapezoids mounted orthogonally on top, the whole being probably ca. 20–25 centimeters high (Fig. 3.4a–b). As Digby (ibid.: 271–272) describes it, the device combines the properties of a sundial (using the shadow of a vertical element as a gnomon to indicate the time of day) and an astrolabe (using angles to measure the altitude of celestial bodies). When the instrument is oriented to the cardinal directions, with one trapezoid north-south and the other east-west, the shadow cast by the north-south trapezoid moves from west to east as the sun traverses the sky. At the same time, the shadow of the bar of the east-west trapezoid moves north-south during the day, its position at noon indicating the position of the sun. Over the course of the year, the distance of the bar's shadow relative to the axis of the device increases or decreases, thus indicating the sun's height in the sky and, ultimately, the season.

Digby (ibid.:279–282; also Edmonson 1988:111) notes the ninety-one days between solstice and equinox, meaning that the year can be divided into approximately four equal units of ninety-one days, and these in turn can be divided into seven units of thirteen days. He constructed an experimental crossed-trapezoid instrument and had a number of individuals make observations of the shadows it cast at thirteen-day intervals. The results were surprisingly accurate except for the two intervals before and the two after the solstice, when the sun's visible movement slows. The significance of such a thirteen-day count may be highlighted on a Late Classic polychrome vase (Kerr No. 2082) with a column of day signs separated by multiples of thirteen days—7 Kimi', 7 Chuwen, 7 Ak'b'al, and 7 Ajaw—which in turn is similar to an almanac in Dresden Codex 30c–33c (Boot 2003:4).

Digby (1974:280) surmises that the trapezoidal device might have been worn over or on the head; if true, that might account for its common depiction in headdresses, for example, in Classic portrayals of Teotihuacanos. This possibility gains further credence from a stone statue of Xiuhtecuhtli, the central Mexican god of fire and time (Miller and Taube 1993:189), who wears on his back an upside-down trapezoidal device fastened by a tie around his neck (Fig. 3.4f; Solís 2004:28). Digby (1974:278–282) further suggests that the device might be related to the *patolli* board "game," which has seven divisions on each arm, each of which might correspond to a thirteen-day interval. The penultimate divisions of the game board are marked with an X, corresponding to the four intervals around the solstice when accurate observations are difficult to make.

Pecked Circles

Hypothetical crossed-trapezoid instruments—"cross-in-circle" or "pecked-cross" symbols—also can be considered in relation to unusual features found in various places in Mesoamerica and beyond (Fig. 3.5a). These are typically double (sometimes triple) concentric circles (rarely squares) divided into four quarters by a centered set of generally orthogonal axes. Some of the axes appear to be aligned to the solar solstices; others exhibit a definite skew from the right angle, which calls to mind the "bent cross" asterism in the constellation Sagittarius recognized by the K'iche' in the dry season (B. Tedlock 1992a:188). The cross-in-circle shapes are created by small (ca. one-centimeter diameter) depressions pecked by percussion into stone outcrops or plaster floors of ceremonial buildings, often on elevations or areas providing unobstructed views of the horizon. In size, the circles range from ca. fifty centimeters to two and a half meters, averaging just under a square meter (Aveni, Hartung, and Buckingham 1978).

The common functional interpretation of these devices is calendrical, as the number of pecked holes typically totals 260, providing a material connection to the 260-day almanac. The numbers in the individual quadrants of the inner and outer circles vary, apparently corresponding to varying numbers of days between solar zeniths and separating them from fixed solstices and equinoxes (Aveni 2000:258–259). The axes typically consist of ten holes plus four between the circles and another four beyond the outer one. The emphasis on counts of four, eighteen, and twenty is significant in these designs.

It has not escaped attention that the pecked crosses resemble calendrical diagrams known in Maya books of the *chilam b'alams*, in Mexican and Maya Postclassic codices, in common quadripartite glyphs for completion (Fig. 3.5b), and in the *k'an* cross, and they demonstrate east-west connections between the axis of the cross and the summer-solstice sunrise or sunset (ibid.:260–261; Aveni, Hartung, and Buckingham 1978; Coggins 1980; A. Smith 1950:21–22). These 260-hole devices also can accommodate calculations of periods in the 365-day solar calendar (Worthy and Dickens 1983). Further experimentation might reveal their use with other relevant periods of time, such as lunar, Venus, Mars, or eclipse cycles.

Pecked circles might be considered the basal footprint for more elaborate three-dimensional devices. Perhaps a vertical shaft was set in the center, or vertical and horizontal poles were lashed together and set above them; the dots might represent positions for marking the shadow at given intervals of days, as among the Kenyah of Borneo (Nilsson 1920:318). Alternatively, perhaps large versions of the crossed-trapezoid devices Digby describes were set on these circles for making observations.

Pecked crosses have been found in the Maya lowlands at Uaxactún (A. Smith 1950), Seibal (Aveni, Hartung, and Buckingham 1978), in Belize (Wanyerka 1999), and also in western North America (Aveni, Hartung, and Buckingham 1978:275). At least sixty-eight examples have been found at Teotihuacan, which is often presumed to be the center of origin and spread of this device (Aveni 2000; Aveni, Hartung, and Buckingham 1978; Cabrera Castro 2000:203; Cowgill 1997:142–143). Two petroglyphs at Teotihuacan lie three kilometers apart in an east-west line perpendicular to the Street of the Dead, suggesting their importance in astronomical alignments and surveying; Sugiyama (2004:103) calls the crosses "benchmarks." The example(s) on Structure A-V at Uaxactún have an orientation of 17.5° east of north, 2° off that of the Teotihuacan Street of the Dead (Aveni, Hartung, and Buckingham 1978:267). Dating the petroglyphs is difficult: although most seem to be Early Classic—the time of Teotihuacan expansion—some at Tlalancaleca, Puebla, may date considerably earlier, ca. 500–100 B.C. (Aveni, Hartung, and Buckingham 1978:273).

These pecked circles could have been used in calendrical divination, with daykeepers moving seeds or pebbles around the holes. A feature in modern western highland Guatemala might be similar, where a Q'anjob'al ritual site was "composed of a circle of stones, each stone representing a day god." The "owner," presumably a daykeeper, recited the names of days in order as he moved around the circle (Neuenswander 1981:128).

The Las Bocas "Mirror"

An unusual artifact known as the Las Bocas 'Mirror' (Fig. 3.6a) is of interest in the context of early devices used in calendrical calculations. Supposedly found in a burial at the heavily looted Formative "Olmec cemetery" site of Las Bocas, in

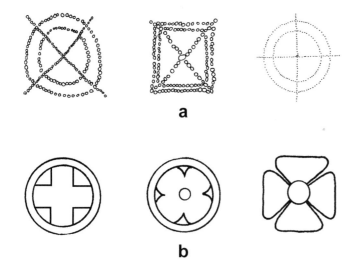

a

b

3.5. (a) Pecked circles (drawn from Aveni, Hartung, and Buckingham 1978) and (b) figures for completion (drawn from Coggins 1980:fig. 2).

the Mexican highlands of Puebla, the mirror is of unknown date and provenience (D. Grove, pers. com., May 1, 2004), and because of its questionable pedigree it has been little studied (cf. Marshack 1977).

This object is a rectangular plaque composed of 334 tiny polygonal pyrite tesserae set into a lime "cement" over a ceramic base. Unlike most early ore mirrors, which are either carved and highly polished circular concavities in a single block of ore (Carlson 1981) or are composed of random polygons, this plaque displays the tesserae in three vertical panels, left, center, and right (Fig. 3.6b). The left and center panels consist of regular arrangements of units of four tiny polygons which were multiplied into larger units of eight, sixteen, and so on, such that each panel can be considered to present two columns of sixty-four tesserae, for a total of 128 per panel. The right-hand panel is considerably different in conception, presenting atypical (compared to right and center) groupings of tesserae for a total of seventy-eight.

Marshack (1977:356), who studied the mirror in great detail, observes that the mosaic pieces fit so closely together that a razor blade could not be inserted between them. Perforations in the ceramic backing and on one edge indicate that the mirror was intended to be suspended, probably to be worn as a pendant. He concludes from the direction of inlay that the piece was intended to be used by the wearer by lifting it up to look at it from left to right, whereas when viewed by other observers it would be backwards (ibid.:367). Marshack concludes that the object could have been used to calculate lunar cycles. His study is based in part on his opinion that the "mirror" was initially larger in order for the right panel to accommodate additional tesserae, perhaps totaling the 128 in the other two panels. Ultimately, he considers that the 256 polygons in the left and center panels, plus some 98 that he calculates in his reconstruction of the right panel, represent the number of days in twelve observational lunar months.

My own analysis of the mosaic plaque (Rice N.d.a) leads me to conclude that the unusual groupings of nine, thirteen, and thirty-one tesserae in the right panel were intentional and accommodated counts or multiples of days in the Mesoamerican 260-day calendar, the 365-day

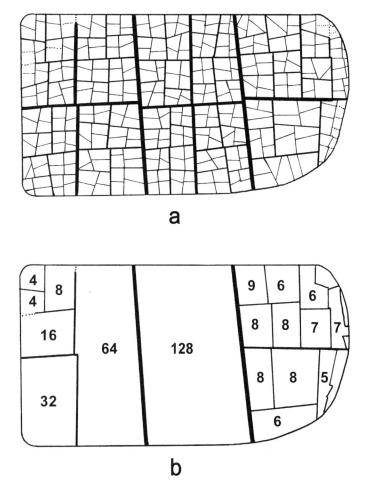

a

b

3.6. Las Bocas "mirror": (a) placement of the tightly interfitting mosaic tesserae (drawn from Marshack 1977:fig. 9); decreasing width of lines indicates hypothesized successive cuts; (b) number of tesserae in units, groups, blocks, and panels.

calendar, and various lunar, Venus, Mars, and other calculations. It is unfortunate that, although the mosaic pieces "work" as a sort of calculator for calendrical intervals, the plaque cannot be dated and might be from the Formative period or the Postclassic period or any time in between. The fact that this is a unique artifact in Mesoamerican archaeology might signify its singular importance . . . or confirm that it is an elaborate fake.

Architectural Patterns

Another way of marking and recording time's passage is through the orientations, layouts, and features of sites and individual structures. For ancient practitioners of naked-eye astronomy throughout this region—largely between about 14° and 21° north latitude—sun angles varied very little over three millennia, from 1500 B.C. to A.D. 1500. Thus the angle or azimuth of summer-solstice sunrise and sunset can be considered everywhere to be 64° to 65°50′ east and west of north, or azimuth 64° to 65°50′ and 294°50′ to 296°, respectively (this includes variations based on altitudes up to 3° above the horizon); similarly, winter-solstice sunrise and sunset occur at azimuth 115° to 116°50′ and 243°50′ to 245°, respectively (Aveni 2001:108–111; also Malmström 1997:77).

Structure orientations and alignments might constitute "orientation calendars" (Aveni and Hartung 1986:1–2; also Aveni, Dowd, and Vining 2003) or "observational calendars" (Sprajc 2000: 404). According to this concept, sites and buildings are oriented to landscape features marking the various positions of the sun on the horizon during its annual cycle. These alignments then constitute permanent records (materializations) and a kind of "calendar." Vincent Malmström (1997), for example, has proposed that many Mesoamerican sites were situated such that points of solstice sunrise or sunset—the points when the sun reversed direction in its annual back-and-forth movement along the horizons—were marked by a distant mountain, especially a volcanic peak. Ivan Sprajc (2005:211) concludes, from observations at thirty-seven central Mexican sites, that major civic-ceremonial structures were both situated and oriented astronomically, specifically toward sunrise and sunset dates, and typically at intervals of multiples of thirteen and twenty days.[11]

In addition, building orientations can stand as meridians, permanent markers of daily zenith passage. For example, the west walls of buildings can be oriented north-south such that they are in shade in the morning and then are relatively abruptly illuminated in midday as the sun passes the zenith (e.g., Malmström 1997:96).[12] Such constructions and their hierophanies might provide a way of marking the start of the day (or a season, or a new year), or, if somehow used as a basis for calibrating midnight, they might mark the start of a new day in the middle of the night, as Westerners do at present.

Certain distinctive structural features at sites throughout Mesoamerica seem to have functioned in solar observations and/or day counts. For example, a "zenith-sighting tube" was built as a vertical tunnel into the stairway of Structure P at Monte Albán, in Oaxaca (Aveni 2001:265–270). Two similar tubes were built into a cave at Xochicalco, one of which, tellingly, illuminates the cave for 105 days (ibid.:266, 269; Manzanilla 2000). Excavations in the Maya lowlands have led to discovery of the possible location of a gnomon: the shadow of a post set into a posthole in the center of a structure fell on an embedded stone in a platform to the southwest at the summer solstice sunrise (Zaro and Lohse 2005).

Calendars, Writing, and Power

The accumulating body of special knowledge derived from regular observation of the movements of the sun, moon, Venus, and other heavenly bodies begun in the Archaic period or earlier would have been passed down and expanded through generation after generation, leading to the emergence of specialists such as daykeepers. For Late Archaic peoples, hunters and gatherers increasingly dependent on cultigens, regular observation of seasonal phenomena—such as annual cycles of hot/cold and wet/dry and animal movements and migrations and accurate counts of the passage of days between them—would be highly valued because they determined the scheduling of subsistence cycles and whether the future held feast or famine . . . as well as reassurance of the continuing cosmic order. Recognition of harbingers of seasonal changes, such as the positions of the sun, the phases of the moon, and the movements of other celestial bodies, accompanied these observations. Individuals who possessed specialized knowledge of the timing of such changes and movements, and hence the ability to predict the appropriate times for shifting campsites and later for planting (particularly the arrival of the life-giving rains) and harvesting, accrued power and status in early horticultural groups in the transition from egalitarian to rank societies. With reference to the order-legitimacy-wealth model, an ideology was developing that would come to underwrite political authority and legitimacy, with early personal-wealth objects such as mirrors as part of the materialization of that ideology.

There are persuasive reasons to believe that the origins of "government" in Mesoamerica, as elsewhere, began with oral record-keeping and that tracking time would have been critical for early agricultural societies. Worldwide, before the invention of writing and in many nonliterate societies thereafter, the history of a people, including genealogies, important events, and economic activities, was maintained by oral traditions and storytelling, likely enlivened by music or performances. Recitations were probably enhanced by a variety of mnemonics such as notches or colored marks on wood, bone, or antler; knotted strings; painted marks on animal skins; or tufts of feathers. Creating names for days and periods—thereby animating and personifying them—would also make it easier to maintain such accounts. The greatest accuracy, of course, is through a permanent written system.

Indeed, according to John Justeson (1986), the origins of Mesoamerican writing lie in the calendrical system. He hypothesizes a stage of "incipient writing" during which graphic representational systems consisting of visual symbols or icons were gradually encoded with meanings, and he suggests that this stage can be recognized in Mesoamerica in Olmec-style iconography by about 1100 B.C. In particular, he connects the beginnings of writing to the 260-day almanac, noting that the earliest appearance of numbers is in association with the day names in this calendar. These day names, in turn, are "the only element of content shared by all Mesoamerican scripts, apart from numerals, probably inherited from the ancestral representational system," as illustrated by the fact that they are conventionally shown by single, fairly simple, signs (ibid.:445).

Justeson (ibid.:446) takes his argument farther, linking early writing and daykeeping with elite statuses and power. The individuals who developed the earliest scripts would have been elite males who were also ritual specialists, and one of their major roles would have been that of daykeeper, or "calendar priest." Not only would these early scribes/calendar priests have had responsibility for keeping counts of the days and tracking celestial movements, but, surely, a critical duty would have been that of manipulating the 260-day calendar and its auguries to determine propitious times or probable outcomes for important elite or group activities. By making permanent and public records of these pronouncements in written form, the early daykeepers/scribes/calendar priests could "promote a public perception of supernatural sanction" for the activity as well as its outcome (Justeson gives the example of mustering group support for a raid on a neighboring community). "Representation of day names therefore assists an elite in consolidating power over group action in the guise of scheduling" (ibid.). In other words, the materialization (in numbers and writing) of an ideology (calendars, cycling of time) was an efficient armature undergirding supernatural order and elite power, wealth, and legitimacy.

How might the role of counting days and daykeeper/calendar priests be recognized archaeologically in early Mesoamerica? One possibility, of course, is through artifacts: objects that might be interpreted as having uses in making or recording observations of solar, lunar, or other celestial phenomena. Such objects, particularly if found in burials, would be of inestimable value in reconstructing the role of the calendar in early societies, but because they are likely to have been made of perishable materials such as wood or fiber they are not likely to have survived except in extreme contexts.

Another possibility is based on historical linguistics, vocabularies, and etymologies. A particularly intriguing illustration is the Yukatekan Maya word *xoc* or *xok*, which means "to count, enumerate, number, order, sum" and "to read" or (as a noun) "a reading" (*Diccionario maya-español*). Marcus (1992a:80) calls attention to the Yukateko word *xokhun* 'to read', which comes from *xok* 'count' plus *hun* 'book': "[t]his use of the verb *xoc* is important, because it suggests that many books embedded the events they covered in a calendric framework." *Xok* (and *k'anxok*) also means "fish," probably a shark.[13] Sharks are present in the offshore waters of Mesoamerica and they, like other marine fishes, are known to enter the mouths of its larger rivers and lakes; for example, cub shark, sawfish, tarpon, and snapper have been reported in the waters of Lake Izabal in southeastern Petén, Guatemala (Stuart 1964:335). Similarly, in the Gulf coastal region, sharks are known to enter the Río Coatzacoalcos and its tributary, the Río Chiquito as far as Tenochtitlán in times of low water (Coe and Diehl 1980, 2:122). It is of no little interest, then, that a sharklike fish appears in Preclassic Mesoamerican art, particularly in head-dresses. Such headdresses appear to define the wearer—a chief? a priest?—as a "counter" and "reader," presumably bearing the responsibility for counting days and reading their auguries. This possibility is pursued in succeeding chapters.

DISCUSSION

The importance of formal calendars accompanies the development of elites and complex, bureaucratic, stratified societies (Aveni 2002b), but it is probable that humans began recording time's passage much earlier, even before the growing importance of cultivated plants and animals in their subsistence systems. Indeed, in discussing the timekeeping of the seminomadic pastoral Nuer of Sudan, East Africa, E. E. Evans-Pritchard (1939) makes the useful distinction between "ecological time" and "structural time." Borrowing these concepts, Aveni (2002a:148–149) notes that the former, eco-time, is strongly cyclical and "connects people with the environment through changes in nature to which they react"; structural time, on the other hand, is a much longer framework that "seems to deal with social rather than ecological concerns."[14] By this distinction, the Mesoamerican 260-day calendar is a register of eco-time while the 365-day calendar, following Edmonson (1988:214), and the Calendar Round record structural time through public and social ritual.

Counts of units of 260 (or, perhaps better said, counts of multiples of thirteen and twenty) seem to have been extremely important in early Mesoamerica, and from this remove it may be impossible to distinguish among solar, lunar, and gestational explanations for the 260-day calendar. The widespread sharing of names of days in this calendar indicates that it began to be compiled well before major ethnolinguistic separations and sedentarization around 2000 B.C. The fact that a 360- or 365-day solar calendar can be parsed into meaningful intervals of 260 days suggests that the two were closely intertwined from the very earliest efforts at counting time.

At some point, Mesoamericans differentiated these two concurrent counts into separate systems

of record keeping. How, when, and why this development occurred is, in hindsight, simultaneously intuitively logical and totally unfathomable. It is tempting, but perhaps erroneous, to conclude that the creation of a distinctive solar calendar coincided with the increasing importance of maize agriculture in the economy, and that the 365-day ja'ab' was a late "agricultural calendar." Edmonson (1988:214; cf. Lamb 2002) concludes that this calendar does "not constitute an agricultural calendar and probably never did. There is considerable evidence, in fact, that it was the divinatory calendar of the [260-]day count that was most closely related to agricultural decision making. The year count was primarily a ritual calendar for general civic ceremonial, and its primary focus was on the New Year rites."

A similar conclusion was reached by Stross (1994:32–33), who notes that the day names of the so-called ritual calendar (tzolk'in) and the month names of the so-called agricultural calendar (ja'ab') appear to encode similar amounts of agricultural as well as nonagricultural information, particularly in relation to maize. This allows both to serve "ritual and mnemonic functions related to agriculture in ways quite unsuspected, such as in scheduling maize planting activities from beginning to end of the maize cycle, and generating the times for ceremonial activities engaged in to secure the favor of the gods in order to ensure a good harvest." He concludes (ibid.:33) that "it appears that maize symbolism was even more closely incorporated into elite ritual during Preclassic times in Mesoamerica than previously thought."

In any event, early Mesoamerican daykeepers seem to have devoted considerable effort to perfecting their calendars by including five "dead days" (wayeb', nemontemi) in the 360-day "year" for closer approximation to the annual solar cycle and by creating the Calendar Round. Over the following centuries and millennia, the ensuing proliferation of scores of variant calendars throughout Mesoamerica took on "political and ethnic significance [in that] calendric knowledge . . . as well as the keeping of local history were handled at the level of the ethnic group" (Marcus 1992a:118).

Bricker (1982:102–103) observes that the proper seasonal alignment of the Yukatekan solar calendar month names occurs when a day 0 Pop, the first day of the first month of the 365-day year, occurs around the winter solstice. The last time that happened was around A.D. 950–960, a date she acknowledges is well past the origins of the 365-day calendar. Because the correlation of 0 Pop and the winter solstice occurs only every 1,507 years, if this event actually marked the origin of the calendar, it is necessary to go back to roughly 550 B.C. The origin of the 365-day solar calendar indubitably antedated that, and I think that an even earlier correlation, around 2060 B.C., is not an entirely unreasonable estimate. This seems to be a major transition in Mesoamerica, when populations were becoming more sedentary, languages were beginning to differentiate, and maize agriculture was assuming a critical role in an emerging Mesoamerican political economy.

I argue that the two main Mesoamerican calendars, one of 260 days and the other of 365, had nearly simultaneous (in archaeological time) but sequential origins, and their foundations can be traced back into the Late Archaic period as compilations of observations about regular seasonal changes, availability of foodstuffs, and celestial cycling. This information would have been compared, verified, adjusted, and more widely disseminated at the seasonal aggregations occurring around late-summer zenith and in times of food abundance. Until further data can be accumulated, this argument—that the two primary Mesoamerican calendars originally developed nearly simultaneously—seems to be the most logical and parsimonious explanation of their origins. They developed together, one within the other, very early in Mesoamerican history; they were later disarticulated into two calendars to permit greater specificity of the functions, agricultural and ritual, of each. And then, still later, they were carefully interrelated and reintegrated in very different ways that became, among the Maya, a cosmic mandate inextricably tied to order, ritual, and power. These steps, with the exception of creation of the Long Count, appear to be evident in the archaeological record by the beginning of the Formative/Preclassic period, around 1600 B.C.

Maya Calendar Developments in Broader Context

4 The 365-day calendar can be envisioned as incorporating three intervals of approximately 260 days. The first is that between zeniths, from the late-summer zenith to the spring zenith in the lower latitudes of Mesoamerica (Fig. 4.1; see Table 3.3).

During the Archaic period in this region the summer zenith coincided approximately with the scheduling of seasonal settlement aggregations and also with the reconstructed base date of the Maya Long Count calendar. It is possible that this festive event, occurring in the equivalent of our early August, established the beginning of the earliest precursors of the Mesoamerican calendar(s), timed from second zenith/harvest/macroband settlement to first, or spring, zenith/planting/end of the dry season at the beginning of May.

Another 260-day period is the so-called agrarian year, or main growing season, from February through October, which incorporates extended counts of days before and after distinct solar phenomena such as zeniths and the summer solstice. The timing of these solar positions is fairly easily measured by observing changing positions of the sun at sunrise or sunset, lengths of the shadow of a stick or a human, and so on. Such changes are far more obvious to people living in higher latitudes than in the tropics, however, and this system of marking the passage of time could have extremely ancient origins antedating the dominance of agriculture in human subsistence economies.

A third 260-day sequence in the Mesoamerican 365-day calendar, which can be considered a variant of the second, is the full maize-growing cycle (Stross 1994). This cycle consists of thirteen stages corresponding to thirteen periods of twenty days, with the names of the stages corresponding to thirteen day names as mnemonics (Table 3.5). This sequence merits further attention in terms of calendrical origins.

ORIGINALLY THIRTEEN MONTHS?

Stross's (1994) elucidation of the maize cycle raises the possibility that the 365-day calendar began as a luni-solar calendar which was an expansion of thirteen core months of twenty days. To examine this proposition, we can combine and modify the various suggestions about calendrical origins to create a model in which thirteen of the

The further the calendar develops, the less does it become a common possession.

—Martin P. Nilsson,
Primitive Time-Reckoning

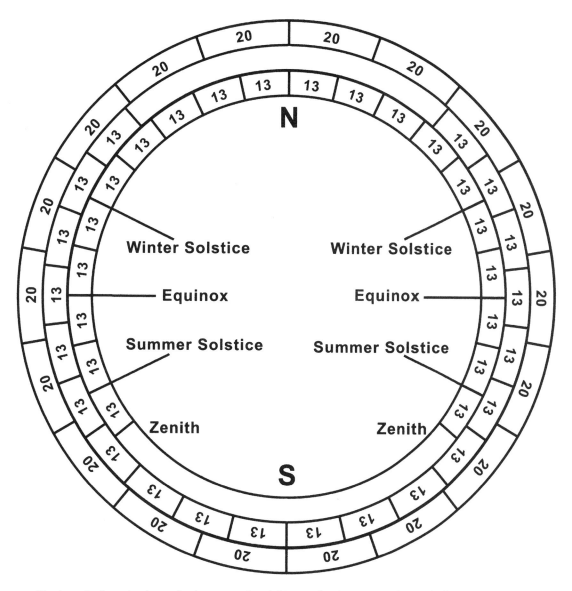

4.1. Nesting 260-day calendar cycles (twenty units of thirteen days) into a 360-day cycle (for ease of illustration, the extra five days of the tropical year are excluded). The inner ring shows the 260-day interval beginning and ending with the solar zeniths at 15° north latitude (April 30 and August 13). The outer ring shows the eighteen months of the 365-day year minus Wayeb'. Azimuths of solar sunrises and sunsets on equinoxes and summer and winter solstices, which are roughly identical throughout Mesoamerica, are shown in the interior.

Maya day names summarize the entire 365-day year. Several clues to this process—that is, to the calendars' early relations—already have been mentioned:

- The number 13 is ritually important, perhaps having been drawn from the thirteen days of the waxing of the moon. The Classic Maya used at least thirteen forms of one glyph to record named lunations, and thirteen is the number of levels of the celestial realm.

- A sequence of thirteen of the twenty day names in the 260-day almanac corresponds to the head variants—probably supernaturals or symbolic ancestors—for the numbers 1 through 13.

- At least eleven of the day names in the 260-day calendar have virtually the same meaning and occur in the same sequence throughout Mesoamerica (Table 3.2). Stross (1994) identifies a core sequence of thirteen day names in the Maya calendar that encompass the "agrarian year" from February through October (Table 3.7).

Another key point is found in a discussion about the "seemingly nonastronomical" twenty-day months of the Mexican solar calendar being derived from lunar phenomena. Citing the earlier work of Alfonso Caso (1967) and others, J. D. Stewart (1981) notes that several of the named Mexican months are paired, as, for example, "little fiesta of the dead" and "great fiesta of the dead." He (ibid., emphasis added) concludes convincingly that, "if each of the five pairs of *meztli* [20-day months] is counted as one, the sequence is reduced from 18 to 13 items. Thus, the structure of the sequence may imply that the *meztlipohualli* was created by *expanding an earlier luni-solar calendar of 13 named 'moons.'*"

Such pairing of month names is widespread cross-culturally (Nilsson 1920:224–225) and can be found in some ethnographically known highland Maya calendars (where it may reflect the late impact of Nawatl influence; Edmonson 1988:216–217; Lamb 2002:250–254). For example, in the Kaqchikel 365-day calendar (Edmonson 1988:216–217; Recinos and Goetz 1953:30–31), the months *tumuzuz*, *mam*, *tokic*, and *pach* occur twice, each prefaced by either *nabe* 'first' or *ru cab* 'second'. If these four pairs are counted as single months, the result is fourteen months: thirteen plus the unlucky five-day month. A similar phenomenon can be seen in other Maya calendars (Table 3.7): the K'iche' calendar has three pairs plus a triplet, resulting in thirteen months plus the unlucky period. The Tzeltal calendar (Villa Rojas 1988:146–149) has only one pair (male and female opossum), but five months incorporate the term *winkil* (referencing *winal* 'month' or *winik* 'man'?), each distinguished by a prefatory number 7, 6, 5, 4, or 3.[1] Counting the pair as one month and the five as another, the sequence is reduced to thirteen plus the five-day month. Similarly, in the Ch'olan

calendar there is one pair of month names plus four distinguished by incorporating color terms (black, green, white, red) with *zih*;[2] if the pair is counted as one and the four color months are counted as one, the total is fourteen month names.

In contrast to their highland colleagues, Classic lowland Maya daykeepers/calendar priests seem to have expanded the solar calendar into eighteen months not by doubling certain names as big and little or first and second months but, rather, by creating a series of nineteen uniquely named months. The mechanism by which they accomplished this can be recognized in Classic inscriptions: they incorporated the day-name signs of the 260-day almanac as infixes in eleven month signs. For example (see Figs. 3.1 and 3.2):

- The glyph for the month of Mol has an infixed day sign, Muluk, from the 260-day calendar.
- The glyphs for the next four months, Ch'en, Yax, Sak, and Kej, all incorporate a Kawak day sign (equivalent to the *ja'ab'* component in the four Ch'olan color-month names).
- The glyph for the month of Mak has both Ajaw and Imix day infixes; in the 260-day calendar the days following Kawak are Ajaw and Imix.
- Three months incorporate *k'an* signs in their glyphs—two with *k'an*, meaning "yellow" (K'ayab' and Pop) and one with *k'an* as a day sign—separated by the five days of Wayeb'.
- The *k'an* months are followed by Wo and Sip, both with *k'at* crossed-bands infixes; in K'iche' *k'at* refers to a net for maize (Lamb 2002:16).

It is evident from these observations that, if the months in the Classic Maya calendar are grouped by these day-sign infixes, there are actually only fourteen unique months or month groups—Yaxk'in, Mol, the Kawak month(s), Mak, K'ank'in, Muwan, Pax, the *k'an* (yellow) month(s), Kumk'u, the crossed-bands months, Sotz', Sek,

Wayeb', and Xul—a pattern similar to that of the ethnographic calendars described above. This suggests that these day names and months originally had a shared meaning or referent, and they provide a basis for hypothesizing correspondences with an observable solar-seasonal cycle and the months of the Gregorian calendar.

I suggest that the thirteen day names of the 260-day almanac were the original mnemonic basis for the Mesoamerican 365-day solar calendar. This calendar would have been initiated with a series of thirteen named months based on expanding the thirteen day names (Table 4.1), the twenty-day months covering the 260-day period of the agricultural season. When Mesoamerican diviners or daykeepers began to realize that the solar year was closer to 360 days long, they apparently decided to maintain their original thirteen month names while at the same time increasing the number and names of months to cover the nonagricultural season. Most of them accomplished this by doubling certain month names and prefixing them with "first" and "second," or "great" and "little." The final step would have been adding the extra

five days to the calendar to most closely approximate the length of the solar year.

There is some evidence that the multiplication of month names goes back at least to Epi-Olmec times, as the inscription on the O'Boyle Mask refers to Longlip 1, Longlip 2, Longlip 3 as months for harvesting rainy-season beans (Kaufman and Justeson 2001:2.83–2.85). But it seems there was considerable latitude concerning which months might be chosen for the process of multiplying and, judging from the variability in month names, the whole endeavor was probably undertaken at different times in different places throughout Mesoamerica. The dates of creation of the solar calendar and the dates of creation of month names in that calendar need not necessarily correspond, of course, and as Lamb (2002) has shown, month names continued to be modified throughout the Classic and Postclassic periods.

BEGINNINGS AND ENDINGS

In general, the lowland Maya recorded the passage of time by the termination or completion of units,

TABLE 4.1. *Derivational model of correspondences between* ja'ab' *month names and* tzolk'in *day names based on day sign and other infixes*

JA'AB' (365-DAY) MONTH	TZOLK'IN (260-) DAY	SENSE/SEASON
Yaxk'in	?	Spring zenith?; dry season; year "born"
Mol (Muluk infix)	Muluk	Clouds gather; pile up felled trees in milpa
Ch'en (Kawak + black)	Kab'an	Rainy season; prepare earth for planting
Yax (Kawak + green)	Etz'nab'	Rainy season; plant
Sak (Kawak + white)	Kawak	(Kawak: thunder, lightning, rain)
Kej (Kawak + ?)	Kawak	?
Mak (Ajaw + Imix infix)	Ajaw	Flowering
K'ank'in	Imix	Flowering
Muwan	Ik'	?Wind, breath, fruitfulness
Pax (drum)	Ak'b'al	Music, drum
K'ayab' (K'an)	K'an	Music, drum
Kumk'u (K'an)	K'an	Pot, granary
Wayeb' (drum)	K'an	Lost days
Pop (K'an)	Chikchan?	
Wo	Kimi	?
Sip	Manik'	?
Sotz'	Manik'	?
Sek	Lamat	Sink; sun in Underworld
Xul	Ok	End; dog

Note: Days Chuwen, Eb', B'en, Ix, Men, and Kib' are not included in this model. The model is based on day-sign and other infixes.

but it is not clear how they conceived of the starting or ending points of the day. Some Mesoamerican groups counted their days as running from midday to midday, that is, from the sun at zenith, its highest point in the sky, a pattern found at Chan Kom in Yucatán (Redfield and Villa Rojas 1962:184) and perhaps among the Aztec and Zapotec (León-Portilla 1988:143–145). J. Eric S. Thompson (1966:179) believed the lowland Maya counted days by sunrises, but there is little support for this view. Among some highland Maya, including contemporary Mam speakers of Huehuetenango, Guatemala, the day begins at sundown (Watanabe 1983:716, 723–724). The K'iche' in Momostenango, however, welcome new yearbearers at midnight (B. Tedlock 1992c:26), suggesting that the new day or new year begins then, as it does for the Chamulas in Chiapas (Gossen 1974b:227).

Peter Mathews (2001:406) raises the possibility that the two Maya calendars, 260- and 365-day, began at different times, an idea that has been echoed by David Stuart (2004). The monuments that prompted such thinking, Dos Pilas Stela 8 and an unprovenienced lintel in Campeche, use the Late Classic Campeche or Puuc calendar in which the *tzolk'in* day (260-day calendar) is one day later than in the Classic (or Tikal) calendar. Following Mathews, Stuart (ibid.) suggests that the *tzolk'in* might have begun at sunset while the *ja'ab'* (365-day calendar) might have begun at sunrise. Thus an event occurring during the night would have been in the new day in the *tzolk'in*, but the new day in the *ja'ab'* would not yet have begun. In their view, the Puuc dating system is not a separate calendar per se but, rather, a method of carefully specifying certain nighttime rituals before the entering of the (*ja'ab'*) day at sunrise.

Completion is a key concept in Maya beliefs about time and its passage, and various symbols signify completion in different contexts (see Fig. 3.5b). An oval "shell" symbol signified both null and completion in counting: in other words, if a period or position that could have twenty units in it did have those twenty, it was full, or complete. Because of the importance of vigesimal counting, the number 20 itself and its glyphic representations—a toad (*wo* or *uo*) glyph for the twenty-day period of a *winal*—also came to represent completion. Another sign that means

completion (including death) as well as the number 20 is a glyph of a head with a hand at the lower mouth and jaw. One wonders if covering the mouth might have been an ancient gesture used in rituals or performances to signify the end of an act of speech or oral performance or some other ceremonial act. Another important completion sign is the "quincunx," an arrangement of four dots (or other symbols or units) with a fifth in the center. The quincunx generally is considered to represent the four cardinal directions plus the center, or axis, joining the celestial and earthly realms, often conceived as a World Tree; it thus signifies an encompassing sense of the four winds, the whole world, or the total cosmos. It also could be conceived as representing the sun's four extreme rising and setting points on the horizon (solstices) plus a zenith point in the center, or the central position of a gnomon for measuring those solar points. In any case, it is easy to envision this sign as a simplified cross-in-circle, which is also a *k'an* cross or sign ("yellow, precious"), signaling a relation with the sun.

It is problematic to determine which month began the calendar cycle (see Thompson 1966: 101–102), given that different Maya calendars have different beginnings and endings. In addition, some modern calendars, particularly in the highlands, are "non-sequential" in that the Wayeb' days do not immediately precede the first month, a peculiarity that has been attributed to Mexican contacts in the Postclassic period (see Lamb 2002:295–298) or to Spanish missionaries who wanted to move the pagan festivals to correspond to Carnaval in the pre-Lent period (Gossen 1974b:233–234, 247). In addition, Barbara Tedlock (1992a:93–97) notes that K'iche' daykeepers generally start their recitations of the almanac with the name and number of whatever day it actually is.

Nonetheless, it is intriguing to attempt to correlate the calendar(s) with the agricultural seasons. My arguments about the importance of the seasonal settlement aggregations beginning in August during the Archaic period suggest that the second solar zenith, occurring in late summer, could have been the starting point of the earliest Mesoamerican calendrical record-keeping (see Aveni and Hartung 1986:57–64). Other evidence suggests that later Mesoamericans took the winter solstice as their formal starting point, a decision that might have been made in the sixth century B.C., when the rainy season month names correlated with the seasons (Bricker 1982; Lamb 2002:331). But as will be seen below, it seems likely that, with the increasing role of agriculture in these societies, as well as the use of solar positions in calendrical reckoning, a shift may have occurred to orient the calendar toward the growing season, beginning it with the spring zenith and the start of the rains.

As a starting month, several possibilities are suggested. Yaxk'in and Mol could have been either the first or the last day/month (assuming the scenario of months evolving from day names). Kab'an is a possible starting day, because its glyphic sign represents the god whose head stands for the number 1. Bishop Landa said the 260-day cycle began with 1 Imix, which makes sense, given that the lowland Maya had long ended their calendrical cycles on the preceding Ajaw days. The story of the origin of the *winal* in the *Chilam Balam of Chumayel*, however, begins the count with 12/13 Ok, which might illustrate Tedlock's point: perhaps this tale was first committed to writing on a day Ok.

THE MONTHS AND THE DAY NAMES: A DERIVATIONAL MODEL

The possibility that Maya month names were derived from day names and signs suggests the following model.

Yaxk'in

I begin discussion of the month sequence with Yaxk'in (refer to Table 4.1), a month name that changed very little during its time of use (Lamb 2002:205, 329, 386, 394). The glyph for the month has two morphemes, *yax* (first; *ya'ax* 'green, new') and *k'in* (sun, day, time), readily interpretable as referring to the beginning of the agricultural year. Edmonson (1982:179n4981), in fact, comments that Yaxk'in is the only month referred to by the Maya as being "born." In Ch'olan and Yukatekan, Yaxk'in has the sense of "dry season," perhaps the time of burning. These points suggest the likelihood that at some point the month Yaxk'in could have begun the 365-day calendar.

During the Colonial period, however, Yaxk'in fell in November. Alfred Tozzer (1941:158n811),

commenting on Landa, remarks of Yaxk'in, "This month, coming in November-December and meaning 'the new sun,' or 'the new day,' begins the new agricultural year when the bush is cut down in preparation for making the *milpa*. . . . Yaxkin may have begun a year at some remote time." Ralph Roys (1967:85) refers to the procedure of *tze yaxk'in*, the bending down (*doblando*) of the corn stalks, on November 13: "Until the fall rains are over, the corn is said to keep better in this manner than in the granary." Gossen (1974b:240) reports that among the Chamulas the month *yask'in* is the time of harvest.

Mol

The next *ja'ab'* month, Mol, with its infixed Muluk day sign (jade, water, collect), would refer to the beginning of the rainy season. J. Eric S. Thompson (1966:110) not unreasonably interprets this as the gathering storm clouds that signal the beginning of the rains. Spring zenith occurs in early May in lower Mesoamerica, probably between the Maya months of Mol and Ch'en, just before the beginning of the rainy season. Lamb (2002:18, 202, 385, 393) suggests "collect, harvest" as a meaning, noting that *mol* means "harvest" in both Itzaj and Mopan, and also "pile" in the sense of the piles of cut trees in the milpas before burning.

Ch'en, Yax, Sak, and Kej

As noted above, the hieroglyphic signs for the next four months, Ch'en, Yax, Sak, and Kej, bear the sign of the Kawak day name, which I interpret as indicating their expansion from the day Kawak to refer to the rainy season months (see Bricker 1982; Lamb 2002:331). Lamb (2002:11, 18–21, 233) links this sign, glyph T528,[3] to Proto-Mayan and Proto-Yukatekan "lightning, thunder, rain," noting also that it may represent either Ch'olan *kum* 'stone' or Yukatekan *kúum* 'thunder', thus possibly indicating the rainy season. Indeed, around 600 B.C., the rainy season months from June through November would have corresponded to the Yukatekan Maya months of late Mol, Ch'en, Yax, Sak, and Kej through Mak, K'ank'in, and Muwan. In 2000 B.C., the rainy season would have fallen in the months of Ch'en through K'ayab' (a day 2.16.10.0.0 8 Ajaw 13 Ch'en, for example, would be May 23). Among the Chamulas, *c'un* was the first month of the year, beginning after the winter solstice (Gossen 1974b:231–232).

Besides sharing the Kawak sign, the glyphs for the months Ch'en, Yax, Sak, and Kej carry prefixes that reference a color of the cardinal or intercardinal directions plus center/zenith, perhaps in homage to the rains and rain gods of the four quarters. These months represent expansion and elaboration of the day name Kawak from the 260-day calendar, perhaps a mnemonic for the rainy season, into an eighty-day sequence of activities that occur during the rainy season (see the similar pattern for numbered rainy season months in the modern Tzeltal calendar, Table 4.1). It may be relevant here that the word *ja'ab'* could be derived from words for rain in Kekchi and Kaqchikel (Fields 1989:85).

However, the day Kab'an precedes Kawak in the 260-day sequence and corresponds, in this proposed model of month-name derivations, to the month of Ch'en; the following day, Etz'nab', would correspond to the month Yax. That these two months are paired might be reflected in the *oknaj* ceremony to the Chaaks (rain gods) that the Maya of Yucatán held in the months of Ch'en and Yax (Sharer 1994:532). In Colonial times, this ceremony involved renewal of idols, *incensarios*, and the temple to the Chaaks. In any case, Kawak is the next day name in the *tzolk'in*, serving, as discussed above, as a mnemonic for the next two months, Sak and Kej,[4] both of which include the Kawak sign in their glyphs.

Mak

The next month, Mak, corresponds to the next day name in the *tzolk'in* sequence, Ajaw. The glyph for Mak has a "comb" suffix that is usually read *ka* 'count' and combines the Ajaw and Imix glyphs. One interpretation is that *mak* is a verb meaning "to cover, to close," and J. Eric S. Thompson (1966:118) has read the glyph as "count set in order" and "end of 260 days." Lamb (2002:21) interprets *mak* as "enclosure, storage room, or granary." The ideas of "setting the count in order" and storing grain are congruent with the idea that, during late summers several millennia earlier, the remotest ancestors of the Maya gathered at the time of harvest to exchange information and began to develop the order of the counts of the days.

Among the twentieth-century Tzotzil-speaking Chamulas, the corresponding month Mok is the time of sowing crops, and the name has the sense of a fence to keep animals out of milpas (Gossen 1974b:235).

K'ank'in

The month of K'ank'in corresponds to the next sequential *tzolk'in* day name, Imix. Imix refers to earthly abundance while K'ank'in translates directly as "yellow sun/day/time," perhaps a dual reference to both the yellow heat of later summer zenith and the ripening of plant foods.[5] Lamb (2002:22, 28, 136) describes K'ank'in as a Yukatekan innovation, the original name being Ch'olan *uniw* or *unew*, from a Mixe-Zoquean and/or Tzeltal word meaning "avocado."

Muwan

The following month is Muwan (the Maya *moan* bird, perhaps an owl or hawk?), corresponding in this sequential progression to the day name Ik' (wind, breath; fruitfulness). Perhaps related to this, both *mujan* and *i'* in Itzaj Mayan mean hawk (C. A. Hofling, pers. com., July 14, 2004). In the *Popol Vuh*, the owl (*moan* bird?) is an emissary from the Underworld;[6] in the Dresden Codex the *moan* bird is referred to as "Thirteen Sky" (Thompson 1966:114). In this calendrical context it might reference a harbinger of the autumnal equinox and the sun's position lower in the sky toward the Underworld. If the *moan* bird were a hawk, this month could correspond to the southward migration of Swainson's hawks across Central America in late October through early November (B. Tedlock 1992a:188). In the Classic period, an inexplicably large proportion of inscriptions recording "warfare" events were dated to the month of Muwan, which fell in October, with none in the preceding K'ank'in (P. Rice 2007). Perhaps this relates to the *Popol Vuh*, in which owls are the "Military Keepers of the Mat" (D. Tedlock 1996:348).

Pax

Next comes the month Pax, equivalent in sequence to the day Ak'b'al. While Ak'b'al usually means darkness or night, it can also refer to a drum, and the glyph for Pax is a *tun* 'drum'. Lamb (2002:11, 23, 202, 347) says *pax* means "tap-instrument," music, hollow log drum, upright drum played with the fingers, and a decoy whistle for birds and deer; he reads the month name as *pa'ax-hab'*.

K'ayab' and Pop

The following three months in the Yukatekan calendar, K'ayab', Kumk'u, and Pop, incorporate a *k'an* cross or *k'an* sign infix, with Kumk'u and Pop separated by the five days of Wayeb'. In K'ayab' and Pop the sign means "yellow," while in Kumk'u it corresponds to the day K'an, perhaps a grain of ripe maize. These months might be interpreted as a reference to the ancient increasing fall–through–early winter role of maize, particularly dried and stored maize, in the diet.

The glyph for K'ayab' is usually identified as the head of a parrot, macaw, or turtle, although in Ch'olan the meaning is *kanazi* and appears to reference cicadas or vultures (Lamb 2002:23–24). Broader meanings relate to singing (the call of cicadas?), music, and a drum, specifically, a horizontally held drum made of turtle plastron (Lamb 2002:200–201). The conflation of turtle and parrot could relate to a belief in Chan Kom that in September tortoises turn into parrots and parrots into tortoises, and then back again (Lamb 2002:201, citing Redfield and Villa Rojas 1962:208–209).

Pop is generally considered to be the first month of the *ja'ab'*, or "'base' of the new year" (Lamb 2002:207). It seems more appropriate in the current argument, however, to group it with the other *k'an* months. I find no logical correspondence between month and day names here; the day Chikchan (the celestial serpent) follows the day K'an in the *tzolk'in*, suggesting the near homophone *kan* (Yuk.; Ch'olan *chan*), which also means "snake." The day Chikchan is followed by Kimi, meaning "death"; the month following Pop is Wo, which incorporates the sign *ek'*, meaning black and also star. It is not difficult to think of winter and the winter solstice as a time of death and long nights of black, starry skies.

Kumk'u

As noted, the sequential correspondence of Kumk'u is to the day K'an, meaning "ripe maize." The glyph for Kumk'u might refer to a pot, oven, or granary (Yuk. *kuum* 'pot'), although the Ch'olan month name is Ol, meaning "heart, ball" and also a portal to the Otherworld (Lamb 2002:25). Here we can recall too that the beginning of the Maya Long Count in 3114 B.C. is a day 4 Ajaw 8 Kumk'u, perhaps a reference to fall storage of seeds and grains. Alternatively, Lamb (ibid.:198–199) mentions *kum* in Yukatekan (Ch'olan *chum*) as meaning "to seat," *k'uj* as "god, temple," and *k'u* as "nest," suggesting that the last might be a metaphor for a cave. This raises the possibility that certain kingly accession and seating rites might have taken place in such locations and also supports the metaphorical associations of temple sanctuaries with caves. The significance of a day 8 Kumk'u for the ancient initiation of the 365-day calendar and Long Count, then, could be polyvalent, referring to the "seating" of time (perhaps in a cave ritual) in the same way that rulers are seated, and the birth of time in a protective "nest" or cave (see Manzanilla 2000).

Wayeb'

Wayeb', perhaps *way-ab'* or *way-hab'* 'bed, sleep/vision of the year' (Lamb 2002:211), falls between Kumk'u and Pop in the Yukatekan calendar. These Wayeb' days might be better interpreted as the five days before or encompassing the winter solstice, perhaps originally situated between the months of Pop and Wo, which were followed by new year's celebrations when the sun began moving northward after staying at the southern extreme of its journey. The five-day Wayeb' "month" has variable placement in modern Maya calendars (Bricker 1982:102; Lamb 2002:295–298), and it is possible that another month began or ended the year in ancient times. The Wayeb' days might have been moved by Spanish missionaries so as to occur before the Catholic rituals of Lent (Gossen 1974b:233–234, 247).

Throughout Mesoamerica, these extra days, whatever they are called, are commonly considered unlucky or dangerous. From the viewpoint of calendrical history, it bears remembering that these five days likely were not part of the fundamental cosmic order established by the original spirits or gods of the days and multiples of thirteen and twenty creating the 260- and 360-day calendars. Instead, they were late additions by humans, thus perhaps having negative connotations as violations of the gods' initial structuring of the cosmos . . . and hence dangerous.

Wo and Sip

The glyph for the month of Wo (*wo* 'frog, toad') has a crossed-bands (*k'at*) component, which is also shared by the following month, Sip, suggesting that they might have some original pairing. While the glyph for Wo would be read "black cross" in Ch'ol, that for Sip would be "red cross." *K'at* refers to a "large net for maize" in K'iche' (Lamb 2002:16) while the *k'at* crossed-bands sign, or Saint Andrew's cross, has been identified as symbolizing the sun's positions at solstitial rises and settings (Aveni 2001:151). During a period of some 130 years, from around 450 B.C. to 320 B.C., the winter solstice would have occurred during the months of Wo and Sip. Reference to *wo* frogs, found only in the Maya lowlands, might have been a late addition to the calendar. Their calls are common in the rainy season.

Sip is associated with hunting because Sip (or T'zip in the highlands) is the name for a Maya deer god or guardian of deer (L. Brown 2005). The corresponding day name in the *tzolk'in* sequence is Manik', which is also associated with deer. The Manik' glyph is a hand with thumb and forefinger touching, perhaps referring to the position of the hand in the mouth while whistling, a traditional technique used by Maya deer hunters. The reference to deer hunting in winter, in what would correspond to our month of January, corresponds to archaeologists' reconstructions of highland winter subsistence patterns in the Archaic period, when vegetal foods were scarce and deer, peccary, and other animals were hunted. Justeson and colleagues (1985:21, 57) claim that this day name came into the Maya calendar sometime after 500 B.C., perhaps from the Otomanguean language, because *manik'* is not a Maya word. The Otomanguean meaning is "to eat (meat)," suggesting reference to both deer and the touching fingers while putting food to the mouth, as seen in the glyph.

Sotz'

The month following Sip is Sotz'. The name and glyph refer to a leaf-nosed bat, but the "patron" of the month is the *xok* fish (perhaps a shark?). As Thompson (1966:108) remarks with some understatement, "It is very strange that one animal should form the glyph and another, totally unrelated to it, should be the patron of the month." Possibly one or the other animal was substituted at some point, but I can find no basis for associating the bat or shark with the day name Manik' or the following day, Lamat.

Sek

The next *ja'ab'* month, Sek, corresponds to the day Lamat in the *tzolk'in* sequence. One meaning of *sek* is "skull," but in the hieroglyphic (Ch'olan) spellings the month name reads *Kasew*, the Pacaya palm tree (*Chamaedorea tepejilote*) (Lamb 2002:128), the unopened male flowers of which are edible. Another sense of *sek* is "end" or, according to Eric Thompson (1966:118), "end of the 260-day count." The glyph for the month Sek has a "comb" prefix, like Mak, which is combined with a *winal* (month) sign. The day Lamat is most specifically associated with Venus, but also with "star" and "rabbit." However, *lamat* has been said to be a non-Maya word and is believed to have come into Mayan (as *lambat*) from Zapotec about the same time as did *manik'* (Justeson et al. 1985:21). The *Diccionario maya-español* (Yukatekan), on the other hand, gives *lam* as "flood" and *lamats* as "to sink" (as in a boat sinking below the water, or the sun setting below the horizon). This solar interpretation, rather than that of Venus or stars, relates fairly well to an interpretation that Sek/Lamat ended a cycle at some point, with the sun figuratively in (or ready to begin to move out of) the Underworld, that is, below zenith.

Xul

The following month, Xul, parallels in sequence the day Ok 'dog'; Xul also means "end" in Yukatekan, and in Itzaj Mayan it refers to the summer solstice (Lamb 2002:120). Lamb (ibid.:17–18) associates the animal head of the Xul month sign with a wide range of rodentlike creatures, including the coatimundi, rat, mouse, gopher, mole, agouti, and paca, although it might also relate (through Ch'olan) to bird (*chichin* or *tz'ikin*). Eric Thompson (1966:109) describes the glyph for Xul as the head of a dog with an attached "sun tail" (actually a syllabic sign) and associates it with the Mexican canine god Xolotl (identified as a twin), who "led the sun each evening into the underworld, and in time came to be associated with the sun immediately after setting." This interpretation, then, has Sek as the dead sun (or, figuratively, the old year) being led to the Underworld by a dog (*xul, ok*) and also refers to the southward movement of the sun sinking, that is, moving south—or downward below the equinox position to its solstice point in December.

In the model developed here, Yaxk'in simultaneously completes this annual cycle and begins a new one, as the name means "new sun" and marks the spring equinox heralding the approach of the rainy season and new growth.

Summary

Six of the twenty day names are not accounted for in this reconstruction, and one can only speculate, along with Eric Thompson, that they were added sometime after the original thirteen names were established. These six days, which currently follow Muluk in the sequence, are Chuwen (monkey), Eb' (jaw, tooth; grass; stairway), B'en (cane, reed), Ix (jaguar), Men (eagle), and Kib' (buzzard, vulture). Some of them are non-Maya names: Justeson and colleagues (1985:21, 24) note that the day name B'en may come from Zapotec, and Ix and Chuwen (and also Ok) from Mixe or Mixe-Zoquean. The addition of these days might have been to tighten up the overlap with the months and also to "account for" the winter months, which were, in the model, correlated in multiples with the first thirteen day names. If some of the non-Maya day names came in late, after 500 B.C., they were substitutions for earlier names, now discarded.

The fit between days and months in this day-to-month derivational model is not perfect, of course, because there are twenty day names and only nineteen months. One issue that calls the model into question is Edmonson's (1986a:169) observation that three of the putatively "added" day names—monkey, jaguar, and eagle—are among the eleven that seem to be nearly universal among all Mesoamerican calendars; this suggests substitution of names and concepts very early in calendrical development. The day name Kib' generally is interpreted as a buzzard/vulture or wax (although *cib* can mean smoke in Kaqchikel; see Recinos and Goetz 1953:30), but its glyph is the shell sign for completion (Thompson 1966:84–85), suggesting that at one point it might have been the last day of the complete sequence.

In terms of human agency and decision making, all of the foregoing information supports the likelihood that ancient daykeepers conferred about calendrical matters and compared calendars on a semiregular basis, and probably had done so for hundreds if not a few thousand years. Linguistic evidence suggests that many changes in month names were made after the Classic period (Lamb 2002), calling into question the use of ethnographically known 365-day calendars for comparative purposes. Nevertheless, in their nascent form by the end of the Archaic-Formative transition, early Mesoamerican calendars appear to have been related to significant events in eco-time, such as the beginning of the rainy season, the timing of the second solar zenith, fall settlement aggregation, and harvest. These events coincide with a period of increasingly plentiful vegetal foods and encompass roughly 120–140 days of the modern months of May through August or September. In the months of today's Yukatekan Maya calendar, this would have begun with Yaxk'in (first/new day/sun; dry season) or Mol (Muluk rain/water infix) and the building of storm clouds, and ended with K'ank'in (*k'an* 'yellow, harvest, ripe maize'), a sequence of seven named months of twenty days each.

CALENDRICAL ORIGINS AND THE *POPOL VUH*

The highland K'iche' Maya creation story or mythic history known as the *Popol Vuh* was written in its alphabetic form, Dennis Tedlock (1996:56) asserts, in the mid-sixteenth century. Before that, it was probably formalized in hieroglyphic manuscripts, and even earlier versions would have existed as oral tradition. Numerous scenes from the myth can be recognized on Classic Maya polychrome pottery (Kerr 1992). Given the content, it is likely that the first parts of it were of very early date and minimally pan-Maya (if not pan-Isthmian or pan-Mesoamerican) in scope, while later parts are specific to late K'iche' history. One study of the origin of the *Popol Vuh* myth suggests that it began in a dry and highly seasonal environment,[7] perhaps like that of central and southern Mexico, and supports the proposed start of the solar calendar in the dry season (i.e., Yaxk'in).

Tedlock's (1996) Parts 1 through 3 of the *Popol Vuh* are summarized in Chapter 1 because of their relevance to various arguments presented here. For example, elements of the story can be recognized in the images on early monuments at sites such as Izapa in the southeastern Isthmian region (see Chap. 6). These hint that the *Popol Vuh* tale was recited or proclaimed as part of processions that moved through the site's plazas, from stela to stela, in the course of calendrical celebrations. This in turn relates to Tedlock's (ibid.:28, 29) observations that "at times the writers of the . . . Popol Vuh seem to be describing pictures, especially when they begin new episodes in narratives" and that "there were also occasions on which writers [of the original hieroglyphic manuscript of the *Popol Vuh*] offered 'a long performance and account'" of the narrative. Such pictures might have been carvings or paintings on stelae.

Tedlock and others have emphasized how the events and creatures of the *Popol Vuh* explain various celestial phenomena, such as the Big and Little Dippers, the Pleiades, the moon, and the movements of Venus. The Hero Twins Hunahpu (or Hun Ajaw, One Ajaw[8]) and Xbalanque (Yax B'alam) are given various celestial or godly attributions, for example, as maize gods. Aveni (2002b:67; also D. Tedlock 1992) identifies the Hero Twins as the sun and Venus when they are in the Underworld, but as the sun and the moon in the sky above earth. He (ibid.) is interested in the role of Venus in the story, as the sets of twins make "five journeys to Xib'alb'a, one to match each of the five unique paths that Venus takes in the twilight sky. . . . Every time Venus [Xbalanque] appears as morning star to announce the arrival of his twin brother, the sun, he resketches for us the cycle of creation that led to the present-day Maya lineage."

I propose something broader: that the story related in the *Popol Vuh* recapitulates, subtly and allegorically, the history of the creation of the Mesoamerican calendars. That is, the various events and characters in this mythistory serve as keys or mnemonics that encode the day names in the 260-day *tzolk'in* and also, but less clearly, the names of the months in the *ja'ab'*. Public performances of this narrative drama would have reinforced social and cosmic order, proclaiming connections between humans and the cosmos and telling and retelling the creation not only of the world, humans, and animals, but also of the origins and human control of time itself.

This proposition, if correct, underscores the idea that the *Popol Vuh* has a very ancient history, the seeds of which could have been planted five thousand or more years ago as Archaic daykeepers scanned the skies and memorized the recurring journeys of celestial bodies bearing the burden of time's passage. Over the millennia, there would have been tens of thousands of opportunities for this oral history to become garbled or for the events and characters to change, resembling a multi-millennia-long version of the old parlor game Telephone. In addition, the calendars themselves underwent significant transformations during these millennia before they achieved the forms recorded by Classic scribes and modern ethnographers, and this too distorted precise correspondences. Nonetheless, with these caveats in place we can begin to evaluate this proposition by examining the events of the first three parts of Tedlock's 1996 edition.

Parts 1 and 2

The cosmogenetic events of Parts 1–3 of the *Popol Vuh* take place in darkness and culminate in the appearance of the sun, which brings light to the cosmos. This could, perhaps, indicate that the earliest calendar was lunar and the solar calendar developed later. Part 1 begins with nothing but primordial sea and sky; everything is **dark**. Heart of Sky, the principal deity also known as Huracan (Christenson 2003:69n56), came to Plumed Serpent, and by their **thought** and words the **earth** was created and mountains rose out of the water. Then they created animals, including **deer** and **birds**,[9] followed by efforts to create humans,[10] first of **mud** and then of wood (male) and rushes or **reeds** (female).[11] Because these early humanlike creations did not worship the gods and "keep the days," as intended, they were not pleasing to the gods, who sent a **flood**, heavy **rains**, and other misfortunes, including an uprising of talking cookpots and **dogs**, to destroy the wooden people. Those who were not destroyed became **monkeys**.

Part 2 begins with the story of Seven **Macaw**, who has grandiose pretensions to be the sun and moon but is shot from his perch in a tree by the Hero Twins, the **blowgun** shot severely damaging his **jaw** and **teeth**. The next episode concerns the Four Hundred Boys, gods of alcoholic beverages, who were building a **house**. After calling on the aid of **Zipacna**, son of Seven Macaw, to haul a large **log** for them, the Twins try to kill him. He survives and avenges himself by bringing the house down, killing all the Boys at their celebration. But then he is killed pursuing an artificial **crab** that the Twins have created to entrap him; he heaves a great **sigh** of death beneath a mountain. Next, the second son of Seven Macaw, **Earthquake**, dies after eating one of the **birds** the Twins had roasted.

Some of the bold-faced words above correspond to the meanings of day names in the lowland (Yucatán) Maya *tzolk'in* (see Table 3.2): dark, Ak'b'al; earth, Kab'an; deer, Manik'; birds, Men and Kib'; reeds, B'en; flood, Lamat; rain, Muluk (water); dog, Ok; monkey, Chuwen; jaw or teeth, Eb'; wind, breath, Ik'; earth monster (Zipacna), Imix or Kawak; and earthquake, Kab'an. Other concepts in these portions of the *Popol Vuh* are found in highland Maya calendars (see Table 3.2), both as day names in the 260-day calendar—thought (K'iche'); house (Tzeltal); birds (Tzeltal, K'iche') —and month names of the 365-day calendar: mud (Tzeltal); log, wood, tree (K'iche'); blowgun (K'iche').

It is noteworthy that Parts 1 and 2 of the *Popol Vuh* incorporate reference to fourteen to sixteen day names of the series of 20 in the 260-day calendar. Could thirteen of these be the earliest day names that accompanied the thirteen numbered gods? Also of interest is the *Popol Vuh* sequence flood, rain, dog, monkey (Lamat, Muluk, Ok, and Chuwen), because these four days are sequential in the 260-day calendar (also see note 16). This particular day sequence is likely very old in Mesoamerican calendars in general. Eight month names are suggested in Parts 1 and 2: Kej and Sip (deer), Xul (dog), and K'ayab' (Seven Macaw) in the lowland calendars, and mud (Tzeltal), wood/tree

(K'iche'), blowgun (K'iche'), and crab (equivalent to Pax) in three highland calendars.[12]

A number of astronomical phenomena and directional symbols are woven into Part 2 of the *Popol Vuh* (D. Tedlock 1992; idem 1996:34– 35). As noted previously, various events mark the position of Venus rising in the east as morning star. Zipacna's burial place is associated with the west and his brother Earthquake's with the east. Seven Macaw is of particular interest: he becomes the seven stars of the Big Dipper at his death, while his wife, Chimalmat, becomes the Little Dipper, both lying in the north. His falling from the tree is said to mark the onset of the hurricane season in mid-July, and even the word *hurricane* comes from Huracan, another name for the principal sky god. Seven Macaw boasts that he is the sun and the moon, brightens the face of the earth, and sheds light for all the earth's creatures, including humans. Allen Christenson (2003: 92n153) considers that the authors of the *Popol Vuh* "apparently also meant to emphasize that Seven Macaw saw himself as the means of marking the passage of time." However, Seven Macaw represents a false calendar: "His vision did not reach beyond where he sat. It did not really reach everywhere beneath the sky" (ibid.:93). This could reference an early solar calendar that did not accurately commensurate time and so was abandoned ("killed").

Another interesting element is the death of the Four Hundred Boys, associated with alcohol, who rise into the sky to become the Pleiades. I suggest that they also represent the abandonment, or "death," of an early 400-day calendar, as hypothesized by Edmonson, in favor of one comprising 360–365 days, which more closely approximates the solar year. A similar reference occurs in Aztec myths:[13] Coyolxauhqui has four hundred relatives, the Four Hundred Southerners, who live south of the Aztec capital and who join her against her mother, Coatlicue, and her newborn brother Huitzilopochtli. The infant Huitzilopochtli defeats the Four Hundred, his brothers, and beheads and dismembers his sister Coyolxauhqui, throwing her down a mountain (Schele and Guernsey Kappelman 2001:32–34). In addition, the alcoholic beverage pulque, made from the fermented sap of the agave cactus, is "personified by gods known as the Centzon Totochtin," or 400 Rabbits (Christenson 2003:103:197).

Part 3

Part 3 of the *Popol Vuh*, as Dennis Tedlock has edited it, is long and complex, perhaps reflecting the greater socio-politico-economic complexity of the later Mesoamerican world. It tells the story of the Hero Twins and their families, and the cast of characters includes the following:

- Xpiyacoc and Xmucane: grandparents and daykeeper-diviners
- One Hunahpu and Seven Hunahpu: their sons, joint fathers of Hero Twins Hunahpu and Xbalanque
- Xb'aqiyalo (Egret Woman): wife of One Hunahpu; little is known of her
- One Monkey and One Artisan: sons of One Hunahpu and Xb'aqiyalo; craftsmen, artisans, writers
- Blood Moon (or Blood Woman): pregnant via One and Seven Hunahpu; mother of Hero Twins
- Hunahpu and Xbalanque: Hero Twins, younger stepbrothers of One Monkey and One Artisan
- In addition, there are the denizens of the Underworld, including One and Seven Death, Demon of Pus and Demon of Jaundice, Bone Scepter and Skull Scepter, Scab Stripper, Blood Gatherer, Demon of Filth and Demon of Woe, Wing, and Packstrap.

The events of Part 3 are a series of adventures—primarily ballgames—of One and Seven Hunahpu and their sons **Hunahpu** and Xbalanque, which take place on the earth's surface and in the Underworld, or Xib'alb'a. One Hunahpu and Seven Hunahpu play ball in their aboveground court, which offends the lords of Xib'alb'a, One and Seven **Death**, who send four **owls**, the "Military Keepers of the **Mat**," to summon them to the Underworld to play ball there. In their

descent to Xib'alb'a, One and Seven Hunahpu pass through Canyons, the Scorpion Rapids, and Blood River and choose a path at the Crossroads. They fail several tests and traps set for them in Xib'alb'a and spend the night in **Dark House**. The next day, instead of playing ball, One and Seven Hunahpu are sacrificed and buried in the Place of Ball Game Sacrifice. The head of One Hunahpu is removed and placed in a calabash tree in Xib'alb'a.

A young maiden, Blood Moon (Blood Woman), visits the calabash tree, and the **skull** spits saliva into her hand, impregnating her. When her father, Blood Gatherer, discovers her pregnancy six months later, he sends her to be sacrificed by the owls, who are instructed to bring back her **heart**. Blood Moon dissuades the owls from sacrificing her and prepares a nodule of **incense** from the red sap of the cochineal croton tree (*Croton sanguifluus*) as a substitute for her heart. This successfully fools the Lords of Xib'alb'a.

Blood Moon is then able to travel to the earth's surface, where she goes to Xmucane and announces that she is going to bear her grandchild. Xmucane, disbelieving, gives her a test: she must go to the garden and **gather** a big **net** full of ripe corn. Blood Moon sees only a single ear of maize in the field and cries out in despair to the "guardians of the food," goddesses of the days **Toj**, **Q'anil**, and **Tz'i'** along with Lady Cacao and One **B'atz'** (Christenson 2003:137). She brings back quantities of maize to a still-skeptical Xmucane, but when the grandmother goes to the garden and sees the imprint of the net, she is finally convinced that Blood Moon is indeed pregnant with her grandchild(ren).

After Blood Moon's twin sons, Hunahpu and Xbalanque, are born, they are ill-treated by their brothers One Monkey and One Artisan, and by their grandmother. One day, instead of bringing back the birds they shot, they tell an angry Xmucane that the birds were caught in a tree and they need One Monkey and One Artisan to help bring them down. Hunahpu and Xbalanque send their brothers up into a **yellow** tree,[14] which quickly begins to grow taller and taller so that One Monkey and One Artisan cannot descend. They become **monkeys**, and the Twins' efforts to lure them out of the trees to their grandmother by singing and **drum**ming are unsuccessful.

The story continues with the boys' efforts to establish a garden: each day they clear the brush, but overnight the animals—pumas and jaguars, deer and rabbits, foxes, coyotes, peccaries, birds—contrive to regrow all the trees and bushes. Hunahpu and Xbalanque spend a night in the garden to catch the animals, but they all get away except a **rat**. The rat shows them the location of the ballgame equipment that had belonged to their fathers, One and Seven Hunahpu, in the rafters of their house. At lunchtime they send their grandmother to fetch water, and they arrange a delay—a leaky water **jar**—that allows the rat to climb into the rafters and lower the ball and other equipment.

Hunahpu and Xbalanque go back to the ballcourt where their fathers had played, and once again their rambunctious play raises the ire of the lords of the Underworld, who summon them to play a game with them in seven days. This message is issued to their grandmother, Xmucane, who, distraught, passes on the message to a louse, which is swallowed by a **toad**,[15] which is swallowed by a **snake**, which is swallowed by a laughing **falcon**. The boys shoot the falcon in the eye with their blowgun and, after they treat his eye, he disgorges the snake, which vomits the toad. The louse is found in the toad's mouth and delivers the summons to Hunahpu and Xbalanque.

The boys, with the aid of a **mosquito,** successfully navigate the journey to Xib'alb'a and the tricks the lords set out for them. They survive a night in Dark House and next day they play a ballgame with the lords, using a ball the Xib'alb'ans put into play. But the ball is really a **skull** containing the White **Dagger** of sacrifice. Hunahpu and Xbalanque are uninjured, so they agree to play another game, this time using their own ball. A wager is placed on the game's outcome: four bowls of **flowers**. The boys allow themselves to be defeated and then, after surviving a stay in **Razor** House, they summon the ants to cut flowers from the garden of One and Seven Death, right under the eyes of the garden's guardians, the whip-poor-wills. The lords are amazed that their own flowers have been stolen. They play yet another ballgame, which finishes in a tie.

Hunahpu and Xbalanque survive the night in **Cold** House, **Jaguar** House, and a house of fire, and then enter **Bat** House, all of this while waiting for sunrise. But when Hunahpu lifts his head to see how long until dawn, his head is seized by a bat and sent rolling into the ballcourt. A **coatimundi** brings a **squash** to Xbalanque, who has it carved into a simulated head for Hunahpu.

At this point, the nocturnal **opossum**, presented as an old man, makes four red streaks indicating the approaching dawn and the rise of the sun.

Hunahpu's head is then dropped into the court to begin a ballgame. When it rolls out of the court the Xib'alb'ans mistake a hopping **rabbit** for the ball, allowing Hunahpu's head to be retrieved and put back on his shoulders. The Xib'alb'ans return to the court, and the ballgame resumes with the squash as a ball; the Xib'alb'an lords are defeated. The lords then create a huge stone **pit** oven to make a beverage and challenge the boys to a game of leaping across the pit. But Hunahpu and Xbalanque, anticipating their fate, dive in headfirst and die. Their bones are ground up and deposited in a river.

On the **fifth day** they reappear first as catfish and then as vagabonds, **dancing** and performing magical feats. They are summoned by One and Seven Death to perform before them, and Hunahpu and Xbalanque give them a show: dancing; setting fire to a house without burning anyone; and sacrificing a dog, a human, and even Hunahpu and then reviving them. On seeing this, One and Seven Death demand that they themselves be sacrificed and brought back to life. Hunahpu and Xbalanque comply in sacrificing the two but do not resurrect them, and thus the Twins' true identity is revealed to all the Xib'alb'ans.

In the final act of Part 3, Hunahpu and Xbalanque return to the Place of Ball Game Sacrifice, where Seven Hunahpu was buried, to try to revive him. Because Seven Hunahpu is unable to name all the parts of his face, he cannot be fully revived and is left where he was buried. After this, "the two boys ascended this way, here into the middle of the light, and they ascended straight on into the sky, and the sun belongs to one and the moon to the other. When it became light within the sky, on the face of the earth, they were there in the sky" (D. Tedlock 1996:141).

It can be seen from this extended summary of Part 3 of the *Popol Vuh* that its events and characters also incorporate names of days and months in the Maya calendars (see Table 4.2). These include six new day names in the Yucatán calendar and at least four in the K'iche' and other related highland calendars.[16] Part 3 seems to emphasize the months, with thirteen new lowland and at least eight highland names added to the four lowland (and four highland) names of Parts 1 and 2. The emphasis on the months in Part 3 of the *Popol Vuh* may be considered to reflect the later development of a precise solar-year calendar, perhaps developing out of the thirteen day names of the 260-day calendar as described above, or, minimally, integrated with it. I was unable to discern references to two Yukatekan Maya months in the *Popol Vuh*, Ch'en and Yax.

The Underworld lord Skull corresponds to the month Sek, and the month Sotz' is Bat (House). The owl messengers compare to the month of Muwan (see note 6). The Hero Twins' singing and drumming is a reference to the month Pax (or K'ayab'), and their disappearance for five days can be seen as a reference to the five "lost" days of Wayeb' (D. Tedlock 1996:209). Many of the month references seem old and related to months in highland calendars, either as highland additions/substitutions or as having been lost in the lowlands. For example, the months Wo and Sip might be referenced by their *k'at* signs in the Classic glyphs, *k'at* being a K'iche'an word for a large net to hold corn,[17] but *wo* can also mean frog or toad.[18] The coatimundi that brings the squash head to the ballcourt might be the creature depicted as an animal head in the month sign Xul; alternatively, Xul might be referenced by the rat that gives the Twins their fathers' ballgame equipment. Mol refers to Blood Woman gathering maize in Xmucane's field. Highland month names include incense, cold, squash, mosquito, and opossum, which are referenced in Part 3, plus crab in Part 2.

Birds play a significant role in Part 3 of the *Popol Vuh*: the falcon as messenger of the sky god Huracan; owls as "Military Keepers of the Mat" and messengers from Xib'alb'a; "throng birds," perhaps the migratory Swainson's hawk heralding the approach of both the rainy and the dry seasons (B. Tedlock 1992a:187–188; D. Tedlock 1996:272); and whip-poor-wills, which failed to guard the flower gardens of the Underworld. Bird day-names in the lowland Maya 260-day calendar include eagle (Men) and buzzard (Kib'), plus others in highland calendars, while in the lowland 365-day

calendar they are represented by the month names Muwan (owl) and K'ayab' (macaw, parrot; Seven Macaw of Part 2). Kent Reilly (2000:375) notes that, as part of shamanic transformations, shamans frequently take on the symbols of avians, especially raptors such as owls and eagles. In the calendars that have come down to the present, however, avians are poorly differentiated; owls might be represented by the month Muwan, but Muwan as the Maya Principal Bird Deity (or the Classic-period Itzam-Yeh) is identified as a scarlet macaw (Freidel, Reese-Taylor, and Mora-Marín 2002:46, 48) and is primarily a celestial, rather than an Underworld, deity.

As in Parts 1 and 2, Part 3 also incorporates numerous references to astronomical affairs. The Underworld lord Seven Death has associations with the moon: the waning ("dying") moon lasts seven days before disappearing into the Underworld. Merideth Paxton's (2001:54–56) analysis of the personifications of the moon in the *Popol Vuh* leads her to support the lunar origins of the Maya calendar: the young woman Blood Moon, representing the moon from first visibility to full moon; the Hero Twin Xbalanque, who rises to become the full moon; and Xmucane, the grandmother-midwife-diviner of the waning moon.

There are also allusions to the movements of the planet Venus in the *Popol Vuh*. Because Venus's movements are extremely complex and cover a long period of time, it is likely that the Maya did not achieve a complete understanding until fairly late (i.e., the Classic period; Bricker [1982] says ca. A.D. 934). This could have resulted in significant alterations to earlier texts of the *Popol Vuh*:

> Venus rose as the morning star on a day named Hunahpu, corresponding to the ball playing of Xmucane's sons, One and Seven Hunahpu, in the east; then, after being out of sight in Xibalba, Venus reappeared as the evening star on a day named Death, corresponding to the defeat of her sons by One and Seven Death and the placement of One Hunahpu's head in a tree in the west (D. Tedlock 1996:37). . . .

TABLE 4.2 *Correspondences between* Popol Vuh *characters and events and Maya day and month names*

Popol Vuh	YUKATEKAN OR CLASSIC		OTHER MAYA
Popol Vuh	**Day**	**Month***	**Day/Month**
Part 1			
Dark	Ak'b'al		
Thought			K'iche' day
Earth	Kab'an		
Deer	Manik'	Kej, Sip	
Bird	Men, Kib'		Tzeltal, K'iche' day
Mud			Tzeltal month
Flood	Lamat		
Rain	Muluk (water)		
Dog	Ok	Xul	
Monkey	Chuwen		
Part 2			
Macaw		K'ayab'	
Blowgun			K'iche' month
Jaw, teeth	Eb'		
House			Tzeltal day
Log, wood, tree			K'iche' month
Crab			Chuj, Q'anjob'al, Q'eqchi' month
Sigh, breath	Ik' (wind)		
Earthquake	Kab'an		
Part 3			
Hunahpu	Ajaw		
Death	Kimi		
Owl		Muwan	
Mat		Pop	
Dark	Ak'b'al	Kumk'u	
Skull		Sek	
Heart			Ch'olan month
Incense			Tzeltal month
Gather		Mol	
Net			K'iche' month
Yellow	K'an	K'ank'in	
Monkey	Chuwen		
Drum		Pax, K'ayab'	
Rat			Ixil month
Jar		Kumk'u?	
Toad		Wo?	
Snake	Chikchan		
Falcon			K'iche?
Mosquito			Q'eqchi' month
Dagger	Etz'nab'	Sak	
Flower	Ajaw?		
Razor	Etz'nab'		
Cold			Zapotec day
Jaguar	Ix		(Day in many calendars)
Bat		Sotz'	
Coatimundi		Xul?	
Squash			Pokom, Mixe month
Opossum			Tzeltal month
Rabbit	Lamat		
Pit		Mak	
Five days' disappearance		Wayeb'	
Dance			Q'anjob'al month
Sun appears		Yaxk'in	

Source: Edmonson 1988:174–177, 216–217; Lamb 2002.
*The lowland months of Ch'en and Yax are not identified in this model.

whenever Venus rises as the morning star on a day named Net, corresponding to the appearance of Hunahpu and Xbalanque on the earth [from the Underworld], its next descent into the underworld will always fall on a day named Hunahpu. (Ibid.:39)

Venus as morning star may be linked to the planting of maize, while Venus as evening star relates the growth of maize through One Hunahpu's decapitation and his skull's fertilization of Blood Moon (Milbrath 1999:159–160; also Sprajc 1996). One Hunahpu has been identified with the Maya Maize God (Taube 1992:48), and the twentieth-century Chamula believe the sun is composed of maize.

In sum, I argue that calendars played a deeper role than hitherto suspected in many aspects of Mesoamerican and, specifically, Maya culture in structuring the interrelations of order, legitimacy, and wealth evident in their sociopolitical formations. The mythic history of the *Popol Vuh* narrative covers not only the origins of the world and its creatures in historical time, but also key points in the development of the calendars. The Long Count not only provided a linear measure of the passage of time but also structured geopolitical relations.

In a provocative but largely ignored essay published in 1979, Edmonson poses "some Postclassic questions about the Classic Maya" and raises the possibility that the Classic Maya observed *may* cycles. It has long been known that the Late Classic Maya celebrated the completion of *k'atuns* by erecting carved, dated monuments, often in distinctive architectural arrangements, such as twin-pyramid complexes (see, e.g., C. Jones 1969). My review of sculpted monuments and architecture at selected lowland sites supports the idea that not only *k'atuns* but also *may* cycles were widely recognized and celebrated by rulers in the Classic period (Rice 2004). Edmonson suggests the possibility that calendrical cycling played a role in the Preclassic period, with *may* cycles possibly explaining the rise and fall of sites as well as the widely noted destruction of monuments.

I now turn to two Isthmian regions and sites that are of interest in terms of exploring the origin and development of the *may*: the Middle Preclassic Gulf coast Olmec area, especially the site of La Venta; and the Pacific slopes of Chiapas and Guatemala, particularly the Late Preclassic site of Izapa.

Middle and Late Preclassic
The Gulf Coast Olmec and Epi-Olmec

 The theme pursued in this book is that basic principles of Maya geopolitical organization were shared with those of the Isthmian region in the Formative period and were expressions of ideological/calendrical structures developed by and during that time. Thus it is necessary to review some of these developments in the Isthmian region, where they are archaeologically recognizable earlier and more extensively than in the Maya area. The late Early and Middle Preclassic/Formative periods, dating from approximately 1200 to 400/300 B.C., were a time of dramatic cultural transformations in Mesoamerica, with the emergence of what anthropologists and archaeologists refer to as complex societies. Complex societies may be briefly characterized by greatly differentiated sociopolitical and socioeconomic roles and statuses, three- or more tiered site-size hierarchies, monumental art, and formal site planning with public or "civic-ceremonial" architecture in the form of temples, platforms, plazas, and ballcourts.

Mesoamerican complex societies developed out of the late Archaic and Early Formative sedentary village traditions archaeologically evident by 2000–1600 B.C. and even earlier in some favored locales. Paleobotanical analyses reveal that this sedentarization was accompanied by increasing dependence on agriculture, although domesticated maize was not necessarily a dietary staple. Interregional trade networks transported early exotic, or wealth, goods, such as obsidian and iron ores; these were circulated through interregional trade networks overland and by canoe along waterways. Such goods constitute evidence for the beginnings of ranking and the symbolism of statuses and may signal the existence of specialized roles such as shaman and/or shamanic chief. In addition, elements of later Mesoamerican ritual and worldview, such as an emphasis on dualism and quadripartition, infant sacrifice, incipient ceremonial architecture in the form of dance grounds and/or ballcourts, and probably the notion of caves as sacred places, were already in place.

Early complex societies emerged in numerous places in Mesoamerica but are best known in four areas. Two are in highland Mexico—the Oaxaca highlands (Flannery 1976; Flannery and Marcus 1983, 2000) and central Mexico (see, e.g., Niederberger 1996; Tolstoy 1989)—and are not discussed further here. The other two are in the Isthmus of Tehuantepec: the Olmec culture along the southern coast

The appropriation of caves iconographically by the [Olmec] political elite is contemporaneous with the emergence of complex society itself so the relationship would appear to be both ancient and intimate.

—Ann M. Scott and James E. Brady,
"Formative Cave Utilization"

of the Gulf of Mexico in Veracruz and Tabasco (Fig. 5.1), and the advanced culture of probable Proto-Mixe-Zoquean speakers in the Pacific piedmont and coastal regions of Chiapas, Mexico, and adjacent Guatemala (see, e.g., Blake et al. 1995; Clark 1991). During the Middle Formative all these groups seem to have maintained extensive contacts with each other, to judge from the widespread distribution of raw materials and the finished artifacts that constituted elite wealth.

In the southern Gulf lowlands, two to as many as five "independent, contemporaneous kingdoms" may have developed during the twelfth to tenth centuries B.C., including San Lorenzo, Laguna de los Cerros, La Venta, Las Limas, and Tres Zapotes

(Clark 1997:217). They occupied a "patchy landscape" of slow-moving and annually flooded "bifurcating, meandering, and braided streams, seasonally or permanently flooded back-swamps, oxbow lakes, interfluve savannas, mangrove-bordered estuaries, and coastal beach-ridge formations" (von Nagy 1997:254). This rich, complex, and dynamic wetland environment provided fertile alluvial soils for farming, salt domes, and an abundance of terrestrial and avifauna as well as fish, shellfish, and reptiles. On the western edge of this Olmec heartland, the Tuxtlas, a volcanic massif rising some seventeen hundred meters above sea level (Pool 1997:44), provided the columns and boulders of basalt so important to their monumental art. Sites in the

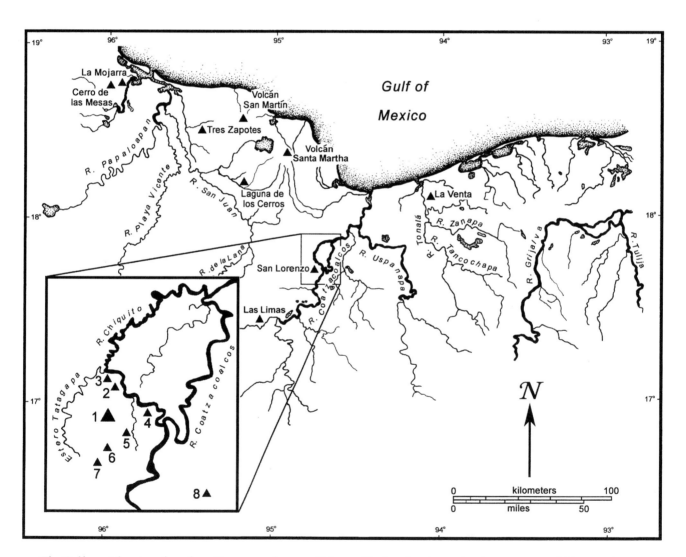

5.1. The Gulf coastal region of southern Veracruz and eastern Tabasco, Mexico, showing regional waterways and Olmec and Epi-Olmec sites. Inset: sites in the San Lorenzo region: (1) San Lorenzo, (2) Tenochtitlán, (3) El Remolino, (4) El Azuzul, (5) Potrero Nuevo, (6) Loma del Zapote, (7) Las Camelias, (8) El Manatí.

Tuxtlas, where pollen in lake sediments suggests maize cultivation ca. 3000 B.C., had largely egalitarian settlement in the Early Formative (Santley, Arnold, and Barrett 1997:178–179).

Since the Olmec culture was first investigated by archaeologists (see Benson [1996] for a history), discussions have focused on its extraordinary art style, especially the monolithic basalt monuments and their iconographic themes. These include portraitlike "colossal heads" and flat-topped "tabletop altars" now regarded as thrones. Until the late twentieth century, relatively little attention was devoted to architectural arrangements and virtually none to the role of calendrical ritual in Olmec history as a charter for societal order and legitimacy of rulers. In addition, until the 1980s, pre-Olmec occupation along the Gulf coast was poorly known and even more poorly dated.

ARCHITECTURAL PATTERNS

The spatial patterning of archaeological sites and their architecture may be analyzed from innumerable perspectives. Olmec sites have been studied with respect to their location, relation to other natural features, layout or dispersion of built features, and orientations of architectural complexes and individual structures (see, e.g., Aveni, Dowd, and Vining 2003; Aveni and Hartung 1986, 2000; Malmström 1997). There is also considerable interest in the creation of "sacred landscapes" by the Olmec through the directions of placement and themes of monuments (Grove 1999; Reilly 1999, 2000; Rodríguez and Ortiz C. 1997), expressions of the materialization of ideology (including cosmologies) on a grandiose scale.

San Lorenzo Tenochtitlán, Veracruz

San Lorenzo (Coe 1968a, 1981a, 1981b; Coe and Diehl 1980; Cyphers 1996, 1997; Diehl 1981) is located in southern Veracruz, some 60 kilometers from the coast amid past and present tributaries of the lower Río Coatzacoalcos. The site and its surrounding area are often referred to as San Lorenzo Tenochtitlán, incorporating a minor site northeast of San Lorenzo proper (Fig. 5.1[1]). A survey of 403 square kilometers in this region revealed rapid population growth in the Early Preclassic period, with 106 sites in the 90 square kilometers around San

Lorenzo and 29 in its "outer hinterland" (Symonds 1995:567). One large secondary site, Loma del Zapote (Fig. 5.1[6]), has monuments and monumental architecture, including the El Azuzul acropolis and its sculptures (Fig. 5.1[4]); another possible secondary site is Las Camelias (Fig. 5.1[7]). Numerous tertiary sites include Tenochtitlán, Potrero Nuevo (part of Loma del Zapote), and El Tigrito, thus indicating a three-level settlement hierarchy (ibid.: 572), although some of these, such as Tenochtitlán, date later than the primary Olmec florescence. In addition, the sacred spring of El Manatí (Ortiz C. and Rodríguez 1999) is located a short distance southeast of San Lorenzo (Fig. 5.1[8]).

San Lorenzo dates to the late Early Preclassic/ Early Olmec period, with occupation beginning around 1500 B.C. and lasting through the Middle Preclassic, until about 500/400 B.C. At that point the site was virtually abandoned, perhaps in part because of the seventh-century eruption of the nearby San Martín Pajapan volcano and deposition of an ash layer, and it may have been largely vacant during the Late Preclassic, 400 B.C. to A.D. 200 (Diehl 2004:31; Symonds 1995:611, 694, 696; Weiant 1943). Throughout the Preclassic, settlement appears to have been oriented toward the region's waterways (Symonds and Lunagómez 1997:153–160, 171–172). The Early and Middle Preclassic occupation of San Lorenzo is divided into six phases: Ojochi—1500–1350 B.C.; Bajío—1350–1250 B.C.; Chicharras—1250–1150 B.C.; San Lorenzo—1150–900/800 B.C. (two subphases); Nacaste—900/800–675 B.C.; hiatus in occupation; Palangana—600–400 B.C.

Materials recovered from the first two phases appear to be related to contemporaneous cultures on the Pacific coast of Guatemala and Chiapas, leading archaeologists to trace the earliest origins of the Olmec back to this region. During the Chicharras phase, San Lorenzo covered some twenty hectares or more, with more than one hundred satellite sites demonstrating a three-tiered settlement hierarchy in the surrounding area (Diehl 2004:27). Some new iconographic motifs and art forms characteristic of later ritual and status systems in the Gulf coast appeared, resulting in this phase's being dubbed "proto-Olmec." These elements were initially linked to an in-migration of groups external to the Gulf coast (Coe and Diehl 1980, 1:150; Malmström 1997:66–71), but more recent research has pointed to continuity and stability during this early period. In particular, excavations at the nearby El Manatí spring revealed Early Formative ritual offerings, including "Gulf Olmec–related ritual paraphernalia." This suggests that the activity at this site represents the beginning of material expressions of Olmec identity (Arnold 2003:41–42; Ortiz C. and Rodríguez 1999). The Olmec florescence began during the San Lorenzo phase, and the site of San Lorenzo has been described as the "capital" of the lower Coatzacoalcos drainage area (Cyphers 1996:65). The site's decline around 900 B.C. is marked by significant monument destruction or recarving (Porter 1989, 1990) and regional depopulation (Symonds and Lunagómez 1997:158).

San Lorenzo (Fig. 5.2) was built on a plateau, and Malmström (1997:78–79) proposes that its location was dictated by a view to the southwest (azimuth 245°) to Cerro Zempoaltepec, the point of winter solstice sunset. The site might have had a master plan, perhaps unfinished: some scholars think the site represents the modification of a natural promontory to create a platform with six ridges and valleys, resulting in an effigy of a large bird flying east (Coe and Diehl 1980, 1:387). According to this proposition, the platform was created by raising and leveling the natural surface with artificial fill, which reached a depth of at least seven meters in some places. Alternatively, the strong bilateral symmetry of the ridges might be a result of post-Preclassic activity, with the ridges and ravines formed by a combination of geological processes of erosion, uplift, and settling, rather than human action (Cyphers 1997:104–105). In any case, as an early example of public architecture this one kilometer–long platform represents an enormous amount of human labor (Diehl 1981:74).

Until the late 1990s, San Lorenzo was identified as a ceremonial center, which is to say, it displayed primarily public-ceremonial architecture and yielded comparatively little evidence for domestic occupation. Public architecture consists of four complexes, including more than twenty earthen mounds, although most were built after 600 B.C. and/or during an Early Postclassic occupation of the site. Much of the construction in the area used blocks of local bentonite (Cyphers 1997:99), a soft, highly absorbent clay formed by

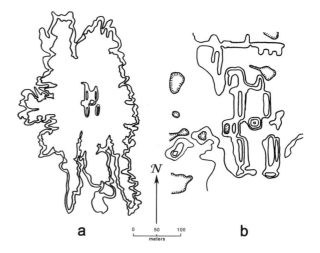

5.2. The site of San Lorenzo, Veracruz: (a) the San Lorenzo plateau; (b) the central portion of San Lorenzo, showing mounds and lagoons (baseline contour 75 m).

the decomposition of volcanic ash. Although several ridges have concentrations of small, low mounds thought to be residential housemounds, totaling approximately two hundred (Coe and Diehl 1980, 1: 29), and wattle-and-daub apsidal construction dated as early as 1000 B.C. (ibid.:388), early work suggested very low populations for San Lorenzo, both at the site and in the region. More recent efforts have focused on domestic settlement and revised these estimates considerably upward. Ann Cyphers (1996:67, 1997:106, 1999:158) indicates that "intense" Early Preclassic settlement existed on terraces created on the sides of the San Lorenzo platform, and by the tenth century B.C. it covered about 690 hectares, or 7 square kilometers. Clark (1997:217) estimates the population at 10,500–17,500, but most Preclassic structures are buried under one to one and a half meters of overburden, making population estimates risky (Cyphers 1997:102).

Structure Group A, in the center of the site, exhibits a typical Formative layout, with a strong north-south axis, pairs of long, narrow mounds defining rectilinear plazas, and a pyramid at the end of the plaza.[1] The distinctive feature of this early plan is its strong east-west bilateral symmetry about the central axis; in addition, the four long mounds with a pyramid at the center might represent a quincunx arrangement, a Maya symbol of completion. Group A was constructed late in the

Middle Preclassic occupation of the site, during the Palangana phase, 600–400 B.C. (Coe and Diehl 1980, 1:201–202), which appears to have followed a settlement hiatus and is characterized by relatively small populations. A similar north-south axis and symmetry can be seen at roughly contemporaneous Laguna de los Cerros (Bove 1978) and La Venta (below), and Michael Coe and Richard Diehl (1980, 1:29) posit that Group A at San Lorenzo might be a copy of Group A at La Venta. Circular Mound C3-1, in the center of San Lorenzo's Group A, was rebuilt in three stages during the Villa Alta phase (A.D. 900–1100), a reoccupation of the site after a hiatus of about a millennium (ibid.:213). In fact, Grove (1999:276) suggests that the entire Group A complex might date to the Early Postclassic. However, the presence of Palangana-phase sherds in the late fills hints that an early version of Mound C was originally built in the late Middle Preclassic (Coe and Diehl 1980, 1:53, 388) as part of the Group A construction. Interestingly, a sherd of "Mars Orange ware" (now called Savanna Orange), a common ware in the Middle Preclassic Belize Valley, was recovered in a Palangana-phase context (ibid.:202).

One of the most distinctive features of San Lorenzo is its waterworks, consisting of twenty ponds, or *lagunas* (lagoons), and systems of drains. At least some of these postdate Formative occupation and may be the result of modern ranching activity (Cyphers 1997:108, 110). The lagoons vary in plan from irregular to geometric (hexagonal); some occur in north-south lines; and at least one may have been lined with blocks of bentonite (Coe and Diehl 1980, 1:30). The drains are troughs lined with slabs of basalt, creating a U-shaped section, and are covered with additional slabs of stone; at least one was lined with clay. One drain in the west-central part of the site extends 170 meters east-west with three subsidiary canals, and the weight of the basalt in the canal is estimated at more than thirty tons.

The functions of these *lagunas* and canal structures are not clearly understood: they may have served for water storage or as ritual baths, or, given the torrential rains that fall in this region, perhaps to carry away rainwater (Adams 1991:62). One has an associated sculpture of a duck, and Karl Taube (2001:110) notes that the "duck is an important

rain-bringer" in Mesoamerica. Cyphers (1999:165) hypothesizes that the foundation of San Lorenzo's rulers' power was water management, with the water perhaps drawn from a spring at the upper (east) end of the canals, thereby supplying potable water from a spring for ritual and quotidian use, as well as control of labor.

The ritual importance of water is apparent earlier at El Manatí, the sacred spring at the western base of Cerro Manatí, a salt dome seventeen kilometers southeast of San Lorenzo. There, excavations in the organic, anaerobic sediments of the spring revealed three phases of deposits: (1) dispersed greenstone celts above sandstone rocks, covered by (2) an organic layer with carefully arranged celts on cardinal axes, underlying (3) carved wooden busts wrapped in reeds as if mortuary bundles (Rodríguez and Ortiz C. 1997:83–84, 93). Other finds include wooden scepters, greenstone and jade tools, beads, and other objects, rubber balls, stone knives, and infant burials that appear to be sacrifices (Ortiz C. and Rodríguez 1999; Rodríguez and Ortiz C. 1997). Two uncorrected radiocarbon dates suggest that the ritual deposition of artifacts in the spring area began as early as 1790–1760 b.c. (Ortiz C. and Rodríguez 1999:228). The investigators conclude that "we have at El Manatí the remains of activities associated with the worship of natural elements, especially of water in the form of springs, of the hills as attractors of the clouds and the rain, and the possible linking of these with communication with the ancestors, here represented by images carved in wood" (ibid.:251). In addition, the positioning of a body of water at the base of a hill seems to have been replicated in the ceremonial architecture of some later Formative sites, such as Izapa.

Although San Lorenzo yielded few caches or artifacts of jade or serpentine, numerous large stone sculptures have been found at the site, including ten colossal heads and five thrones. Arranged in groups, or tableaux, for viewing in processionals, the monuments convey different mythological or historical themes in varied areas, contributing to the interpretation of a sacred landscape (Cyphers 1996:68; Grove 1999:280). Most monuments, particularly colossal heads, occur in the southern half of the site, as well as east of a line established by two thrones; the latter display rulership themes or expressions concerned with legitimacy. In the central western part of San Lorenzo there is evidence of monument storage and a workshop for recarving/recycling basalt monuments, perhaps where "attached specialists" worked (Cyphers 1996:66; idem 1999:167).

Outside San Lorenzo, some eighty or more sculpted monuments have been found in the surrounding region (Coe 1981c:139; Coe and Diehl 1980, 1:30–31; Cyphers 1996), including jaguars and human athletes. One well-known sculpture from Potrero Nuevo is thought to show a jaguar copulating with a human female. Toward the end of the Early Formative occupation of the site, most of these monuments were defaced and buried, a task involving considerable labor expenditure. Around 700 B.C. or shortly thereafter, San Lorenzo experienced an approximately 150-year hiatus in construction activity and settlement, perhaps the consequence of a volcanic eruption, after which the center was reoccupied.

The distribution of hinterland sites on elevated terrain along rivercourses points to the importance of trade to the San Lorenzo Tenochtitlán region, as does the presence of causewaylike dikes and docks at some locales, for example, El Tigrito and Potrero Nuevo (Cyphers 1997:108–109, 111; Symonds 1995:570, 588; Symonds and Lunagómez 1997:157). San Lorenzo's obsidian came from the Guadalupe Victoria (Puebla), Otumba (central Mexico), and El Chayal (Guatemala) sources (Cyphers 1996:66). San Lorenzo might have specialized in making beads of ilmenite, magnetite, and other ferric minerals (Symonds 1995:587) such as hematite. A possible ilmenite workshop or storage area was located at Loma del Zapote (ibid.:587, citing Cyphers).

An unusual magnetic object was recovered in excavations into Mound B2-1 at San Lorenzo, the largest mound in an isolated, small complex on the Northwest Ridge (Coe and Diehl 1980, 1:71–78): a small fragment of a bar of highly polished magnetic hematite ore, 3.4 centimeters long and with a polygonal cross-section (9 x 3 x 8.5 x 4 millimeters). The bar has an incised longitudinal groove and, when free-floated on water or liquid mercury, the groove points to 35.5° west of magnetic north (Carlson 1975:758). Analyses revealed that the bar could have been a lodestone ("any iron ore mineral with a geomagnetic remanent magnetization"; ibid.:754) used as a "geomagnetically directed pointer," the earliest technological step in development of a magnetically oriented compass (quotation, Fuson 1969:508; see also Carlson 1975:759). This compasslike artifact was dated, on the basis of associated ceramics, to the San Lorenzo phase (Coe and Diehl 1980, 1:245).

Other unusual artifacts of iron ore are small, multiperforated, drilled cubes. Only fourteen were found in the Yale excavations at San Lorenzo (Coe and Diehl 1980, 1:242), but later excavations uncovered three pits containing six metric tons of them (Cyphers 1999; Lesure 2004:82). Apparently manufactured from ore sources in the Central Depression of Chiapas at the sites of Mirador, Plumajillo, and elsewhere (Lee 1989:214, citing Pierre Agrinier), such cubes also have been found at Tres Zapotes in the Gulf coast region (Lowe 1989b:51). Their use is unknown, although it has been suggested that they were used in stoneworking (Lesure 2004:82), as fishnet weights, beads, hammers, *atlatl* weights, amulets, or fire-drilling apparatus (Lee 1989:214; Lowe 1989b:53). Another possibility is that they were beads woven into the netlike headgear seen on some of the colossal heads (Fig. 5.9a) or other items of regalia (Coe and Diehl 1980, 1:242, 324). Whatever their function, the ritual deposition of some 13,600 pounds of these tiny worked pieces of ore is hard to fathom in terms of an ideology, although it clearly represents accumulation of wealth in the form of skillfully crafted exotic goods (Helms 1993).

La Venta, Tabasco

The site of La Venta, described variously as occupying an island in the Río Tonalá or perched on a north-south natural ridge surrounded by swamp, lies fifteen kilometers from the Gulf coast. Three major volcanic peaks of the Tuxtla Mountains, of which two mark important solar alignments, are visible from the site; San Martín volcano, at azimuth 295°, marks the position of summer-solstice sunset, while Cerro Santa Martha marks sunset on August 13 (one possible start date for the Long Count; Malmström 1997:81, 83–84). Archaeological surveys of the roughly forty kilometers around La Venta revealed more than one hundred settlements, at least fifty of which date to Formative times (González Lauck 1996:80, citing Rust).

La Venta (Fig. 5.3) originally covered two hundred hectares (ca. five hundred acres) and, compared with San Lorenzo, has far more and larger ceremonial platforms, with "formally marked entrances at the north and south, 40 earth mounds forming 9 architectural complexes, [and] 90 known stone sculptures" (Diehl 2004:62). The site's ceremonial center shares a north-south linear layout with San Lorenzo, but the emphasis on bilateral symmetry is variable. The best-known portion of the site, Group A and the thirty-two-meter-high Mound C, lies north of the Main Plaza. The Main Plaza is bounded on its east side by the Stirling Acropolis platform, possibly the living area of the chief or ruler, and Group B on the west. South of the central plaza is Group D, an arrangement of mounds (elite residences?) in three north-south lines (Grove 1999:272–275; Reilly 1999). Group E, to the east of Group A, is a residential area (González Lauck 1989:83). Evidence of domestic occupation, including house floors, storage pits, burials, and pottery, can be found in the civic-ceremonial core of the site, and corn pollen was found in deposits dating to 2250 B.C. (Rust and Leyden 1994). Vast quantities of exotic goods, such as jade, serpentine, ferric-ore mirrors, and other materials, often carefully secreted in buried caches, indicate that the site's elite maintained extensive economic ties with distant areas of Mesoamerica and, it is important to note, these can be linked to an inferred belief system or ideology.

Except for the Stirling Acropolis, the main civic-ceremonial structures are oriented 8° west of magnetic north (the same orientation as the Tierras Largas–phase Structure 6 at San José Mogote, Oaxaca). This orientation is not easy to explain. It might have been based on a sighting south to the mountain nearest the site (Tate 2001:142) or on the setting azimuth of the Big Dipper at midnight of the summer solstice (Hatch 1971:10). Damon Peeler and Marcus Winter (1992) suggest that this orientation was based on the position of the three stars in the Belt of Orion. First, they argue that conceptualizing this orientation as 8° west of north is an imposition of modern Western values and orientations—toward north—

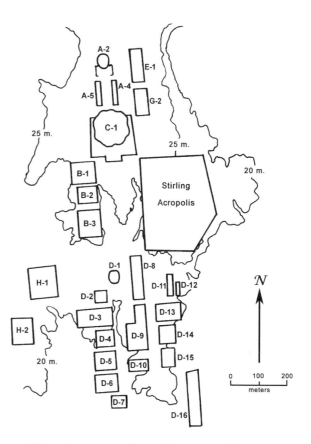

5.3. The main ceremonial core of La Venta, Tabasco (after González Lauck 1996:fig. 1).

on ancient Mesoamericans, who, instead, emphasized east as the primary direction. Thus what we think of as 8° west of north can also be considered azimuths 82° (east of north) and 262°, with an approximately north-south line derived as a right angle to that axis (ibid.:40). Noting that there are no significant lunar or solar positions (equinoxes, solstices, zeniths) at these azimuths, they observe that, around 1000–900 B.C. at 18° north latitude, the three roughly equally spaced stars of Orion's Belt rose in a nearly vertical line, and that the setting of the middle star, Alnilam (Epsilon Orionis), occurred at azimuth 262° (or 8° south of west) around November 11–12 (ibid.:42–43).

La Venta flourished from roughly 1000 to 400 B.C., or, more narrowly, during the late La Venta period, 850/800 to 500 B.C. Although early occupation along the Gulf coast has not been well dated chronometrically (see González Lauck 1996; Grove 1997, 1999; Rust and Sharer 1988), dates from the La Venta region (Rust 1992) reveal an Early Preclassic (ca. 2250–1150 B.C.) or pre-Olmec occupation, followed by Middle Preclassic florescence. The chronological division in Table 5.1 loosely follows Lowe (1989b). The most common scenario for La Venta, derived from early excavations, sees four construction phases, I through IV, each about one hundred years long; these correspond to the Intermediate and early Terminal Olmec periods.

Further surveys and excavations at La Venta and its surroundings have dispelled many long-standing beliefs about the site's origins and growth. For example, it was previously thought that little to no Early Formative occupation existed in the swampy vicinity of the site, and that it blossomed relatively suddenly. More recent hydrological and geomorphological studies, however, have revealed that at the time of La Venta's florescence it was surrounded by a complex network of swamps, bays, small lakes, estuaries, rivers, and streams, which not only facilitated trade but were sources of valued aquatic resources (González Lauck 1989:85). Nine sites with evidence of Early and Middle Formative settlement were located on raised islandlike areas along a previously little known rivercourse north of La Venta (Rust and Sharer 1988). One of these is San Andrés, five kilometers northeast of La Venta, where soil cores yielded domesticated maize pollen around 5000 cal. B.C., domesticated manioc pollen dated to 4600 cal. B.C., and maize macrofossils around 2500 cal. B.C. (Diehl 2004:24, 86; Pohl 2001); pottery dates to 2300 B.C. (Diehl 2004:89). A three-tiered settlement-size hierarchy might have existed in the area by 800–500 B.C. (Rust and Sharer 1988:104).

The Ceremonial Court Complex

La Venta Group A/C has a north-south axis and bilateral symmetry, as emphasized by two long, linear "range mounds" (labeled A4 and A5 on Fig. 5.3) (Reilly 1999:20), but the axis is embellished with a "Ceremonial Court" complex (Fig. 5.4a) on the north and an enormous mound, either rectangular or truncated-conical in plan, on the south (Mound C; labeled C1 on Fig. 5.3). This complex, partially enclosed by a "fence" of basalt columns, was explored in 1942–1943 and intensively excavated in 1955 (Drucker, Heizer, and Squier 1959), revealing sequential elaborations in a series of four superimposed constructions, floorings of colored sands, and rich tombs and caches. Each phase of construction (La Venta Phases I, II, III, and IV) was initiated by depositing "massive offerings": tons of blocks of nonlocal serpentine stone layered in huge pits (ibid.:46). Two of these offerings were made in Phase II, under the Southwest and Southeast platforms, and were topped by mosaic jaguar masks of serpentine. The other offerings were under or in front of northern Structure A-2. The four-phase construction sequence is thought to have been executed between 1000/900 and 600/500 B.C., but a much shorter interval of 100–150 years has been suggested (Diehl 2004:69). This abbreviated chronology might suggest that a refurbishment was undertaken on completion of Calendar Rounds every fifty-two years. The Complex A area was ritually "terminated" by being covered with a thirty-centimeter cap of red clay (ibid.:70).

The five platforms in the Ceremonial Court might be considered to represent a quincunx arrangement, with four at the intercardinal corners and one at the center. The central mound in this

TABLE 5.I. *Gulf coast Preclassic chronology*

PRECLASSIC PERIOD DIVISION	GENERAL CULTURAL PERIOD	ESTIMATED DATES
Early Preclassic	Pre-Olmec	2250–1200/1150 B.C.
Middle Preclassic	Early Olmec	1200/1150–900 B.C.
	Intermed. Olmec	900–600 B.C.
	Terminal Olmec	600–300 B.C.
Late Preclassic	Epi-Olmec	300 B.C.–A.D. 300

Source: Loosely based on Lowe (1989b).

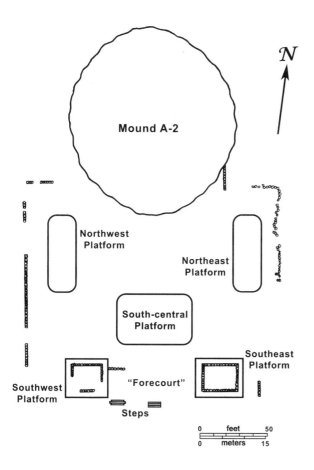

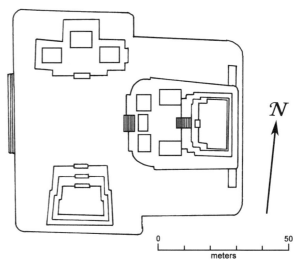

5.4. (a) La Venta Complex A and Ceremonial Court (drawn from Drucker, Heizer, and Squier 1959:fig. 4); (b) Uaxactún Group H (drawn from Schele and Freidel 1990:fig. 4.6).

configuration, identified as the South-central Platform, had two monuments (Monument 12 and Stela 3) lying at its base on the north and west sides, respectively. Archaeological explorations into the east end of this mound revealed two partially overlapping pits (Drucker, Heizer, and Squier 1959:fig. 7, 24, 26). Perhaps the sculpted stones, Monument 12 and Stela 3, were originally placed in these pits, or a stone or wooden pillar serving as a World Tree or gnomon could have been erected there as a sighting/shadowing device to mark solar positions.

Offerings 9 and 11 were found above Massive Offering 2, at Mound A-2 at the north end of the ceremonial court (Drucker, Heizer, and Squier 1959:176–184, pl. 42). These offerings, positioned on either side of the site centerline and dated to Phase IV, consist of nine jade celts lying on their flat sides, bits to the north, in two rows of four, with the ninth at the north end. North of this single celt was a large, concave pyrite mirror. Offering 1943-E, excavated in the 1943 field season south of Mound A-2, and dated to Phase II, consisted of

twenty jade and serpentine celts in a cruciform arrangement, with a concave mirror at the north arm of the cross. This offering was oriented precisely 8° west of north (Carlson 1981:130)—the same orientation as the axis of La Venta itself—suggesting the importance of the magnetic orienting properties of the concave pyrite mirrors.

Excavations in the Northeast Platform, in front (west) of which was found the famous Offering No. 4, identified six large postholes and three offerings of jade earflares, beads, and maskettes on cinnabar or ochre (Drucker, Heizer, and Squier 1959:162–179). F. Kent Reilly (2005:34) proposes that the postholes are indicators of a wooden scaffolding erected for a ruler's accession, similar to those known from the Maya area, and the artifacts were his accompanying regalia. These were dated to Phase III, the penultimate construction of the complex.

In a sense, La Venta's closed Ceremonial Court complex might be considered a microcosm of the overall Group A plan (see also Clark 2001:189). One enters from the south, climbing low basalt steps to enter a "forecourt," the plaza of a "triadic group": three structures arranged at right angles in a U-shape, usually on a single platform (Hansen 1990:171; idem 1998:77–78, 2000:59). The north side of the forecourt is formed by the South-central Platform, with Stela 3 (Fig. 5.5), an undated but late Terminal Olmec– or Epi-Olmec–period (ca. 400 B.C.) monument, set into its northwestern corner. North of this platform is another triadic group, the Ceremonial Court proper, flanked by linear platforms to the east and west and Mound

5.5. Restoration drawing of the eroded sculpture on La Venta Stela 3 (drawn from Drucker, Heizer, and Squier 1959:fig. 68). The original clearly shows two facing figures carrying clubs, the one to the right wearing a fish-head headdress and standing in front of a niche, with several club-wielding figures in the sky; other details of costuming and features are conjectural.

A-2 on the north side. As described by Grove (1999), this entire court complex represents the celestial realm—sky and the home of the ancestors—with numerous lavish burials of presumably important Olmec leaders and buried caches and offerings. The enclosing "fence" of basalt columns physically and symbolically sets it apart from the lower earthly realm.

Complexes similar to La Venta's Ceremonial Court existed in the Maya lowlands at Middle Preclassic Nakbe (Hansen 1991a, 2000) and at Late Preclassic Uaxactún, but with east-west orientations. At Uaxactún, the acropolis on the east side of the Group H triadic complex (Fig. 5.4b), east of Group E and dating ca. 150–100 B.C. (Valdés and Fahsen 1995), is entered from the west (not from the south, as at La Venta) by low steps. The visitor does not enter a "forecourt" but faces the central mound in a north-south line of three small temples. Beyond is another triadic group: two linear structures flank a plaza on the north and south sides, with a large tiered pyramid, Structure H3, on the east side. This acropolis exhibits north-south bilateral symmetry and greatly emphasizes the eastern structure (rather than the northern), as compared with La Venta.

Reilly (1994, 1999) interprets the La Venta Group A/C complex in light of ideological principles found in Maya studies (e.g., Freidel, Schele, and Parker 1993). He sees Mound C as the Olmec version of the Maya "First True Mountain" (or a Coatépec, Snake Mountain), the "range mounds" to the north in Group A as "liminal space," and the Ceremonial Court complex with its greenstone deposits as a primordial sea and watery otherworld. More specifically, he (1999:28) interprets the enclosed court as a Formative "Lying-down-Sky, First-Three-Stone-Place" where, the Maya believed, the current creation began and First Father, the Maize Lord, raised the World Tree. In particular, the sumptuous elite burials in the courtyard—including artifacts that seemingly represent the trefoil element that is an "Olmec prototype for the Maya Jester God" headband (ibid.:31; see also Freidel 1992) worn by rulers—reveal this area as home of the ancestors (see also Grove 1999).

Finally, the triadic-structure arrangements in the court suggest the three stones the Maya gods set up during the act of creation. In other words, the sacred location built by the rulers of La Venta represents a re-creation of the mythic primordium which "provided the cosmic validation for their elevated social status and political authority, establishing a basic pattern that was modified by later Classic Maya polities" (Reilly 1999:38).

These interpretations can be expanded with respect to the Baines and Yoffee (1998, 2000) model. It is apparent that La Venta, especially the Ceremonial Court complex, materializes an ideology that establishes cosmic and social order with creation stones and ancestors in the north, which legitimizes rulers and serves as a context for the display and consumption of exotic wealth goods. However, one important element is missing: time. If La Venta was created as a sacred landscape and place of cosmic creation, we might also expect that it would be the place of the beginning of time. How might this be recognized archaeologically? One way is through a possible specialized "observatory" architectural complex at the site.

The "Observatory Complex"

La Venta's largely unexplored complexes in the southern part of the site, Groups B and D, are believed to date to the late Terminal Olmec period, possibly 500–400 B.C. Two structures, D-1 and

D-8 at the southern end of the Main Plaza (Fig. 5.3), are believed to be part of the earliest site construction, however (Clark 2001:fig. 2b). Structure D-8, formerly referred to as the "Long Mound" in Group B, is a long, narrow "range mound" with its axis north-south; a low truncated conical (?) structure (D-1) sits to the west on the same central axis. A basalt column (Monument 49) was set on the southern end of Structure D-8, and two large thrones were found on either side on its central axis. Throne ("Altar") 4 (Fig. 5.6), on the east centerline of this structure facing east, shows an individual seated in a cave or the mouth of a large feline and holding a rope attached to several smaller figures around the sides of the stone. Ninety-nine cylindrical and spherical jade beads and one round amethyst bead were recovered in front of Throne 4, suggesting that the monument marked an important event (Lowe 1989b:61). Throne ("Altar") 5 (Fig. 5.7), on the structure's west centerline, shows a number of seated figures holding infants.

The linear-mound-plus-western-platform combination of La Venta Structures D-1 and D-8 is unusual in the Gulf coast region, but it can be noted in widespread areas of Mesoamerica at approximately the same time (Clark and Hansen 2001), from the Mundo Perdido complex of Tikal in

5.6. La Venta Throne ("Altar") 4, on the east centerline of Structure D-8 (drawn from photograph, de la Fuente 1996:23).

5.7. Scene on side of La Venta Throne ("Altar") 5, on the west centerline of Structure D-8 (drawn from photograph, Grove 1995:31).

the Maya lowlands to the site of Tlalancaleca in the Mexican highlands (García Cook 1981:251). In the Isthmian region, the arrangement is found during the Escalera phase, ca. 600–450 B.C., at sites in Chiapas that also display typical linear layouts: San Isidro, La Libertad, Finca Acapulco, and Chiapa de Corzo in the Central Depression of the Río Grijalva, and also at Mirador, Tzutzuculi, Ocozocoautla, Vistahermosa, and five or more other sites, where the complexes typically occur in the center of the community (Clark and Hansen 2001; Lee 1989:207, 225).[2]

One structure at San Isidro also had a La Venta–style centerline cache of celts in cruciform arrangements and burials (Lowe 1981, 1998). The linear mound is occasionally cruciform, emphasizing the transverse centerline rather than the ends,

as did the placement of thrones at La Venta Structure D-8. Some of the Chiapas sites also have structures vaguely resembling those in La Venta's Ceremonial Court: "large squarish or rectangular basal 'acropolis' platforms with one or more superstructures" in the site centers, and at some sites, ballcourts also make an early appearance (Lee 1989:207). One such site, Tzutzuculi, has twenty-five earthen platforms in a linear arrangement, including a triadic group; the site's orientation of 38° east of north is aligned to Tres Picos mountain (McDonald 1977:560–561). There, two carved monuments flank a stairway on the south face of a Middle Preclassic structure; the one on the right (east) appears to depict a feline, and the other, west of the stair, may show a stylized profile of a serpent's head (ibid.).

Philip Drucker (1952:9; see also Lowe 1989b:fig 4.10) hypothesizes that the "Long Mound" at La Venta, Structure D-8, originally might have had three basalt columns set in a north-south line on top, but only the southern one was recovered archaeologically. If this is true, then the Structure D-1/D-8 arrangement could have functioned like the putative observatory complexes of the Maya "E-Group" assemblages, with the three columns on the range mound marking sight lines from the western platform to sunrise on the solstices and equinoxes. The linear mound-plus-platform arrangements in Chiapas and elsewhere, including the early one at Tikal, originally might have supported similar markers—perhaps smaller stone columns or perishable wooden poles—erected to identify sunrise sight lines (or positions for backsighting to sunsets). Such stones or poles also could have been used to mark the solar zeniths in the region. This interpretation would suggest that all these sites might have been considered local sacred places of creation.

An alternative interpretation of the La Venta complex suggests that it was oriented toward summer-solstice sunset over San Martín volcano (Malmström 1997:83–84) on the coast of Veracruz: sunset would be viewed by a sight line over Structure D-1 from the position marked by the column of stone on the southern end of Structure D-8. A sculpture atop the San Martín volcano (Fig. 5.8) in an opening that leads to the crater (Benson and de la Fuente 1996:162–163), presumably placed after its early-seventh-century eruption, depicts a robust Olmec lord wearing an enormous "were-jaguar"/Maize God headdress and crouching on one knee, with his hands grasping a thick, cylindrical, possibly ophidian, horizontal bar in front of him. One hand is under the bar, the other is over it; it is evident that he is preparing to stand and raise the bar to the vertical position. This appears to be a representation of one of the duties, responsibilities, and powers of Olmec paramounts: raising a World Tree (Fields and Reents-Budet 2005b:24; Reilly 1994, 2005).

I suggest that World Tree (or maize stalk) imagery seen in later Mesoamerican iconography might be a result of animating ("botanomorphizing") the stone or wooden poles erected as gnomons to mark solar phenomena such as zeniths, solstices, and equinoxes. The occurrence of this sculpture in a volcanic crater suggests relations with an earth deity or spirit, given the sinking of the sun into the mouth of this volcano at solstice sunset. Perhaps the vertical gnomons, set into the earth, were viewed as conduits for the sun to move into and out of the Underworld.

MONUMENTS, ICONOGRAPHY, AND THEMES

Most of the attention archaeologists and art historians have devoted to the Olmec has been directed toward elucidating what *is* Olmec: how to identify, describe, and define the constellation of artistic media, forms, motifs, and relationships that characterize Gulf coastal and neighboring Isthmian cultures and their more distant contemporaries elsewhere in Mesoamerica. The basis for most of these discussions and debates has been an iconographic program—"widely but unevenly distributed across Mesoamerica" from 1200 to 400 B.C.

5.8. San Martín Pajapan Monument 1, showing a crouching Olmec figure preparing to raise a zoomorphic bar (drawn from photograph in Benson and de la Fuente 1996:162).

(Lesure 2004:74)—that appears on stone sculptures and pottery. Their differential occurrences and varied expressions represent local choices of elements drawn from varied traditions, some of which were Gulf coast Olmec and some of which were not.

Sculpted monuments in the Olmec area include colossal heads, thrones, anthropomorphic and zoomorphic figures, reliefs, and stelae. These materializations are large and public, primarily constructed of nonlocal but regional resources (basalt), meant to be viewed with awe, and perhaps the central features of ritual performances, all of which underwrote the elites' legitimacy and their institutions of control. Besides monumental sculpture, Olmec art includes smaller objects of stone, pottery, and jade, the styles and iconography of which varied through time. Early Preclassic San Lorenzo is known for three-dimensional stone sculpture, including individuals with powerful bodies, perhaps ballplayers, with large iron-ore mirror chest pendants; jade was rarely used (Coe 1989a:69).

Flora Clancy (1990:22) observes that a major artistic transformation occurred in Mesoamerica with the beginning of the Middle Preclassic period in the Isthmian region, as stone sculpture in the round gave way to low-relief, narrative carving. At La Venta, relief carving appeared on a variety of basalt objects, of which stelae are the most distinctive and have the closest relationship to Maya art, although sculpture in the round continued to be created. Relief-sculpted stelae and altars continued into the Epi-Olmec period along the Gulf coast as well as more broadly in the Late Preclassic throughout the Pacific piedmont of Guatemala, including Izapa in Chiapas, and in the Guatemala highlands.

Monuments and Portraiture

Freestanding sculpted stone monuments throughout the Gulf coast Olmec area display what Beatriz de la Fuente (1996) has called "homocentrism." The most distinctive of these monuments, the colossal portrait heads (Stirling 1955), are primarily a late Early Formative expression and are particularly common at San Lorenzo, where there are ten; four are known at La Venta and two at Tres Zapotes. These heads (Fig. 5.9), some of which might have been recarved thrones

(Porter 1989, 1990), are highly individualized portraits of presumed Olmec paramounts at their respective sites, but they also have been suggested to be ancestors, shamans, warriors, or ballplayers (Cyphers 1999:163). Individual rulers can be identified by the insignia—perhaps lineage-related—on their helmetlike headgear as well as by distinctive facial features. One head at La Venta shows an individual with prominent teeth and an eagle-foot helmet identifier, who also appears on the side of a throne, Monument 14, at San Lorenzo (Grove 1981b:66).[3] Traces of stucco and purplish pigment on La Venta Colossal Head 4 suggest that these monuments were further individualized by painting (Diehl 2004:42). Portraiture was important throughout the Olmec culture, especially in the early period, as it was on the Pacific coast (Blake et al. 1995:171), but although "Olmec influence" extended widely throughout Preclassic Mesoamerica, colossal heads are not found outside the Gulf coastal region.

Through time (i.e., by 600 B.C., toward the end of La Venta's Middle Preclassic florescence), these giant but iconographically simple colossal-head portrait monoliths began to be replaced by the complex iconography of low-relief carvings on stone stelae and large flat-topped thrones, seats of power (Gillespie 1999; Grove 1973). Thrones occur only at the major Olmec heartland centers: San Lorenzo with five and La Venta with nine.

Grove (1999:267) divides them into two types. Type A shows a single person seated in a niche or cave, depicted as the mouth of an earth monster (the Underworld) and displays rulers' role as guarantors of order, their "pivotal position in the cosmos as mediators between society and the supernatural forces associated with rain and fertility" (Grove and Gillespie 1992:26). In the case of Throne ("Altar") 4 (Fig. 5.6), on the east centerline of La Venta Structure D-8, the figure seated in the cave mouth could relate to the emergence of the sun out of the Underworld at dawn every day. He is wearing a bird headdress that probably represents a harpy eagle (*Harpia harpyja*), associated with the sun (Grove 1973:130; Reilly 2000:392). Reilly (2000:392) believes the individual may be a captive. Type B thrones depict the seated figure in the niche/cave holding a "baby," as exemplified by Throne ("Altar") 5 on the west centerline of Structure D-8 (Fig. 5.7). Type A and B thrones are

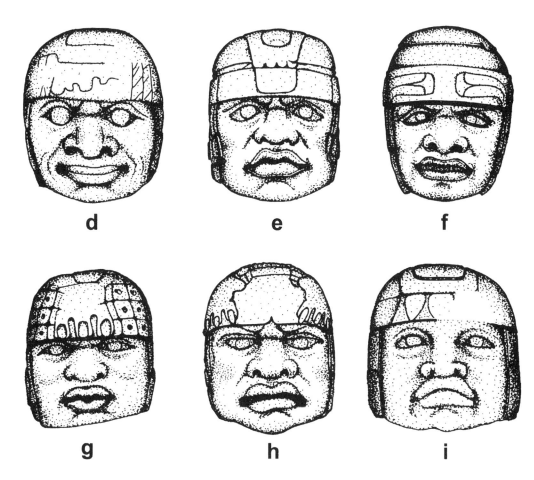

5.9. Olmec colossal heads, showing variations in facial and headdress features indicating portraiture (not to scale). (a) San Lorenzo Monument 17; the beads on the headdress might be drilled iron-ore beads, seven of which were found cached near the monument (drawn from Coe and Diehl 1980, 1:fig. 443); (b) San Lorenzo Monument 4 (drawn from ibid.:fig. 427); (c) San Lorenzo Monument 2, very badly pockmarked; the headband bears macaw-head medallions (drawn from ibid.:fig. 425); (d) San Lorenzo Head 9 (Monument 1; drawn from photograph in Cyphers 1995:45); (e) San Lorenzo Monument 1, "El Rey" (drawn from Coe and Diehl 1980, 1:fig. 423); (f) San Lorenzo Monument 61 (drawn from photograph in Benson and de la Fuente 1996:155); (g) San Lorenzo Colossal Head 10 (drawn from photograph in Cyphers 1995:43); (h) San Lorenzo Monument 5; the woven headdress features two jaguar paws (drawn from Coe and Diehl 1980:fig. 428); (i) La Venta Monument 1 (drawn from photograph in Cyphers 1995:46).

often positioned so as to face in opposite directions (Grove 1999:270), as do Altars 4 and 5.

Grove (1999:272–273, 275; see also Reilly 2005:31) observes that La Venta's major monuments are located south of the Group A/C complex in a "processional arrangement" in Group B, and the themes of these monuments are those of rulership. The northern part of La Venta, particularly the enclosed Ceremonial Court, is the location of major burials, with three colossal heads farther to the north in an east-west line. Grove (1999:275n6) notes that north represents the "celestial otherworld" and that in some Mesoamerican cosmologies "north" equates with "the past." Further, he (ibid.:276) identifies an east-west division, with altars to the east and colossal heads and stelae in the west. Some of these patterns, particularly north as home of the ancestors, continue throughout the Classic and Postclassic periods among the Maya.

Other examples of portraiture come from the site of Arroyo Pesquero, which Carolyn Tate (2001:153) suggests was "La Venta's sacred spring." Twenty-five life-sized jade masks and hundreds of jade and serpentine celts have been found, many of them portraits and many with incising (possible tattooing?). The portraits show young, middle-aged, and aged versions of the same leaders (Coe 1989a:78). The "Lord of the Double Scroll" is the focus of one portrait group; this epithet is also found in highland Mexico and Guerrero.

These objects exemplify an important characteristic of the Middle Formative in general and La Venta in particular: the sumptuous use of imported jade and greenstone. These exotic materials reveal the existence of extensive trade networks and the greater ability of elites to develop "new codes of communication that establish the ability to trade with foreigners and connect these distant people in a community of interests" (Baines and Yoffee 1998:253; also Helms 1988). In contrast to the Early Formative, when iconographic symbols appeared primarily on pottery, during the Middle Formative such motifs were incised on objects or goods from distant sources and with far more restricted distribution (Grove and Gillespie 1992:30). "Celts"—small rectangular slabs of jade and greenstone bearing these motifs and constituting items of personal wealth and display—are

particularly common and continue to be items of elite regalia in the Maya area. Coe (1989a:69) proposes an association between jade and other precious goods, especially maize, given that jade celts resemble maize cobs. It also has been suggested that Olmec and later Maya stelae are essentially supersized celts, carved and uncarved, that were buried in caches, positioned upright and often in cruciform arrangements (Porter 1996; Reilly 2005:36; Taube 1996).

Iconography

The unending quest to define Olmec or "Olmecoid" art and iconography (see, e.g., Covarrubias 1946; Joralemon 1971, 1976; Lesure 2004; Pohorilenko 1996; Quirarte 1981; Reilly 2000) has drawn attention to many points of variability, but some commonalities exist. One fundamental point is the use of fauna of the tropical lowlands (jaguars, toads, caimans, birds), which are frequently conflated and incorporate human elements, resulting in depictions of various polymorphs. This has made it difficult not only to identify exactly what is being represented, but also to interpret meanings in the context of an overall Olmec or Middle Formative ideology or worldview and to track changes in these representations through time (Pohorilenko 1996:130–131). It is commonly assumed that the creatures represent Olmec deities (Coe 1989a:75–76; Joralemon 1971, 1976; Taube 1996), with considerable effort expended in linking them to later deities in Mesoamerica.

"Were-Jaguars," Toads, and Earth

The most discussed imagery has long been known as a "were-jaguar" (Benson 1972; Coe 1965c, 1968b; Covarrubias 1946) (Fig. 5.10a): "basically a human infant with felinized facial characteristics, . . . [with] a cleft in the top of his head, slanted almond eyes in enlarged sockets, and a large flared upper lip with downturned corners. At times, the gums lack teeth but a few representations depict large fangs" (Diehl 2004:104). The hands are sometimes pawlike, and the eyebrows greatly exaggerated ("flame eyebrows"). One interpretation of the were-jaguar is that it shows the transformations of shamans from humans into their supernatural companions—variously known among Mesoamericanists as a *way* or *nawal* (*nagual*)—which are typically "power animals" such as a jaguar or an eagle (Reilly 2000:374–375). There is a widespread belief in jaguars as alter egos of shamans in the tropical Americas; shamans could have used tobacco or hallucinogenic substances to enhance this transformative experience (Furst 1968).

While the feline interpretation of this creature is extensively discussed in the literature, a more recent and less well known interpretation is that it represents a toad, in particular, *Bufo marinus* (Furst 1981; Kennedy 1982; Miller and Taube 1993:168). The key elements behind the batrachian identification are the depictions of the toad's pronounced

U- or V-shaped intraocular cleft; supraorbital crests (flame eyebrows?); wide, down-turned mouth; forelimbs bent inward; and conspicuous paratoid glands on the shoulders (Fig. 5.11).

Several aspects of *Bufo*'s appearance and behavior can be highlighted in terms of its representations in Olmec iconography. One is that the paratoid glands, which also occur in the tibial region, exude bufotenine, a toxic and psychoactive (hallucinogenic) substance (Guernsey Kappelman 2003:116–117n40; Kennedy 1982) that might have been used by ancient shamans in transformation-ritual performances. Another is the toad's extraordinary reproductive success. As a symbol of fecundity, *marinus* toads can live up to forty years, and their annual breeding, which occurs in June and July in Veracruz, can produce up to thirty-five

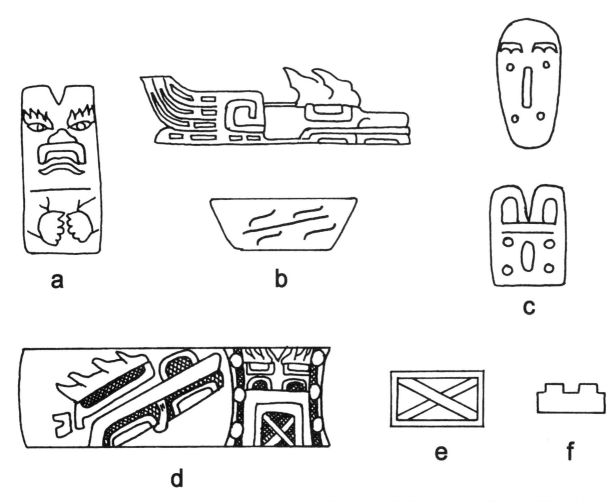

5.10. Common Olmec and Olmec-related motifs: (a) were-jaguar; (b) paw-wing (top) and angry-sky (lightning; below); (c) four-dots-and-bar; (d) profile and frontal views of zoomorph on a vessel from Tlapacoya; (e) crossed bands; (f) double merlon.

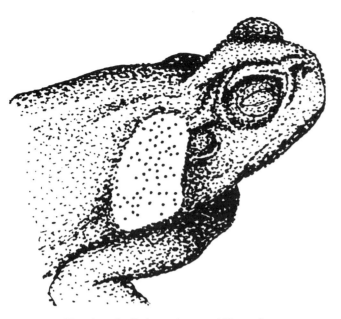

5.11. Drawing of a *Bufo marinus* toad (drawn from photograph, http://www.livingunderworld.org/gallery/photos/anura/bufonidae/bufo/marinus/index.shtml

thousand eggs in a "staggered double-row pattern" in two gelatinous strips (Kennedy 1982:273, 275, 283). A final point is their molting, which can occur four to six times a year in adults: the toad "yawns extravagantly" and hunches down to loosen the skin; the skin splits longitudinally over the dorsal and ventral regions; and the animal sucks the skin into its mouth, both sides simultaneously, with the back legs being the last to be consumed (Furst 1981:158–160; Kennedy 1982:281, 282). The result is that, at the end of the brief process, only the toes stick out of the corners of the mouth, giving the appearance of fangs. On a metaphoric level, both Peter Furst (1981:158) and Alison Kennedy (1982:281) note that *marinus* is a fine symbol of cyclical renewal: "in shedding its skin it periodically reenacts the cosmic drama of transformation and renewal" (ibid.). Whether feline or toad, the Olmec representation is usually interpreted in terms of earth (Marcus 1989:169–173) and earthly, particularly female, fertility; Furst (1981) suggests that it is the ancestor of the Aztec earth goddess Toci, Our Grandmother, in her feline toad-monster manifestation.

In Middle Formative iconography, the zoomorphic were-jaguar/toad is found incised on personal items such as celts or pectorals of jade or serpentine, or in low-relief carving.[4] More iconic symbols

believed to relate to the creature are a series of motifs, known by various terms, which also occur on these objects as well as on pottery. Joyce Marcus (1989:169–173) suggests that these motifs, possibly pan-Mesoamerican, represent a fundamental duality—sky and earth—and appear in what she refers to as their "angry" form: sky as storms and lightning and earth as earthquake. The angry-sky motif consists of grouped diagonal, lightninglike incised lines and also has been interpreted as a "fire-serpent" (or "paw-wing") motif (Fig. 5.10b). The earth/earthquake spirit(s) appears in two main motifs: the were-jaguar (or toad) (Fig. 5.10a) and a glyphlike sign incorporating four dots and a central bar (Fig. 5.10c). The four-dots-and-bar motif may represent the four quarters or directions, plus center (Marcus 1989:172); another view sees it as a symbol of the earth's surface and antecedent to the quincunx (Tate 2001), which appears on Monument 43 at San Lorenzo; Susan Milbrath (1999:211, also 187) suggests that it might have been an "Olmec form of a Venus symbol." Elizabeth Benson (1971:2) regards the motif as a toponym for La Venta. Kennedy (1982:277) concludes that the four-dots-and-bar motif is an icon for the toad viewed from above: the four paratoid glands on shoulders and legs, and the conspicuous light stripe running down its back.

At San José Mogote, Oaxaca, during the San José phase (1150–850 B.C.), the earth (were-jaguar) and sky (fire-serpent) motifs had distinctly different patterns of occurrence, particularly in burials (Pyne 1976). Pottery in burials in the eastern and western residential wards of the site exhibited the fire-serpent (sky) motif, while those in the southern ward depicted the were-jaguar. Marcus (1989:169) interprets this to indicate "at least two major descent groups in the San José phase, with the 'fire-serpent' and 'were-jaguar' serving as apical ancestors." A variant perspective comes from a painted pottery vessel (Fig. 5.10d) from Tlapacoya, central Mexico, which shows both motifs, fire-serpent and were-jaguar; this suggests that they are profile and frontal views of an earth saurian with caiman characteristics (see Grove 1993:89–92). In this light, the fact that at San José Mogote the sky-serpent/profile motif was found in eastern and western wards and the were-jaguar in the south suggests that the community was effectively viewed as or atop the earth saurian, portrayed in profile from east and west perspectives but frontally with open mouth in the south (direction of the Underworld).

The Olmecs' apparent elaboration of earth symbolism reflects an early preoccupation with the Underworld and caves, most distinctively seen in the images on thrones (and elsewhere) of an individual, presumably a ruler, emerging from the mouth of an earth-monster/cave. Such imagery is central to his legitimation (Grove 1973), demonstrating that the ruler is descended from an earth deity (Scott and Brady 2000:149). Related imagery is tied to agriculture, maize, and the later Maya Maize God. There also may be references to actual earthquakes or volcanic eruptions, for example, the eruption of San Martín in the early seventh century—clearly an angry earth—that were retained in historical memory.

In the end, it is impossible to make definitive statements about what the Formative infant/were-jaguar/batrachian imagery represents, given its polymorphic expressions. The possibility that these supernaturals are dyads is intriguing.[5] There seem to be two earth motifs, were-jaguar/toad and four-dots-and-bar, and two earth-related saurians are found in the *Popol Vuh*, Zipacna and Cabracan (Earthquake). These latter appear in the early part of the myth and are dispatched to the western and eastern sky, respectively, perhaps reflecting a deemphasis of earth deities in Formative cosmology (being replaced, it appears, by avians). One wonders, however, whether, if the sky-earth dyad appeared most commonly in an angry aspect, there was also a benevolent aspect? Such might be denoted by the frequent presence of vegetation—a maize plant?—sprouting from the sagittal crevice in the were-jaguar/saurian representation. This, in turn, supports Taube's (1996) idea that this image is related to maize and possibly a maize god, also identified with Hun Hunahpu in the *Popol Vuh*. At the same time, he (ibid.:78; idem 2001) associates the Formative reptilian/saurian creature with wind, referring to it as an "Olmec rainmaker" and noting that it is often depicted with its snout raised, breathing rain clouds; it thus may have sky associations.

The Shark

Another composite zoomorph exists but has received less attention than the were-jaguar: a piscine or selachian zoomorph (see T. Jones 1985; Joralemon's [1976] God VIII; Joyce et al. 1991: 145–148). The fish or shark zoomorph appears in the Olmec heartland (e.g., on San Lorenzo Monument 58) as well as in Formative art from other regions of Mesoamerica (Fig. 5.12). It commonly displays other infixed iconographic elements such as crossed bands and a crescent or U-shaped eye. The shark interpretation of this zoomorph comes from the occasional depiction of a dorsal fin and the prominent delineation of teeth, often serrated, and particularly a pointed front tooth. The fish zoomorph is associated with bloodletting and frequently has conflated serpent or crocodilian characteristics (ibid.:146–147). Different variants of these motifs may be specific to certain vessel forms (Joyce et al. 1991:147–148).

Crossed Bands

Another repeated design element in Middle Formative—especially Olmec—art is the crossed-bands motif, often referred to as the Saint Andrew's cross. One interpretation associates the crossed-bands motif with a serpent, particularly the diamond patterns found on their skin (Quirarte 1981:301n4; Taube 1986:59, citing M. Coe), while another associates it with an "Olmec storm god" without further explanation (Joralemon in Benson and de la Fuente 1996:232). Reilly (2000:384) gives the motif celestial associations, perhaps as a symbol of the crossing point of the ecliptic and the Milky Way, while Julia Guernsey Kappelman (2001:102) regards it as marking a portal to the otherworld. In their decipherment of the Epi-Olmec text on La Mojarra Stela 1, Terrence Kaufman and Justeson (2001) associate this sign variously with a macaw and a badge or title; it is especially common at the Late Preclassic site of Izapa.

Anthony Aveni (1980:156–157, following Barthel 1968a:190) posits that the four arms of this arrangement refer to the intercardinal directions and, more specifically, to the extremes of the sun's movement along the horizon between solstice sunrises and sunsets. The motif might represent the crossed-sticks sighting device discussed in Chapter 3, used for observing distant objects (such as celestial phenomena) on the horizon. Crossed bands frequently appear in the eyes of Olmec creatures, perhaps alluding to this sighting

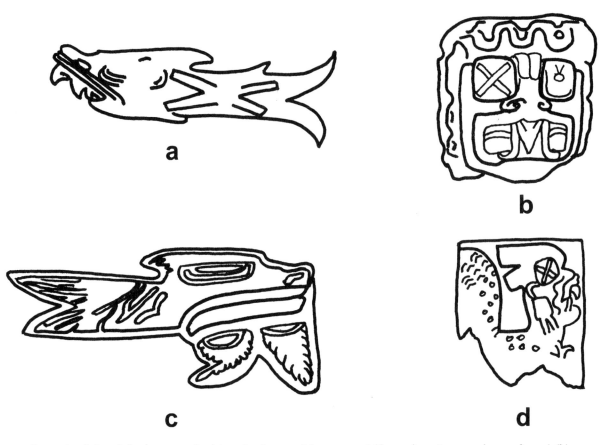

5.12. Formative fish and shark zoomorphs: (a) on San Lorenzo Monument 58 (drawn from Joyce et al. 1991:fig. 4a); (b) on *tecomate* from Las Bocas, Puebla (drawn from Joyce et al. 1991:fig. 4b); (c) on Laguna de los Cerros Monument 1 (drawn from ibid.:fig. 5c); (d) on San Lorenzo Monument 30 (drawn from ibid.:fig. 5d).

function. They are more commonly displayed by humans as rectangular ornaments with crossed bands, probably mirrors suspended at the neck or decorating a cumberbund-like belt (Fig. 5.10e). Virginia Fields (1989:112) suggests that they represent "regalia borrowed from supernatural contexts and utilized by human rulers as an expression of divine sanction and power." In particular, they seem to have solar associations.

The unprovenienced "Humboldt Celt," generally regarded as early Olmec in date, bears a complex series of cosmological symbols, including a large cruciform, badgelike motif (Fig. 5.13). At the center of the badge is an element consisting of two concentric circles with a cross (the Maya *k'an* cross) in the center; surrounding the central element are four glyphlike compounds that may reference the cardinal directions (Headrick 2004:371, citing Reilly 1994). Each has an identical basal component with varying signs above. The uppermost compound may represent north (ibid.) or zenith and is distinguished by a crossed-bands motif surmounted by a crownlike sheaf of vegetation. Moving clockwise, perhaps east, the next compound displays a tied headband, which is the Zapotec year sign as well as a Maya symbol of rulership, atop the common basal element. The bottommost or south (?) glyph has what looks vaguely like a Maya Chuwen day sign over the basal element, while the leftmost, or west, compound has an element resembling eyeglasses over the base. All in all, this cruciform motif can be read not only cosmologically but also technologically, being centered on an equivalent of the pecked-cross motif with the solar crossed-bands motif marking up, or zenith, and the other glyph-like compounds designating the other cardinal directions.

5.13. The Humboldt celt, ca. 900 B.C.(?)
(drawn from Joyce et al. 1991:149).

Themes

Olmec monuments share some significant themes of order (de la Fuente 1996) and legitimation (Grove 1973, 1999) that continue to resonate in the iconographic programs of later Mesoamerican cultures, particularly among the Maya (see, e.g., Fields and Reents-Budet 2005a; Schele and Miller 1986:104–105).

Rulership, Legitimation, and Power

The primary theme of Olmec monuments is rulership and the power and legitimacy of the paramount. This is shown in two ways: as massive individual portraits, and as depictions of rulers in supernatural legitimation contexts, typically seated in the mouths of caves, symbolic entrances to the Underworld. As we have seen, portraiture had early importance throughout the Isthmian region, while Middle Preclassic elites portrayed themselves in connection with rituals commemorating order and supernatural symbols of legitimacy. La Venta stelae and thrones depict extravagantly attired rulers, with ostentatious displays of wealth and ritual paraphernalia, as the pivotal actors in scenes of ceremonial activity, just as Classic Maya monuments continued to do.

Innovations in styles of chiefly portrayal can be interpreted as reflecting changes occurring in the leadership position itself, specifically as these differences relate to the sources of power, as symbolic (control of ideology, ritual, etc.) rather than objective and economic (Gillespie 1999:232). Among the early Olmec, power was in the hands of charismatic leaders and/or shamans (see Reilly 2000:374–376), who were individually personalized on monumental art. Positions might have been based on descent (from an important ancestor or founder) or personal power (such as specific knowledge and skills, or both). Through time, perhaps as that venerated ancestor became a part of the distant mythic past, authority came to be hereditary, based more on ascribed status. Rulership evolved into a formalized office defined independently by its duties and paraphernalia rather than solely by the skills or charisma of the individual who held it. Power became vested in more formal institutions of statecraft, such as titles and offices, descent/genealogy, and manipulation of symbols of power, wealth, and legitimation, including ritual costuming and other regalia. By the Middle Preclassic, depictions of a Mesoamerican leader revealed that he "represented the ordering forces of the different regions of the cosmos and the territory of the kingdom. He summoned rain and fertility; he enjoyed the protection of the founding ancestors and held the power to make those forces work on behalf of the kingdom's people" (Florescano 2005:17). Yet instability continued to threaten, and complex ideologies and cosmologies were created—emphasizing, in the Olmec case, earth supernaturals—which provided charters for rulers to display their legitimacy and control of world order, particularly relating to agricultural success.

Domination

A related theme of Olmec art might be called "domination" (Drucker 1981:46; Grove 1999), manifest as relations among humans (power and legitimacy) as well as between humans and nature (order), specifically, animals. Concerning the former, La Venta Throne ("Altar") 4 (Fig. 5.6), on the east side of observatory structure D-8, shows captives bound by a continuous rope around its sides; a similar scene appears on San Lorenzo Monument 14. Grove (1981b:66) calls it a "rope of kinship." Numerous representations of animals, particularly snarling felines, atop human figures are found at sites around San Lorenzo, such as Potrero Nuevo and El Azuzul (see Grove 1999:284; Reilly and Garber 2003), and in highland Mexico, and the images have sometimes been interpreted as depicting copulation (Stirling 1955). Rather than portraying sexual relations, however, these scenes might illustrate mythical events in a shared Middle Preclassic cosmogony (Grove 1999:261), such as the jaguar supernatural of Olmec paramounts, whose overpowering of a human is a metaphor for rulers overcoming enemies in warfare (Reilly and Garber 2003:146–147). Alternatively, they might have astronomical significance in representing conjunctions of astral bodies, such as eclipses in the Moon Goddess almanacs of the Dresden Codex (Hofling and O'Neil 1992).

Contact with "Foreigners"

Several monuments at La Venta seem to celebrate outsiders (Drucker 1981:44–46), their "foreignness" indicated by distinctive items of dress. For example, late-dating La Venta Stela 3 (Fig. 5.5), found on the west-northwest corner of the south-central platform in the Ceremonial Court, depicts two standing figures facing each other. The right-hand figure, bearded, barefoot, and wearing a fish-head headdress, stands in front of a niche or cave mouth, suggesting that he represents an Olmec or Epi-Olmec ruler. The figure on the left wears pointed-toe footgear, a chest ornament, belt, and kilt and holds a short, paddlelike baton next to his lower right leg.[6] The differences in attire might indicate "a face-to-face encounter of Olmec with non-Olmec" (Drucker 1981:44).

La Venta Monument 13 (Fig. 5.14), the "Ambassador," shows a striding figure carrying a banner and wearing sandals and an elaborate turbanlike headdress resembling that on figurines from the Escalon-phase (650–450 B.C.) refuse at Izapa (Lowe, Lee, and Martínez 1982:figs. 7.7b, d). This round basalt altar was found as an apparently late placement on the site centerline in the Ceremonial Court at the southern edge of the A-2 platform (Drucker, Heizer, and Squier 1959:41, 43) above an arrangement of twenty serpentine celts.

Finally, La Venta Monument 19 (Fig. 5.15), a large carved basalt boulder, shows a seated individual, possibly bearded, wearing a jaguar headdress and wrapped by a giant plumed rattlesnake (ibid.:197–200). Because images of feathered serpents are rare in Olmec art (Taube 1986:59)—indeed, this sculpture might be the earliest—the individual depicted might be non-Olmec. Taube (ibid.) identifies an element on this monument, two quetzals flanking two crossed-bands signs, as a nominal glyph for Quetzalcoatl.

Another meeting between local and possibly foreign dignitaries is represented by La Venta Offering 4 (Fig. 5.16), a cache in front of the Northeast Platform in the Ceremonial Court, which consists of sixteen human figurines and six celts, all well worn as if heirlooms (Diehl 2004:74). The celts (symbolic stelae?) had been set in a line along the eastern edge of the deposit, backed by the mound; four were cut and shaped from a single larger, carved piece (ibid.:73). The figurines—thirteen of serpentine, two of jade, and one of granitic sandstone or conglomerate—were arranged roughly in a semicircle around them. Figure number 7, of sandstone, stands with his back to the line of celts, facing west; to his right (i.e., north) a line of four figures (nos. 8–11) proceed toward a jade figurine (no. 22), facing them at the southern end of the semicircle. The remaining ten figures form a group of onlookers. Given the differences in raw materials and colors among the figurines, I see them as representing thirteen local and/or lower-status individuals (serpentine) and three high elites and/or outsiders (distinguished by jade and sandstone). Brown sandstone figure number 7, a foreigner (Drucker, Heizer, and Squier 1959:152–161), watches a local (no. 8, of serpentine) lead three individuals, the first of which (no. 9) is of light blue green jade and thus an elite or outsider, southward toward dark green jade figure number 22, also a distinguished elite or foreigner.

5.14. La Venta Monument 13, the "Ambassador" altar.

This diorama-like cache was emplaced under the floor of the court during construction Phase III, and sometime later a hole was excavated precisely over the cache to the figurines' heads, presumably to verify its continued presence, and then refilled. This carefully curated cache suggests broader interpretations. For example, the thirteen figurines of serpentine, which I interpret as local personages, might represent *k'atun* lords from the thirteen *k'atun* seats in the La Venta realm in an idealized *may* model. The group of four locals (nos. 18–21) standing near jade figure no. 22 might indicate a fourfold division of priestly or other leadership roles, such as, for example, the four *b'atab*'s (chiefs) of later Maya times.

La Venta's interactions with "foreigners" become salient in the context of Mary W. Helms's (1988) cross-cultural discussions of the prestige accorded to those who have firsthand knowledge of distant places and peoples. Although "exoticizing the Other" is unfashionable in postmodern academic circles, the knowledge and material goods acquired in travels to distant places and, more important, the increasing power to control access to such knowledge and goods became key early elements in the legitimation of politico-religious authority. Olmec travel to exotic places in Mesoamerica might have been undertaken for a variety of reasons, including access to precious goods (iron ores, greenstone, jade) as well as

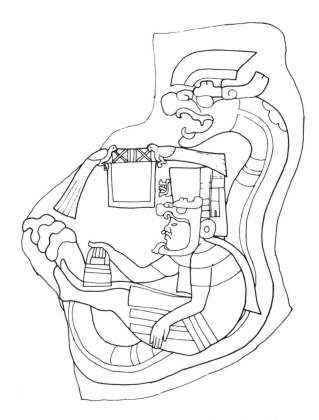

5.15. La Venta Monument 19 (drawing by Linda Schele, © David Schele, courtesy Foundation for the Advancement of Mesoamerican Studies, Inc., www.famsi.org).

5.16. La Venta Offering 4 (drawn from Drucker, Heizer, and Squier 1959:fig. 38). Figure 7 watches a procession of four individuals (8, 9, 10, 11) move southward toward figure 22, while ten figures look on. (For interpretations, see text.)

esoteric knowledge (see ibid.:130) such as that related to calendrics, numeracy, and writing. Similarly, for outsiders, travel to Olmec centers such as La Venta might have been closely related to pilgrimages. This raises a question: Who were the foreigners commemorated on La Venta's monuments? They might have been traders, ballplayers, or elites; they might have come from various areas in Mesoamerica; Richard Hansen (2005:66) suggests that they might have been lowland Maya. Interestingly, the Epi-Olmec text on the Tuxtla Statuette begins with the query, "Who should go on a trip?" (Kaufman and Justeson 2001:2.75– 2.81). Whether such travels were trading expeditions, pilgrimages, chiefly rituals related to legitimation, calendrical celebrations, or undertaken for other purposes is unknown, but they clearly seem to have been part of elite culture, power, legitimation, and wealth.

Ballgame

In Mesoamerican creation myths, and also in the temporal affairs of Maya rulers, one of the key rituals—performed in a key architectural complex—is the ballgame (Schele and Miller 1986:241–263). The ballgame is a contest, part ritual and part sport, played in different ways at different times in different parts of Mesoamerica. At least five forms of the game have been identified, including handball, stickball, hipball, kickball, and "keep-away" (Hill and Clark 2001:334). The size of the teams may have varied, as may have the equipment. In some games, particularly on the Gulf coast, a stick was used, whereas the Maya played it as a soccer-like football game in which the hands could not touch the ball. But it is generally agreed that the game often concluded with the sacrifice of one or more individuals.

In the *Popol Vuh*, the ballgame was played in a ballcourt envisioned as a crack or crevice in the Creation Mountain, which gave humans access to the Underworld, or Xib'alb'a (Schele and Mathews 1998:207). The game was played by the Hero Twins against the Lords of the Underworld, and in one of these games a skull was used as a ball; the twins' father was buried in the Place of Ball Game Sacrifice. In an Aztec origin myth, the Mexica stopped at a place called Coatépec (Snake Mountain), where they built a temple on top of a mountain with a ballcourt at its base and a nearby pit called "skull place" (Schele and Guernsey Kappelman 2001:31). Symbolically, the ballgame reenacts creation, and the back-and-forth movement of the bouncing ball is a metaphor for the movement of celestial bodies.

The Mesoamerican ballgame may have its ultimate origins in Archaic times, as the so-called dance ground identified at Gheo-Shih, Oaxaca, also could have served as a ballcourt. The earliest recognizable formal architectural complex for the ballgame is at Paso de la Amada around 1400 B.C. (Hill, Blake, and Clark 1998; Hill and Clark 2001). The presence of ballcourts at Olmec sites is uncertain: Richard A. Diehl (2004:105) suggests that the only known ballcourt dates to Middle Formative San Lorenzo, where residue from a rubber ball was found in the Palangana mound group, while Reilly (1994) proposes that the long parallel mounds of Group A at La Venta might have demarcated an area for playing the game.

The distinctive iconography associated with the Mesoamerican ballgame—garb including the thick belts known as yokes, protective padding for the arms and legs, and helmets, as well as sticks for hitting the ball—developed during the Middle Preclassic period in the Gulf coastal region. Much of it appears on portable objects removed from their original contexts, however, and thus is not datable. The stela from the site of Alvarado is interpreted as an Olmec captive seated in front of a ruler attired as a ballplayer (Covarrubias 1966: fig. 29, cited in Coggins 1996:27n30); one of the figures on late La Venta Stela 3 might be a ballplayer. Hill and Clark (2001:333–334) have suggested that the personages represented by the Olmec colossal heads are sporting leather helmets worn during ballgame competition. The appearance of the ballgame and its distinctive apparatus in monumental and portable art underscores its importance in sustaining elite power and legitimation.

Termination Ritual

Termination ritual—acts carried out to destroy the supernatural power imbued in buildings and monuments when they were initially dedicated and periodically reanimated—was widespread in ancient Mesoamerica (Mock 1998). Termination activities could be reverential or desecratory, each with different causes and outcomes (Freidel, Suhler, and Cobos P. 1998; Pagliaro, Garber, and Stanton 2003). Reverential termination is typically associated with calendrical cycling and renewal, the beginning and simultaneous ending of various significant periods of time, and also may be associated with new phases of construction of a building. Desecratory termination ritual, typically more intense, is intended to achieve final destruction, death (without renewal), and delegitimation of monuments, structures, sites, or ruling dynasties (e.g., by damaging tombs) and the ideologies and wealth they represent. Desecratory termination frequently accompanied warfare and conquest.

Termination ritual is of interest because much of the vast corpus of Olmec monuments—colossal heads, stelae, altars/thrones, zoomorphic and anthropomorphic statues, carvings in relief and in the round—was damaged in antiquity (Grove 1981b). Dating the destruction is difficult, because the monuments also may have been moved, but the earliest evidence for defacement appears to occur around 1250–1150 B.C. at San Lorenzo (ibid.:62). Later, around 900 B.C., "all of the great basalt monuments of San Lorenzo [were] mutilated and then laid out in long lines on ridges around the peripheries of the site" (Coe 1967:25). Similarly, monuments at La Venta were also heavily damaged. An inventory of the monuments and the kinds of harm they suffered indicates that, in particular, "stylized-religious monuments remain relatively unmutilated . . . [but] with the exception of colossal heads, almost all portrait monuments are broken, decapitated, or effaced. . . . Among portrait carvings one particular feature was the target of destruction: the head" (Grove 1981b:61).

Grove (ibid.:63) proffered three explanations for monument destruction: termination of calendrical cycles; change in ruling dynasties; or death of chiefs. He favored the last explanation. More recent studies (Diehl 2004:58; Porter 1989, 1990) indicate that monuments were frequently recarved and reused, and the "mutilation" was simply interrupted recarving. I suggest that the first of Grove's alternatives—termination of the monuments at the ending of calendrical cycles, perhaps some kind of "proto-*may*"—is also valid.

Infants, Twins, and Fetuses

One of the major themes of Olmec and Olmec-related art, monumental and portable, is the depiction of infants or young children. Sometimes these are youths, seated or standing, typically distinguished from adults by their less-brawny torsos. Mostly, they are infants or babies appearing in stone sculpture or as pottery figurines. Typically, they are chubby with puffy cheeks and bald heads, but many look limp, lifeless, and sexless as they are held in the outstretched arms of youths or adults. As discussed ad infinitum, these infants often bear a confusing and bizarre combination of human and feline traits, leading them to be dubbed "were-jaguars."

I wonder if some of these infants and children might have been twins. Although twins are not widely highlighted in studies of Olmec art, their depiction is significant from the point of view of calendrical origins and mythic history, specifically, the *Popol Vuh*. De la Fuente (1996:47–48) discusses three Olmec representations of twins. One, on the El Azuzul acropolis at Loma del Zapote, near San Lorenzo, consists of four sculptures: twin males facing east toward a feline, with a larger feline sculpture a few meters away. The twins are seated in a position common in Olmec art: leaning forward with hands on a thick horizontal bar or staff; their headgear was mutilated in antiquity, but it bears the distinctive wavy or pleated side ornamentation associated with the were-jaguar. De la Fuente refers to the twins vaguely as "mediators" between the powers of humans and the gods. Cyphers (1996:68; idem 1999:172) suggests that they relate to the Hero Twins of the *Popol Vuh* and "a ritual reenactment of a historical or mythical event with possible astronomical symbolism," which I interpret as raising a gnomon. The feline sculptures, perhaps recarved earlier monuments, might be "viewed as a metaphor for shamanistic animal transformation" (Cyphers 1999:172). The association of twins with felines recalls the name of one Hero Twin, Xbalanque, or "little jaguar/sun."

Other twins appear as dwarfs bearing the flat slab surfaces of basalt thrones. On one well-preserved throne, Monument 2 (Fig. 5.17), variously attributed to Potrero Nuevo, San Lorenzo, and Loma del Zapote (Coe and Diehl 1980, 1:368), the two figures differ slightly in details of costuming, particularly in their headgear, which might indicate distinct identities or perhaps political roles. Another such throne is the badly mutilated T-(or Maya Ik'-) shaped Monument 18 on the south-central ridge at San Lorenzo (Coe and Diehl 1980, 1:326), on which dwarf twins support the throne platform with one arm and hold an object (torch? scepter? knife?) in the other. Twin sculptures are also found at San Martín and La Venta (Monument 44).

The role of twins in Mesoamerican and particularly Mayan mythology has unquestioned importance, given the three sets of twins in the *Popol Vuh*. Twins are often liminal creatures: because they are relatively rare, they do not belong to the normal, secular world and fall into the same category of other ambiguous beings such as tricksters and bisexuals (Gillespie 1989:133, citing Lévi-Strauss). Susan Gillespie (1989:133, 143, 145) notes that the Nawatl word *coatl* (Sp. *cuate*) means "serpent" but also "twin," particularly along the lines of female twin or female counterpart.[7] She translates "Quetzalcoatl" as "precious twin." The Aztec paired rulers, *tlatoani* (primary ruler) and *cihuacoatl* (serpent-woman), are a dyad and may have been viewed as twins: the native historian Chimalpahin, in his seventh *Relación*, claims that *tlatoani* Motecuhzoma I was born at sunrise to one of his father's wives, and *cihuacoatl* Tlacaelel was born just before dawn to another wife. They are thus half-brothers but viewed as twins, associated, respectively, with male/female and sun/Venus (ibid.). Cihuacoatl is also the name of a goddess who was the mother of twins (Gillespie 1989:133).[8]

5.17. Potrero Nuevo Monument 2, showing twins and/or dwarfs supporting a slab (drawn from Coe and Diehl 1980, 1:fig. 496).

Despite these important roles, Mesoamericanists have paid scant attention to the biology of twins or how twins might have fit into the lifeways and belief systems of hunter-gatherer peoples, those beginning to adopt a sedentary lifestyle, or early civilizations.[9] Twin births carry risks for both the infants and their mothers (http://www .babycenter.com; accessed September 7, 2006): birth defect and miscarriage rates are approximately twice as high as for singletons, and babies are frequently born prematurely (before week thirty-seven) and at low birth weights. Today, twins are often delivered by Caesarean section, an option that would not have been safely available to pregnant women in prehistory. For mothers of twins, there were issues of difficult births and the additional burden of providing sufficient milk for two babies at the same time, one or both likely to be in fragile health. Twins are often feared among hunter-gatherer groups because feeding them places a very high energy demand on the mothers; even if they survive the birth process, one or both may be killed (H. Kaplan 2001:809). Twins also may have been feared in Mesoamerica. The Aztecs considered them a "malevolent omen" and felt that one should be killed at birth (Miller and Taube 1993:175, 190; cf. Gillespie 1989). Bringing both individuals past infancy and childhood into adolescence doubtless would have required extraordinary pre- and postnatal care.

Tate and Bendersky (1999) hypothesize that certain Olmec sculptures represent human fetuses or neonates. More than two dozen small stone sculptures, believed to date between 900–600 B.C., show medically recognized fetal characteristics, such as a disproportionately large head and small, flexed limbs, and some depict deformities (see also Murdy 1981). Exploring parallels between the human and maize life cycles, Tate and Bendersky (1999:9) conclude that the figures represent a "fascination with the developmental stages of life." I raise the possibility that these figurines might represent miscarried or stillborn infants who were a twin, or perhaps talismans for invoking protection for twins or against bearing them.

DISCUSSION: CALENDRICAL IMPLICATIONS

There is general agreement that the Olmec and other peoples in the Isthmian area in the Middle Formative period spoke some variant of an ancestral Mixe-Zoquean language, whether pre-, proto-, or pre-proto- (Campbell and Kaufman 1976; Kaufman 1976; Kaufman and Justeson 2004). This proto-language eventually (ca. A.D. 500) differentiated into Mixean and Zoquean, both of which developed still later into various subgroups spoken in Chiapas, Veracruz, Oaxaca, and the Guatemala highlands. Lyle Campbell and Terrence Kaufman (1976) list numerous Proto-Mixe-Zoquean (PMZ) words incorporated into other languages, particularly Mayan, and many of these are words for items and practices characteristic of Mesoamerica as a culture area. For example, although the word for maize might be Uto-Aztecan (Hill 2001) rather than Mixe-Zoquean, Mayan words for maize preparation, such as grinding corn, are PMZ.

Søren Wichmann (1995:222–226), on the basis of exhaustive linguistic studies of Mixe-Zoquean languages and their history, proposes some corrections to Campbell and Kaufman's original listing. He argues that many terms are not PMZ but, rather, later developments after the two languages, Mixe and Zoque, began to differentiate. These words include *plantain* (Proto-Zoquean), *zapote* (Proto-Mixean), *avocado*, *fish*, *dog*, *mat*, *year*, *fox*, *coyote*, and *tobacco*. Wichmann does agree, however, that many of Campbell and Kaufman's terms are indeed PMZ and therefore likely to have been vocabulary used by the Olmec, including "milpa; to clear land; to sow (plant); seed; to harvest, etc.; chile; beans; honey; to spin thread; to twist rope, etc.; holy; to write; to count/divine; drum; complex numeral system, *zontle*; cigar; to cost; remedy; house pole; sandals." This linguistic evidence—particularly the existence of words revealing early literacy and

numeracy—combined with the archaeological, iconographic, and calendrical data reviewed herein, broadens the context for investigating the role of Mesoamerican calendars during Olmec times.

As noted, distinguishing what is artistically, culturally, and ethnically "Olmec" in the widely dispersed corpus of related artifacts in Formative Mesoamerica has been a continuing problem, matched only by the difficulty of ascertaining their origins. Grove (1993:91, citing Donald Lathrap) issues a provocative proposition: that certain Olmec ideas, beliefs, and symbols, including representations of caimans, jaguars, serpents, and anthropomorphized versions of these creatures, "lie deep in antiquity" and are part of a more ancient belief system widely shared by agricultural societies throughout Mesoamerica and South America. If true, these widespread symbols "do not represent the creation of a new ideology or the borrowing or intrusion of a new religion, but perhaps signify instead (a) the placement on *non-perishable* media of symbols reflecting long-held beliefs, and (b) the rapid adoption by many societies of certain visual or material symbols to express concepts they already held in common" (ibid., emphasis in original).

Grove's suggestion helps explain the spatial variability in manifestations of Formative symbols and styles, in that different regions emphasized different components of this common belief system. He goes on to support the notion that the Olmec symbol system was so widely accepted because in varied societies it helped people clarify internal social divisions, particularly underscoring the structure of (highly personalized) rulership (ibid.: 92–93).

I would modify Grove's proposition in two ways. First, the dissemination of so-called Olmec symbols might have been part of a widespread custom in nonstate societies of travel for acquisition of knowledge as well as goods. Such journeys, undertaken by elite and nonelite individuals, confer on the returned traveler a certain authority and status (Helms 1988:131–171). Second, the long-held common concepts would include the body of knowledge and practices related to time and calendrics, the role of increasingly powerful leaders in controlling or manipulating such information, and the millennia of celestial observations underlying such systematized practice. In the Baines and

Yoffee (1998, 2000) model, such knowledge and practices were the basis for establishing order among social segments, ancestors, and the cosmos, and they, along with imported wealth goods like jade, established the basis for legitimacy of elites and rulers.

It is of interest to look at the stylistic changes in Olmec art and iconography in the context of calendrical development. Anatole Pohorilenko (1996:130–131) notes an end to reptilian/saurian motifs—associated with mountains and caves—by the end of the late Early Formative and an emerging emphasis on avian and serpent motifs after about 600 B.C. In terms of the *Popol Vuh* and its subtext of recapitulating the history of Mesoamerican calendrical development, the discontinuation of reptile imagery would be represented by the death of Seven Macaw's saurian sons, Zipacna and Cabracan, which then became the two-headed celestial monster of the Classic Maya. The subsequent use of avian elements in La Venta art would relate to the emphasis on birds in the "ecstatic journey or shaman's flight." It is also echoed in the increasing emphasis on avians of various sorts in Part 2 and especially Part 3 of Tedlock's (1996) edition of the *Popol Vuh* and in the art of Late Preclassic Izapa. There seems to be, in other words, a transition from earth to sky imagery and evocations from the Middle to the Late Preclassic periods.

THE EPI-OLMEC

The Olmec florescence in the Gulf coast is followed by the Late Formative "Epi-Olmec" period, beginning around 400/300 B.C. and extending into the first few centuries A.D. This can be characterized archaeologically by the florescence of new archaeological sites as regional "capitals." Most of them lie in the western Gulf coastal area of Veracruz, west of San Lorenzo, and include Tres Zapotes, Laguna de los Cerros, and Cerro de las Mesas (see Fig. 5.1). This western focus suggests an intensification or formalization of the "east-west style zone" noted by Flannery and Marcus (2000:9–11), dating many centuries earlier, and might relate to post-Olmec language dispersions.

Cerro de las Mesas, a large site with earthen mounds and stone monuments at the far western edge of the Olmec heartland, was occupied in the Middle Formative but reached its peak in the "Protoclassic" and Early Classic (Coe 1965a:696–697, 701–703; idem 1994:113). Stelae 6 and 8 have early Cycle 8 Long Count dates (Coe 1957:606). Malmström (1997:90–92) asserts that the alignment of Cerro de las Mesas is toward the peak of Orizaba (or Citlaltepetl) to the west-northwest (at 285°), which marks sunset on August 13.

Tres Zapotes lies west of Lake Catemaco at the foot of the Tuxtla Mountains, about 220 kilometers (100 miles) northwest of La Venta (Bove 1978:4–6; Coe 1994:74–76). San Martín volcano to the northeast may mark the point of summer-solstice sunrise. Tres Zapotes boasts some fifty mounds over a distance of three kilometers and has a long mound like those at La Venta, Tenochtitlán, and Laguna de los Cerros (Pool 2000, 2003). Two colossal heads are found in one part of the site, but most of the monuments are carved in the Late Preclassic style of Izapa, including the well-known Stela C (Coe 1965a:695–696; idem 1965b:773). This monument, often remarked as bearing the oldest complete Long Count date in Mesoamerica, records a date of 7.16.6.16.18 6 Etz'nab' (see Fig. 6.21a), equivalent to September 3, 32 B.C.,[10] and uses Epi-Olmec script. A distinctive feature of this Long Count date, as well as those on other early monuments (the Tuxtla Statuette, Cerro de las Mesas stelae, El Baúl Stela 1, La Mojarra Stela 1) is that the month names and day numbers in the 365-day calendar are not presented (Coe 1957:606). Stela C was reused in later times and bears an abstract were-jaguar mask on the reverse side in a style that Michael Coe (1994:75) calls "derivative" from Olmec. A bedrock carving at the site appears to bear a single date 6 Ik' (Coe 1957:599).

Laguna de los Cerros lies south of Lake Catemaco at the foot of the Tuxtlas, between Tres Zapotes and San Lorenzo. The site covers approximately 95 to 100 acres, with ninety-five mounds ranging in height from one to thirty meters (Bove 1978:6, 9). Some five smaller centers are arranged around it. The summer-solstice sun rises over Cerro Santa Martha, as viewed from Laguna de los Cerros (Malmström 1997:81, 85). The main group has a strong north-south linear layout oriented 8° west of north, the same as that of La Venta, but does not display such strong bilateral symmetry. Twenty-eight stone monuments have been found at the site, at least ten of them Olmec in date and style, including a colossal head, but also many that are not Olmec; numerous monuments appear to have been reset by later Late Classic and Postclassic occupants (Bove 1978:9). Frederick Bove (ibid.:32) concludes, on the basis of analysis of monuments, drainage canals, and pottery, that Laguna de los Cerros was a "major Olmec center, contemporaneous with at least the San Lorenzo phases at San Lorenzo . . . and probably the earliest phases at Tres Zapotes." Either Laguna de los Cerros or Tres Zapotes may have controlled the source of the basalt used in Olmec monuments (Grove and Gillespie 1992:26).

One of the most significant occurrences in the Epi-Olmec period in the Isthmian region was the development of a hieroglyphic writing system. As noted in Chapter 3 (see also Chapter 8), Justeson (1986) proposes that the origins of Mesoamerican writing reside in the calendrical system, specifically, the 260-day calendar. He hypothesizes a stage of "incipient writing" during which graphic representational systems consisting of visual symbols or icons were gradually encoded with meanings and can be recognized in Olmec-style iconography by about 1100 B.C. Marcus and others (Flannery et al. 2005:11222) argue that Mesoamerican writing might have originated with the signs carved on stone roller stamps or cylinder seals. Several hundred of these, dating around 1000 B.C., have been found at the central Mexican site of Tlatilco. One bears two "Olmec" earth motifs—the angry spirit and the bar-and-four-dots—plus an early version of the Maya *k'in* (day, sun, time) glyph, which perhaps supports Justeson's suggestion. A later roller stamp found near La Venta bears carved signs possibly related to writing and is believed to date ca. 490–340 B.C. (Pohl, Pope, and von Nagy 2002), but it is long preceded by the central Mexican examples.

Out of these early symbols, a full script developed many centuries later in the Gulf coastal region. This Epi-Olmec (or "Tuxtla" or "Isthmian") script was first recognized on the Tuxtla Statuette (8.6.2.4.17 8 Quake [o Kank'in]; March 12, A.D. 162), but sixteen or so glyphs were incised on a pottery fragment from Chiapa de Corzo that may date as early as 300 B.C. (Kaufman and Justeson 2001); the longest text is on La Mojarra

Stela 1. The script is hieroglyphic and logosyllabic (Kaufman and Justeson 2004) or logographic (Houston and Coe 2003:155), and its angular, rectilinear style suggests that it developed out of a wood-carving tradition (ibid.:155, 157). This might explain why so few examples of the script survive. More than two hundred signs are known (Macri and Stark 1993), and a syllabary has been published. Linguistically, Epi-Olmec can be called pre-Proto-Zoquean (or -Sokean); that is, it "belongs to the Sokean branch of the Mije-Sokean family" (Kaufman and Justeson 2004:1079, 1104; Wichmann 1995).[11]

La Mojarra Stela 1 (Fig. 5.18) was discovered in the Acula River in Veracruz (Winfield Capitaine 1988). This basalt monument portrays an elaborately garbed individual, presumably a ruler, standing facing forward but with his head in profile, facing the viewer's right, and wearing a cape and a towering headdress. His name or title is Harvester Mountain-Lord, reflecting the long-standing responsibility of Mesoamerican paramounts to ensure bountiful supplies of food as evidence of direct communication with, and the beneficence of, the gods. The lower part of the figure is destroyed, but he stands on a basal register that shows four dots edged by double-merlon bars, similar to the Preclassic four-dots-and-bar earth motif. The ruler's headdress carries the heads of four (probably six, were it not in profile) long-snouted creatures, and he wears a nearly identical head as a pectoral. Another head, more anthropomorphic, on the front of the headdress displays a prominent front tooth and resembles the later Maya God III. Stephen Houston and Michael Coe (2003:152, citing pers. com. from Karl Taube) claim the headdress and/or the figure wearing it is Ehecatl. The heads resemble an Epi-Olmec glyph that Kaufman and Justeson (2001:2.45) identify as "Longlip," equating it with a macaw or "Macaw monster" (and also the name of a rainy-season month). To me, however, all the long-lipped heads (perhaps excluding the GIII-like one) equally appear to be sharks, with prominently delineated fins.

The text of La Mojarra Stela 1 consists of more than five hundred glyphs in twenty-one columns above and in front of the ruler and continuing on the right side. It has been partially deciphered by John Justeson and Terrence Kaufman (1993, 1997;

5.18. La Mojarra Stela 1 (drawing by George Stuart; used by permission).

Kaufman and Justeson 2001, 2004), who use analo- gies with Olmec iconography as well as compar- isons with Mixe-Zoquean to interpret many of the glyphs.[12] Interrupted in places by effaced glyphs, the text is narrated by noble supporters of "King" Harvester Mountain-Lord (HML, presum- ably the individual portrayed), who say they erect- ed the monument to celebrate his victory over rebels/usurpers thirteen years earlier and to com- memorate the one-year anniversary of his acces- sion. Apparently, the usurpers had toppled the carved monuments (ancestral "symbol-stones" "set in order" by Longlip/Macaw Monster) and their leader, or one of the leaders, is identified near the end of the text as HML's brother-in- law. This individual was imprisoned for thir- teen "years" (*tuns*) and six "months" before being "chopped" (beheaded and/or dismembered). Soon thereafter, the young HML took office after four *winals* of preparation.

Most of the text describes the rituals celebrat- ing the end of HML's first year of rule, which took place over a period of about fifty-two days. HML "scattered" and was seated on the throne beside the god(s) Macaw Monster (and) Scorpius. His offi- cial regalia included a "skin-drum" headdress and a hummingbird,[13] a Macaw sign, an eccentric flint, and a pectoral. The last three of these might be dif- ferent terms for the same object, as the pectoral is also described as a sacred heirloom "badge" that had apparently conferred some special status on HML for the past year. Associated rituals involved the taking of twenty-three jaguars in as many days, HML's singing, and what seems to be the folding (perhaps counting?) of garments or knotted cloth.[14] HML appears to hold several titles, including flower lord, beard-mask wearer, and star-warrior. Besides Macaw Monster/Scorpius, other supernat- urals mentioned in the text are Sky Quetzal and Ten Sky (a rainy-season god).

HML's ritual bloodletting ("piercing of his but- tocks") is related three times, accompanied by the "sharing-out" of the materials on which his blood dripped. In the first telling, Scorpius, Venus, and Mercury ("heavenly jaguar") are bright in the sky. In the second telling, his rival is portrayed as a bird, whose wing (arm?) "quivered/flapped blood- ily." This might refer to something like the inci- dent in the *Popol Vuh* in which, after Seven Macaw was shot by the Hero Twins, the bird tore out the arm of Hunahpu; a similar episode is hint- ed at by Stela 25 in Group A at Izapa (see Chap. 6). When all this was done, HML stood "on tip-toe" and proclaimed himself the sun; presumably, this is the moment he is shown on the stela. At the end of the text, HML is identified by his supporters with an unknown title, as a twelve- or thirteen-*tun* something (perhaps relating to the Early Classic Maya celebration of thirteen *tuns*; see Fahsen and Grube 1999), and having a divinely sent animal spirit companion (a *way*) appearing on his body.

Only two of these events are specifically dated by the Long Count, although Kaufman and Justeson (2001) interpolated from the narrative to date other events. A distinctive feature is that the two Long Count dates appear in the center of the monument, with the rest of the text in single columns on either side; Tak'alik Ab'aj Stela 5 also features two central columns of Long Count dates. This may indicate that the calendrical dates are of central importance and that the text is almost embellishment. The La Mojarra story begins with a Long Count date of 8.5.3.3.5 13 Snake (13 Chikchan 3 K'ayab' in the Yucatán or Tikal calendar; May 19, A.D. 143), which was the day after a solar eclipse, when Venus shone brightly as the evening star. HML's brother-in-law was "chopped" on 8.5.16.9.7 5 Deer (5 Manik' 15 Pop; July 11, A.D. 156), specified both by a Long Count date and reference to thirteen *tuns*, six *winals*, and two days after the first date. For the next four "months" (i.e., up to 8.5.16.13.7 7 Manik' [15 Sek; September 29, A.D. 156]) the accession preparations were carried out, at which point HML took the throne. One year later (on 8.5.17.13.7 3 Manik' [10 Sek; September 24, A.D. 157]) there occurred the celebration of the end of his first year in office ("bundling," presumably, the ritual ending of the count of days). Oddly, given that this anniversary is what is being commemorated by the monument, this date is not specified by Long Count.

The story ends with the taking of the twenty-third jaguar on a day calculated as 8.5.17.15.2 12 Wind (5 Yaxk'in; October 29, A.D. 157). There is a possibility that the monument might have been dedicated some years later, with what might be a reference to a date 8.6.10.0.0, a *lajuntun* 9 Ajaw (3 Yaxk'in; October 24, A.D. 169) (Kaufman and Justeson 2001:2.68).

"I am the sun," proclaimed Harvest Mountain-Lord, as does the arrogant Seven Macaw in the *Popol Vuh*. But by the Late and Terminal Preclassic periods in the Gulf coast and Maya areas, it seems that rulers were indeed sun kings, and I propose that the roots of this development began by or during the Middle Preclassic. One line of argument comes from changes in portrayals of Olmec (and earlier) leaders from highly individualized portraits (colossal heads) toward emphasis on the symbols of office they bear. Some of these symbols include feline or jaguar imagery, which calls to mind the name of one of the Hero Twins, Xbalanque, or "little jaguar/sun." In particular, in the Middle Formative, certain children (of certain elites?) were depicted as having feline attributes, perhaps

indicating an association of the jaguar with the young/rising sun. These "were-jaguar babies" commonly display the crossed-bands element as a pectoral on their upper chest and/or on a belt or loincloth, a symbol that refers to the extreme points of the sun's movement along the horizon at the solstices (Aveni 1980:156–157; Barthel 1968a:190).

The Epi-Olmec—that is to say, Mixe-Zoquean or, more specifically, pre-Proto-Zoquean—vocabulary of La Mojarra Stela 1, albeit only partially deciphered, builds on what is known about the vocabulary of the Olmec, discussed above. Together, they provide fascinating insights into legitimacy, wealth, order, and associated rituals in the Late Preclassic period. Rivals were imprisoned and dismembered. Heirloom pectorals were displayed. Inscribed stones were set in order and toppled. Various kinds of cloth and garments, whether knotted, folded, or bundled, were of ritual importance. Land was measured in hand spans. Sprinkling/scattering were ritual activities. Blood was let. And dating political events and the activities of royalty, even disgraced noble usurpers, was of supreme importance.

DISCUSSION

Archaeological and iconographic data from the Late Early Formative and Middle Formative Gulf coast provide ample evidence for the creation and display of wealth related to political legitimation and maintenance of social and cosmic order as bound up in an ideology related to time and calendrics. While presumed elites in the Initial Early Formative in the Isthmian region wore sun-reflecting iron-ore mirrors on their heads or chests to proclaim their access to wealth—exotic goods with a high labor investment in manufacturing—later paramounts were able to involve the local populace in massive work projects that involved moving and carving multiton boulders of basalt into their own portraits or thrones they sat (or stood, or danced) on while overseeing community rituals. At the same time, the trappings of elite status and chiefly office came to encompass extravagant objects denoting personal wealth, particularly items of jade and other nonlocal greenstones, such as celts and earplugs, which were further elaborated with incised designs. The incised motifs frequently reference calendrical information, including dates in the 260-day calendar, earth supernaturals, and ballgame paraphernalia.

Besides glorifying individual rulers, in numerous Middle Formative sites construction was begun on distinctive architectural complexes—a western platform centered opposite a north-south linear mound—that appear to have functioned to observe or commemorate sunrise positions on the horizon on solstices and equinoxes. It is not difficult to see the western structure in these early complexes as an architectural embodiment of the later widespread Mesoamerican calendrical and surveying device known as the pecked-cross symbol or the cross-in-circle symbol: typically, double concentric circles divided into quarters by a centered set of orthogonal axes. At La Venta, Mound D-1, the platform opposite the linear structure, is illustrated in site maps as a truncated cone, which can be envisioned in plan as concentric circles; the radial structure at Tikal and the linear structures at other sites emphasize the axial cross. Unfortunately, because of imprecise dating, it is currently impossible to identify the location of the earliest of these assemblages—in central Mexico, on the Gulf coast, in Chiapas, in the Maya lowlands—and the most conservative position is that they are all Middle Preclassic. This broad contemporaneity suggests that the complex represents the materialization of a widely shared belief system: a "solar cult," with increased emphasis on the sun, the east, and eastern structures as the focal direction of cosmology, sacred landscapes, and ritual.

The beginnings of this "cult," if such it were, might be seen in the iron-ore mirrors worn by presumed early elites in the Initial Early Formative. It may also coincide with the celebration of calendrical cycles, such as *may* cycles, through formal architectural commemoration. The dates of florescence and decline at the two important Olmec sites of San Lorenzo and La Venta, described as urban, regal-ritual "capitals" of large realms (Diehl 2004:29, 60–62), are suggestive in terms of the *may* model. The end of the Intermediate Olmec–period occupation of La Venta is estimated to date ca. 600 B.C., remarkably close to the 590 B.C. ending year of a K'atun 8 Ajaw (as retrodicted from Classic and Postclassic times; see Edmonson 1979:14).

If we project the 256-year *may* (or a hypothetical proto-*may*) cycle back from 590 B.C., we reach 846 B.C., which is not too far from the estimated date for the beginning of La Venta's florescence and also the end of the early occupation of San Lorenzo. At San Lorenzo, colossal heads might be considered that site's "signature" for celebrating what later became *k'atun* or *may* cycles, commemorated at Late Classic Tikal by construction of elaborate architectural complexes (P. Rice 2004). Around this time there was a marked change in artifact assemblages (particularly an increase in exotics such as jade and greenstone) in many areas of Mesoamerica, the conspicuous mutilation (or recarving) of monuments at San Lorenzo, and an apparent shift of demographic and ritual emphasis to La Venta (see Grove 1993). We can tentatively postulate that some predecessor of what later became a 256-year *may* cycle would have been established at La Venta around 900–846 B.C. and lasted until 590 B.C., and may have extended another 128 or 256 years (see Drucker, Heizer, and Squier 1959:127, for suggestions of calendrical ritual). In the succeeding Epi-Olmec period, this geopolitical pattern seems to have been followed by the florescence of sites in the western Gulf coastal area and in Pacific coastal Chiapas and Guatemala.

Late Preclassic
Izapa and Kaminaljuyú

We now move to the other side of the Isthmus, where, by 1350 B.C., in the Mazatán region of southeastern Chiapas, the site of Paso de la Amada was the seat of a large chiefdom with a population of three thousand to five thousand people (Clark 1997:228). Around 1100–1050 B.C., this area may have experienced "an aggressive takeover" by the Olmec, former trade allies: "All the formerly independent simple chiefdoms were consolidated into one complex chiefdom directed from a new regional center. . . . Most of the former head villages of the traditional simple chiefdoms were abandoned, and their inhabitants were relocated to newly founded villages nearby" (ibid.). It is not clear how or why this subjugation was realized, but John Clark (ibid.:229) surmises that it was directed by an Olmec king, given the area's continuing ties to Olmec symbolism and goods, and it might have been for the purpose of controlling the Pacific cacao trade.

Subsequently, in the Pacific coastal and piedmont strip of Chiapas and Guatemala known as the Soconusco, the pattern of creating monumental relief sculptures as part of the Olmec and Epi-Olmec florescence in the Gulf coast was also widely seen in the Late Preclassic, as well as in the adjacent highlands. As compared to the early Middle Preclassic, these later sculptures continued to deemphasize individual portraiture in favor of scenes with a distinct narrative quality; they depict multiple individuals engaged in various types of action, most evident at the site of Izapa. Clearly, the charters of elite legitimation were different from those of earlier periods and from the Gulf coastal region: elites anchored themselves and their rulership to myths and powerful mythic creatures, and also to the grand cycles of cosmic order, as a few of the region's stelae, altars, and other monuments bear bar-dot dates in the Long Count.

IZAPA, CHIAPAS

Izapa lies on the Pacific piedmont slope of Chiapas, near Mexico's border with Guatemala.[1] Its occupants probably spoke Proto-Mixe or some Mixe-Zoquean language, which was likely the dominant language at least as far south as Chalchuapa in western El Salvador (Campbell 1997:162; Justeson et al. 1985:4). Barbara Voorhies

Our ancestors probably initiated the tally [of lunar counting] with the appearance of the thin crescent of the "new moon" in the west after sunset. . . . At least, this seems the most logical and decisive point to begin the count cycle: either you see it or you don't.

—Anthony F. Aveni, *Empires of Time*

(1989b:14) refers to Izapa as the "cultural and probable political center of the Soconusco," noting its role in cacao production and trade. The site also might have controlled distribution of ignimbrite, a low-quality variety of obsidian, from the nearby Tajumulco source. One of the site's toponyms might have been "misty water," judging from the monuments' basal bands of water with rising smoke scrolls and zoomorphic heads at either end (Stuart and Houston 1994:60, 64).

Izapa was occupied from late Early Preclassic through Early Postclassic times, but it is best known as a Late Preclassic center (Guernsey Kappelman 2001:108n1), with its monuments erected in the Guillen phase (Lowe 1982a:23; Laughton 1997). Lee Allen Parsons (1986:45), however, dates the Izapan art style to the Terminal Preclassic from 200 B.C. to A.D. 200. The general chronology is Frontera phase—450–300 B.C.; Guillen phase—300–50 B.C.; Hato phase—50 B.C.–A.D. 100; and Itstapa phase—A.D. 100–250. Most deposits of artifacts dating to the Early and Middle Preclassic occupation of Izapa were incorporated into the fills of later structures (Ekholm 1969:4).

Izapa has six major plazas—Groups A, B, C, D, G, and H—plus Group F to the north (Fig. 6.1). The site has a linear layout that deviates considerably (ca. 21° east of north) from north-south: its northern point of reference was the Tacaná volcano, and the alignment was established by Mounds 25 and 60 of Group H. As an example of site plan materializing ideology—in this case, cosmology, the calendar, and, in particular, the sun—Izapa was laid out such that summer-solstice sunrise is marked by Tajumulco volcano to the northeast (Malmström 1997:76), and the axis of the winter-solstice sunrise and summer solstice sunset lies at an approximate right angle to the north-south alignment. This axis was established by Mounds 55 and 57 in Group A and Mounds 60, 61, and 62 in Group G (Lowe 1982a:32). As discussed below, most of Izapa's sculpted monuments were found in Groups A, B, and D.

Group H, in the central portion of the site, may have replicated some important cosmogrammatic features found at La Venta. The huge Mound 60 can be viewed as the Primordial Mountain, a Coatépec, with an apparent reservoir, the watery

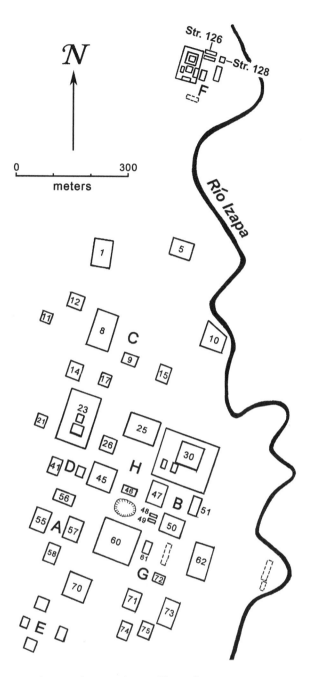

6.1. The site of Izapa, Chiapas (drawn from Lowe, Lee, and Martínez 1982:endmap).

Underworld, created by the borrow pit (excavation of earthen fill for the mound) to its north (Lowe, Lee, and Martínez 1982:263). To the northeast of Mound 60 and east of the reservoir are small, low Mounds 48 and 49, which form a ballcourt.

The two plaza groupings on the east side of Izapa, B and G, taken together, can be considered to generally mimic the linear layout of La Venta's complexes A/C and D (Fig. 5.3) but with little concern for bilateral symmetry. Group B is a linear plaza with a raised "ceremonial court" at the north end. The north side of the court, in turn, is bounded by the imposing Mound 30, which had five phases of construction and remodeling, including a Middle Preclassic structure; Early Preclassic sherds were recovered from the fills (Ekholm 1969). At the southern end of Group B is a sizeable mound (50), beyond which lies Group G to the south on the same axis.

Monuments and Iconographic Programs

Izapa has an enormous corpus of more than 250 stone monuments, originally inventoried as 87 stelae, 89 altars, 68 other miscellaneous monuments, and 3 four-legged thrones (Norman 1973:1), but since this count three decades ago new monuments, including a carved stela (no. 90; Gómez Rueda and Sierra 1997), have been recovered. The site is said to represent the origin of the enduring Mesoamerican stela-altar "cult" (Guernsey Kappelman 2003).

Some forty of Izapa's stelae are carved, of which more than half are well preserved; only about a dozen of the altars are carved. Unlike Olmec sculpture, which emphasizes rulers and portraiture, the scenes on Izapa's carved monuments are highly narrative and emphasize a variety of creatures, particularly avians (ibid.; Pohorilenko 1996), but also serpents, reptiles (including toads), and felines (Laughton 1997). It is important that, instead of portraying portraits of individual rulers, these monuments are tied to an ideology of myths and creation stories, many of which appear to be events later recorded in the Maya *Popol Vuh* (Coggins 1996; Guernsey Kappelman 2003; Kerr 1992; Lowe 1982b).

The narrative qualities of the Izapa monuments and their arrangements in plazas have led to suggestions that they were organized by a formal ritual circuit or circumambulation (Grove 1997; Lowe 1982a:31; Laughton 1997), discussed below. These processions and performances would have been expressions of elite power and cosmic sanction for their rule.

U Shapes

One important symbol in Izapan iconography is a crescentic, or flattened, U-shaped element. It appears in the main scene of three monuments as canoelike boats carrying a human head but is more common in upper and basal panels. It has been suggested that these U shapes derive from Olmec earth-monster imagery, particularly the feline snout (see Quirarte 1977:261–264), or from a serpent (Quirarte 1981:301). In the Maya lowlands a U appears in the face and mouth of early versions of the Ajaw glyph (e.g., on a Middle Preclassic sherd from El Mirador in northern Petén (Stone 1989:321–322, citing Demarest 1984:fig. 47), and a glyph in Loltún cave, in the Puuc region of northwest Yucatán, has a bar-dot number 8 above a U, perhaps a day or name 8 Muluk (Stone 1989:321–322). Reilly (1991:157) likens the U element to the double merlon (Fig. 5.10f), which, among the Olmec, was a symbolic entrance to the Underworld. He (ibid.) also states that the "puzzling geometric shape" of the double merlon is a cross-sectional rendering of walled and sunken courts at some Middle Formative sites. Annabeth Headrick (2004) sees the U as the cross-section of a "divining bowl."

U symbols seem to have "combined earth-jaguar-moon-fertility connotations" (L. Parsons 1986:67) and are particularly associated with the moon, especially the new moon, as Aveni (2002a:94) suggests for a counting program. In the *Popol Vuh*, Blood Moon or Blood Woman symbolizes the rising moon as she ascended from the Underworld to become mother of the Hero Twins. Because, according to this myth, Xbalanque became the full moon ("little sun") upon his death, Blood Woman is primarily the moon in its dark, or Underworld, aspect. Gareth Lowe (1982a:36–40) calls attention to the Maya word *u* or *uj* for moon (although this seems to require that ancient Izapans had some knowledge of the Roman alphabet), which might also be the base for the twenty-day interval *winal* or *uinal* (Lowe 1982b:287, citing Spinden 1946:112). A nearly closed crescent-moon glyph represents the number 20 in Maya script (Glyph T683; see Thompson 1970:283–289). A similar reading has been given for a crescent-shaped symbol on the Epi-Olmec La Mojarra stela, as both "twenty" and "moon" (Justeson and Kaufman 1993:figs. 6D, 8A, 8B;

Kaufman and Justeson 2001:2.34). Lowe (1982a) raises the possibility that some of the carved stelae in Izapa Groups A, B, and D are *k'atun* markers. In particular, thirteen monuments have these distinctive crescentic, new moon–like U symbols in their upper "sky" panels; these could mark the *k'atuns* of a 256-year *may* cycle. Thus the U symbol on Izapa monuments could designate the number 20, a "month" of twenty days, and also a *k'atun* of twenty years, which is significant in the context of calendrical development and the origins of *may* cycling.

U shapes appear on Early Classic Maya monuments, where they mark objects that are iconographically identifiable as shiny stone—probably jade—jewels, particularly beads, and are symbolic of rulership (Freidel, Reese-Taylor, and Mora-Marín 2002:55; Freidel and Schele 1988a:555). (One wonders if they might also mark stone mirrors worn as ornaments, in which case the U shape in Formative art might refer to the cross section of concave mirrors.) The U symbol ceased to be used in the Maya Late Classic period and was replaced, in part, by the parallel curving elements that art historians recognize as indicating something shiny or a reflective surface (Schele and Miller 1986:43).

Border Panels

Scenes on Izapa monuments are bordered on top, and sometimes on the bottom, side, or all three, with stylized horizontal bands which have been called the Izapa "signature" band or a "skyband" panel (Lowe 1982:31). This skyband consists of one or more horizontal bands with various elements in or around them, including diagonal stripes, a U-shaped motif, outward-curving scrolls, and rectangular tabs (Laughton 1977:43–44). The presence and positioning of these elements can vary considerably. They resemble patterns on some Olmec altars/thrones, particularly the band above the niche on La Venta Throne 4.

This band has had several interpretations. One sees it as representing the mouth or snout of a jaguar/earth monster, with the enclosed scene taking place within the earth or the Underworld, much as the Olmec depicted their rulers seated in niches as earth-monster mouths or caves (Norman 1976; Quirarte 1979). It has also been identified as celestial and terrestrial boundaries; the latter appears as the Epi-Olmec sign *na*, meaning "my" and also "earth" (Zoquean *nas*) (Kaufman and Justeson 2001:2.5, 2.18, 2.27). Timothy Laughton (1997:74) has persuasively argued that this band represents a "threshold" between the natural and supernatural worlds, demarcating a scene that allowed viewers to peer into the supernatural realm and see the gods. As such, it is an extremely widespread motif in Mesoamerica: "one specific, albeit specialised, manifestation of a set of symbols found continuously over a period stretching from ca. 1200 B.C. to A.D. 1000 or perhaps later; and geographically from the Olmec heartland to Guerrero and Morelos, at Monte Alban and the Zapotec area, and in the Maya region from northern Yucatan to the southern highlands" (ibid.:41).

Of the twenty-eight relatively well preserved Izapa stelae illustrated by Garth Norman (1973), nineteen have the upper panel (or some variant) and three have a lower panel, but only two have both. The basal panels of five monuments depict water and three include triangles, perhaps mountains; fifteen stelae lack basal panels.

Crossed Bands

Another early glyphic element in Izapa art is the crossed-bands sign (Glyph T552) (see Fig. 5.10e). This sign is known from Olmec monuments and may refer to the extreme positions of the sun at the solstice positions and/or the intercardinal directions (Aveni 1980). It occurs with reference to felines (the jaguar/earth-monster mouth of La Venta Throne 4, perhaps the sun in the Underworld, as in the later Maya Jaguar Sun God of the Underworld, or JGU); it also occurs with humans, presumably as some sort of insignia or identifier, as it is displayed in the headdress or as a chest or belt ornament (e.g., La Venta Monument 77 and four monoliths from Teopantecuanitlan, Guerrero, Mexico). At Izapa, this cross is associated with saurians (Quirarte 1981:301) and depictions of a "celestial bird" or Principal Bird Deity, probably Seven Macaw or the falcon/hawk messenger of Heart of Sky (the sky gods) of the *Popol Vuh* (Hellmuth 1987, cited in Milbrath 1999:274). Crossed bands also appear on Throne 1, on the centerline in the plaza of Group B.

Other Elements

Besides these glyphs or proto-glyphs, many Izapa monuments display recurrent themes, such as world creation, fertility, and rebirth (Newsome 2001:18). Others portray seated figures gesturing and probably conversing, sometimes with incense burners between them, a theme seen on a few Olmec monuments. Depictions of incense burners raise the possibility of Burner or New Fire ceremonies being celebrated on the monuments. Fragments of the kinds of incense burners depicted on the monuments were recovered at the base of Miscellaneous Monument 2 (Group B) and under Mound 25 (Lowe, Lee, and Martínez 1982:133–134) and are also known elsewhere (J. Clark, pers.com., September 2005).

Another theme is the transformation of rulers into birds—the Principal Bird Deity—in ritual performances recorded on the stelae (Guernsey Kappelman 2003:114). References to the Olmec theme of foreigners or outsiders, however, are opaque if they exist at all at Izapa. Paired individuals (twins? the Hero Twins?) appear on at least six and perhaps as many as twelve monuments at Izapa (Lowe 1982a:31).

Dates and Numbers

None of the Izapa monuments bear inscribed hieroglyphic texts, and only a few bear possible dates, a peculiar omission that demands explanation, given contemporaneous texts elsewhere in the Isthmian region. Elizabeth Newsome (2001:18) attributes it to the fact that the monuments' imagery treats events in cosmic time, "outside historical time." Guernsey and Love (2005:37) suggest that the lack of texts was a strategy employed by the rulers to situate the monuments beyond the limits of language-dependent interpretation. Instead, because Izapa sat at the boundary of two major language and cultural traditions, Mixe-Zoquean and Mayan, the monuments featured "well-established pan-Mesoamerican concepts of sacred knowledge that were broadly understood."

One Izapa monument may register the day Seven Death, the name of one of the lords of the Underworld in the *Popol Vuh*, and it is likely that fairly simple glyphic elements appearing in various places on the carved scenes might have served in naming or dating individuals and events. Given the Maya fondness for numerology, the frequent use of the number 7 at Izapa is significant. Several individuals named in the late Maya *Popol Vuh* creation myth have names beginning with the number 7, for example, Seven Hunahpu, Seven Macaw, and Seven Death, and the number appears to be associated with death or weakness. Seven is the number of days of the waning ("dying") moon before it begins to disappear into the Underworld, and the deaths of Seven Hunahpu and Seven Macaw are major elements in the extant story. Seven Hunahpu is described as "just secondary" or a "servant" (Chap. 5, note 7). Given the strong correspondence between the scenes on the Izapa monuments and the *Popol Vuh*, the appearance of the number 7, often as a bar with two tabs (a merlon or double merlon), becomes apparent.

Ritual Processions and Monuments

It has long been suggested that Izapa's monuments were viewed as part of ritual processions; Suzanne Miles (1965:258) proposes that Stelae 2, 21, 22, 7, 12, 18, and 5 "seem to be almost a sequence." Processions among monuments likely accompanied festivals celebrating social and cosmic order and elite wealth and legitimacy. More specifically, ritual perambulations at Izapa might have taken place in celebrations that involved narration of a creation myth like that in the *Popol Vuh* (see Laughton 1997). If so, it might be expected that monuments in each of the plazas narrated a particular set of episodes.

One difficulty in hypothesizing a route through the site is determining where such a course would have started. Lowe, Lee, and Martínez (1982:257–259) note a stone-paved ramp leading up the west bank of the Río Izapa toward the site, suggesting an entry into the site via the eastern side of Group G. Within that complex, Mound 61, a small but unusually well constructed platform with plaster floors and cut-stone walls (ibid.:254) at the eastern base of Mound 60, might have had some role in site entry (Guernsey Kappelman 2001:87).

Maya processions in the Postclassic period were typically conducted in a counterclockwise route, and I propose that a similar direction of circumambulation was employed at Late Preclassic Izapa. If such were the case, this movement would have begun in the southeast part of the ceremonial complex at Group G, continued northward to Group B, then west to Group D, south to Group A, and then east to finish in Group G.

Groups Outside a Processional

Before proceeding to a plaza-by-plaza discussion, it is necessary to note certain structural complexes that do not fit into such a hypothetical processional scheme. Group C, for example, is somewhat suspect: monuments were found primarily around Structure C-9, atop a Middle Preclassic structure, and all but two were uncarved. The two carved monuments display the T-shaped Ik' glyph: one, Altar 13, has the Ik' sign alone; the other, Stela 14, shows two seated figures inside an Ik'-shaped cartouche, with a snarling feline above. Group E also is out of the proposed scheme; although monuments were found in the group, they were not carved and would have had narrative functions only if painted.

In the far southern part of Izapa, the lower portion of a monument, Stela 90 (Fig. 6.2), was found on the south side of northern Structure 92, originally facing south (Gómez Rueda and Grazioso Sierra 1997). It shows a striding figure with an enormous serpent emerging from his loincloth; the figure's left thigh has a smooth, polished area, as if it has been reverently stroked by thousands of hands. The investigators (ibid.:226–229) suggest that the left foot is separated from the calf just above the ankle, calling attention to Maya traditions referencing beings with only one leg or foot, including Huracan (hun rakan, 'One Leg') in the Popol Vuh and the serpent-footed Manikin Scepter (God K; Bolon Dz'akab) brandished by Classic Maya kings. They propose that Stela 90 may represent an archetypal figure given considerable elaboration in later myth and rulership. Figure 6.2 does not indicate such a separation.

Group F, nearly two kilometers north of the main ceremonial core, might have been the location of rituals celebrating mythological components different from, or a distinct subset of, those of the site center. Its architectural layout—the western part is a La Venta–style Ceremonial Court complex, and the eastern half is a ballcourt and possible "observatory complex" (see Lowe, Lee, and Martínez 1982:224–245, fig. 13.1)—suggests

Middle Preclassic origins. In addition, there are several low, square structures called "monument platforms" (ibid.:239). Monuments include stelae, altars, two of the three four-legged thrones known from the site, and miscellaneous sculptures, including zoomorphs, tenoned serpent heads, and a stone basin with a braid motif. Virtually all monuments were fragmentary and heavily damaged at the time of their discovery, perhaps due to sectarian violence or later Classic construction and occupation. Many were incorporated into fills, while others may have been moved and reset to fulfill later shrine functions. Timothy Laughton (1997:6, 12, 125) suggests that Group F represents a new settlement begun in the first century A.D., after the main part of the site was abandoned, and that many monuments were moved there.

Stela 22 in Group F—broken, incomplete, and reworked—shows a very eroded figure, the Maize God or an impersonator (Guernsey Kappelman 2002:67, 77) or the "Izapan rain, water, and storm deity" (Laughton 1997:226), sitting in a "boat" or canoe floating on water coming out of a deity mask. Two fish are in the water, perhaps relating to the episode of the Popol Vuh in which the Hero Twins reappear as catfish after the Lords of Death toss their bones into the river.[2] Stela 67, closely related to Stela 22, also depicts the Maize God or rainstorm god (Guernsey Kappelman 2002:67, 77; Laughton 1997:226) seated in a boat suspended over water with ropes. Two fish (the Hero Twins?) swim in the water below, which emerges from a long-nosed deity (Chaak?) with crossed bands in his headdress and possibly the number 9 in his ear. Guernsey Kappelman (ibid.:67–74) identifies these monuments as materializations of creation narrative, specifically, the "transportation, sacrifice, and rebirth of the Maize God from a watery realm that was marked by a cosmic portal." Stela 67 was found in Mound 126, the northern ballcourt structure of Group F, facing south.

Stela 60 (Fig. 6.3), on the western face of Mound 128 at the eastern end of the ballcourt (Lowe, Lee, and Martínez 1982:233), is known only from its broken lower portion. It depicts a fallen winged deity with a crossed-bands sun/sky glyph in one wing; above, a human figure faces a "fallen ballgame contender(?)" (Norman 1973:pl. 51). At the bottom is the typical "jaguar mouth" or skyband panel with an inverted three-lobed element

6.2. Izapa Stela 90, Group G, facing south, on the south side of northern Structure 92 (Gómez Rueda and Grazioso Sierra 1997:fig. 2) (drawing by Ayax Moreno, New World Archaeological Foundation, used by permission of John E. Clark).

in the center, but it may be a celestial band (Guernsey Kappelman 2003:106). Reilly (2000:386) interprets the scene as occurring in the celestial realm. According to Dennis Tedlock (1985:132), Stela 60 shows the falcon that was the messenger of Heart of Sky, Huracan, and the other sky gods, after it was shot by the Hero Twins as they were playing ball in the ballcourt.

Three, possibly four, monuments in this group are reptilian or toad zoomorphs. Altars 53 and 54 are accompanied by plain stelae and sit in the southern end of the plaza; Altar 54 exhibits pronounced magnetism in its head (Malmström

1997:36–37). Miscellaneous Monument 3, west of the main ceremonial group, is a large trough ending in a "serpent's head" (Lowe, Lee, and Martínez 1982:226), but it more closely resembles the head of a *Bufo marinus* toad with paratoid glands on the shoulder (see Fig. 5.11).

Group G

Group G, where I hypothesize that processions began, may be considered to comprise four individual plazas, of which Group G-a represents a solar-solstitial "observatory" comprising Mounds 61

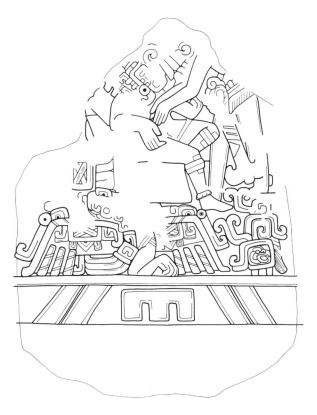

6.3. Izapa Stela 60, Group F, facing east, set at eastern end of east-west-oriented ballcourt (drawing by Ayax Moreno, New World Archaeological Foundation, used by permission of John E. Clark).

and 62, aligned with and resting on the same terrace as the huge Mound 60. Two linear mounds, Structures 48 and 49, aligned east-west, lie west of Mound 50, which separates Groups G and B. They constitute a ballcourt, suggesting that a ballgame might have been an important component of the start or end of processional ceremonies. Mound 61, at the base of Mound 60, was a small but very well constructed platform with plaster floors and dressed stone walls (Lowe, Lee, and Martínez 1982:254). Altars 43, 46, and 38 lie at the base of Mound 61, while two stela-altar pairs and one other altar (Stelae 47, 48; Altars 39, 40, 41) were placed in a roughly north-south line in the center of the plaza. These monuments are generally roughly shaped stones or boulders, and none exhibit relief carving.

In a ritual walk, participants could have gazed southeastward from Mound 61 to observe the sunrise on the winter solstice over Mound 62, and/or northwestward to view the sunset from atop

Mound 61 on the summer solstice. Because the monuments in Group G are all plain, it is impossible to place this complex into a narrative, but an observatory function certainly could have played a major role in any ritual promenade, leaving sculpted narrative stelae unnecessary. In fact, given the critical role of dawn in the extant *Popol Vuh* myth, it is very likely that these ceremonies took place at night, both starting at Group G and finishing there for observation of sunrise.

East of Mound 60, the plaza of subgroup G-a appears to have been cleared and remodeled during or just after the late Guillen phase, perhaps for fill to expand Mound 60 (Lowe, Lee, and Martínez 1982:247).

Group B

If there were an ancient, counterclockwise, plaza-to-plaza perambulation for viewing Izapa's Late Preclassic monuments, then such a ritual circuit should have moved north(east)ward from Group G into Group B. Group B, a linear plaza with a raised ceremonial court–type arrangement at its northern end, is thought to be the earliest occupied portion of Izapa (Lowe 1965:54; Lowe, Lee, and Martínez 1982:119), and many of its monuments are stylistically early.

Thirteen carved stones were recovered in Group B, including stelae, altars, miscellaneous monuments, and a four-legged throne (Lowe, Lee, and Martínez 1982:179). Lowe (1982b:283) suggests that the central stela in each of two lines of three in Group B is a potential yearbearer, while Coggins (1996:30) hypothesizes that the east-facing stelae in front of Structure 47 on the west side of the plaza celebrated the emergence of celestial bodies. Guernsey Kappelman (2001:99, 101) refers to them as metaphors for the three-stone hearth at the center of the universe. No monuments were found in front of the easternmost structure, Mound 51, and only plain ones in front of the southernmost Mound 50. Laughton (1997: 92–142) considers the sculptural program of Group B to focus on the birth and rebirth of the sun.

Most monuments in the Plaza B group were found in and in front (south) of the northern La Venta–like ceremonial court complex, dominated by the large Mound 30 to the north with numerous lower secondary mounds (30b-2). It appears that construction began in the Early Formative Ocós phase (ca. 1500–1200 B.C.), culminating in a structure some twelve meters high in the Late Preclassic Guillen phase, ca. 300–50 B.C. (Lowe 1965:54; Lowe, Lee, and Martínez 1982:119, 184). Three stone balls on pillars stood in front of this mound, and Lee Parsons (1986:64) suggests that they might have been ballgame markers. Laughton (1997:216) and Taube (1998:439), on the other hand, associate them and their triangular arrangement with the three hearthstones of creation. Throne 1 (Fig. 6.4) stands in front as an altar with a plain stela. This throne has five long-lipped gods carved in low relief on its sides, while the top has an eroded crossed-bands motif in a cartouche with crenellated or spiked edges (Lowe, Lee, and Martínez 1982:92; Norman 1973:pl. 63). Presumably, the ruler, physically linking the supernatural and earthly realms, would have been seated here during the rituals taking place in the plaza; Taube (1998:439) describes him as symbolically "enthroned in the center of the cosmos." While this is not an unlikely scenario, one might also speculate that the crossed bands on the throne are solar symbolism as well as calling forth the symbol of the mat as a seat of power; the stone ball–topped pillars could have acted as gnomons.[3]

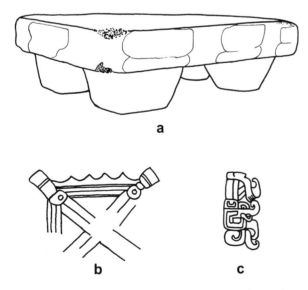

6.4. Izapa Throne 1, Plaza B, facing south, set in front of Structure 30 platform, with crossed bands on the upper surface (b), and downward facing deity heads on the edges (c) (drawn from Norman 1973:pl. 63).

Monument 2, dubbed "El León," stood in the extreme northeast corner of the basal platform in front of secondary Mound 30i. Badly damaged, it is characterized as one of the oldest sculptures at Izapa (perhaps 700–500 B.C.; L. Parsons 1986:19; also Laughton 1997:29) and shows an "Olmec-appearing human (or humanized jaguar)" in the jaws of a serpent or jaguar, possibly originally holding an offering in its now-missing arms (Lowe, Lee, and Martínez 1982:95, 100). Fragments of two cylindrical censers with three loops were found at the monument's base (Lowe 1965:57, 134).

Izapa Miscellaneous Monument 60 (Fig. 6.5), facing west, was found on the western (front) edge of Mound 30e in Group B, a low platform in the southeast corner of the ceremonial court arrangement. The carving is a bar-and-dot numeral 7 above a skull in a cartouche, apparently reading 7 Death: perhaps a day or a reference to the name of one of the lords of Xib'alb'a in the later *Popol Vuh* (Edmonson 1988:187; Lowe, Lee, and Martínez 1982:194). This glyph is strikingly similar to two oversized day glyphs on Kaminaljuyú "Stela" 10 (actually an altar; Fig. 6.19a), distinguished by an embellished trilobate element below the cartouche. Except for being rendered upside down, these day signs resemble early versions of the Initial Series Introducing Glyph (see below; also Fig. 6.21): triple scrolls atop a variable sign, resting on a number. Laughton (1997:10), who notes that the tri-lobed element is a semantic determiner indicating a day name in the 260-day calendar, suggests that Monument 60 may have been brought to Izapa from Kaminaljuyú because it is basalt rather than the local andesite or volcanic tuff used at Izapa.

In the southwest corner of the ceremonial court platform in the northern part of Plaza B were two plain altars and a carved stela. The latter, Stela 28, has been described (Norman 1973:pl. 47) as the "metamorphosis of an insect shown as it emerged from the pupal stage." Coggins (1996:30) sees it as the emergence of a butterfly from its chrysalis. Alternatively, it could be a reference to the "artificial crab," which, in the later *Popol Vuh*, was created by the Hero Twins and placed in a tight crevice to trick Zipacna in revenge for killing the Four Hundred Boys (D. Tedlock 1996:84–85). Given the references to Scorpius in the text of La Mojarra Stela 1, perhaps the creature is a scorpion.

6.5. Izapa Miscellaneous Monument 60, Plaza B, facing west, set in front (west) of Structure 30e on the southeast corner of Structure 30 Platform (drawn from Edmonson 1988:29).

On the front (south) centerline of this complex, Stela 24 was paired with Altar 20. Only a very small part of the lower portion of the stela is undamaged; it shows human feet wearing net stockings and perhaps dancing. On either side are small, seated figures attending smoking incense burners. This might represent the performance of the Hero Twins as dancers before the lords of Xib'alb'a after they were sacrificed, transformed into catfish, and then reborn as "dancers and vagabonds"; because only one figure is shown, it may be Xbalanque after he pretended to sacrifice Hunahpu (ibid.:136–137). Altar 20 features a seated human figure (on a throne?) raising his arms toward

a bird deity holding a ball in its feet. Lowe (1982a:19) identifies this bird as a Crested Guan (*Penelope purpurascens purpurascens*) and suggests that, "if the scrolled basal bar and its two tabs here can represent the number 7, then this altar and Altar 3 may bear prototypes of 7 Macaw in the Popol Vuh." The ball held in the bird's feet may be a symbol of the sun, which he arrogantly pretended to be (Laughton 1997:223).

Several groups of stelae and altars were placed, facing south, on the low, front-central platform at the base of this Mound 30 ceremonial court complex. Stela 10, the easternmost, shows two small personages, probably twins, holding a curved stick to the abdomen of a figure leaning against a tree. Laughton (1997:208) associates this monument with the final episode in the *Popol Vuh*, in which the Twins try to revive their father, and sees this as a "fitting conclusion to the ritual procession." It was paired with plain Altar 7. Stela 9, the center monument of this group, shows an anthropomorphic winged individual with Medusa-like hair and carrying a curved stick or club in one hand; on his back he carries a small, limp, upward-gazing human, perhaps a child sacrifice. Laughton (1997:129) says the figure is "the fully fleshed sun after it has risen and the small figure on the back is Venus, which pulled the sun out of the Underworld." The stick held by these figures might be the same "batons" or sticks held by the individuals on La Venta Stela 3 and could represent ballgame apparatus or fending sticks. Izapa Stela 9 was paired with plain Altar 6, directly behind Throne 1. Thus the ruler, seated on his throne, is framed by the newly reborn sun (Laughton 1997:125).

The westernmost monument, Stela 8, depicts a human seated on a legged throne in a quatrefoil (*k'an* cross cartouche) in the belly of an earth monster. Above is a defaced cartouche that cannot be read, although the crenellations on the right side suggest that it may be similar to the cartouche on Throne 1, which held a crossed-bands sign. The stela was paired with plain Altar 5.

In the open plaza area of Group B, three stela-altar pairs stand in front of Mound 47 on the west side, facing east toward the winter-solstice sunrise. Stela 11 (Fig. 6.6), in the northernmost of these pairs, shows a bearded anthropomorph with arms outstretched and four featherlike elements rising from his arms. He rises from the mouth of

6.6. Izapa Stela 11, "Dawn," Plaza B, facing west, set as northern monument in front (west) of east-facing Structure 47 (drawing by Ayax Moreno, New World Archaeological Foundation, used by permission of John E. Clark).

a saurian that bears a crossed-bands (T552) sky glyph on his abdomen and squats on a double-headed U-shaped earth serpent. The monument has had several interpretations: Milbrath (1999:181) sees it as "a bearded god (Venus?) positioned in the jaws of the earth monster;" Norman (1976) suggests that it was the descent of the sky deity into the Underworld, and Laughton (1997:107) similarly interprets it as the sun setting into the mouth of a toad/earth monster; Lowe (1982b:285) indicates that it represents the fourteenth day Ix and patron of the month Ch'en; and Taube (1996:62), not surprisingly, identifies it as the Maize God. Coggins (1996:30) comes closest

when she says it represents the ascent of the sun from the jaws of crocodilian earth. I believe the scene represents dawn and the birth of the sun as described in the *Popol Vuh* (D. Tedlock 1996:127–128): the "old man" (an opossum) makes four dark streaks along the horizon, heralding the rising of the sun. The four streaks stand for the four yearbearers that correspond to the first days of the solar year.

Stela 12 (Fig. 6.7), with plain Altar 8, is the middle monument in this east-facing group. According to Garth Norman (1973:pl. 23), the sculpted scene features a "limp jaguar on a mat, suspended by ropes from the heads of a double-headed earth serpent above a fire attended by two human figures; blood or water pours from the jaguar's mouth and a rain cycle glyph appears at the right of the serpent's body." Laughton (1997:109–116) interprets the scene in terms of Xbalanque ("little jaguar") being sacrificed by fire. Lowe (1982b:285), noting the calendrical glyph 1 Reed in the sky panel above, observes that One Reed is also Hun Aj (or Yukatekan One Ajaw) as well as *huná*, the highland four hundred–day cycle.

Lowe (ibid.) reads the monument's basal panel, from left, as a bar representing a multiplier of 5, then five triangles each with a bar and three dots representing 8, yielding either 200 or 400. The number 400 recalls the incident in the *Popol Vuh* in which the "Four Hundred Boys" become the stars of the Pleiades, which set in the west in the early evening; for the modern K'iche' Maya, their disappearance marks the time for sowing crops (D. Tedlock 1996:35). As suggested, the death of the Four Hundred Boys might represent the abandonment of a hypothetical four hundred–day calendar. A very different interpretation comes from Laughton (1997:189–190), who sees it as a topographical representation of the eastern horizon as viewed from Izapa: the triangles represent the mountains and volcanoes, then a flat area representing the piedmont plain.

Stela 50 (Fig. 6.8), paired with plain Altar 44, is the southernmost of three stela-altar pairs in front of Mound 47. It shows a winged human figure in the upper left holding onto the umbilical cord (?) of a skeletal "god of death" in the lower right, slumped on a decorative panel. Coggins (1996: 30n38) interprets the scene in terms of the heliacal rise of Venus after its disappearance into the

Underworld; the quadripartite pelvis of the skeletal figure is a completion sign, and the monument itself symbolizes completion of various calendars. Laughton (1997:131–132) embellishes this theme, claiming that Stela 50 shows the rise of Venus on the summer solstice, pulling the umbilical cord of the sun, both appearing to come out of the mouth of Tajumulco volcano. Joralemon (1981:176–177) suggests that the skeleton is a woman in the birthing position, while Lowe (1982b:285) finds a calendrical representation in the day Eb' and a patron for month Yaxk'in. Arthur Miller (1974: 179) calls attention to parallels with Postclassic representations of umbilical cords, noting also that the position of the skeleton is virtually the same as that on page 19 of the Paris Codex and that the winged figure might be related to the descending deities of Tulum.

In terms of the later *Popol Vuh* myth, this monument might represent the visit of Hunahpu and Xbalanque to the grave of their uncle, Seven Hunahpu, in the sacred Place of Ball Game Sacrifice, in an unsuccessful effort to revive him. Astronomically, the Twins' visit to Seven Hunahpu's grave marks the beginning of a new round of Venus cycles on a day named Hunahpu or Ajaw (D. Tedlock 1996:43), and the stela portrays death and apotheosis through the umbilical connection.

6.7. Izapa Stela 12, Plaza B, facing west, set as central monument in front (west) of east-facing Structure 47 (drawing by Ayax Moreno, New World Archaeological Foundation, used by permission of John E. Clark).

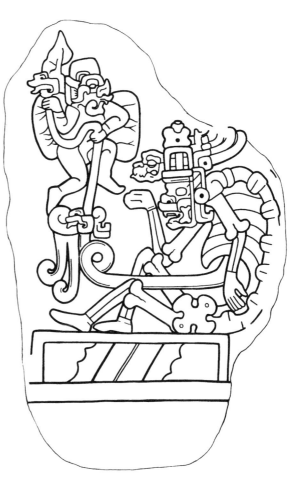

6.8. Izapa Stela 50, Plaza B, facing west, set as southern monument in front (east) of west-facing Structure 50 (drawing by Ayax Moreno, New World Archaeological Foundation, used by permission of John E. Clark).

Group D

From Group B, a counterclockwise procession would pass into Group D, in the northwestern site center. The stela-altar pairs of Group D are found in two areas: on the south centerline of the lower platform of Mound 23 at the north side of the plaza; and on the west face of the large Mound 45 platform(s), facing other structures lying to the west.

Stela 18, in front of Structure 23, has a badly damaged upper portion, but the lower half shows the theme of meeting and presumed conversation noted on earlier monuments at La Venta: two seated priests or nobles face each other, with an image censer between them and an attendant behind each; this might relate to a Burner or New Fire theme. Skyband panels appear above and below

6.9. Izapa Stela 21, Plaza D, facing west, southernmost monument in front of west-facing Structure 45 (drawing by Ayax Moreno, New World Archaeological Foundation, used by permission of John E. Clark).

the scene on this monument, indicating that the figures are supernaturals (Laughton 1997), and the stela is accompanied by plain Altar 14.

Stela 21 (Fig. 6.9), facing west, was positioned with plain Altar 18 on the southwestern side of the Mound 45 platform. In a scene reminiscent of the ballcourt panels at Terminal Classic Chich'en Itza in Yucatán, this monument shows a collapsed, decapitated human figure with blood spurting from his neck. Above him stands another individual brandishing the triangular knife of sacrifice in his left hand and holding the victim's head in his right. To the left, the "victim's spirit is possibly being transported to the land of the dead in a sedan chair" (Norman 1973:pl. 33) or palanquin, with a jaguar crouching on top. The curled signs below the upper skyband panel have been interpreted as rain but are more likely predecessors of the Maya Kab'an sign for "earth." The presence of these signs above the scene indicates that the sacrifice is taking place in the Underworld, and it could represent the sacrifice of Hunahpu by Xbalanque, after which Hunahpu comes back to life. Lowe (1982a:31) refers to the sacrificer, the sacrificed, and the litter bearers as "symbolic twins." Laughton (1997:133–136) sees clear astronomical associations, the position of head, shoulders, and legs corresponding to the stars of Orion rising on the night of the summer solstice.

The Stela 21–Altar 18 pair is the southernmost in a line of three such pairings southwest of Mound 45: Stela 23 and plain Altar 19 are the central pair, and the northernmost consists of two unsculpted monuments on the west side of the mound itself. Stela 23 portrays a descending anthropomorphic storm (?) god flanked by a "double-headed-U" sky serpent pouring columns of rain into the water panel below. Arthur Miller (1974) notes similarities between this stela and diving gods and umbilical cords on Tulum structures.

Group A

Counterclockwise movement from Group D takes a procession south into Group A, where the abundance of carved monuments, some of which are stylistically late, has given rise to varied interpretations. Coggins (1996:31) sees the stelae in Group A, on the southwestern part of the site, as celebrating the descent of celestial bodies, a position that follows logically from the orientation of the central mounds of this grouping—55, 57, and 60—along the western solstice axis of the site. Alternatively, Lowe (1982b:283) suggests that the central stela in each of the lines of monuments in Group A (as in Group B) represents a yearbearer. A third interpretation comes from Laughton (1997:143–196), who says they portray creation as described in the *Popol Vuh.*

Stela 27, at the base of Mound 57 on the east side of the plaza, facing west, shows two humans (twins?) interacting with a seated animal (dog?) between them. Behind the large left-hand figure is a reptile tree bearing a *k'an* cross cartouche enclosing a possible descending winged deity. Guernsey and Love (2005:42) claim the *k'an* cross marks "the location of the Maize God's rebirth." Above the individual on the right is a large square glyph cartouche; the glyph is not readable, but two bars, probably signifying the number 10, are above it. This may represent "the tenth day sign dog (Itzcuintli or Ok) or else the god of Number 10, the day Death" (Lowe 1982b:285). An upper register is created by a probable four-legged throne with two seated, gesturing figures in conversation, as indicated by a speech scroll in front of the left individual. The panel below shows a terrestrial saurian. Lowe (1982b:285) considers that the "Underground scene, death-like tree-root mask, owl (?) in diving position, and possible fire in mouth of dog (?) all support the idea of death." Laughton (1997:193–196), on the other hand, suggests the scene refers to the conception of the Hero Twins in an early version of the *Popol Vuh.* The larger figure is the decapitated father of the Twins; the smaller figure is Blood Moon; and the tree is the croton, the sap of which was used to make the fake "heart" to take to Blood Moon's father. The doglike creature holding the "heart" was replaced in later versions of the myth by owls.

On the north side of the plaza, six stelae and five altars were placed on the south side of Mound 56, facing into the plaza. The carved monuments can be related to the "aboveground" episodes of the later *Popol Vuh,* particularly those involving Seven Macaw. Their location on the north side of the plaza is significant because after Seven Macaw's death he became the seven stars of the Big Dipper (D. Tedlock 1996:34, 35).

Stela 26, on the lower terrace of Structure 56, is the easternmost in the line and paired with Altar 21. Because its face is very badly damaged, the scene is nearly impossible to read. Rain symbols can be discerned at the top and on the right; eroded human figures (twins?) with upraised arms are evident along the base panel with triangles, and a single personage sits above in a U symbol. Lowe (1982b:285) interprets the five "teeth," or peaks, at the base and the "rainy sky serpent" above as indicating the fifth day sign, Snake or Chikchan.

The next monument in the line, Stela 25 (Fig. 6.10), shows a human figure minus his left arm, standing in a rectangular panel above the nose of an alligator tree. He holds a stylized staff/tree in an olla which supports a great masked bird connected to the staff and alligator by a twining, ropelike serpent. The scene has been widely identified with the episode in the *Popol Vuh* in which the Hero Twins shoot at Seven Macaw as he is feeding in the nance tree, after he has broken Hunahpu's arm (Coe 1989b:163; Coggins 1996:31; Freidel, Schele, and Parker 1993:88–89; Kerr 1992:109–111; Lowe 1982b:297–299). The small bird perched on top of the tree might be the falcon messenger from Huracan who watched the Twins play ball (D. Tedlock 1996:35); note the Venus glyph in the wing. The twining serpentlike cord could be a "metaphorical cosmic umbilicus" that highlights the bird as a "conduit to and denizen of the supernatural realm" (Guernsey Kappelman 2001:94). Stylistically, this stela is thought to be "late," dating ca. A.D. 100–200. Of the accompanying Altar 60, "almost certainly the remains of a broken stela" (Laughton 1997: 41n1), only the lower right corner remains. This shows a figure in ballgame pose, left foot resting on a glyph that might include the number 7.

Stela 4 (Fig. 6.11) shows a striding individual in the costume of the Principal Bird Deity (Guernsey Kappelman 2003:105), with a beaked mask and headdress and an enormous feathered back ornament displaying the crossed-bands sun/sky glyph. His paraphernalia resembles that associated with the ballgame: a curved stick in his right arm and a hockey stick–like club in his upraised left arm. Above, an anthropomorphic winged creature, also with crossed bands in one wing, descends from a celestial band. Perhaps a yearbearer (Lowe 1982b:285), Stela 4 is said to be

6.10. Izapa Stela 25, Plaza A, facing south, set east of the centerline on the south-facing apron of northern Structure 56 (drawing by Ayax Moreno, New World Archaeological Foundation, used by permission of John E. Clark).

6.11. Izapa Stela 4, Plaza A, facing south, set on centerline of the south-facing apron of northern Structure 56 (drawing by Ayax Moreno, New World Archaeological Foundation, used by permission of John E. Clark).

late—Terminal Preclassic—in date (Clancy 1990:30), which may be correct because Guernsey Kappelman (2001:90) notes that the glyph on the right wing of the bird reads 'owa, or "macaw," in Epi-Olmec script. She (ibid.:90–92; idem 2003; also Reilly 2000:375) relates the scene to shamanic ritual transformation, with the ruler assuming the characteristics of the Principal Bird Deity, a macaw. Laughton (1997:166) suggests that the monument depicts the fight between Seven Macaw and Hunahpu.

Stela 7 is badly broken, and the central portion of the scene has been effaced so that only the carving around the edges is visible. According to Norman (1973:pl. 13), a downward-gazing deity

mask in the upper panel overlooks a double-headed earth serpent–saurian. On the right, a figure stands on the upside-down head of the serpent. Altar 3, paired with this stela, shows a large birdlike creature with a human head in its mouth, perhaps one of the owl messengers of the lords of Xib'alb'a. This bird is perched atop a rectangle, perhaps a throne or a ballcourt.

Stela 5 (Fig. 6.12), the westernmost of the monuments on the basal platform of Structure 56, is iconographically and compositionally complex. The scene is dominated by a World Tree, with numerous groups of conversing figures; the sky-band above indicates that events are taking place in the supernatural realm. The scene, according to Laughton (1997:179–191), shows creation as it was told in the *Popol Vuh*, when the sky begins to rise from its position lying on the water:

> The moment of the separation of the sky and sea at the beginning of the creation process is indicated by the inclusion of the two fish hanging from the "skyband". The presence of the pelican perched by the top branches of the tree emphasises the former close connection between the two domains in that it has the ability to fly into the sky, and yet relies on fish, and therefore the river, for food. The World Tree is then raised and from this, in the middle ground of the relief, humans are created. At the base of the stela, in the [left] foreground, the newly created humans are then instructed by the gods in the proper manner of religious observance. (Laughton 1997:191)

This is perhaps a shaman instructing an apprentice, given the similarity of the hats they wear. On the right side is a figure with an elaborate headdress holding an indeterminate implement. Schele and Mary Miller (1986:140) describe him as a "scribe in a spangled turban shaping a human body" while Laughton (1997:191) suggests it might be "a deity carving the first idol for use by the Izapeños." Alternatively, Stela 5 might depict the gods seeking counsel of Xpiyacoc and Xmucane, the elderly couple who are diviners/daykeepers and grandparents of the Hero Twins, before their third try to make humans.

One of the most interesting aspects of Stela 5 is its basal panel. As with that on Stela 12, this panel "is a remarkably accurate depiction of a new 180° view of the eastern horizon as observed from Izapa. . . . The triangles represent the mountain range visible from Izapa, including the two largest volcanoes, Tacaná and Tajumulco. These mountains appear to diminish in size . . . The eastern horizon continues as a flat plane to the south

which is indicated on the right-hand side of the base panel by the horizontal line. The Río Izapa flows along the eastern edge of the site from north to south. . . . The scrolls of the water band correctly indicate the direction of flow" (ibid.:189). Because the artist extended the roots of the World Tree into this topographic panel, they inform viewers that the act of creation took place at Izapa itself (ibid.:191). Monument 5, paired with Altar 36, shows relatively little damage, suggesting that it was revered for nearly two millennia.

Stela 6 (Fig. 6.13) stands in front (south) of Mound 56, before the low platform that held the other stelae and altars and on the same centerline as Stela 4. This monument depicts a *Bufo marinus* toad, as indicated by the conspicuous paratoid glands on the shoulder, with the toxic bufotenine issuing from them. According to Coggins (1996:31) and Laughton (1997:193), the setting moon—symbolized by a U symbol, perhaps with a human in it—is about to be received in the creature's open mouth. Lowe (1982b:285) notes that "a moon scroll, a flower, and a water or rain mask" are "in apparent birth," suggesting references to an eclipse. This scene might represent some early version of the *Popol Vuh* incident in which the toad swallows the louse bearing the Xib'alb'a lords' message to the Hero Twins. Failing to cough up the louse, the toad is kicked by the boys: "they kicked him in the rear, and they crushed the bones of his rear end with their feet. When he tried again, he just sort of spit" (D. Tedlock 1996:115). The U shape above the toad's tongue may symbolize the message from the Underworld. This monument was found with plain Altar 4.

Several monuments were placed on the south side of the Group A plaza, on the north side of Mound 58 and facing north. Stela 1 (Fig. 6.14) shows a god or priest wearing an elaborate mask and snouted and toothed sandals and lifting a basket, with water and fish spilling from it, out of the basal water panel. He also carries a large jar in a net on his back. There is widespread agreement that the figure is the Maya rain god Chaak (Coe 1978:77; Milbrath 1999:208; Taube 1993:65) or a precursor to Chaak and K'awil (Laughton 1997:149–150), which may be also a fishing god and which appears in both the Dresden and the Madrid codices. In particular, Laughton (ibid.: 162) claims that "Stela 1 shows a world in which nothing exists but sky in the form of clouds and water, just as it was at the beginning of the *Popol Vuh*," before the present creation, and the figure fishing is a Preclassic version of Heart of Sky. The scene is remarkably similar to that on a carved bone found in the tomb of Tikal's Late Classic ruler Jasaw Kan K'awil (Montgomery 2001a: 162; Newsome 2001:226n14). The upper panel is the typical jaguar snout or skyband, indicating a view into the supernatural setting, above which is a seated individual holding a snake with five dots below the snake's head, possibly representing the day 5 Snake (Lowe 1982b:286). Arthur Miller (1974:181), however, suggests that the figure is holding his own umbilical cord and placenta, and the date may represent the day the umbilical cord was cut. Stela 1 was paired with Altar 1, a boulder carved as a hunched toad or frog.

Stela 2 (Fig. 6.15) shows two humans in the branches of a tree with crocodilian roots, a descending winged supernatural above. This scene has been interpreted in light of the *Popol Vuh* as

6.12. Izapa Stela 5, Plaza A, facing south, set on western end of the south-facing apron of northern Structure 56 (drawing by Ayax Moreno, New World Archaeological Foundation, used by permission of John E. Clark).

6.13. Izapa Stela 6, Plaza A, facing south, set on front (south) centerline of northern Structure 56 (drawing by Ayax Moreno, New World Archaeological Foundation, used by permission of John E. Clark).

6.14. Izapa Stela 1, Plaza A, facing north, set at eastern end in front (north) of southern Structure 58 (drawing by Ayax Moreno, New World Archaeological Foundation, used by permission of John E. Clark).

the Hero Twins in a tree; the avian would be Seven Macaw (Norman 1976:92–94). Guernsey Kappelman (2003:114) sees the descending deity as an Izapa ruler transformed into the Principal Bird Deity. The monument has a typical jaguar-mouth or skyband panel above with volutes and a U moon (?) but no basal panel. It could have been paired with Stela 25 on the north side of the plaza, given the comparable scenes.

Stela 3 (Fig. 6.16) shows a personage wearing a long-nosed god mask resembling a Manikin Scepter, standing astride an earth serpent. In his upraised left arm he holds a hockey stick–like

club, perhaps a ballgame stick. A human head is shown in a U symbol above the serpent's open mouth. Clancy (1990:30) says this stela is earlier than Stela 4 and Late Preclassic in date. Laughton

6.15. Izapa Stela 2, Plaza A, facing north, set at center front (north) of southern Structure 58 (drawing by Ayax Moreno, New World Archaeological Foundation, used by permission of John E. Clark).

6.16. Izapa Stela 3, Plaza A, facing north, set at the western end in front (north) of southern Structure 58 (drawing by Ayax Moreno, New World Archaeological Foundation, used by permission of John E. Clark).

(1997:199) sees it as closely paired with Stela 1 in showing the "Heart of Earth, Heart of Sky" deities as the creator couple in the precreation world. The monument was paired with Altar 2, a boulder carved as the hunched body of a *Bufo marinus* toad.

Discussion

As suggested earlier, it is generally assumed that ritual activity at Izapa involved public processionals through the site, with declamations of mythic history related to the *Popol Vuh* at the various monuments and perhaps performances in the plazas. The Baines and Yoffee (2000:16) order, legitimacy, and wealth model indicates that processions through the site center and its stelae celebrate and reenact "an order that may not be fully itself without such celebration. In joyfully reaffirming order and legitimacy, the actors use wealth [the carved monuments] to counter fragility [of the sociopolitical system] . . . . Without celebration, order may be threatened."

Two questions in proposing this processional route are its starting place and, as always in archaeology, the contemporaneity of the structures, complexes, and monuments. In general, mound groups G, B, D, and A seem to have experienced maximal construction and use in the Late Preclassic period Guillen phase, ca. 300–50 B.C. (Lowe, Lee, and Martínez 1982:164, 167, 184, 188, 196, 211, 215, 247, 254), although Late Classic and Early Postclassic activity is also evident.[4]

Dating the monuments is more difficult: Newsome (2001:18) considers them all to have been erected during the Guillen phase, although some may be earlier (e.g., Monument 2, "El León"), and Clancy (1990) believes some date as late as the first centuries A.D. Laughton (1997:138–142), on the other hand, argues on the basis of Chinese astronomical records that an unusual period of comet activity between 148 and 134 B.C. was registered on Stelae 21 and 23. He (ibid.:142) believes the Izapa monuments were "mainly carved within a relatively short period of perhaps twenty years after the 147–145 BC astronomical events."

None of the plazas has Classic-period monuments; they are all believed, on the basis of various style-dating schemes, to be Late (or Terminal) Preclassic. Although these schemes are hardly precise, they indicate mixed dates, some earlier and some later, for the monument corpus in each of the plazas. It is likely, then, that during the 250-year Late Preclassic florescence of Izapa, monuments were regularly carved and erected in different ceremonial groups to illustrate various myths or events that were later compiled and redacted by the Maya into what became the *Popol Vuh*.

Laughton (1997) discusses processions through Izapa primarily in terms of the Group A and Group B plazas, as well as with reference to his sequencing of monuments. He proposes that Group B, the earliest architectural group at the site, focused on solar events, with Group A to the west constructed later and focusing on creation as narrated in the *Popol Vuh*. There might have been separate processions in each plaza, one on the summer solstice in Group B, focusing on solar movement and sunrise out of Tajumulco, and the other on what would have been the day of creation, according to the Long Count, in August, taking place in Group A (ibid.:221). He also proposes an intrasite circuit that would have begun in Group A, specifically at Stelae 1 and 3. These monuments, he believes, show the cosmos as it was before the present creation, only sky and water, and the fishing figures

represent the creators Heart of Sky and Heart of Earth (ibid.:199). From these two stelae in the southern part of the plaza, a procession would move clockwise to the northwest corner and Stela 5, showing the moment of creation itself. The ritual trek would then move through the "Group D corridor" to end in Group B.

The logic of this movement is based on Laughton's perceptive interpretations of the themes of the monuments. However, it would involve a clockwise circuit, which is atypical for the Maya, as most ethnohistorically and historically known perambulations follow a counterclockwise path. In addition, many other monuments stand between and among the ones he discusses, and the images and scenes on them disrupt a smooth narrative. Although he (1997:199–201) has an explanation for the interruption of the Plaza A discussion of creation by the Seven Macaw battle with the Hero Twins, other monuments are left unexplained. Possibly his sequencing of the monuments of Groups A and B is correct for a period in the mid–first century B.C., and the other monuments were subsequently added.

I suggest that ritual processions through Izapa consisted of multiple counterclockwise circuits through the site core,[5] beginning with arrival at Group G and moving through the plazas. They would have involved performances at the various monuments and in the plazas, and these would have changed as monuments were added or moved over time. Ceremonies took place during the night, participants peering into carved scenes of the supernatural world by means of the skyband threshold device, animated by the flickering lights of ritual fires and torches. Perhaps beginning or ending with a ballgame, the drama culminated at dawn in Group G, where participants could observe sunrise: on the summer solstice the sun rose out of Tajumulco, and on the winter solstice it was commemorated architecturally.

Seventeen carved monuments at Izapa seem to correspond to events or creatures of the *Popol Vuh*, and perhaps as many as a dozen display twins, presumably Hunahpu and Xbalanque (or their predecessors). Only three seem to represent events in Xib'alb'a or the Underworld: Altar 3, with the owl messengers (?); Stela 21 in Group D, showing the sacrifice of Hunahpu by Xbalanque; and Stela 24 in Plaza B, with Xbalanque dancing in the

Underworld after pretending to sacrifice Hunahpu. The other monuments show aboveground scenes. Although thirteen Izapa monuments have U-elements (moon? *k'atun*?), only five monuments with presumed *Popol Vuh*–related scenes have U-elements.

Some scenes on Izapa monuments suggest parts of a proto–*Popol Vuh* or similar myth that did not survive to the modern era, that changed significantly through time, or that did not enter Maya belief systems. Perhaps the mythistory of the Late Preclassic Izapans was more concerned with, and therefore materialized in stone, the earlier creations—and earlier calendars—mentioned only briefly in the extant *Popol Vuh*, the episodes in which humans were made of wood or mud. Also, the several scenes of water on the Izapa monuments exceed those in the extant Maya myth. Wetlands and water were key features of San Lorenzo and La Venta, in their settings and numerous water-management constructions, so perhaps the scenes on the Izapa stelae reflect a near relationship with the Gulf coast that has since been lost. On the other hand, Izapa has Middle Formative drains, "fountain stones," and other features reminiscent of Gulf coastal waterworks (Lowe, Lee, and Martínez 1982:206–207, 258). Also, some *Popol Vuh* scenes could have been painted on plain monuments or carved on monuments too heavily damaged to recognize or that remain buried.

The number, location, and iconographic characteristics of monuments at Izapa reveal adherence not only to a strong ideocosmological program, but also to highly developed ritual performances keyed to the positioning of the monuments throughout the site center. Much of the display seems interpretable in the context of the *Popol Vuh*, but other rituals also might have been involved. Monuments in Group F, for example, many of which may have been removed from the site center, relate to the sacrifice and rebirth of the Maize God (Guernsey Kappelman 2002). Another is Burner ceremonies, best known from the Colonial period (see P. Rice 2004:246–248). Burner rituals divide the 260-day calendar into four periods of sixty-five days and occur on only four days—Chikchan, Ok, Men, and Ajaw—which were yearbearers in the Olmec calendar (Edmonson 1988:21, 231), suggesting great

antiquity. Three monuments in Izapa Group A display symbols and/or day names relating to this sequence: Chikchan (Stela 26), Ok (Stela 27), and birds on various monuments (especially Altar 3). The many depictions of incense burners, including those on Stela 5 in Group A, may further indicate the importance of fire or Burner rituals in this particular sector of the site.

Early Olmec iconographic programs stressed composite saurian/feline/serpent creatures, and these fauna continued to be present in later sculpted scenes, frequently as framing devices and less commonly as central elements or themes. But later Olmecs (after 600 B.C.) and Izapans placed greater emphasis on avian imagery (as does the *Popol Vuh*) (Pohorilenko 1996) as well as on toads. The birds, particularly the one that later became the Maya Principal Bird Deity, often combine avian features with human, feline, and reptilian elements (Cortez 2005), but they are fundamentally avians as evident from the widespread wings. There is no clear correlation among the birds in the *Popol Vuh* and those on the Izapa monuments. Birds in the former include owls, falcons, macaws, and possibly hawks, while the avian most prominently displayed on the monuments is a large bird with crossed bands (the sun/sky symbol) on its wings. While this creature could be the sky messenger falcon, it is typically interpreted as Seven Macaw and as precursor of the later Classic Maya Principal Bird Deity (Hellmuth 1987:365, cited in Milbrath 1999:274) associated with God D, or Itzamna, the creator god (Guernsey Kappelman 2003:114).

Guernsey Kappelman (2001:95, 2003) discusses shamanic leaders in avian transformations, suggesting that "Late Formative rulers not only adopted the garb of the bird while performing shamanic feats but actually performed certain passages from the [*Popol Vuh*] creation story in the persona of the avian deity," probably as components of ritual circumambulations. The transformation scenes on Stelae 2, 4, and 60 may be performances by Late Preclassic Isthmian rulers, who were demonstrating their legitimacy through their ability to communicate with the supernatural, a standard claim of rulers in asserting order (Baines and Yoffee 1998:213; idem 2000:234). The anthropomorphic "birdman" is clearly Seven

Macaw, who, on the Izapa monuments and elsewhere, as at Oxtotitlán and Kaminaljuyú, seems to represent an esteemed figure. Yet in the late *Popol Vuh*, Seven Macaw is regarded as a pretender to the role of the sun and celestial light, an arrogant false sun that the Hero Twins must eliminate because of his "self-magnification." Perhaps Seven Macaw is an allusion to an early, unsatisfactory solar calendar, or to conflict between Mixe-Zoquean and Mayan speakers/factions who refused to accept a new calendar or the Long Count. One might also speculate that the Seven Macaw episode refers to a major change in the role of kings between the Late Preclassic period and the Early Classic, such as their new divine status within the solar cult. Early shamanic kings in the Izapa region might have presented themselves as giant birds (macaws) bringing light to the world in Late Preclassic mythic history and cosmology. With the institution of *ajaw* and divine kingship, however, the early basis of rulership would have been repudiated—hence the killing of Seven Macaw in the *Popol Vuh* myth.

KAMINALJUYÚ AND RELATED SITES

Kaminaljuyú, lying at almost exactly 90°30′, is considerably east of the eastern boundary I have drawn for the Isthmian region of Mesoamerica (Fig. 1.2), but because of its importance and that of nearby Pacific piedmont sites to the arguments herein, and to the Maya lowlands, I include it. Kaminaljuyú is—or was, before modern development—a large city in the western "valley" of Guatemala, now largely destroyed by the urban expansion of the capital, Guatemala City. Beginning with occupation in the late Early Preclassic period (Arévalo phase, 1200–1000 B.C.), the site flourished in the Preclassic and Classic periods as the largest (ca. five square kilometers) and most powerful chiefdom in the Maya highlands (Demarest 2004:75; Hatch 1991). It is perhaps best known because of its relations with the immense city of Teotihuacan in central Mexico in the Early Classic period.

During the Preclassic period several lakes existed in the valley; the largest, Lake Miraflores, covered some twenty-five hectares and occupied the center of Kaminaljuyú until its waters dried

up around A.D. 100 (Hatch et al. 2001). Canals drained water from the lake to fields in the southern valley. The earliest, Canal Miraflores, more than half a kilometer long and nearly 6 meters deep, was in use by 700 B.C. and abandoned around 400 B.C. (ibid.:103, 106; Valdés and Wright 2004:340–341); to the west, Canal San Jorge, some 1,750 meters in length, functioned until abandonment around A.D. 100. Hatch and her colleagues (2001:108–109) note that the irrigated fields might have been raised beds and that, while there was sufficient rainfall in the valley for maize cultivation, irrigation might have permitted year-round cultivation of vegetables.

Kaminaljuyú's early growth and long florescence were due in part to its convenient location in a mountain pass, which facilitated extensive trade and other contacts with sites along the Pacific coast and eastward into El Salvador, as well as with the lowlands to the north. These relations were broken at the end of the Terminal Preclassic period, approximately A.D. 200, after which population declined. By the Early Classic period three major sites in the valley, Kaminaljuyú, Solano, and Frutal, may have functioned together in such a way as to create a port of trade (K. Brown 1975), and Early Classic pottery shows closer ties to the western highlands (Hatch 1991). Major trade goods thought to be controlled by Kaminaljuyú include the El Chayal obsidian source to the northeast, the Motagua jade source beyond, and cacao production in the rich soils of the southern piedmont. Kaminaljuyú's location also would have facilitated interactions among the various "proto"-linguistic groups that were emerging in the region in the Middle Preclassic: Mixean, Xincan, Lencan, Zoquean, Ch'olan-Tzeltalan, and Poqom. Coggins (1996:33), in fact, sees the site as a meeting ground for multiple cultural groups that shared common creation myths and cosmology but had competing beliefs about calendars and ritual.

Kaminaljuyú's two hundred-plus monumental structures were built of earth rather than stone, using a mixture of volcanic sand, *talpetate* (a hard, compacted, weathering product of volcanic sand), and clay (Michels 1979:139). Their construction began in the late Middle Formative period (around 500 B.C.), with parallel linear arrangements of these structures alone or in two or three plazas along an axis roughly 20° east of north.[6] This lin-ear site plan, already noted at Olmec sites and at Izapa, was shared by other sites in the valley of Guatemala (e.g., Canchón, Piedra Parada, Santa Isabel, Cuyá, and Virginia; Valdés 1992:74), as well as at contemporaneous sites in the Pacific pied-mont such as Tak'alik Ab'aj (Orrego Corzo 1992:9) and Monte Alto (L. Parsons 1986:145). It is also noteworthy that the early "observatory" structur-al arrangement can be found in the Terminal Preclassic valley of Guatemala at the sites of Rincón, Rosario-Naranjo, Cruz de Cotió, San Isidro II, and Las Charcas (Valdés 1992:74), and at Kaminaljuyú itself, where the linear mound is replaced by three structures (J. Valdés 1997).

Kaminaljuyú has twelve ballcourts, eight ori-ented northwest-southeast and four oriented northeast-southwest, but these were apparently

constructed and used in the Middle and Late Classic periods (Michels 1979:230). Ballcourts are present at other sites in the general region, includ-ing a Middle Preclassic court at Tak'alik Ab'aj (Orrego Corzo 1992:9; Schieber de Lavarreda 1994). The population of the Late Formative Kaminaljuyú chiefdom was estimated at ca. forty-five hundred persons, with twenty-five hundred living in Kaminaljuyú (Michels 1979:144; I have been unable to find more recent estimates).

In a synthesis of data from Pennsylvania State University's archaeological research at Kaminal-juyú from 1968 through 1971, Joseph W. Michels (1979) proposes a "conical clan" chiefdom model for the sociopolitical organization of the site. He divides the site into two "districts," northeast and southwest, which encompass five "precincts"—El Incienso, Santa Rosita, Catarina Pinula, San Carlos,

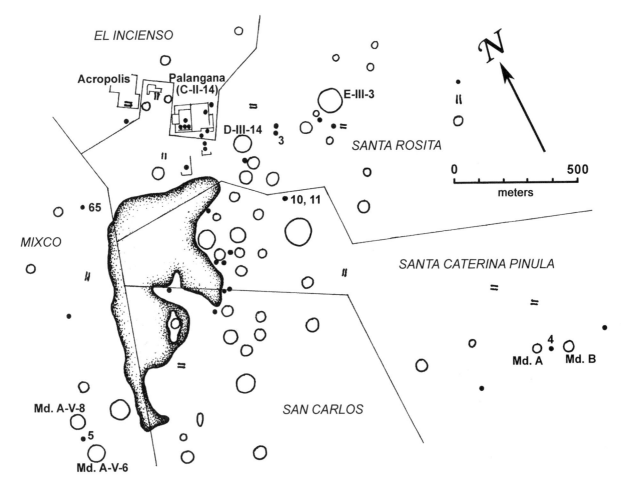

6.17. The site of Kaminaljuyú, Guatemala (drawn from Parsons 1986:fig. 4), showing the extinct lake in the center of the site and Michels's (1979) hypothesized precincts. Numbered dots are locations of stelae discussed in text. Mounds are indicated by circles; monuments, by dots; ballcourts, by parallel lines.

and Mixco (Fig. 6.17) in clockwise order from the north—based on five distinct groupings of Late Formative mounds. These precincts had different statuses (high to low as listed) and involvement in craft activities. For example, the percentage of households involved in Late Formative obsidian blade production varied significantly (ibid.:153): El Incienso (20 percent); Santa Rosita, which is believed to have controlled the Chayal obsidian source (7 percent); Catarina Pinula (25 percent); San Carlos (75 percent); and Mixco (0 percent). By the Late Terminal Formative period (A.D. 1–200), Michels (ibid.:157) deduces evidence for dual organization or moieties in the precincts, via differential involvement in craft activities (e.g., one moiety responsible for production and the other for distribution of obsidian; ibid.:186). By the Middle and early Late Classic, when Kaminaljuyú's ballcourts were constructed, every moiety chief had a ballcourt (ibid.:230).

Kaminaljuyú Sculptures

One frequently debated feature of Kaminaljuyú is its sculptural corpus, the points of disagreement being the dates and the degree to which the monuments display stylistic ties to Izapa and lowland Maya sculpture (see, e.g., J. Kaplan 1995; L. Parsons 1986; Prater 1989). As compared with Izapa, the iconographic program at Kaminaljuyú and related sites appears to glorify rulership rather than mythical themes, with stelae depicting rulers engaged in various kinds of ritual (Newsome 2001:19–21). This links them to Maya sites, but certain motifs—earth basal panels, incense burn-

ers, long-lipped heads in headdresses, toad altars—betray clear ties to Izapa.

Lee Parsons's (1986) study of Kaminaljuyú monuments and sculpture at several Pacific piedmont sites created four chronological "style divisions" for the early material: Early Olmec (no examples), Late Olmec, Post-Olmec, and Izapan, most with subdivisions or substyles. Kaminaljuyú's sculptures originated during a Late Olmec–Post-Olmec Transitional phase (n = ~15), with more (n = ~25) in the Post-Olmec period (ibid.:26, 27). Parsons sees the Terminal Preclassic sculptures from Kaminaljuyú and Pacific slope sites as "more explicitly 'proto-Maya'" in style than are those of Izapa. In particular, he (ibid.:49–50, 94–97) identifies three sculptural substyles in the Terminal Formative Guatemala-Chiapas region: an Izapan "narrative" style centered at Izapa, and the Miraflores and Arenal "proto-Maya" styles at Kaminaljuyú in early and late facets. Differences between these presumably contemporaneous substyles prompted him (ibid.:96) to wonder whether they reflected competing lineages at Kaminaljuyú. However, when his styles are mapped over Michels's hypothesized districts and precincts there is no clear pattern of distribution.

The corpus of monuments from this region is extremely large. Parsons's study incorporated 127 monuments from Kaminaljuyú, including low-relief-carved stelae, altars, and wall panels, plus sculpture in the round, including potbelly figures, ballcourt markers, "giant three-pronged incense burners," mushroom stones, and human and animal figures, especially toads. In addition, more than one hundred sculptures were known from

TABLE 6.1. *Sculptural chronology at Kaminaljuyú and Pacific region sites*

SCULPTURAL STYLE	DATES
Early Olmec	pre-900 B.C.
Late Olmec	900–700 B.C.
Transition	700–500 B.C.
Post-Olmec	500–200 B.C.
Terminal Preclassic/Izapan	200 B.C.–A.D. 200
Early Arenal substyle (or Early Miraflores)	200 B.C.–A.D. 1
Arenal phase	A.D. 1–200
Early Classic	A.D. 200–400
Middle Classic	A.D. 400–600

Source: L. Parsons (1986).

Tak'alik Ab'aj at the time of his analysis (ibid.:8). The numbers increase at both sites as more excavation and salvage work is done every year.

The greatest concentration of recovered monuments at Kaminaljuyú—four stelae, four altars (including two toad altars), and four monuments—is in the acropolis known as the Palangana (the C-II-14 mound complex) in the northern part of the site in Michels's (1979) high-status El Incienso precinct. The Palangana was constructed in the Middle Classic period over an earlier late Terminal Preclassic (Arenal-phase) structure, and some of the monuments were found in an early Middle Classic tomb under a shrine. The entire corpus dates to the first millennium B.C. (see L. Parsons 1986:table 3), but the stylistic and chronological variability suggest that either new monuments were sculpted and added to this architectural complex every few centuries over a span of some seven hundred years, or that they reflect different but roughly contemporaneous ethnic sculpture traditions.

Kaminaljuyú Stela 65 (Fig. 6.18) shows an overtly political scene, with eight seated humans in three tiers. The central figure of each tier is richly attired, facing left and seated cross-legged on a four-legged throne and gesturing with the index finger of the right hand. Facing the central individuals, right and left, are kneeling captives, naked or nearly so, with their outstretched arms bound at the wrists. The hair of the three central figures is nearly identical, pulled back into a knot or bun, but, interestingly, their headdresses vary: that of the central figure has an infixed *k'in* sign, while the lower figure has a leaf (cacao?) in the mouth of a profile dragon (ibid.:58). The headdress of one of the captives on the right side is that of a long-beaked and -necked bird, probably aquatic. The central personages might illustrate the importance of being "seated" (*chum*) in office in Classic times; the captives might be foreign elites, and their headgear, perhaps predecessors of Emblem Glyphs indicating a place and/or ruling elite, could indicate their names (J. Kaplan 1996:453–454). It is difficult to determine, however, whether this scene is intended to be historical in nature, the central figures representing three successive rulers of Kaminaljuyú, or—given their different headdresses and Coggins's (1996:33) suggestion of the site as a meeting ground for competing groups—the leaders

of major groups with interests in this advantageously sited city. Lee Parsons (1986) dates Stela 65 to the Early Arenal period.

Kaminaljuyú "Stela" 10, now identified as an altar or throne rather than a stela (Prater 1989:128), was uncovered in a large open area between two mounds, D-IV-2 and D-III-10, about one hundred meters south of the latter, close to the postulated boundary between the Santa Rosita and Catarina Pinula precincts. Stela 11 was later discovered only one meter away; perhaps they were originally a stela-altar pair. They both date to the Miraflores phase/style of Kaminaljuyú florescence, although Lee Parsons (1986:50) sees Stela 11 as earlier than Stela 10. Stela 11 shows a ruler standing on an Izapa-like basal/earth band, with identical incense burners in front of and behind his feet. He wears an elaborate belt, loincloth, and large mask of a hook-beaked (avian?) creature with crossed bands as an earplug; he holds an upraised staff of some sort.

6.18. Kaminaljuyú Stela 65 (drawn from L. Parsons 1986:fig. 149).

Above him is a winged deity. Guernsey Kappelman (2003:103) comments that this costuming and pairing with the Principal Bird Deity demonstrates that "the ruler's ability to communicate with the supernatural was central to the display and legitimation of rulership."

The altar of this possible pair, "Stela" 10 (Fig. 6.19a), depicts two personages: the main figure, dressed in the avian guise of the "Sacrificer Rain God," standing on a mountain, with a kneeling female behind him (Mora-Marín 2005:82). This central scene is bounded by a three-strand mat motif. The monument has two glyphic text panels closely resembling Epi-Olmec and lowland Mayan scripts, suggesting "some currently unspecifiable historical relation" among the three (Kaufman and Justeson 2004:1075). The text is not fully intelligible; while it appears to exhibit regular glyph block size, it is not clear if it is read in single- (J. Kaplan 1995:194) or double-column (Mora-Marín 2005) format. Both texts begin with oversize day glyphs; the first is unreadable and the second may be 8 Muluk. The larger glyph panel (Fig. 6.19b; J. Kaplan 1995:194; Mora-Marín 2005:71–78) might include a reference to autosacrifice (G4), an early version of the scattering glyph (H3), "completion"/moon/20 (H4), *winal* glyphs at H1 and I7, and three numbers—15, 6, and 10 (at G1, I4, and J5, respectively). This suggests the typical Late Classic Maya ritual of scattering on a period ending. David Mora-Marín (2005) interprets the last two numbers as pertaining to *tzolk'in* dates, 6 Imix and 10 Chikchan, following Stuart (Mora-Marín, pers. com., April 27, 2005). He also notes the apparent nominal of the main personage, which includes the epithet Mountain Lord (I3–J3); this calls to mind the name Harvester Mountain-Lord of the personage on La Mojarra Stela 1.[7] Mora-Marín dates "Stela" 10 to 400–200 B.C. (cf. L. Parsons 1986:50, who dates it to the Terminal Preclassic Miraflores style) and believes the script is Ch'olan, closely related to lowland Mayan script. Fahsen and Grube (2005:78), noting the combination of logographic and syllabic signs, also conclude that "Cholan, or at least a western Mayan language" was used by scribes of Kaminaljuyú.

Another monument dump, this one dating to ca. 200 B.C.–A.D. 100, was found on what appears to be a peninsula jutting into the extinct lake from its southeastern shore. The recovered monuments, Altars 9 and 10, plus full-round sculptures 51–54, lie approximately on the boundary between Michels's (1979) Catarina Pinula and San Carlos residential precincts (as do Monuments 6 and 7, not discussed further here). Altar 10, the better preserved of what Lee Parsons (1986:54) sees as a pair, may show an Izapan-style profiled saurian "behind" the Izapan-like bird monster, but the cartouches in the wings are proto-Maya day signs: *k'in* (sun, day) and *ak'ab'* (*ak'b'al* 'darkness, night') instead of the crossed bands noted at Izapa (Cortez 2005:45; L. Parsons 1986:55). The same is true of Altar 11.

Seven, possibly nine, toad altars were found at Kaminaljuyú, plus at least one at the site of El Tejar in Chimaltenango to the west, and Lee Parsons (1986:130–131) dates them to the Early Miraflores phase/style, ca. 200–1 B.C. Three of the Kaminaljuyú altars are of unknown provenience, but the others are from the northern and eastern part of the site: fragmentary Altars 11 and 13, and possibly Monument 2, were redeposited in the lower plaza of the Palangana; Altar 3, a plain toad, was recovered east of Mound D-III-14; Altar 4, a small toad with a basin on its back, possibly reused, was found between Mounds A and B; and Altar 5, a large *Bufo marinus* toad altar with a basin, was found between Mounds A-V-6 and A-V-8.

Pacific Piedmont Sites

Other large and important sites in the Pacific piedmont of Guatemala include La Blanca, Ujuxte, Tak'alik Ab'aj, El Baúl, El Balsamo, and Monte Alto (Fig. 6.20). La Blanca, located close to the coast near the western border of Guatemala, appears to have preceded Izapa as a major regional center, with the construction of earthen mounds as much as twenty-five meters high during the early Middle Formative, ca. 900–600 B.C. (Guernsey and Love 2005; Love 1999). La Blanca declined rapidly after 600 B.C., and the new power to emerge in the area was Ujuxte, twelve kilometers to the east. Ujuxte has an unusual grid layout with an orientation 35° east of north (Love 1999:140–141). Unlike La Blanca and Ujuxte, which have few examples of monumental sculpture, Tak'alik Ab'aj, some forty kilometers east of

6.19. Kaminaljuyú "Stela" 10, actually an altar: (above) carving on the altar face (drawn from drawing by James Porter, published in Mora-Marín 2005:fig. 2a); (right) lower-right glyph panel; see text for reading of some glyphs (drawn from ibid.:fig. 2c).

La Blanca, has an enormous corpus of monuments, including two colossal heads, but most of these monuments were reset in post-Preclassic times (ibid.:142).

As many scholars have observed, there are striking similarities between Izapa stelae and monuments at some of these sites, especially Kaminaljuyú Stelae 4, 10, 11, and 19 and Tak'alik Ab'aj Stelae 1, 2, 3, and 4 (see Guernsey Kappelman 2002:77–80), El Baúl Stela 1 (V. Smith 1984:36), and the Epi-Olmec La Mojarra Stela 1 (Guernsey Kappelman 2003; Mora-Marín 2005). The monuments also exhibit traits that are not found at Izapa but that are characteristic of later Classic Maya art (V. Smith 1984:36–37). For example, the human figures on some monuments hold one or both hands in the distinctive "crab-claw" position of many Classic Maya stelae, as at Copán: backs together against the upper chest with fingers curled outward. Downward-peering heads and U

elements are found on some of these monuments and also appear on Izapa monuments and Early Classic stelae in the Maya lowlands.

Another significant trait is the presence of early Long Count dates, which appear in the last quarter of B'ak'tun 7 in the Isthmian and Pacific piedmont regions. They exhibit a number of striking differences compared with later Maya Long Count dates and show considerable internal variability: (1) they consist of a single (rather than a double) column of bar-dot numbers; (2) they frequently appear in the center of monuments, for example, between two standing figures, rather than to the side; (3) glyphs for the "bundles" of days or the temporal units themselves (b'ak'tun, k'atun, etc.) are not inscribed with the numbers, suggesting that these units were understood by viewers on the basis of their vertical placement; and (4) the calendrical specifics extend only to the day name and number in the 260-day calendar; the

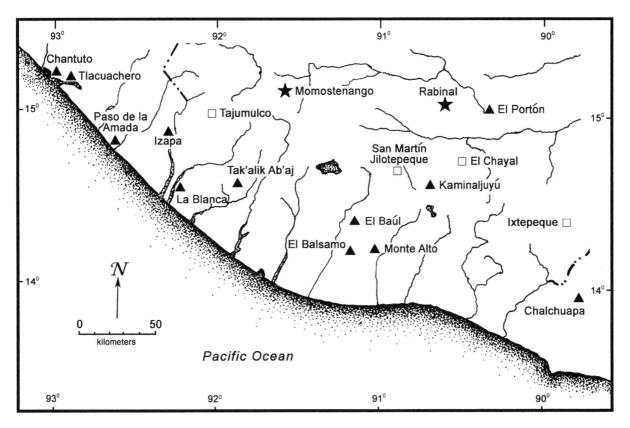

6.20. Pacific coastal Chiapas, Guatemala, and western El Salvador, showing sites mentioned in text and obsidian sources. Triangles indicate archaeological sites; stars, modern cities; squares, obsidian sources.

day numbers and month names in the 365-day calendar are absent. Examples of late Cycle 7 Long Count dates exhibiting these characteristics include a fragmentary date equivalent to 36 B.C. on Stela 2 from Chiapa de Corzo, Tres Zapotes Stela C (32 B.C.; Fig. 6.21a), El Baúl Stela 1 (A.D. 37; Fig. 6.21b), Tak'alik Ab'aj Stela 5 (A.D. 126), and the Tuxtla Statuette (A.D. 162; Fig. 6.21c) (Coe 1957; Edmonson 1988:27, 28, 30).

One element of the Long Count that begins to appear in the Late Preclassic is the Initial Series Introducing Glyph, or ISIG. Characteristic of Classic lowland Maya Long Count dates, the Maya ISIG is an oversized glyph appearing at the start of a Long Count date. It has three components (see Chap. 8): a trefoil element atop a month glyph atop a *tun*/year sign. In some early Long Count inscriptions on the Pacific slopes, dates begin with an inverted ISIG-like oversized collocation consisting of a bar-dot number atop an upside-down day cartouche above a tri-lobed or trefoil element (see Figs 6.5, 6.19). Elsewhere on the Pacific piedmont and in Epi-Olmec script, however, the ISIG starts with the trefoil, sometimes appearing as three curls, fronds, or ornate fleur-de-lis-like trefoil elements above a month sign, followed by a bar-dot number, which more closely resembles the Maya pattern.

An aspect of the archaeology of the highlands and Pacific piedmont and coast that has received comparatively little attention is the occurrence of plain (uncarved) stelae at numerous sites (Borhegyi 1965:13; Bove 1999; idem 2005:104). These monuments range from rough unworked stone shafts to dressed stone stelae, and Borhegyi (1965:13n13) believes they may have begun to be erected in the late Early or Middle Formative. At Monte Alto, some fifteen plain stelae were found; one arrangement of three sat in a north-south line, with the southernmost monument marking the position of

6.21. Early Long Count dates: (a) Tres Zapotes Stela C (after Edmonson 1988:280); (b) El Baúl Stela 1 (after ibid.:28); (c) Tuxtla Statuette (after ibid.:30).

the winter solstice sunrise when viewed from the main mound (Bove 1999:2, citing E. Shook), suggesting the "E-Group" observatory arrangement.

DISCUSSION: CALENDRICAL IMPLICATIONS

My argument here has been about the development of calendars, and about the role of an astrocalendrical ideology in underwriting elite wealth, power, and legitimacy and establishing social and political order. In previous chapters I discuss Early and Middle Formative objects of personal ornamentation and status, and distinctive site plans and orientations, as archaeologically visible evidence of such a foundational ideology. Data from the Late and Terminal Preclassic periods in the Pacific piedmont and the Maya highlands support the idea that this emphasis continued and was elaborated in southern Mesoamerica.

The two major Late Formative sites in the extended eastern Isthmian region, Izapa and Kaminaljuyú, share similar linear site plans with similar orientations, and both may have played important roles in development of the Mesoamerican calendars. Izapa and its rulers merit particular attention in this regard because of the site's location at 15° north latitude and consideration of the sun's position at zeniths. Izapa's architecture, monuments, and iconography appear to be materializations of an ideology focused in part on solar movements (Izapa has one and perhaps two of the early "observatory" commemorative architectural complexes and the "Dawn" monument, Stela 11; Fig. 6.6) and in part to lunar symbolism (if the crescent element is taken as a moon icon). Two monuments at Izapa and one at Tak'alik Ab'aj relate to the Maize God, and Guernsey Kappelman (2002:80) asserts that the "narrative of the Maize God's sacrifice and rebirth was central to the display and legitimation of power in both Mayan- and Mixe-Zoquean-speaking regions during the Late Preclassic." I am not confident that three monuments in the region are sufficient to establish "centrality," and in the case of Izapa, the two monuments in question were found at Group F, some distance north of the site center. This, plus the fact that the monuments in Group F were damaged and buried, suggests that any elite group there claiming legitimacy through the Maize God myth might have been a disfavored faction.

It is generally thought that the Izapan art style per se, with its narrations of pre- or proto-*Popol Vuh* episodes, is quite restricted spatially. The earliest version of the *Popol Vuh* narrative could have begun there, in the sense of the site's rulers declaring as their charter of order and legitimacy the synthesis of much mythic history and many calendrical elements that had been widely circulated and known in oral performances for centuries. If so, the Mixe-Zoquean-speaking rulers at Izapa played a central role in memorializing, in material form and at a very early date, this important and long-lived creation story of the Maya.

The monumental art of Izapa, Kaminaljuyú, and related sites continues the earlier emphasis on polymorphic creatures that combine ophidian, feline, batrachian, avian, and human characteristics in ways that are nearly impossible to parse into individual supernaturals and a coherent belief system. Avians seem to gain importance in the Late and Terminal Preclassic, as seen in various "bird-man" depictions. In this regard, it is of interest that the head variants and "full-figure" glyphs for periods in the Maya Long Count, the *b'ak'tun* and *k'atun*, and some depictions of the *tun*, are birds. Similarly, *Bufo marinus* toads and other batrachians or anurans, or selected attributes of these creatures, appear in Middle, Late, and Terminal Preclassic art, particularly as altars. "Toadiness" is not a highly valued esthetic concept in most of today's Western world, but, clearly, these creatures represented something very important (at the very least an earth symbol) to ancient Mesoamericans. In many parts of the world, however, marine toads are valued for pest control and also for their hallucinogenic exudates, and shamans of the Tacana of Brazil kept toads in captivity (Furst 1981; Kennedy 1982); such a practice could have been followed in Mesoamerica as well. Toads or frogs are seen in full-figure variants of the *winal* glyph, and the fact that four zoomorphic altars at Late Classic Quiriguá marked *k'atun* divisions raises the possibility that the toad altars at Izapa, Kaminaljuyú, and elsewhere played a similar role in commemorating period endings.[8]

What is the significance of the widespread sharing of sculptural art styles of the Guatemala highlands and Pacific piedmont areas from Chiapas to El Salvador? Over the decades, various art historians have downplayed the similarities between the styles in efforts to highlight the uniqueness of one versus the other. Their methods and conclusions are reminiscent of those of scholars engaged in any sort of comparative—especially taxonomic—exercise: some are "lumpers" (preferring to emphasize similarities) and some are "splitters" (preferring to emphasize differences), generally as a result of their theoretical persuasions. In this situation, I am a lumper. To me, the similarities and continuities between Olmec, Epi-Olmec, Izapan, Kaminaljuyú, and lowland Maya styles of art and epigraphy cannot be denied. The kinds and degrees of similarities are certainly variable, but they clearly indicate both distinct ethno-linguistico-epigraphic traditions and considerable interaction—social, economic, and linguistic—over a wide area in the Late and Terminal Preclassic periods.

If some proto-*may*-type geopolitical organization can be hypothesized for the Preclassic period, it is likely that, as part of this unique role, Izapa was a Pacific regional politico-ritual capital, the seat of the *may*, in the Late Preclassic period, just as La Venta was for the Gulf coast in the Middle Preclassic. The problem is to determine the dates of this seating: Izapa's florescence dates from roughly 300 B.C. to 50 B.C., which is only thirty-some years from the proposed K'atun 8 Ajaw *may* seating of 334 to 79 B.C. The site's excavators (Lowe, Lee, and Martínez 1982:139) note a settlement shift and intrusion of a new ceramic complex in the interval from about 50 B.C. to A.D. 100. I take this to mean that the Izapa Late Preclassic *may* seating ended at the time of this shift. However, the site has evidence of mound construction dating to the Middle Preclassic period, and several monuments appear to be late dating, as they bear glyphs associated with the Epi-Olmec writing tradition (Guernsey Kappelman 2003). The possibility arises, then, that Izapa dominated the Pacific coastal Chiapas region for a period of five hundred years, or two terms as *may* seat, although it is equally likely that La Blanca played this role in the Middle Preclassic. Perhaps these two sites fit into the successional process of "host" and "guest" (P. Rice 2004:112–114).

To the east, in the Guatemala highlands, Kaminaljuyú could have been another early *may* seat, perhaps beginning as early as did Izapa, in the fourth century B.C. or before, as the site has significant Middle Preclassic occupation. Unlike the situation with Izapa, the Kaminaljuyú sculptural and epigraphic style seems to have been both more eclectic and more widely shared. This stylistic sharing was paralleled by patterns of ceramic exchange—particularly trade in Usulután pottery, which is characterized by resist decoration—in the Terminal Preclassic period as far south as Chalchuapa in El Salvador and north into the Maya lowlands (Sharer 1994:101–102).

The two sites, Izapa and Kaminaljuyú, differ dramatically in the events that accompanied the end of their hypothesized *may* seating. As Lowe (1982a:28) notes, one of the most intriguing aspects of Izapa's monument program is how relatively few of the sculptures were damaged over the millennia. Some of them, such as Stela 5, are astonishingly well preserved, suggesting that the scenes they registered continued to be important to myth and history through the Classic and Postclassic periods and into modern times. El Baúl and Tak'alik Ab'aj also have well-preserved monuments.

At Kaminaljuyú, however, monuments were defaced, broken, and buried. Here and at some other Late and Terminal Preclassic sites, such as Tres Zapotes, Chiapa de Corzo, Chinkultic, El Portón, La Lagunita, and Chalchuapa (ibid.), monuments were damaged, sites were abandoned, settlements shifted, and new styles of ceramics began to appear. What do these transformations represent, and what were the causes?

At Kaminaljuyú, hypothesized as a cosmopolitan meeting ground for various ethnolinguistic groups, presumably with competing politico-economic goals, interethnic or factional rivalries might have played a part. David Mora-Marín (2005), for example, posits that the valley of Guatemala was populated by speakers of two Maya languages, Ch'olan (or Ch'olan-Tzeltalan) and Poqom, during the Late and Terminal Preclassic, with Ch'olan speakers having greater political power. Alternatively, the eruption of Ilopango volcano near Chalchuapa might have been considered a sign that the earth spirit was angry and bent on destruction. The desiccation of Kaminaljuyú's lake, and the accompanying decline of the intensive agricultural enterprise it fed, also must have played a critical role. By A.D. 200 the so-called Miraflores sphere of trade and interaction in Pacific piedmont Guatemala and western El Salvador, ostensibly headed by Kaminaljuyú, was permanently disrupted and never returned to its former importance. Along with it, the coastal piedmont writing tradition disappeared (Fahsen and Grube 2005:76), perhaps linked to the in-migration of speakers of K'iche'an languages from the west. There are some arguments (Valdés and Wright 2004:344) that Kaminaljuyú elites migrated to northwestern Honduras and Copán following these K'iche'an incursions.

Why were Izapa's monuments spared and Kaminaljuyú's not? The careful curation of the *Popol Vuh* narration monuments at Izapa suggests that that site long might have been a key pilgrimage site for the Maya or for Mesoamericans in general. Monuments suffered major destruction in only one sector of Izapa, Group F. Kaminaljuyú apparently played a different, and perhaps ultimately controversial, geopolitical role in the highlands. The destruction and site abandonments in this interaction sphere between A.D. 100 and 200 suggest a widespread episode of termination ritual of the sort seen earlier at Olmec sites.

The roughly 250-year periods of regional dominance of Late and Terminal Preclassic sites such as Izapa, Kaminaljuyú, and their satellites suggest the possibility of 256-year, or 260-*tun, may* cycles, one of which would have ended and another begun at a K'atun 8 Ajaw ending in September 179, A.D. (according to the Classic or Tikal calendar). In addition, if, as Mora-Marín (2005) proposes, the valley of Guatemala was populated by speakers of Ch'olan and Poqom, the former having greater political and presumably also ritual power, it is not inconceivable that disagreements vis-à-vis Ch'olan dominance—including a Ch'olan-supported calendar—could have resulted in factionalism and monument destruction.

The Early Maya Lowlands
Origins and Settlements

 The Maya lowlands (Fig. 7.1) are centered on the Yucatán peninsula, incorporating the Mexican states of Yucatán, Quintana Roo, Campeche, and northeastern Chiapas, along with the country of Belize and the northern part of Guatemala known as the Department of El Petén. The lowlands also stretch southeastward to include northwestern Honduras. Geologically, the lowlands are a shelf of limestone interspersed with dolomite and chert and characterized by karst topography: low hills, subsurface drainage, and sinkholes (Yuk. *tz'ono'ot*; Sp. *cenote*). Comparatively little surface water is found in the region, especially in the northern peninsula, where cenotes are common sources of water and the focal point of settlements. To the south and west, however, the region is traversed by the Río Usumacinta and its tributaries (including the Río San Pedro Mártir and Río Pasión), which flow into the Gulf of Mexico. In the east, the Río Hondo, New River, and Belize River drain eastward into the Caribbean Sea. There is a strong rainfall gradient over the lowlands, with highest precipitation in the southeast (southern Belize) and least in the northwest (around Mérida).

ORIGIN MYTHS

The foundation of social, natural, and cosmic order in many societies is reflected in their creation myths. Myths' structures and narratives transmit the "shared knowledge of origins" of a people and establish the core "validity" of events and experiences (Parker Pearson and Richards 1994b:11). The Maya origin myth *Popol Vuh*, generally considered to be late and specific to the highland K'iche' Maya, is discussed in Chapters 1 and 4, but many other Maya creation stories are known (Gossen 2002; Thompson 1970:330–373). Most include similar elements: three or four creations of humans who do not please the gods; destructions by flood; battles between lords of the sky and the Underworld; tales about the sun and the moon; conflicts between early humans and animals; support of the world at its four corners; and the origin of maize. A Yucatán creation story suggests that the first humans were dwarfs who were ultimately turned to stone; each of the first three creations ended with floods (Thompson

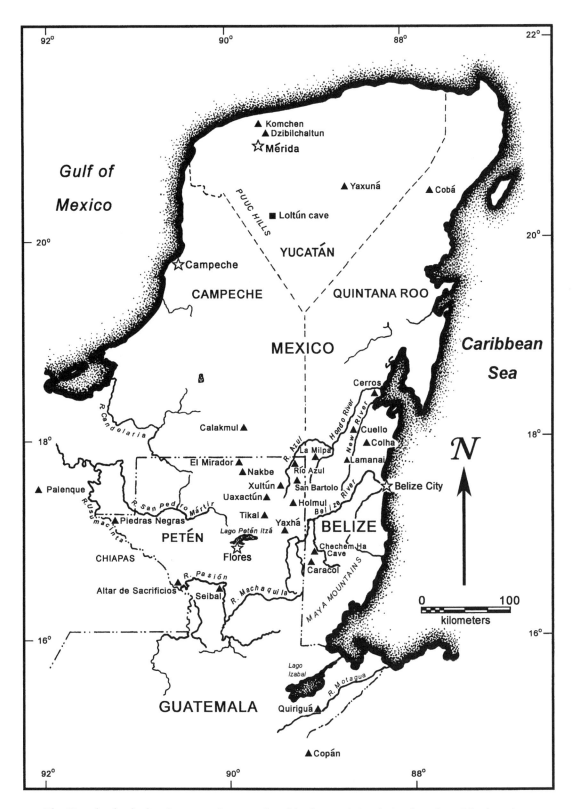

7.1. The Maya lowlands showing some sites mentioned in the text (triangles) and modern cities (stars).

1970:340–342). Another myth reports that the previous creation resulted in "fish-men" (Taube 1986).

In the lowlands, the late books of the *chilam b'alams* provide sketchy and highly syncretistic accounts that parallel some sections of the *Popol Vuh* that describe the origin of the cosmos and of humans. *The Book of Chilam Balam of Chumayel*, for example, includes two creation narratives, "The Creation of the World" and "The Ritual of the Angels" (Roys 1967:98–113; see also Newsome 2001:198–205), also titled "Ceremonial of the B'ak'tun" and "The Sevenfold Creation," respectively (Edmonson 1986:152–168, 228–244). It is evident that the ceremony of *b'ak'tun* completion and renewal, as Edmonson outlines it, is a recitation of Maya creation, ancestry, the setting up of the world directions and trees, competitions among the gods, and so on. The "Ritual of the Angels" describes cosmogenesis in terms of sevens: "Then there were born seven tuns, seven katuns, hanging in the heart of the wind, the seven chosen ones. Then, they say, their seven graces stirred also. Seven also were their holy images" (Roys 1962:98–113).[1]

Unfortunately, nothing approximating these lengthy recent tales dates clearly to the Classic period in the lowlands, but at least three brief Classic-period texts have been deciphered and contribute to our understanding of how the Classic Maya conceptualized cosmic creation (for extended discussion, see Freidel, Schele, and Parker 1993). The extraordinary Stela 1 at Cobá, in northeastern Yucatán, references the creation of the world on the day 4 Ajaw 8 Kumk'u as the speaking of a prophecy (*halah b'ob'a*; see Schele 1992:69; compare with the creation of the world by spoken words in the *Popol Vuh* [Chap. 1 here]). Time's passage since this creation date was calculated by the customary units of thirteen times twenty *tuns* (~years), but carried upward nineteen units beyond the *b'ak'tun* into the billions of years (Fig. 7.2). With regard to origins, however, this calculation may be merely an example of computational virtuosity—the Maya recorded this extraordinarily large number because they *could*—rather than a statement of their view of cosmic history.

Quiriguá Stela C

This same 4 Ajaw date, minus the prefatory calculations, appears on Stela C (Fig. 7.3) at Quiriguá in

7.2. Cobá Stela 1 (drawing by Linda Schele, © David Schele, courtesy Foundation for the Advancement of Mesoamerican Studies, Inc., www.famsi.org).

the Río Motagua valley of eastern Guatemala. This monument, with a dedicatory date on the *hotun* ending 9.17.5.0.0 6 Ajaw 13 Kayab' (December 27, A.D. 775), is one of four monuments placed in front of Structure 1A-3, on the northern end of the long, narrow Great Plaza. It is read first, followed by Stela A to its left and then Zoomorph B, a crocodilian, in front (south) of Stela A dedicated five years later at the *lajuntun* (Looper 2003:158). Stela C's text (Freidel, Schele, and Parker 1993:66–67; Harris and Stearns 1997:153–157;

Looper 2003:158–159) is the Maya's own description of creation as the placement of three stones representing supernatural thrones or platforms:

> On 4 Ajaw 8 Kumk'u the image appeared;
>   three stones were bundled and set.
> Jaguar Paddler and Stingray Paddler planted
>   a stone; it happened at the Five-Sky
>   House (Na Ho Chan) jaguar
>   platform/throne stone (tz'am).
> The Black-House-First-God[?] (Ek' Na Yax[?])
>   planted a stone; it happened at the Earth
>   Place/Large Town[?], the snake
>   platform/throne stone.
> And then Itzamna bundled the stone at the
>   water platform/throne stone.
> Thirteen b'ak'tuns were completed
>   at (Lying-down[?]) Sky, First
>   Three-Stone Place.
> It was supervised by Wak Chan Ajaw
>   ('Six Sky Lord').

This Late Classic text is generally read as describing creation in terms of the bundling, setting, or "planting" of three stones at three places, and of the three gods who placed them. The first is the jaguar throne/platform (Stela C) at First Five-Sky; the second, a snake platform (Stela A) at "Large Town?"; and the third, a water platform (Zoomorph B) at ? Sky, First Three-Stone Place. The deities, respectively, are the Jaguar and Stingray Paddlers, an unknown god (Black-House-First-God), and Itzamna. All of this is related to completion of thirteen b'ak'tuns—a Great Cycle—under the direction of Six Sky Lord. I wonder, given Matthew Looper's interpretation that these three monuments symbolize the Three Stones of Creation, whether the creation event described is actually the ritual of erecting these monuments; the toponyms would refer to names for Quiriguá itself, or places at Quiriguá.

A similar—though more abbreviated as well as eroded—text can be seen on Piedras Negras Altar 1 (Harris and Stearns 1997:158, 160–162). This text appears to reference the 4 Ajaw 8 Kumk'u date, on which an image was made visible by the Paddlers at First Three-Stone Place. The "image" seen at the moment of the setting of these stones might refer to dawn and the Sun God's rise, the momentous event that marked the genesis of the current

7.3. Quiriguá Stela C, showing 13.0.0.0.0 4 Ajaw 8 Kumk'u date (Schele and Freidel 1990:fig. 211) (drawing by Linda Schele, © David Schele, courtesy Foundation for the Advancement of Mesoamerican Studies, Inc., www.famsi.org).

era for the Maya. The altar also mentions the end of nine b'ak'tuns on a day 8 Ajaw 18 Pax, which must fall in a previous Great Cycle (the end of nine b'ak'tuns in the current era falls on a day 8 Ajaw 13 Kej). Reference to the Paddler Gods could be a Late Classic reworking of earlier myths concerning twins.[2]

Freidel, Schele, and Parker (1993:67; see also Taube 1998) identify the three stones of creation as "symbolic prototypes" for the three stones used to create cooking hearths in Maya homes, which are emblematic of the heart of Maya households and the center of life. From the text of Stela C, it seems likely that these three stones also represent the three domains of the Maya universe and their natural symbols or totems (described earlier in this chapter): jaguar/sky, snake/earth, and sea. (This is a bit confusing, however, because Mayanists associate the snake with the sky [the celestial serpent] and the jaguar with the earth/ night.) The three stones also are sometimes interpreted as three stars in a triangular formation in the constellation we call Orion, including one in the belt, in the center of which is the Orion Nebula (Harris and Stearns 1997:163).

Freidel, Schele, and Parker (1993:68–69) call attention to a spectacular Late Classic polychrome vessel painted with images of six gods facing a seventh. The vessel bears the creation date of 4 Ajaw 8 Kumk'u and the text notes that "Black-Is-Its-Center" was put in order. Presumably, this refers to the ordering of a world that was in darkness. While the authors propose that these lords are seated in the heavens, the black background, combined with the traits of the seventh lord, apparently God L, wearing a *muwan* bird headdress and sitting on a jaguar throne "inside a house made of mountain-monsters," would seem to indicate that the scene is cast in a cave in the dark Underworld.

The Palenque Triad

The Late Classic "Cross Group" (Fig. 7.4) at Palenque, Chiapas, was built by ruler K'inich Kan B'alam II, son of and successor to the great K'inich Janab' Pakal I. It consists of three temples arranged as a triadic group, open to the south. The Temple of the Cross is in the north, flanked by the Temple of the Foliated Cross in the east and the smaller Temple of the Sun in the west, facing east toward the rising sun at winter solstice. The buildings were dedicated in A.D. 692 (Martin and Grube 2000:169).

The carved texts on the interiors and exteriors of these buildings describe the birth of three gods

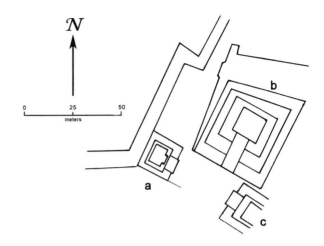

7.4. Palenque "Cross Group": (a) Temple of the Sun; (b) Temple of the Cross; (c) Temple of the Foliated Cross.

known as the Palenque Triad (Table 7.1), their parents, and the descent of Palenque's rulers from these gods. The parents of the Triad, First Father (the Maize God, GI') and First Mother, were born in a previous creation before the August 14, 3114 B.C. genesis of the present universe (Freidel, Schele, and Parker 1993:64–70; Harris and Stearns 1997:141–153; Kerr 1992; Schele and Freidel 1990:245–252. Note the use of a different calendrical correlation coefficient: see the Note on Orthography and Dates). The gods of the Palenque Triad are known as God I, God II, and God III (Berlin 1963; see also Kelley 1965; Lounsbury 1985). The texts also refer to the "Raised-up-Sky Lord," who is mentioned on Quiriguá Stela C.

Some elaboration of the data in Table 7.1 is in order. First Mother is also known as Na Sak or Lady Sak, formerly dubbed "Lady Beastie" by some writers. Seven years after her birth, on 13.0.0.0.0 4 Ajaw 8 Kumk'u (August 11/13, 3114 B.C.), the current creation occurred. The text includes a passage similar to that on Quiriguá's Stela C: "it was made visible, the image at Lying-down-Sky, the First-Three-Stone Place." "Lying-down Sky" (or "Closed Sky") refers to the fact that, as in the *Popol Vuh* narrative, it was still dark, and the sun/light had not been created. The image may be that of a turtle, which is also associated with the Maize God, First Father (Freidel, Schele, and Parker 1993:65). On this same day, an undetermined "deer hoof" event occurred for or by First Father.

TABLE 7.1. *Maya creation events as recorded on Palenque's Cross Group structures*

LONG COUNT DATE		GREGORIAN DATE (B.C.)	EVENT	STRUCTURE
12.18.4.5.1	1 Ajaw 3 Kank'in	3149, May	Itzam Yeh (7 Macaw) defeated (shot from tree)	??
12.19.11.13.0	1 Ajaw 8 Muwan	3122, June 16	Birth of First Father, or GI'	TC
12.19.13.4.0	8 Ajaw 18 Tz'ek	3121, Dec. 7	Birth of First Mother, or Na Sak, Lady Sak	TC
13.0.0.0.0	4 Ajaw 8 Kumk'u	3114, Aug. 11/13	Creation; "Deer Hoof" event for/by GI'	TC
0.0.1.9.2	13 Ik' o Ch'en	3112, Feb. 5	GI' "entered the sky" GI' dedicated Raised-Up Sky Place	TC, TS
1.18.5.3.2	9 Ik' 15 Kej	2360, Oct. 21	Birth of GI	TC
1.18.5.3.6	13 Kimi 19 Kej	2360, Oct. 25	Birth of GIII; arrival at Matawil	TS
1.18.5.4.0	1 Ajaw 13 Mak	2360, Nov. 8	Birth of GII	TFC
2.0.0.0.0	2 Ajaw 3 Wayeb'	2325, Feb. 17	Lady Sak celebrated PE	TFC
???	???	2305, Aug. 13	Lady Sak assumed rule	?

Source: Freidel, Schele, and Parker 1993:64–71; Harris and Stearns 1997:141–153; Schele and Freidel 1990:245–254.

Notes: PE = Period-ending; TC = Temple of the Cross; TS = Temple of the Sun; TFC = Temple of the Foliated Cross. Note that the first three events are dated to a B'ak'tun 12 at the very end of the previous Great Cycle, before the start of the present one at 13.0.0.0.0.

About a year and a half after the creation of the current era, First Father "entered the sky" and prepared or dedicated the Raised-up Sky Place known as 8 House Partition, in the north. In other words, the sky was illuminated. Raised-up Sky is sometimes interpreted as the World Tree or the Milky Way, and 8 House Partition represents the cardinal and intercardinal directions (Freidel, Schele, and Parker 1993:71–75). On October 21, 2360 B.C., God I (or GI) was born to First Mother and First Father, and four days later GIII was born; two weeks after that, GII was born. On February 17, 2325 B.C., First Mother celebrated the *b'ak'tun* ending by autosacrifice and conjuring the gods. A *k'atun* (or twenty years) later, First Mother (Lady Sak) assumed rule at age 815.

God I, the firstborn of the Palenque Triad (Fig. 7.5a; see Schele and Freidel 1990:245, 413–414; Schele and Miller 1986:48–51), has a square eye, a T-shaped or shark's front tooth, a fish fin on his cheek, and a shell earflare, and is associated with Venus and decapitation. Second-born GIII (Fig. 7.5c) is characterized by a jaguar ear, a "cruller" ornament under the eyes and across the nose, and

often a T-shaped tooth; he is typically referred to as the Jaguar God of the Underworld (JGU or JGU/GIII) or the Jaguar Night Sun. GI, whose image appears on Early Classic incense burners, and GIII, whose image is on Late Classic funerary censer stands, often appear together as twins. GII (Fig. 7.5b), the youngest of the Triad, is a zoomorphic deity, typically portrayed with a smoking ax, a mirror, or a cigar, and a human leg transformed into a serpent, that is, the Late Classic Maya manikin scepter, or God K. Frequently identified with K'awil and B'olon Dz'akab', GII is a patron of royal dynasties and associated with bloodletting.

On the Tablet of the Cross, Kan B'alam noted the birth of one U-Kix-Chan on March 11, 993 B.C., and his accession to kingship on March 28, 967 B.C. Schele and Freidel (1990:254) suggest that, given these dates, this individual might have been an Olmec, although in the text he is identified as "divine Palenque lord." Regardless of the specific ethnicity, it is clearly an effort on Kan B'alam's part to situate his ancestry deep in the past. A comparably earlier date appears on the roof comb of the Temple of the Inscriptions (Temple VI)

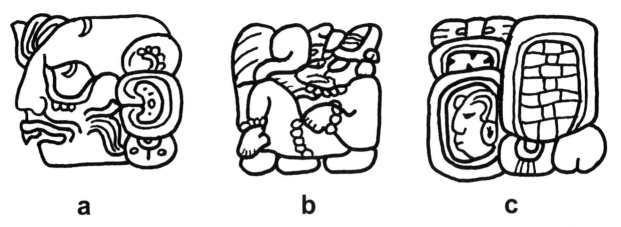

a   **b**   **c**

7.5. The Palenque Triad, from left to right, GI, GII, GIII (drawn from Schele and Miller 1986:fig. 30). Note fish barbels on cheek of GI; GIII is glyphic name.

at Tikal, which mentions the completion of five *b'ak'tuns* (5.0.0.0.0 12 Ajaw 3 Zak, in 1139 B.C.).

The San Bartolo Murals

The spectacular murals at the northeast Petén site of San Bartolo, incompletely studied at the time of this writing, provide additional insights into Maya concepts of creation and rituals surrounding divine kingship. The site of San Bartolo is largely Late Preclassic, although Middle Preclassic construction underlies the buildings, and structures exist in two complexes on an east-west axis. The murals were found in the eastern complex, aptly named Las Pinturas, in a small building at the base of a large, badly looted structure on its east side (Saturno 2006; Saturno, Taube, and Stuart 2005). Style-dated to roughly 100–50 B.C., the brightly painted murals focus on maize and associated symbolism in Maya myth and kingly ritual.

The mural on the north wall (Saturno, Taube, and Stuart 2005) has two scenes in unclear relationship. The left (west) side shows the birth of five babies from a gourd (womb; earth). Although the infants do not have direct color associations, and the theme of birth from a gourd is not a part of known Maya myth, the figures may represent the four cosmic directions and the center (ibid.:12), that is, a quincunx. To the right of this birth scene is a complex depiction of Flower Mountain, with a kneeling woman offering tamales in an unusual painted vase (not a Late Preclassic style). East of the woman, eight anthropomorphic figures ride on

a feathered serpent body with its head to the extreme right. These might be "ancestral couples, the maize god with his mate, and three pairs of young men and women" (ibid.:50).

The thirty-meter-long mural on the west wall has the Maize God, or First Father, as its central figure, appearing seven times. Four individuals—the son or sons of the Maize God—let blood, set up the four World Trees in the cardinal directions, and give offerings of fish, deer, turkey, and flowers (http://www.mesoweb.com/reports/SanBartoloWest.html; accessed September 13, 2006). A great bird perches atop each tree. One fragmentary scene shows the accession of the Maize God, seated on a wooden scaffold, while another scene, accompanied by a hieroglyphic text, shows a human king receiving a headdress: "By acceding to the throne in the company of gods, the mural likely shows the king is claiming the divine right to rule from the gods themselves" (http://www.mesoweb.com/reports/SanBartoloWest.html). The three short columns of glyphs appearing on the murals have not yet been translated, but they include a reference to "star man" (http://www.mesoweb.com/reports/SanBartoloWest.html) and *ajaw* (Sharer and Traxler 2006:263).

Discussion

It is rather surprising that so few known hieroglyphic texts (Stela C at Quiriguá, Stela 1 at Cobá, Altar 1 at Piedras Negras, and the Cross Group at Palenque) discuss the lowland Maya's view of the origins of the cosmos. There is, of course, the likelihood that other texts might have existed but are still buried or have been destroyed; alternatively, such matters may have been deemed more appropriate for exegesis in bark books or even left to oral histories rather than being carved in stone. The Late Classic creation texts provide only a sketchy outline of two fundamental birthings for the Maya—the origins of sacred space and the parturition of the gods—and they display few commonalities with the *Popol Vuh*.

With respect to sacred space, although the three stones or thrones have been interpreted as the prototypical three hearthstones of the Maya household, the three stars of the belt of Orion rose almost due east in ancient times (A. Aveni, pers. com., October 2005), raising the possibility that the three stones mimic the belt stars setting on the horizon (see also Peeler and Winter 1992:42–45). The "stones" of myth might have material referents in the various groupings of three monuments at Formative sites: the possible three markers on Structure D-8 of the early E-Group "observatory" complex at La Venta (and, by extension, on other eastern linear mounds in such complexes); the three aligned stones at Monte Alto and other Pacific coast sites; and the three stone balls at Izapa. If, as I suspect, the widespread Middle Preclassic proto-E-Groups were the earliest architecturally formalized settings for solar-based calendrical rituals (sunrises on solstices and equinoxes), the north-south linear settings of the three marker stones would have carried further cosmic symbolism: the directions of sky and ancestors to the north; the watery Underworld to the south; and the earthly surface in between. The creation texts reference the completion of thirteen *b'ak'-tuns* (the end of the previous era in 3114 B.C.) at Three Stone Place, and the analyses of data from La Venta (Reilly 1999) and Quiriguá (Looper 2003) suggest that all major sites might have had programs of erecting three commemorative monuments. These could have been structures or complexes, such as the Middle Preclassic triadic structures, or the three monuments or, later, edifices erected on the eastern platform of E-Groups from Late Preclassic times onward. Alternatively, the three "throne" stones and their locations may be references to three legendary sites or centers of power known as Five Sky House, Earth Place, and

an unspecified sea (watery Underworld?) place. These could be three geopolitical "capitals" of sorts, or the main towns of three early chiefdoms.

It is significant, in this context, that linguists have noted that the word *tun*, meaning "stone," is very old: it is pre-Proto-Mayan (Justeson and Mathews 1983:587) and so was in the vocabulary prior to 2000 B.C., before the various Mayan language separations. This suggests that the celebration of 360-day year endings by activities involving placement of stones—perhaps used as gnomons or for marking sunrises on solstices, as in later E-Groups—is correspondingly old. It might date to the period when calendrical specialists were attempting to develop more accurate estimations of the solar year. Maya creation myths referencing the setting of stones, then, also reference calendrical creation.

ARCHAEOLOGY: THE EARLIEST LOWLAND SETTLERS AND THEIR LANGUAGES

It is unfortunate that the Paleoindian, Archaic/Preceramic, and Early Formative periods are so poorly known in the Maya lowlands because, absent a fuller understanding of the earliest groups in the area, there is a tendency to oversimplify the region as a vacant, open frontier prior to Middle Preclassic settlement by pottery-making agriculturalists.[3] While it is doubtful that the area was largely uninhabited during the Archaic-Formative transition, there is little hard evidence supporting actual occupation. Most data come from lithics, because pottery was not yet used, leading Harry Iceland (2005) to propose that what is referred to elsewhere in Mesoamerica as the Early Formative should be called "Preceramic" in the Maya lowlands.

Although Gordon Willey (1977:384–385) makes light of the possibility of much settlement before 1000 B.C., Norman Hammond (1986) opines that the Maya lowlands were occupied by agriculturalists by about 3000–2000 B.C., and several archaeological projects in northeastern Belize substantiate his view. Here, as in many areas of the post-Pleistocene world, humans reoriented their settlement and subsistence systems to high-energy (i.e., high-caloric-yield) coastal and aquatic environments. In the Maya lowlands, the shallow coastal shelf of the Yucatán peninsula and other areas would have been inundated by rising sea level prior to 3000 B.C., but archaeological and palynological research in swampy areas of north coastal Belize has yielded evidence of the presence of cultigens (maize, manioc) by around 3500 B.C. (J. Jones 1994). Pollen indicates that, about a millennium later, after 2400 B.C., maize cultivation became common, as did forest disturbance (Pohl et al. 1996:363),[4] and agricultural intensification is evident between 1500 and 1350 B.C. (Pohl et al. 1996:365–366). In the interior of Petén, Guatemala, pollen from sediment cores in Lake Petenxil, south of Lake Petén Itzá, suggests anthropogenic disturbance around 2000 B.C. (Cowgill and Hutchinson 1966). Also, as discussed below, the El Mirador basin farther to the north, characterized by extensive seasonal swamps, or *bajos* (Hansen et al. 2002), exhibits stunning social and architectural precocity. Early cultivation in the lowlands had a wetland focus (Hansen et al. 2002; Pohl et al. 1996:368).

One early explanation for population entry and spread into the interior of the Maya lowlands was the "riverine hypothesis": the earliest migrants moved along the coasts and into the interior along waterways draining into the Gulf of Mexico and the Caribbean Sea (Puleston and Puleston 1971). E. Wyllys Andrews V's (1990) two-pronged model is similar, proposing in-migration from the highlands along eastern and western routes around 1000 B.C., a point that accords well with linguistic reconstructions. Patricia McAnany (2004b:149) sees an analogy with "the colonization of Polynesia by hierarchically organized groups transporting a full suite of domesticates, an elaborated material culture, and a sophisticated cosmology." The general rationale for these hypotheses is that the earliest settlers were swidden agriculturalists, the rivers provided attractive swaths of rich alluvial soil, and the need to move frequently to clear new fields would have led these farmers on a leapfrogging settlement sweep upriver. On the basis of then-available evidence, these hypotheses had considerable validity: some of the earliest settlements known were in the middle valley of the Belize River in the east and in the Río Pasión valley in the west.

Newly discovered palynological evidence for early wetland agriculture, however, demands some rethinking of this proposition. The pollen clearly predates the movements of Mayan-language speakers from the highlands into the lowlands,[5] and it seems unlikely that Early Preclassic cultivators in the highlands, except for the occupants of the valley of Guatemala, would have had (and brought with them) a wetland adaptation. Wetland cultivation seems more closely related to the environment and practices of the Isthmian region, particularly the Gulf coast, although the Belize pollen findings also predate the Olmec florescence. What appears to be indicated is a wide-ranging movement of Early Formative lowland cultivators with an accommodation to wetlands such as coastal, riverine, and swampy environments. The materials found in northeastern Belize are probably only small remnants of far more extensive occupation in these favored zones that have unfortunately been lost to archaeology, as in large parts of the world, by sea-level rise, natural disturbance, and later heavy occupation. The problem remains, though: Who were these early cultivators? How might we give them some sort of identity?

Historical Linguistics

It is worth asking when a distinctive "Maya" identity began to appear in the lowlands, although such questions are notoriously difficult to answer in archaeological contexts. Linguists believe the Mayan language family developed from Proto-Mayan, which was related to Proto-Mixe-Zoquean (PMZ), a language of the Isthmian region. The time of separation of PMZ and Proto-Mayan was once given as forty-seven minimum centuries, or forty-seven hundred years, ago (Swadesh 1969:99–100), but more recent calculations suggest forty-two hundred years (Campbell 2002:56); this, then, would be around 2700–2200 B.C. Because Proto-Mayan has words for plants and animals from both cold/highland and tropical/lowland environments, it is thought that its homeland was in a "highland area not far from the lowlands," specifically, around Soloma in the Cuchumatanes mountains of Huehuetenango in extreme northwestern highland Guatemala (Kaufman 1976:104; see also Campbell 1997:165). This region is a mini "continental divide," as the headwaters of major westward- and northeastward-flowing river systems arise here (Fig. 6.20). Individual Mayan languages would have had their origins during the Early

Formative as a consequence of small groups leaving this homeland and moving downstream along the many rivercourses (Kaufman 1976:104–106), with greater isolation developing among and between populations and the adoption of sedentary lifeways.

The times of these separations (Kaufman 1976) are estimated by glottochronology and are regarded as "no later than" dates at best. But they do indicate that considerable linguistic differentiation began in late Proto-Mayan during the Initial Early Formative period. First, Wastekan split off from Proto-Mayan around 2200 B.C., and the Eastern Mayan languages separated from what was left of Proto-Mayan around 1600 B.C. Then, the separation of the first of the lowland Maya languages, Proto-Yukatekan, occurred around 1400–1000 B.C. (Fig. 7.6), leaving Western Mayan. Around 1000 B.C., Western Mayan divided into Greater Q'anjob'alan and Greater Tzeltalan, existing alongside Proto-Mixe-Zoquean, which began a slow split into two languages (ibid.:106–107; Wichmann 1995). For the next millennium or so, comparatively little language differentiation took place in the Maya area. In the late Late Preclassic, Greater Tzeltalan split into Ch'olan and Tzeltalan, the latter remaining in the highlands and the Ch'olan speakers apparently moving into the southern lowlands. The Middle and Late Preclassic periods, roughly 900 B.C. to A.D. 100, saw considerable interaction between lowland Mayan (Proto-Yukatekan and Greater Tzeltalan) and Proto-Mixe-Zoquean speakers, and many elements of the latter—particularly calendrical terms—were introduced, especially into Ch'olan.[6]

These historical linguistic interpretations need to be evaluated against the palynological data from the lowlands, which suggest the presence of cultivators at least as early as 2000 B.C. and perhaps as far back as 3500 B.C., well predating the development and ingress of Mayan-language speakers. Unfortunately, it is impossible to know if the earliest lowland farmers were descendants of earlier Archaic inhabitants of the region or were later immigrant groups bringing with them cultigens such as maize and manioc. It is also impossible to know what language they spoke, although it has been suggested that the earliest sedentary, pottery-making occupation of both the eastern and the western Maya lowlands might have been

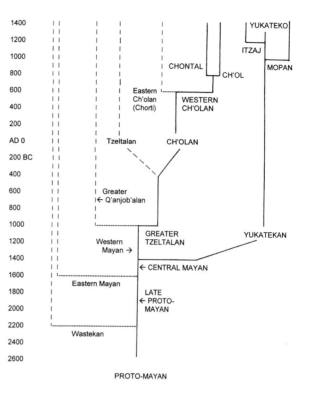

7.6. Linguistic differentiation in Mayan languages through time (Kaufman 1976). Solid lines and capitalized words indicate lowland Maya languages and their predecessors.

Proto-Mixe-Zoquean-speaking. Finally, it cannot be determined if there were appreciable numbers of such early cultivators throughout the lowlands, or if they were few and occupied only small, select niches, such as coastal and riverine wetlands.

Absent such data, it is difficult to characterize the origins of early lowland agriculturalists. If the area was largely unsettled except, perhaps, in coastal wetlands, the early entry of cultivators—speaking an unknown language, but presumably Proto-Mixe-Zoquean or early Proto-Mayan—would appear to conform to the worldwide "farming/language dispersal hypothesis" (Bellwood and Renfrew 2002). More specifically, their entry might be characterized by means of an "initial colonization model" (colonization of previously uninhabited areas or "spread zones"), a process called "demic diffusion" (Cavalli-Sforza 2002; cf. Campbell 2002; also see Table 5.1). However, given the possibility that the area might have been substantially occupied, early and subsequent migrations would argue for a linguistic replacement, or "mosaic" model, of incoming Proto-Yukatekan and Greater Tzeltalan speakers in the lowlands after ca. 1400 B.C.

Irrespective of these models and hypotheses, it is clear that the vocabulary of Yukatekan Maya incorporates a large number of loan words from Mixe-Zoquean (Campbell and Kaufman 1976; Justeson et al. 1985). Many refer to basic traits of the Mesoamerican culture area: cultigens such as beans and squash, maize preparation, and calendrical and ritual items including *may* 'count, divine'. *Tun* 'stone' and 'twin' moved in the opposite direction. It has been suggested that the original name of Tikal—Mutal—might have been the Mixe-Zoquean *mu'ut*, referring to the seasonal swamps that bound the site (Macri 2000). Many loan words reached Mayan languages (Yukatekan and Ch'olan-Tzeltalan) during the Late Preclassic period, between approximately 400 B.C. and A.D. 100 (Justeson et al. 1985:57), which seems unaccountably late. Regardless, it suggests strong and enduring ties between the Maya lowlands and the Isthmian-Pacific coastal region, particularly the sites of Izapa and Kaminaljuyú.[7]

Pottery and Early Maya Ethnicity

Material culture, and particularly pottery, often can shed light on ethnic identity. Although pottery apparently began to be used later in the Maya lowlands than elsewhere in Mesoamerica (see Clark and Gosser 1995), it is ubiquitous from the Middle Preclassic onward. What kind of early pottery reflects a "Maya" ethnolinguistic identity? The pottery that most researchers agree represents the presence of early ethnolinguistic Maya populations is that of the Mamom complex and sphere, characterized by distinctive red, black, and cream slips, sometimes with a waxy tactile quality. Mamom, beginning ca. 700 B.C., is not the earliest pottery in the lowlands, however, and arguments center on disjunction versus continuity between and among the earliest pottery users and those who might be ethnolinguistically Maya.

The earliest pottery in the lowlands is found in northern Belize and is known as the Swasey complex (or phase or sphere). It was initially thought to have begun to be made around 2500 B.C. (Hammond et al. 1979) but has been redated to ca. 1200–1000 cal. B.C. (Andrews and Hammond 1990) and is now recognized as early Middle Preclassic (Kosakowsky and Pring 1998:57) or, better, Late Early Formative. Swasey-like pottery has been found at several sites in northern Belize, including Colha and Cahal Pech, and westward into the Mirador basin of Petén.

Another distinctive early (pre-Mamom) pottery type and group is Jocote Orange-Brown (Garber, Brown, and Hartman 2002; Gifford 1976), found at many sites in the Belize valley and in the eastern lake basins of central Petén. Swasey pottery resembles Mamom pottery in form and slips more than it resembles other Formative ceramics, but clear "Maya"/Mamom identifications are not attested in northern Belize until the López phase, beginning around 700–650 B.C. (Kosakowsky and Pring 1998:57). Andrews and Hammond (1990:580) conclude that Swasey and Mamom ceramics represent different populations with different origins and different times of entry.

In the western lowlands, early (ca. 800 B.C.) pottery is known as the Xe complex (phase, sphere) at Altar de Sacrificios (Richard Adams 1971) and Seibal (Sabloff 1975) and might have had ties to the Isthmian area, either the Veracruz-Tabasco-Chiapas lowlands or the Chiapas-Guatemala highlands.[8] E. Wyllys Andrews V (1990:7) favors a highland relationship and suggests that Xe complex pottery is "not Maya" because the "thin, matte, easily eroded, and powdery slips . . . are dead ringers for Isthmian slips in color, hardness, and dullness of appearance. Xe pastes and slips at Altar [are] . . . indistinguishable from much contemporary pottery in Chiapas." Xe pottery is only weakly comparable to Mamom pottery, suggesting that Mamom replaced Xe rather than evolving out of it (ibid.:10). The Xe ceramic sphere, Andrews concludes, is a product of Mixe-Zoquean speakers.

Joseph Ball and Jennifer Taschek (2003) propose that during the Middle Preclassic period two ethnolinguistic groups, distinguished by differing but coeval full ceramic complexes, coexisted in the Belize valley. One of these (dubbed KXM) is characterized primarily by pottery of the distinctive Jocote Orange-Brown ceramic group and Mars Orange Paste ware, both primarily unslipped and decorated by surface manipulation (fluting, incising, appliqué). KXM is thought to represent household manufacture of domestic and ritual pottery. Comparisons indicate ties to pottery in the Pacific coastal area of El Salvador, and Ball and Taschek propose that this pottery was made by indigenous, local inhabitants of the Belize valley who perhaps spoke Mixe-Zoquean.

The other ceramic group (SBM) displays the distinctive red, cream, and black slips of the Mamom ceramic sphere and is considered to represent "local circulation of exotic vessels produced by non-local [to the Belize valley] Maya potters" (ibid.:195). In fact, these archaeologists believe that the Belize valley was occupied by "two distinct interacting groups competing for ascendancy" and that there was not "a fully and completely continuous 'Maya' occupation of the valley until the *early fifth century A.D.*" (ibid.:210, emphasis added).

Additional data indicating population discontinuities in Belize come from lithic studies, specifically, a discontinuity and lack of shared morphological attributes in projectile point types between the Late Archaic and "Maya" times (Kelly 1993:225): "One can postulate either that the preceramic people were gone before the ceramic-using Maya arrived with an already well-established lithic industry, or that the Maya assimilated and chose not to adopt any of the excellent preceramic lithics" (ibid.). These studies support inferences from palynology indicating an early—that is, late Early Formative, pre-800 B.C.—presence of "non-Maya" pottery-making farmers in the lowlands, at least in its southeastern and southwestern zones. Nonetheless, Harry Iceland (2005) argues that lithic, settlement, and faunal data in northern Belize point to continuities of occupation from Preceramic to Middle Preclassic times by ethnically Maya peoples, and David Cheetham (2005:27) accepts "an indigenous Maya culture horizon preceding Mamom times."

Few of these arguments have taken into account linguistic data, however. As discussed above, Yukatekan was likely heavily influenced by contact with Mixe-Zoquean speakers in the Isthmian region, and inferences about Mixe-Zoquean affiliations of early lowlanders are based on dates around 1000–800 B.C. But it is equally if not more likely that at least some of the early pottery might be the product of early Proto-Yukatekan Mayan speakers. The later migrants and "ceramically 'Maya'" Mamom remains might be those of early speakers of Greater Tzeltalan/Ch'olan.

In sum, the palynological, linguistic, archaeological, ceramic, and lithic evidence suggests the possibility of three or four populations or waves of immigration into the lowlands, resulting in a mosaic of Preclassic ethnolinguistic identities between 1400 and 800 B.C. (see also López Varela 2004:178): (1) unknown numbers of remnant Late Archaic and Early Formative or Preceramic cultivators were in the area, speaking an unknown language; (2) there were likely movements into the lowlands of Early Formative preceramic cultivators, perhaps from the Isthmian region or Pacific coast, who might have spoken Proto-Mixe-Zoquean; (3) in the late Early Formative or early Middle Formative period, groups of pottery-making speakers of early-divergent Proto-Yukatekan entered the lowlands from the highlands; and (4) in the Middle Formative (post-900 B.C.), Greater Tzeltalan (pre-Ch'olan)-speaking groups began moving into the southern lowlands.

ARCHAEOLOGY AND ARCHITECTURE

Remains of early settlements in the lowlands are difficult to locate because Maya towns and cities developed by accretion, with many meters—sometimes spanning nearly two millennia—of superimposed vertically and horizontally expansive construction and occupation overlying those early and often ephemeral living areas. They are usually recovered serendipitously, most commonly as small, thin palimpsests of artifacts in organic soils over bedrock in the very bottom of test excavations through meters of fill, and are read as revealing the earliest settlement or founding of that site. Rarely can large areas of Middle Formative or earlier communities be examined, as they were at K'axob in northern Belize (McAnany 2004a), Nakbe in Petén (Hansen 1991a, 1991b, 2000), and Komchen and Yaxuná in Yucatán (Stanton and Ardren 2005).

Intriguing evidence for early occupation in the lowlands comes from caves. In the Yalahau region of extreme northeastern Yucatán, Middle Preclassic sherds are common on cave floors but are virtually absent at surface sites (Rissolo 2005). Similarly, Chechem Ha cave (Vaca Falls cave) in western Belize began to be used in the Early Preclassic (ca. 1320 cal. B.C.), well before the occupation of surface sites, and activity seemed to focus on removal and stacking of speleothems (Moyes 2004). A miniature uncarved stela, perhaps erected in the Middle Preclassic, stood surrounded by stones in a large "cathedral"-like chamber at the end of the long cave and tunnel system (H. Moyes, pers. com., January 26, 2005). Caves were often the location for Early Formative ossuaries, particularly in the southeastern Maya zone, including Copán (Scott and Brady 2005). In southeastern Petén during the Late Preclassic period, bodies—perhaps of revered ancestors—were placed in walled-in alcoves in caves, but as these were easily desecrated, the practice was discontinued in the Classic, when royal tombs in pyramidal structures constituted "caves" in "mountains" (Garza, Brady, and Christensen 2002). The differences between materials in caves and in surface sites suggest that caves might have been pilgrimage destinations.

An overview of archaeologically derived estimates of population histories in the lowlands (Rice and Culbert 1990:table 1.4) reveals that, except for Becan, all included sites or areas had Middle Preclassic occupation.[9] Mounting evidence for late Early Preclassic occupation dating before 900 B.C. comes from Caracol (D. Chase 1990:211, table 10.1), Copán (Fash 1991:67–70), and sites in northern Belize and the Mirador basin of Petén with Swasey pottery, including Cuello (Kosakowski and Pring 1998), Blackman Eddy (Brown and Garber 2005), and Nakbe (Forsyth 1993). These late Early Preclassic and early Middle Preclassic occupations evince very low population densities, typically less than 10 percent of a theoretical maximum (Rice and Culbert 1990:22). Occupation in the full Middle Preclassic, identified by Mamom pottery, was more extensive and of somewhat higher density, up to 20 percent of maximum (ibid.). Preclassic domestic constructions are not well known, but Cuello may have the earliest dated structure in the lowlands, around 1000 B.C. Its apsidal form reflects similar constructions elsewhere in Belize (K'axob, Blackman Eddy), Yucatán (Yaxuná), and in the Isthmian region, as at Paso de la Amada.

Interestingly, work in northern Belize now demonstrates "the antiquity of formal settlements [and public architecture] that is stratigraphically and chronologically comparable to the Olmec apogee in the Middle Formative period" (Hansen 2005:55). Connections between the early Maya lowlands and the Isthmian region also can be seen in site plans and architecture of early civic-ceremonial centers, such as a north-south linear layout, a "ceremonial court" complex, an E-Group "observatory complex," and placement of burials of important leaders as well as offerings in the north, home of the ancestors (Grove 1999). Middle Preclassic lowland Maya urban planning assuredly had cosmological referents at its base.

Site Plans and Orientations

In western Belize, the site of Blackman Eddy yielded considerable evidence of Middle Preclassic settlement (M. Brown 1997; Brown and Garber 2005). The site has two main structural complexes, A and B, on a north-south axis oriented 8° west of north. Plaza A has a ballcourt and an E-Group. In Plaza B, Structure B1-5th displays a triadic arrangement, and the succeeding Structure, B1-4th, dated 800–415 cal. B.C., has an early example of the façade masks common in the Late Preclassic. The mask was burned and destroyed at some point, which has been interpreted as "desecratory termination events related to warfare" (Brown and Garber 2003:102). Below the Middle Preclassic construction, an Early Preclassic deposit of lithics, shell, and carbon, dated 1395–1015 cal. B.C., has been interpreted as termination ritual along the lines of the burning of the "wooden people" in the *Popol Vuh.*

Because of the difficulty of uncovering substantial late Early Preclassic or Middle Preclassic settlement at lowland sites, their overall layouts are rarely known. Eric von Euw and Ian Graham's (1984) map of Uaxactún, in Petén, suggests a site plan not too dissimilar from that of La Venta: a north-south orientation with significant architectural complexes at the northern and southern ends of a causeway. Group H (see Fig. 5.4b) mimics the ceremonial court at La Venta but is rotated 90° onto an east-west axis: three small structures in a north-south line in the east oppose a large, tiered pyramid in the west, with linear platforms bounding the north and south sides of this plaza.

By the Late Preclassic period at Izapa and in the Maya lowlands, the early north-south focus had diminished, replaced by increasing emphasis on the east-west axis and four or more (rather than three) buildings oriented to the cardinal directions around an open plaza. In Petén, this is most dramatically seen in the El Mirador basin at the Middle Preclassic site of Nakbe and later at El Mirador (Hansen and Guenter 2005:60), both of which have distinct eastern and western sectors.

Why was there this early Mesoamerican stress on north and a north-south axis, and why, in the Maya lowlands, was it replaced by (or why was there created) an emphasis on east-west directionality and quadripartition?[10] As discussed earlier, north in Mesoamerica relates not only to magnetic north but also to "up" and the sun at zenith, and the solar zenith was an early orientation point for time reckoning as it related to changing of settlement with changing seasons. In addition, in the *Popol Vuh*, when Seven Macaw dies he rises to become the seven stars of the asterism we recognize as the Big Dipper and resides in the north.[11] Seven Macaw was a "false sun" and therefore could not occupy a position in the east, home of the true sun.

The two distal stars of the Big Dipper's bowl point to Polaris, currently identified as the North or Pole Star, but in the Early Formative period Polaris was not that indicator. Beginning a few centuries before 2000 B.C., Thuban (Alpha Draconis, in the tail of the dragon constellation Draco) would have been the North Star, and it would have been seen in a line with the two proximal stars of the Big Dipper's bowl. Any association of the Big Dipper and Thuban as North Star would have been lost by 1000 B.C., as the path of the north celestial pole moved slowly counterclockwise (see http://www.astro.wisc.edu/~dolan/constellations/constellations/Ursa_Minor.html; accessed September 14, 2006). Perhaps the decline in importance of north in site layouts (and also the mythological death of Seven Macaw) registers ancient Mesoamericans' recognition of the disappearance of a clear relationship between Seven Macaw (the Big Dipper) and a relatively unmoving star marking north. After the death of Seven Macaw, his sons Zipacna and Cabracan were defeated and rose to take positions in the eastern and western sky. This portion of the *Popol Vuh* myth might be an allegory for the beginnings of the east-west orientation of earthly structures. Indeed, Seven Macaw and his sons occupy places in the northern, eastern, and western sky, a

triangulation echoed by Middle Preclassic triadic architectural arrangements open to the south.

The north-south linear layout can be read either as a lack of attention to solar positions—sunrises and sunsets—or as a dual stress on them, reflected by bilateral symmetry on either side of the axis. The east-west layout, on the other hand, suggests an explicit solar emphasis and, given the florescence of early or prototype E-Groups, it appears that east and solstitial sunrises became the focal orientation. Both the Calendar Round and the Long Count were tallies of the passage of *k'ins*, that is, days or suns. It is likely that, with such increasing emphasis, the sun's daily and seasonal transits came to take on a directive role not only in calendrics but in cosmogony and the re-creation of the cosmos in the sacred landscapes of monumental architecture. In addition to the east being where the sun rises or is reborn every morning, it was the locus of many other phenomena of interest to Mesoamericans: the rising of the moon; the appearance of Venus as morning star; and the direction from which the rains of the rainy season move. North (up) is the home of the ancestors, but east is where all the action is, figuratively speaking. East is the birthplace of cosmic order and therefore, as we shall see, a focus for propitiatory rites and sacred ceremony connected to social order and kingly legitimacy.

Returning to the issue of the identity of the Maya lowlands' early inhabitants, it is tempting to suggest that the north-south axis (and the distinctive 8° west-of-north orientation of Blackman Eddy, like that of La Venta) was particularly associated with early Proto-Mixe-Zoquean speakers in the area, and the later east-west axis with later Maya (Yukatekan or Ch'olan/Greater Tzeltalan) speakers.

Preclassic Structural Complexes

Several distinctive structural complexes found at Middle Preclassic sites in the lowland Maya area are shared with the Isthmian area—E-Groups, triadic structures, and ballcourts—and, like those to the west, they are material representations of an elite ideology underpinning legitimacy, wealth, and power.

The so-called E-Group observatory complex is a distinctive and perduring architectural arrangement in the Maya lowlands. Named after the structural group mapped in Uaxactún's Group E (Ricketson 1928), it also has been called a Commemorative Astronomical Complex (CAC) and Complejo de Ritual Público (CRP). Typically located in civic-ceremonial site cores, E-Groups consist of two platforms opposite each other on the east and west sides of a plaza (Fig. 7.7). The eastern platform is linear and has, in its late form, three structures: one on the north end, one in the center, and one on the south end. The western platform, square in plan and ultimately with stairways on all four sides (a "radial" structure, thought to be associated with rituals in the solar/agricultural calendar; Cohodas 1980), sits on the transverse centerline of the eastern structure. Preclassic and Early Classic E-Groups are found at

sites throughout Petén and Belize, and in some areas (Calakmul [Folan et al. 1995]; Mopan [Laporte 2004]) they continued to be used in the Late and Terminal Classic (see Aimers and Rice 2006).

Perhaps the earliest examples of E-Groups in the Maya lowlands are those dating to the late Middle Preclassic, ca. 600–400 B.C., at Tikal, Nakbe, and Güiro/Wakna (Hansen 1998:66, 70; idem 2005:63), and Kanajau near Holmul (Fialko 2005). In the Mundo Perdido complex at Tikal, the first stage of construction consisted of a small western platform opposite a linear mound with a north-south axis (Laporte and Fialko 1990, 1995). The western platform may be rectangular, and it appears that in the earliest examples of these complexes the western structures were variable in plan (the one at La Venta may be circular, for example). At Nakbe, the early E-Group comprises Structures

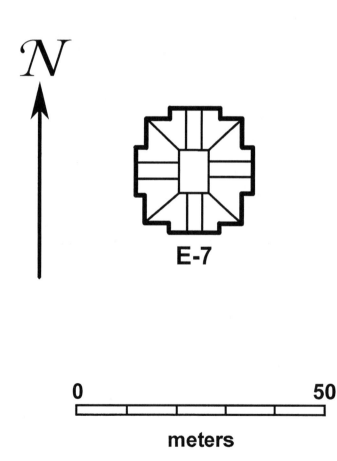

E-7

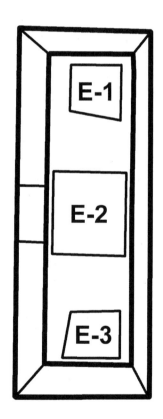

0   50

meters

7.7. The E-Group "observatory" complex at Uaxactún.

47–52. Structure 51 is the long, north-south platform on the east side of the complex, with a building on its center and south end; apparently, nothing was built on the north end of Structure 51, suggesting that it might be unfinished (or that summer-solstice sunrise was not important to commemorate). Structure 52 is a low platform in the plaza on the front (west) centerline of Structure 51; Stela 1 was found on Structure 52, and a large carved altar was sealed below a Mamom floor. The E-Group at nearby Güiro/Wakna is extraordinarily large, with the eastern structure more than two hundred meters long and ten meters high and the western structure thirty meters high (Hansen 1998:66).

At the E-Group at Cival in Petén, an unusual quincunx cache of jade and pottery was placed on the centerline at the base of the eastern structure (Bauer 2005:29; Estrada-Belli 2004:5). Dating sometime before 350 B.C. and dedicating the earliest phase of construction, the cache was found in a tiered, *k'an* cross-shaped pit excavated into limestone bedrock. In the central, deepest, part of the pit, four jade celts were set on end, one at each of the four directions plus one in the center, and pots were placed in the four arms of the cross. The whole was covered with a plaster cap and then a posthole was cut into its center. The excavators interpret the posthole as where a post would have been placed as a World Tree; such a World Tree post might also have served as a gnomon. A Late Preclassic monument was also found in this complex.

Later lowland E-Groups have been interpreted as "observatories" because, for an east-facing observer on the western platform, the sun appears to rise over the northern structure on the summer solstice, over the central structure on the equinoxes, and over the southern platform on the winter solstice. Studies of alignments on reconstructed structures indicate that such observatory functions were imprecise and largely commemorative (Aimers 1993; Aimers and Rice 2006; Aveni, Dowd, and Vining 2003). However, at the time of the arrangement's inception, around 600 B.C. or earlier, it might have had actual solar observatory functions. Stone columns or wooden poles (later elaborated into entire structures) on the eastern linear mound would have corresponded to the different points of the sun's journey back and forth along the eastern horizon from solstice to solstice, and/or as points for backsighting to sunset over a single marker on the western building. Aveni, Dowd, and Vining (2003) believe the complexes were dedicated to zenith observations rather than solstices. Regardless of the phenomenon observed, Middle Preclassic calendar priests might have maintained a ritual like that of twentieth-century daykeepers in Momostenango, highland Guatemala, who observe the positions of the rising and setting sun at twenty-day intervals on each yearbearer day in order to anticipate the zenith (B. Tedlock 1992c:33).

Middle Preclassic structure-pair precursors of E-Group complexes occur widely: in the Isthmian region at La Venta (Structures D-1 and D-8) and at thirteen or more sites in Chiapas dating to 600–450 B.C. (Lee 1989:207, 225); at Tlalancaleca in Puebla, Mexico (García Cook 1981:251); and at six sites in the Valley of Guatemala (Valdés 1997). It is apparent from this broad distribution that (1) formal architectural materialization of solar-solstitial positions came into use around 600–500 B.C. as a critical component of rulers' demonstrating their legitimacy to rule through "control" of the sun's movements; and (2) the complex probably existed at many other sites but is covered by later construction. These complexes are clear demonstrations of the changed cosmic reorientation from emphasis on the north to one on the east and support the notion of the development of a solar "cult" of some sort that dominated chiefly or kingly authority and celebrations of social and cosmic order.

Although not a Preclassic complex, the Late Classic Quincunx site in the hinterland of La Milpa, in northern Belize, reveals another architectural pattern with observatory functions: a quincunx arrangement of five low platforms with a central gnomon. The central structure at Quincunx had a posthole in the center, a post not likely to be a roof support and a feature that survived a series of Late Classic reflooring episodes (Zaro and Lohse 2005). The shadow of a stadia rod (a gnomon) set into this posthole fell across a large stone in the southwestern platform on the summer-solstice sunrise; perhaps other markers of stone or perishable materials sat on the other platforms but did not survive bulldozing operations. The antiquity of this arrangement is unknown.[12]

Triadic architecture (Hansen 1990:171; idem 1998:77–78; idem 2000:59) consists of three structures: a dominant pyramid, often embellished with masks, flanked by two smaller inward-facing buildings. The arrangements are typically found on the south side of a plaza or face south (although not at Middle Preclassic Nakbe, where it faces east); Hansen links this orientation (1990:171) to the "symbolic direction of the solar nadir." This orientation suggests continuing but diminished emphasis on a north/south axis, or on the direction of north. Triadic groupings are particularly common at Late Preclassic lowland Maya sites, including El Mirador (fifteen), Nakbe, Uaxactún, Cerros, Lamanai (Hansen 1998:78, 80), and Dzibilchaltun, as well as in the highlands (e.g., Chiapa de Corzo). The triadic arrangement is also seen in the main structures of the North Acropolis at Tikal, facing south into the Main Plaza and it continues into the Late Classic period. The temples of the Cross Group at Palenque represent a triadic group.

A distinctive architectural embellishment on the façades of Preclassic buildings is the stuccoed and painted deity mask. These occur on structures in triadic groups, for example, at Nakbe (Martínez Hidalgo and Hansen 1992) and El Mirador, and on the western structure of E-Groups, as at Uaxactún Structure E-VII-sub. The masks typically represent zoomorphic creatures' faces, variously, jaguars and avians. On Late Preclassic Structure 5C-2nd at Cerros, in northern Belize, the masks, as blunt-snouted and long-snouted zoomorphs with large ear ornaments, flank the south-facing stairway (Fig. 7.8). They were originally interpreted (Freidel and Schele 1988a, 1988b; Schele and Freidel 1990) in terms of solar cycling and the apotheosis of the Hero Twins of the *Popol Vuh*: the masks on the lower tier were believed to represent the Jaguar Sun, rising on the east and setting on the west, while those on the upper tier represented Venus as morning star (east) and evening star (west). David Freidel (2005) now interprets them as the bundled bones of the Maize God and his twin brother, One (or Hun) Hunahpu and Seven Hunahpu, with the upper gods representing Itzamna and Chaak. Similar masks appear on the western building of Uaxactún's E-Group, while at Tikal two jaguar masks were placed on the center structure of the three buildings on the eastern platform.

Ballcourts were arenas for playing the Meso-american ballgame (see Scarborough and Wilcox 1991). Simple ballcourts consist of two parallel, elongate platforms separated by an open area, the alley or court of play. More complex courts had enclosed "end zones" and, frequently, temple complexes at or on the platforms. The playing court could have vertical or sloping sides and could be elaborated with stone sculptures set into the walls or into the floor of the playing alley and relief-sculpted scenes along the walls; the temples, if any, also could be similarly elaborated. There is a weak tendency for ballcourts to be located near E-Groups (Aimers 1993).

As noted earlier, cleared spaces at Archaic sites might have been used as dance grounds or as areas for an early version of the ballgame, but it is impossible to verify those activities. The earliest known formal ballcourt is at Paso de la Amada, dating approximately 1400 B.C.; otherwise, formal courts are not known until the Middle Preclassic period, when they are components of initial monumental architecture at civic-ceremonial centers. In the Maya lowlands, a Middle Preclassic ballcourt exists at Nakbe (Hansen 1998:74; idem 2000:55), and twenty-five Middle and Late Preclassic courts have been identified in the northwestern Yucatán peninsula (A. Andrews, pers. com., August 14, 2002). Numerous ballcourts are found in the Isthmian-Pacific coastal region, including a Middle Preclassic court at Tak'alik Ab'aj (Schieber de Lavarreda 1994), in the middle Grijalva valley (Lee 1989), and possibly at San Lorenzo (Coe and Diehl 1980, 1:29, 62, 388). Ballplayers, identified by details of costuming, play a prominent role in Olmec iconography.

Ballcourts and the ballgame are of central importance in the *Popol Vuh*, where key events occur in the context of games on earth (the Twins angering the Underworld Lords) and in the court of the Underworld. The ballgame is variously seen as the interplay between the Third and Fourth Creations (Schele and Mathews 1998:207), the sun's entrance into the Underworld (Pasztory 1972), and a ritual carried out "on the equinoxes to represent the battle of celestial and terrestrial forces" (Cohodas 1975:110). Some Late Classic versions of the ballgame may have been played in two different settings, the first with a real ball in a

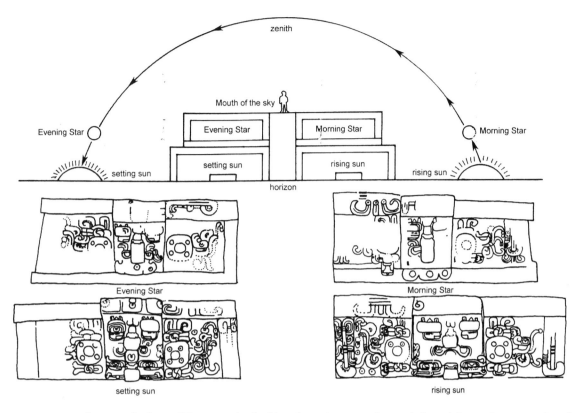

7.8. Reconstruction drawing of solar and Venus masks flanking the stairway on the south face of Cerros Structure 5C-2nd (Schele and Freidel 1990:fig. 3.12). Note Izapa-like framing devices in panels above the earflares (drawing by Linda Schele, © David Schele, courtesy Foundation for the Advancement of Mesoamerican Studies, Inc., www.famsi.org).

formal court and the second on the steps of a temple-pyramid and using the trussed and/or beheaded loser of the game, or his head, as a ball (Miller and Houston 1987; P. Rice 2004:253–256). In any case, sacrifice at the game's conclusion is a salient theme, echoing the events of the *Popol Vuh.*

Some Middle Preclassic Lowland Regions and Sites

Reviewing all archaeological evidence for Middle Preclassic occupation in the Maya lowlands is beyond the scope of this work. Instead, a few examples are briefly highlighted to explore their contributions to the role of calendrics (order) and kingship (wealth and legitimacy).

The Mirador Basin

The Mirador "basin" in northern Petén, adjacent to the border with Mexico, is characterized by large *bajos,* fifty to one hundred square kilometers or more in size, that were probably once wetlands, but no permanent water supplies exist (Hansen et al. 2002:274–278). Despite this seemingly inauspicious environment, numerous sites have impressive Middle and Late Preclassic construction.

Nakbe (Fig. 7.9) is a sizeable Middle Preclassic site with its two main structural complexes on an east-west axis. Radiocarbon dates suggest that occupation may have begun around 1400–1000 B.C., with stone constructions two or three centuries later (Hansen 1998:55–56; Hansen and Guenter 2005). The site has temples eighteen meters high, triadic structures, causeways (including one joining El Mirador, thirteen kilometers distant), and a small ballcourt (Hansen 1998:74, 75). A large mask on one platform façade appears to represent the head of the avian later known as the Principal Bird Deity. The eastern portion of Nakbe has an E-Group, with Stela 1 (Fig. 7.10) on the low western platform (Structure 52). This monument, broken into some forty-five pieces but reconstructed photographically, shows two extravagantly attired standing individuals, perhaps ballplayers,[13] facing each other and gesturing; the right-hand figure wears a Maize God mask (Hansen and Guenter 2005:60). Nakbe had little occupation after its Middle Preclassic florescence. During the Late Classic period, the site was a source of production of the famous "Codex-style" polychrome pottery (Hansen, Bishop, and Fahsen 1991; Reents-Budet 1994).

The nearby site of El Mirador succeeded Nakbe as a major Late Preclassic center in the Mirador basin, with a "massive construction period" from the second century B.C. to about A.D. 100; by A.D. 150 the site was abandoned (Matheny 2001). Like Nakbe, El Mirador has a primary east-west axis, with the Tigre pyramid on the west joined by a causeway to the Danta pyramid some eight hundred meters to the east, an arrangement Ray Matheny (ibid.:473) calls a "cosmological orientation to honor the rising and setting sun." The site is stunning in size, with pyramids as high as seventy meters, a sacred precinct more than three kilometers long, reservoirs, causeways to satellite sites, and a wall around the west precinct (Matheny 1986:332). The Tigre complex, which

covers some fifty-eight thousand square meters, is dominated by a fifty-five-meter-high pyramid, stucco masks, and triadic structural arrangements (Hansen 1990). An early Late Preclassic pottery fragment recovered at El Mirador bears a possible incised *Ajaw* glyph (Justeson, Harmon, and Hammond 1988:97n2; also Stone 1989:322).

Thirteen stelae, twelve plain and one carved, were found in the West Group, an E-Group (Matheny 1986). The carved stela, Monument 18 (Fig. 7.11), broken into many pieces, lay in the south part of the complex at a small mound on top of the encircling wall (Chambers and Hansen 1996). Relief carving appears in three registers: the upper register portrays a downward-gazing head in profile, a motif that continues on Petén monuments into the Terminal Classic period (P. Rice 2004:151–167); the lower register shows two profiled quasi-reptilian heads. The central register is carved in a different style that suggests it could be a later modification of the monument; it might depict a Tlaloc-like figure or a jaguar (god of the Underworld). Another monument at El Mirador, Stela 2 (Fig. 7.12), possibly dating to the early first century B.C., has a standing figure on one face and, on the other, a long-nosed monster figure with a skeletal jaw similar to those on Kaminaljuyú

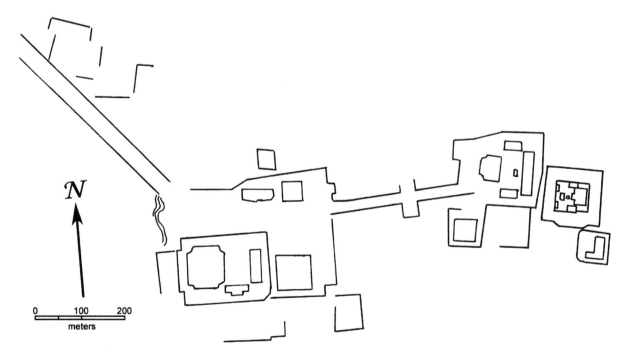

7.9. The site of Nakbe, Petén, showing major platforms, structure complexes, and causeways.

7.10. Nakbe Stela 1 (drawn from Sharer and Traxler 2006:213)

7.11. El Mirador Monument 18, recovered in the site's E-Group (drawn from Chambers and Hansen 1996:fig. 7).

monuments (L. Parsons 1986:78). Stela 1 at the nearby site of Isla depicts the upturned snout of a saurian (Hansen 2005:fig. 5.9).

Aftcr its abandonment, El Mirador apparently experienced some special-purpose reuse during the Early Classic, as thin stucco floors, ritually broken pottery, and green obsidian (from central Mexico) were found on the centerline of the Tigre pyramid and the Central Acropolis. The broken stela and pottery suggest some kind of termination ritual. The original name of the Nakbe–El Mirador polity may have been Chatan Winik (Sharer and Traxler 2006:262–263, citing Grube). This toponym appears with twelve others on Late Classic Altar 3 from the site of Altar de los Reyes in southern

Campeche, which lists thirteen dynastic capitals. Robert Sharer and Loa Traxler (ibid.) consider this polity to be the first lowland Maya state.

Burials: Northern Belize and Copán, Honduras

Additional data on early Middle through Late Preclassic occupation in the lowlands come from burials (Joyce 1999; Joyce and Grove 1999). The site of Cuello, in northern Belize, had a Middle Preclassic population estimated at about five hundred (Hammond 1999:50), and twenty-seven individuals in twenty-three graves dating to the Swasey (1150–900 B.C.) and Bladen phases

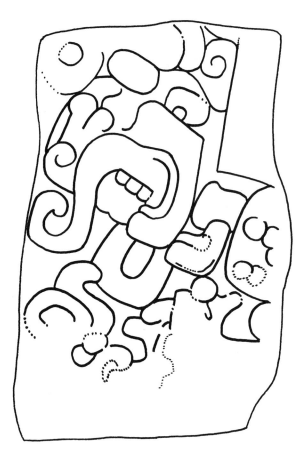

7.12. El Mirador Stela 2 (drawn from L. Parsons 1986:fig. 186). The upper portion shows a long-snouted creature with a fleshless jaw in profile, facing toward the lower right.

(900–650 B.C.) were excavated there. The earliest graves were oriented with head to the north and included skeletons in both flexed and extended positions; grave goods were lacking (Hammond, Clarke, and Donaghey 1995:127). However, mortuary furniture, including pottery vessels; a ceramic bird whistle; jade (some blue), greenstone, and shell jewelry; and tools of chert and ground stone began to be deposited with burials after 900 B.C. (Hammond 1995:50). The remains included all ages and sexes in domestic platforms, suggesting that they were probably family burials, with ancestor veneration beginning around 600 B.C. (ibid.:59; idem 1999:62–63, 64). Furthermore, the lack of age and sex differences in Middle Preclassic burial goods ("wealth") suggests the possibility that "ascribed status may well have existed before 700 B.C." (Hammond 1995:59). Similarly, McAnany

(2001:132) concludes from early burial data that Middle Preclassic settlements in the Maya lowlands were not egalitarian villages but, instead, had a "strongly entrenched" emphasis on descent from an apical ancestor. For example, some males were buried in a seated position at Preclassic Cuello (Hammond 1999:52) and K'axob (McAnany, Storey, and Lockard 1999; also in the late Early Formative in Oaxaca [Marcus 1999:73]); perhaps these were individuals venerated as ancestors (Joyce and Grove 1999:6). As burials became more embellished, "deceased village leaders who were destined to become ancestors may have begun to merge with supernaturals" (McAnany 2001:133).

A complementary picture of the Middle Preclassic emerges from excavations at Copán in northwestern Honduras (Fash 1991:67–70; Hall and Viel 2004). The earliest architecture at the site, discovered under the Acropolis, consists of earth and cobbles and appears to be related to a "general southeastern Maya tradition" evident at Kaminaljuyú and Chalchuapa (Sharer 2003:332, 347). Excavations in Group 9N-8 in the Las Sepulturas area of bottomland settlement, east of the ceremonial center ruins, yielded Early and Middle Preclassic remains of construction as well as burials. A probable house built of perishable materials dated to the late Early Preclassic Rayo phase (1300–900 B.C.) and contained domestic artifacts, including grinding stones, pottery, flint and obsidian tools, mammal bones, and figurines (Fash 1991:65–66). The pottery was similar to ceramics of the Pacific coast and adjacent highland regions, leading to suggestions that the earliest populations might have been Mixe-Zoquean (Clark, Hansen, and Pérez S. 2000; Viel and Hall 2000) or possibly Proto-Mixean (Justeson et al. 1985:5) speakers, rather than Mayan. Passages in the *Popol Vuh* suggest that Copán may have been an important ancestral place of Mixe-Zoque speakers (D. Tedlock 1996:45–47).

In the Middle Preclassic Uir phase (900–400 B.C.), two rectangular platforms were constructed on a north-south axis near the early Rayo-phase house. Poorly preserved subfloor burials were found in each platform, fifteen in the south platform and thirty-two in the north, suggesting that these platforms supported residences constructed of perishable materials (Fash 1991:

67–71). Differences were noted between the burials of the south platform and the north. For example, burials in the south were in stone-lined cists, and pottery decoration (Fig. 7.13) included the so-called paw-wing motif associated with Formative pottery in the Gulf coast and Mexican highlands. Burials under the north platform lacked cists, and pottery was decorated with the flame-eyebrow motif (Fig. 7.13a). In addition, jade was found with northern burials but with only one individual in the south. One of the northern burials, VIII-27, was accompanied by four pots, nine stone celts, and more than three hundred jades, including drilled beads and jaguar-claw effigies; two children's skulls lay under the deposit of jades. Because of the poor condition of the bones, it was not possible to gather reliable age and sex data, but the pottery motifs might indicate lineage or other affiliations as noted at Formative San José Mogote in Oaxaca (Pyne 1976) and, albeit differently, at Tlatilco in the basin of Mexico (Tolstoy 1989).

The total areal extent of Middle Preclassic Uir-phase occupation and construction at Copán is unknown because of heavy Classic-period construction above. Nonetheless, the north-south directional orientation of the two platforms is of interest, as it is characteristic of Middle Preclassic

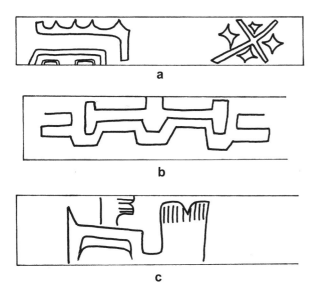

7.13. Motifs on pottery from Middle Formative burials at Copán (drawn from Schele and Miller 1986:119, pl. 30) (a) (flame-eyebrow) and (b) motif from northern burials; (c) possibly a fish or a fish tail, from southern burials.

sites in the Isthmian region. This plus the presence of "Olmec"-style motifs on the pottery suggest a strong influence—and probable Mixe-Zoquean affiliations—in this southeastern region of the Maya lowlands. Such affiliations continued through the Late Preclassic period, with earthen architecture similar to that of Kaminaljuyú, Chalchuapa, and other sites in the highlands and Pacific region (Traxler 2004:58). Retrospective dates at Copán reference the years 321 B.C., A.D. 159, and A.D. 160, all in the Preclassic, but it is not known to whom or to what they refer (Marcus 2004:368).

ARCHAEOLOGY AND EXCHANGE

The presence of nonlocal material goods greatly supplements linguistic and architectural data in providing evidence of interactions between groups speaking varied languages during the Early and Middle Preclassic periods. It also, as Baines and Yoffee (1998:213, 253) note, reinforces the special status of elites in terms of their access to and mobilization of wealth vis-à-vis external groups. Reilly (2005:36) refers to the widely shared ritual objects and ideological concepts, including the materialization of cosmology, as a Middle Formative Ceremonial Complex; similarly, Blanton and colleagues (1996:8) refer to the broad adoption of this Formative artistic-symbolic tradition as an "international style." Long-distance exchange itself confers special status on its participants because they have ventured among "places and people that are increasingly 'different' and, therefore . . . increasingly supernatural, mythical, and powerful" (Helms 1988:4). Returning traders bring back both esoteric knowledge and exotic goods, goods that arc infuscd with thc power of those outsiders who produced them (Helms 1988, 1993). The paths by which these goods moved throughout Preclassic Mesoamerica are not certain, although one might suspect that coastal and/or riverine routes—very likely the same ones used by early Mayan-speaking migrants into the lowlands—would have been involved.

Obsidian provides the most direct evidence of such interactions of lowlanders with outsiders, as well as insights into emerging economic specializations, because this volcanic glass can be traced to its original outcrops or source flows through precise chemical compositional analyses. Blake and colleagues (1995:165–166) indicate that trade in obsidian seems to have begun in the Late Archaic period, while Clark (1987:278–281) suggests that by Middle Formative times Mesoamerican obsidian knappers had formalized core-and-blade production, which hints at some level of consolidated political power. Obsidian is found in the volcanic highlands of Chiapas and Guatemala, as well as in central Mexico, areas where non-Maya languages predominated in the Formative. Four non-Mexican sources are known (Fig. 6.20): Tajumulco (near the Chiapas-Guatemala border); San Martín Jilotepeque (or Río Pixcayá) and El Chayal (northwest and northeast of Kaminaljuyú, respectively); and Ixtepeque (eastern Guatemala, near Copán). Different sources predominated in different areas at different times,[14] indicating complex (but poorly known) trading relationships.

Jade or jadeite was widely valued in Mesoamerica, especially among the Maya. Although sources of jadeite have been hypothesized in Guerrero, Mexico, and in Costa Rica, the best known—and perhaps the only—source of jadeite in Mesoamerica is at Matzanal in the metamorphic region of the Río Motagua valley in eastern Guatemala (Pohorilenko 1996). Although jade has been recovered from Early Formative contexts, it is far more common in the Middle Preclassic, as exemplified by the quantities recovered in burials at La Venta and Copán. The difficulty of cutting and polishing jade, which is extremely hard and tough, suggests that specialists in this activity existed by the Middle Preclassic period. Several other greenstones, including fuchsite and serpentine, were used for ornaments and carved portable objects, but absent secure mineral identifications they are simply dubbed "greenstone." A greenstone offering has been dated to 1400 B.C. at Paso de la Amada (Lesure 2004:93). Deposits of serpentine are known in the northern mountains of Guatemala as well as in Guerrero, Mexico. According to Reilly (2000:373), jade and greenstone objects had two functions: "to act as props in shamanic rituals and to provide, through the symbolic information they bore, visual validation for the political authority of the rulers who manipulated them in these rituals."

Jade and/or greenstone in general seem to be a Middle Formative replacement for Early Formative iron ore as the chief exotic material for personal-wealth displays, ornamentation, and legitimization of elites and rulers. Magnetite and other ores were primarily found as mirrors, either mosaics or concave ground single pieces of stone, depicted on figurines and sculptures as head ornaments or pectorals. Their function is unknown but might include divinatory scrying (Miller and Taube 1993: 114), focusing solar rays to ignite ritual fires (Carlson 1981; Heizer and Gullberg 1981), and establishing magnetic orientations (e.g., 8° west of magnetic north). In any case, the earliest settlers in the Maya lowlands apparently did not share the concave-mirror tradition or lacked access to these artifacts, because they have not been reported from Preclassic Maya sites.

Other raw materials circulating widely in Preclassic Mesoamerica include marine items—stingray spines, marine shell (e.g., *Strombus* [conch]), and sharks' teeth—found at coastal lowland sites and also in the interior highlands (at, e.g., San José Mogote, Oaxaca [Flannery 1976:335–344]). In the Maya lowlands, whole shells and beads of *Spondylus* (thorny oyster, a bright red bivalve mollusk) became the preferred exotic in the Late Preclassic period (Freidel, Reese-Taylor, and Mora-Marín 2002). The reasons for these specific transitions in wealth goods in the Formative are not clear—economic? political? ideological?—but they accompanied a series of other material and ideological transformations involving kingly roles, architecture, and the calendar.

DISCUSSION

The earliest settlers in the Maya lowlands, whoever they were, are nearly invisible archaeologically. They appear to have participated in the same subsistence system and shared the same cultigens as peoples in other areas of Mesoamerica, and limited available evidence suggests an early preference for and adaptation to wetland environments. But it is not known if there was continuity or discontinuity between these Late Archaic or Preceramic peoples, known primarily by pollen data, and the later, archaeologically visible, settlers around 1000–900 B.C. Even though these latter occupants can be better characterized by their material remains, it is also unclear whether or not they were ethnically and linguistically Mayan. Sparse but accumulating evidence suggests the possibility that between about 1500 and 800 B.C. or so, the lowlands might have been occupied by people speaking several possibly closely related ancestral or proto-languages, including Proto-Mixe-Zoquean, Proto-Yukatekan, and Greater Tzeltalan. The "evidence" for this interpretation consists largely of variable ceramic traditions in the eastern and western zones of the lowlands, traditions that suggest ties to the eastern highlands (El Salvador) and Chiapas–western Guatemala, respectively, and, in the case of the latter, perhaps to early divergent Yukatekan speakers. Most archaeologists identify "the Maya" with the primarily monochrome red, black, and cream slipped pottery known as the Mamom complex, which is widespread, particularly in the southern lowlands, after ca. 700 B.C. or so.

Regardless of the uncertainties about the ethnolinguistic identities of the earliest settlers in the Maya lowlands, it is evident that in Mamom times the Maya (and their neighbors) had access to a wide range of exotic goods, particularly jade and obsidian, and participated in the same kinds of trade networks as the Olmec and other Isthmian groups. Judging from later evidence, they also shared symbol systems for elite political authority, symbol systems that had shared cosmological and calendrical referents in the Isthmian region and beyond.

One of the key elements in Maya kingly statements about order and legitimacy concerns the Maize God(s) (Freidel and Schele 1988a; Freidel, Schele, and Parker 1993; Joyce 2000:67). The murals at San Bartolo (Saturno, Stuart, and Beltrán 2006) strengthen iconographic and mythical connections, while the relations among rulership, maize, and the calendar can be contemplated in Stross's (1994) model of thirteen twenty-day months correlating with thirteen day names in the 260-day calendar, based on the agricultural cycle of maize.

I propose a more explicit connection between the sun and Maya *ajaws*, manifest not only in iconography but also in a transition to east-west site orientations and east-focused architectural complexes. An early north-south emphasis may relate to geomancy and the access to and use of lodestone-like minerals with magnetic properties; these in turn appear to tie into ancestor veneration, perhaps as part of the political legitimacy of early paramounts. Affinities with the sun were evident in the Isthmian region in the form of personal objects or accoutrements, such as convex mirrors, and the sun's movement between solstices was often indicated by the crossed-bands motif. But the later Preclassic east-west layouts and structure orientations suggest an explicit solar focus, permitting the ruler and/or his retinue of daykeeper-priests to track more precisely the position of the sun during its annual transit between the solstices and thereby demonstrate "control" of the agricultural season. Concomitantly, the ruler's control of the sun and the solar calendar conferred on him the legitimation of the cosmos, allowing him to claim the sun as his patron, embody the sun god in earthly manifestation, and display the signature attributes of the Maize God in appropriate rituals.

Later lowland Maya creation myths recovered in Classic inscriptions and Postclassic/Colonial written sources do not seem to reference the calendar to the degree I suggest for the highland *Popol Vuh*. Origin myths occupy the "history" sections of the Postclassic *Chilam Balam of Chumayel*, and the Hero Twins are referenced in the Dresden Codex (Coe 1989b:179); Classic lowland Maya mythic history reflects the *Popol Vuh* only selectively, and the Maya seem to have restricted the sources of their mythistories to exegesis on different media and contexts. Rarely can references be found to the *Popol Vuh* myth in inscriptions on stone monuments (as they were in Izapa), which seems to emphasize a rather narrow, celestially focused creation, itself referring to stones. An exception to this exists in ample textual and iconographic references to the Paddler Gods, who may be related to the Hero Twins and traced back to Kaminaljuyú.

Instead, the stories of the late *Popol Vuh* are amply displayed in elaborate scenes—particularly resurrection scenes (Coe 1973, 1978, 1989b; Kerr 1992) on unprovenienced Classic polychrome vases presumably originally deposited in royal tombs—and in the texts and embellishments on select buildings. Among these are the Temple of the Foliated Cross, which reflects on First Father

(Freidel, Schele, and Parker 1993:284–285); the Palenque sarcophagus lid (ibid.:462n34); Temple 20 at Copán, which has been identified as a "Bat House" (ibid.:483n23); and the sets of sculpted macaws (i.e., Seven Macaw) at the Copán Ballcourt (ibid.:365–369, 486–487nn50–51). These contexts seem to suggest that, for the Classic lowland Maya, any early version of the *Popol Vuh* myth was a mythic charter of cosmic and temporal order shared and understood only among elites in ritual and funerary contexts. It was not promulgated to the masses as part of public ceremonies as it seems to have been at Izapa.

Early Lowland Maya Intellectual Culture
Writing, Stelae, and "Government"

One of the key unifying themes in Mesoamerican thought and culture was language and orality. Mesoamericans, including the Maya, "linked language and dialogue to the dawn of consciousness in the creation of the human condition. . . . In effect, beautifully executed speech and song are the only substances, with the possible exception of blood, that the human body can produce which are accessible to, and worthy before, divine beings. . . . If divine beings are pleased, human life is allowed to continue" (Gossen 1986:7).

Before the invention of writing, events and traditions were remembered and passed along orally. The keepers and reciters of such oral histories—and of the kinds of information leading to development of the calendars in Mesoamerica—were likely respected elders, perhaps shamans or daykeepers. Formalized speech can play an important role in maintaining social order, as among the Shuar of Ecuador: "the ability to speak well indicates personal power and possession of spiritual strength, attributes which increase an individual's prestige and, ultimately, political authority" (Helms 1993:26). Moreover, through formal oratory an elder is "transformed into an ancestor speaking eternal truth" (ibid.:222n7).

Given the importance of language and song in Mesoamerica, it is not surprising that the mouth was widely regarded as a source of power (Gossen 1986:7; Stross 1994:20). Among the Maya, the powerful role of oral record-keeping is evident in several ways. One example is found in the Maya term for their rulers, *ajaw*: *aj* is an honorific and *aw* (or *awat*) can mean "to shout"; thus *ajaw* means "he who shouts or proclaims" (Stuart 1995:190–191), in the sense of an orator. In addition, the *ajaw* glyph may represent a human face with an open mouth, in the act of speaking or shouting (Stross 1994:20; Fields [1989:75–76] also suggests that it derives from representations of a jaguar mouth). The glyph appears on numerous Preclassic media, including the Dumbarton Oaks pectoral and the San Bartolo murals, and a Preclassic pottery sherd from El Mirador has an *ajaw* glyph incised on it (Demarest 1984:fig. 47; Matheny 1986. Justeson, Norman, and Hammond [1988:97n2] credit Dorie Reents with the interpretation). The *aw* (or *po*) sign is also a reconstructed pan-Mayan verb root *aw* 'to plant (seeds)' (Fields 1989:104; Justeson et

[Maya monuments portray Classic kings] in a perpetual state of ritual action. . . . [R]ulers were themselves embodiments of time and its passage—a role that was fundamental to the cosmological underpinnings of divine kingship. We find this expressed most directly by the overt solar symbolism that surrounded the office of Maya kingship. . . . The cyclical reappearance of the Ajaw day at each Period Ending in the Long Count calendar was not only a renewal of cosmological time but also a renewal, in effect, of the institution of kingship— an elaboration of the conceptual equation of the ruler and the sun.

—David Stuart, "Kings of Stone"

al. 1985:44; Mathews and Justeson 1984:206), suggesting an alternative reading of *ajaw* as "sower."

The powerful role of speech and oration is highlighted by the role of "the word" in the *Popol Vuh*. The myth begins, "This is the beginning of the Ancient Word" (D. Tedlock 1996:63), and earth and the universe began with a spoken word: "Creation began with the utterance of a word and the appearance of the thing embodied by the word" (Freidel, Schele, and Parker 1993:65). Shortly thereafter the animals were created, and the early deer and birds were ordered by the gods to "name now our names, praise us . . . speak, pray to us, keep our days," but they were unable to so. They "just squawked, they just chattered, they just howled . . . each one gave a different cry," so the gods "changed [their] word" (D. Tedlock 1996:67).

Word also can mean "prophecy," as in the Postclassic *mut* (*mu'ut*), the prophecy for the upcoming *k'atun*, which was declaimed as part of period-ending ceremonies (Edmonson 1986a:x; P. Rice 2004:81, 99). The ancient name for the site of Tikal appears to be Mutul or Mutal 'place of the word' or augury, or sometimes *yax mutul*, designating the place where the first prophecy was spoken. In Postclassic Yucatán, the prophecy, or *mut*, was spoken by the *chilam* 'speaker, spokesman', a term that derives from *ch'i* 'mouth'. (Similarly, in Postclassic central Mexico among the Mexica the emperor's title was *tlatoani* 'speaker' [Fields 1989:75].)

Ritual deposits of human mandibles and teeth can be found in the archaeological record, as in the necklaces of mandibles worn by the buried males at Teotihuacan (Spence et al. 2004), and mandible deposits at Postclassic Zacpetén in the central Petén lakes area (Duncan 2005), suggesting efforts to remove and/or capture the power of speech from an enemy. The many occurrences of animal teeth, particularly those of predators such as jaguars and sharks, in archaeological contexts—including the possible "ceremonial denture" of jaguar or wolf teeth (Roach 2006)—may bespeak a similar theme. A related consideration is the removal of entire human faces, the ultimate in identity capture and disempowerment. Defacement of monuments—literally, removing or damaging the faces and mouths of the individuals portrayed, as with the Olmec colossal heads and Maya stelae—has parallels in the *Popol Vuh*, when another effort to create

humans failed: "They were talking at first but their faces were dry. . . . They were not competent, nor did they speak" (D. Tedlock 1996:70, 71). Then came a great rain and flood and an inversion of order: the kitchen utensils and the animals began to talk to the speechless early humans. Finally, the humans were destroyed: "The mouths and faces of all of them were destroyed and crushed . . . and it used to be said that the monkeys in the forests today are a sign of this. . . . So this is why monkeys look like people" (ibid.:73), that is, why they have humanlike faces that cannot talk to the gods. Speaking and words, then, whether uttered by the ruler or by high-ranking priests, were the quintessential means of assuring the continued beneficence of the gods and the maintenance of cosmic order.

WRITING SYSTEMS

The creation of the precise and concurrently running Mesoamerican calendars was a unique achievement among ancient civilizations, but equally significant was the endogenous creation of a writing system. Justeson (1986:437) defines these as "graphic representational systems whose encoding and decoding of information make crucial reference to language"; they begin with "the introduction of linguistic information into the coding process by which graphic forms are related to meaning." Marcus (1992a:7, following Diringer 1962:20) is careful to distinguish between writing and complex iconography and defines writing as "the graphic counterpart of speech, the 'fixing' of spoken language in a permanent or semi-permanent form." Writing begins when linguistic meanings related to spoken language are assigned to visual symbols arranged in an organized format.

The earliest writing system to develop in Mesoamerica has been debated, with Marcus (1976) favoring the Zapotec in Oaxaca, while Justeson (1986) claims it developed among the Olmec and Olmec-affiliated cultures and all scripts descended from this system. He bases his conclusion on a number of shared features, chiefly, that all Mesoamerican writing occurs from left to right and top to bottom in columns. With respect to Maya writing, Justeson (ibid.:447) proposes that a "Southeastern" script tradition developed from this ancestral incipient writing system in the Isthmian region after about 600–300 B.C. (Figs. 8.1 and 8.2), with two subtraditions: a conservative "Isthmian" or Epi-Olmec one, and a more innovative Greater Izapan/Mayan subtradition. This latter differentiated into two variants after around 250 B.C.: Greater Izapan (probably Mixean or Mixe-Zoquean) and Lowland Mayan (ibid.:451). Lowland Mayan script, he suggests, was adopted from Mixean speakers by Ch'olan-Tzeltalan speakers by A.D. 1, and then by Yukatekan (or Proto-Yukatekan) speakers no later than A.D. 100 (ibid.). Later script developments include the double-column format (255 B.C.–A.D. 36), simple phonetic spelling (around A.D. 400), and the concept of zero.

Another view of the origins of Maya writing comes from Robert J. Sharer, using data from the Salamá valley of Baja Verapaz, Guatemala. The glyph column in the largely destroyed central scene on El Portón Monument 1 preserves seven signs, one of which might be a seating glyph (Sharer 1989b:171–172). Sharer (ibid.:173) dates the monument to 400 B.C. on the basis of its context and suggests that there might have been (at least) "two functionally distinct recording systems in

use in the Maya highlands" in the late Middle Preclassic. In addition, several monuments dated roughly 500–400 B.C. display "cupulate" notations of dots and lines pecked into boulders and outcrops (ibid.:168–169; also Sedat 1992). Other monuments exhibit bar-and-dot configurations, U-shaped elements, and a possible Lamat sign. One repeated motif is the "triadic dot cluster," common in early iconography (Sedat 1992:85–87; see also Peeler and Winter 1992:45–49). Among the Maya, three dots in a triangular arrangement is particularly associated with the *Ajaw* face glyph; David Sedat (1992:86–87) associates it with fire (glyph T672 and three-pronged incense burners); Peeler and Winter (1992:45–49) associate three circles (especially in a line) with the Belt of Orion and with rain or storm gods.[1]

Stephen Houston (2000:146–147) proposes that in the late Late Preclassic and Early Classic periods (Cycle 8), a Maya scribe or scribes intentionally began to create a syllabary of signs,[2] creating graphemes for important words by combining the first consonant and vowel of a word (CV). These graphemes appear earliest on unprovenienced portable objects, such as the Dumbarton Oaks jade

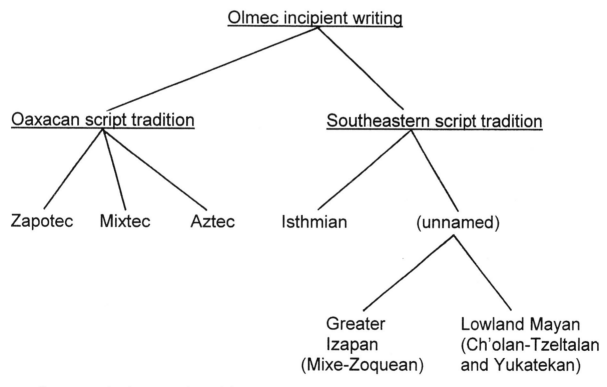

8.1. Differentiation of early script traditions (after Justeson 1986).

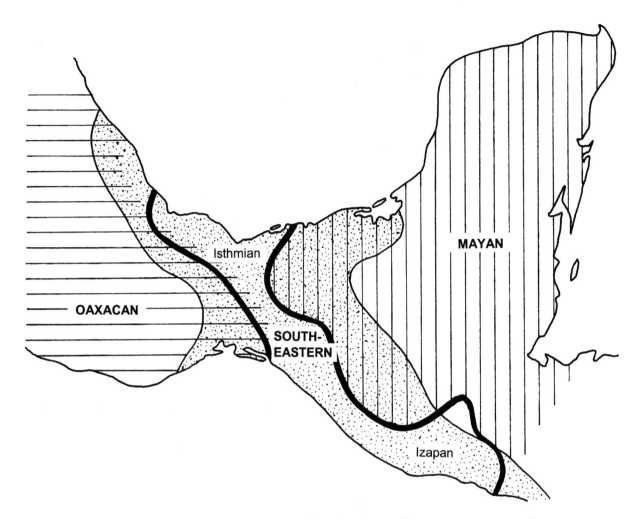

8.2. Geographical distribution of early script traditions, overlying distribution of ca. 1600 B.C. pottery traditions, Locona (stippled area) and red-on-buff to the west (after Clark 1991:fig. 8; Flannery and Marcus 2000:fig. 3).

and the Pomona earflare, but also on provenienced items from Tikal and Uaxactún.

A review of Maya writing by Federico Fahsen and Nikolai Grube (2005:76, 77) notes that early script began with logographs "depicting real things or actions" and appeared primarily on portable objects in the absence of images, indicating that writing was independent of art. Their dates are a bit earlier than Justeson's, as they assert that by the Early Classic period fully phonetic spellings came to be used and "by about AD 300 all features of the Maya script were already present" (ibid.:75, 77). Referencing Houston's (2000:146–147) suggestion about the invention of a syllabary, and noting the similarities between the signs and formats of lowland Maya script and those of the central highlands and Pacific piedmont, they conclude that the

scribes used a shared language, probably Ch'olan (or Greater Tzeltalan) (ibid.:78). These authors do not identify any direct precursor to lowland Maya writing, and, indeed, the texts at San Bartolo (Saturno, Stuart, and Beltrán 2006) underscore the position that Maya writing is not a "unitary system" but a "set of historical practices" accumulated in punctuated equilibrium-like bursts (Houston 2006:1249).

Maya writing has a rounded, curvilinear, or cursive appearance that contrasts with the angular, rectilinear Epi-Olmec or Isthmian script and central Mexican writing (see, e.g., Mora-Marín 2005: figs. 5, 6). This has been interpreted as indicating that Maya writing originated in a painting tradition (on bark, leather, clay, plaster, or plain monuments) rather than in a stone- or wood-carving tradition. Support for this interpretation comes from the fact that the Mayan word for painting, *ts'ib*, is also used for writing; a different word is used for "carving" (Coe and Van Stone 2001: 94–95). In addition, the late Yukatekan word *wooh* (*uooh, wooj*) means "to paint" and also "letter, character, symbol, individual hieroglyph," and a scribe or painter may be called *aj wooj* (Marcus 1992a:79–80). The *aj ts'ib* (Fig. 8.3a) who painted the short glyphic texts at San Bartolo demonstrated considerable calligraphic skill, using thick lines to define the outline of the signs and finer lines for detail (Saturno 2006; Saturno, Taube, and Stuart 2005). The longest text on the west wall mural has not been read, but the signs show similarities to other Preclassic scripts and may represent a name and titles (Saturno, Taube, and Stuart 2005:43–48). An unusual text of ten glyphs painted on a stone block looks similar to Epi-Olmec and dates roughly 300–200 B.C., perhaps several centuries earlier than the murals and earlier than known examples of the Isthmian script (Saturno, Stuart, and Beltrán 2006), and may constitute an example of Justeson's "Isthmian sub-tradition." William Saturno, Taube, and Stuart (2005:47) raise the intriguing possibility that lowland Maya script had an older and independent history apart from that of other Mesoamerican scripts.

Another perspective on writing comes from a Maya title *aj kuju'un* (*aj k'uj ju'un; aj k'ujul nu'n na, aj k'ujul jun*) (Fig. 8.3b) 'one who keeps, guards' or 'he of the holy books' (Coe and Van Stone 2001:97, citing Nikolai Grube; see also Jackson and Stuart 2001). This title is related to the Yukatekan word *xokju'un* 'to read', the key being the knot logogram *ju'un*, which can mean "paper" (book) and "bark-paper headband," presumably indicating a noble scribe. It is also linked to the monkey-faced God C glyph, monkeys being patron deities of artisans. This in turn relates to the *Popol Vuh* and the Hero Twins' brothers One Monkey and One Artisan, who were turned into monkeys by the Twins' trickery.

The derivation of these or similar titles likely begins with an individual responsible for keeping written calendrical records. Specifically, I propose that the Classic Maya *aj kuju'un* title developed from the role variously called daykeeper, skywatcher, or calendar priest: a person responsible for maintaining permanent records of time, the

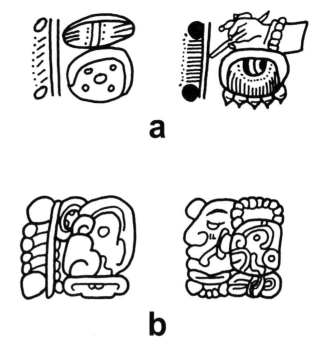

a

b

8.3. Classic Maya titles related to writing and books: (a) *Aj ts'ib* 'the painter, scribe' (drawn from Coe and Van Stone 2001:94); (b) *Aj kuju'un* 'the royal librarian'(?). Glyph on right might indicate a female (drawn from ibid.:97).

calendar, its cycling, and its prophecies. Individuals with such talents and responsibilities would have constituted the earliest elites in Early Formative Mesoamerica and its cultural descendants. Indeed, this elevated status continued into the Late Classic period, when Maya scribes held high social positions and were members of royal families. At the highest scribal rank in the palace, the *aj kuju'un* would have been "royal librarian, historian, genealogist, tribute recorder, marriage arranger, master of ceremonies, and (with more certainty) *astronomer and mathematician*" (Coe and Van Stone 2001:13, emphasis added).

Early Mesoamerican writing frequently appeared as calendar names (J. Justeson, pers. com., September 2005) on personal objects. For example, an earspool from Cuicuilco bears the date or name 2 Lord, and 1 Lord appears on the Tapijulapa ax (Edmonson 1988:20–21). The Pomona earflare, a large (eighteen centimeter–diameter) jadeite ornament from an early tomb in Belize, bears four glyph blocks (Fig. 8.4) loosely read as "The holder of power is the Sun God; the Sun God casts corn to/for the sky god" (Hammond 1987; translation

from Justeson, Norman, and Hammond 1988:143).
The text was "written in pre-Yucatecan, that is, in
a Yucatecan language spoken before the diversification of proto-Yucatecan" (Justeson, Norman,
and Hammond 1988:133), and the meaning likely
"involves actual or metaphorical apotheosis . . .
[it is] a claim of sacred justification for the secular
political activity of the Lowland Maya elite"
(ibid.:143). The "casts corn" phrase could be an
early reference to the scattering rite. A more recent
reading (Freidel, Reese-Taylor, and Mora-Marín
2002:74) suggests that the text reads, "The Maize
God is the heart of the Sun God."

The recovery context of the Pomona flare
included Late Preclassic pottery, suggesting a date
sometime before A.D. 200/250. The inscribing of
individuals' calendrical or birth names and references to deities on early items of elite culture and
personal ornamentation, such as earflares or celts,
especially of jade, reinforces connections between
calendar keeping and status. In the terminology of
the Baines-Yoffee (1998, 2000) model, these
inscriptions on early items of wealth constitute
statements of elite legitimacy and order.

Questions about the language used in the
Classic-period lowland Maya inscriptions have
been debated for decades, with Yukatekan an early
favorite, but since the 1980s epigraphers and linguists have supported Ch'olan, particularly in the
southern lowlands. One proposal suggests that the
inscriptions were written in "Classic Ch'olti'an,"
a "prestige language ancestral to the so-called
Eastern Ch'olan languages—the historically attested Ch'olti' language and its descendant, modern
Ch'orti'" (Houston, Robertson, and Stuart
2000:322). Classic Ch'olti'an would have been
written, read, and spoken by elites and scribes for
the full six hundred years of the Classic period,
perhaps as a "sacred or liturgical language to mediate between people and patron gods," but neither
the language nor the inscriptions on stelae would
have been understood by the general populace
(ibid.:351), further reinforcing the distinctions of
elite legitimacy and power. As Marcus (1992a:28)
comments, it is "not surprising that sacred powers
accrued to those individuals who controlled
knowledge of reading, writing, and books. . . .
Knowledge was passed from the divine world to
the nobles, who, in turn, could interpret and convey to the commoners the necessary message.

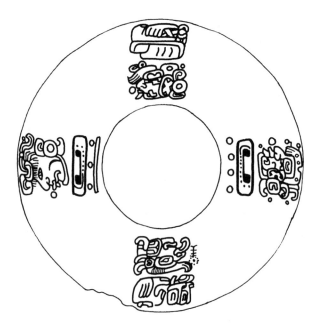

8.4. Inscription on the Pomona flare (Belize), a large jade
earflare (drawn from Justeson, Norman, and Hammond
1988:fig. 3.1).

Since the nobles were descended from the divine
and could interact directly with them, they medi-
ated between the commoners and the 'givers of
knowledge.'" Knowledge of the cosmos comes
from the supernaturals or gods to the rulers and
flows from the ruler's mouth as "the word"; script
enables the materialization and eternalization of
the word, and the ruler's power as the conduit of
divine messages.

THE STELA "CULT" AND CALENDRICS

The lowland Maya stela "cult"—placement of a
vertical slab with a low, round altar in front, both
usually carved—is one of the defining characteristics of Classic Maya civilization. The processes by
which this practice became associated with civic-
ceremonial architecture are unknown, but it is
conspicuous at Late Preclassic Izapa (Guernsey
Kappelman 2003). Evidence suggests that erection
of carved monuments was initiated earlier in the
Maya lowlands than commonly thought. Carved
but undated and stylistically Preclassic monuments have been found at Nakbe (Fig. 7.10), El
Mirador (Fig. 7.12), and La Muerte (Suyuc et al.
2005:fig. 9) in the Mirador basin; Cival (Bauer et al.
2005:fig. 3) and Kanajau (Fialko 2005:fig. 5) in the

Holmul region; Yaxhá, in early low-relief carving below the basal panel on Stela 6 (Fig. 8.5); and Cahal Pech in the Belize valley, where Stela 9, carved in the round, was "ritually buried" in a Late Classic tomb in a plaza group south of the site core (Ball and Taschek 2003:210, 211). It is notable that the early carved stelae at most of these sites were found in E-groups. The styles of some of these carvings resemble those of Izapa and Kaminaljuyú (particularly the crudely carved Stela 1 at Kaminaljuyú). John Montgomery (2001a:41–42) believed ties existed between all early Petén sculpture and Late Preclassic styles of the Pacific piedmont region, although he acknowledges in his book that "differences remain clear and striking."

In the Maya lowlands, Tikal Stela 29, dated 8.12.14.8.15 (9 Men 3 Mol; October 14, A.D. 292), continues to hold the distinction of being the earliest provenienced monument with a Long Count date. However, it is possible that Altar 1 at Polol (Fig. 8.6), in the savannas of central Petén southwest of Lake Petén Itzá, might be earlier. The date on this monument is controversial because the glyphs are difficult to read: it may date in late Cycle 7 (Pahl 1982) or, because of stylistic similarities to monuments at Tak'alik Ab'aj, on the Pacific coast, in early Cycle 8 (Clancy 1999:45–47). On the basis of Gary Pahl's drawing

and photograph, I would put the date of Polol Altar 1 at 7.19.19.9.14 (March 23, A.D. 41), six months before the turning of the *b'ak'tun* on September 5, A.D. 41. Regardless of the date of the Polol altar, the early carved monuments in the lowlands, plus glyphs on portable artifacts and texts on murals at San Bartolo, provide tantalizing hints that Late Preclassic Maya sculpted monuments bearing dates and texts might be more widespread but still unknown in the lowlands, buried under the hundreds of thousands of cubic meters of later Classic construction.

Norman Hammond (1982; also Justeson and Mathews 1983) suggests that the lowland Maya might have had a Late Preclassic cult of erecting plain monuments. This suggestion was prompted by the discovery of a small, plain stela set into the surface of Platform 34 at Cuello, northern Belize, with a stratigraphic date of ca. A.D. 100. Plain monuments were also found at Late Preclassic El Mirador and continued to be erected through the Late Classic period in the lowlands (e.g., at the eastern mounds in Tikal's twin-pyramid groups). Outside of the Maya lowlands, plain stelae were abundant at Izapa and at Preclassic sites on the Pacific coast (Bove 1999).

We will probably never know what public information, if any, might have been conveyed on the early plain stelae in the Isthmian and Mayan regions. The earliest carved and Long Count–dated monuments in both regions bear dates that appear to commemorate specific events rather than calendrical intervals. It is widely known that lowland Maya stelae throughout the Early and Late Classic

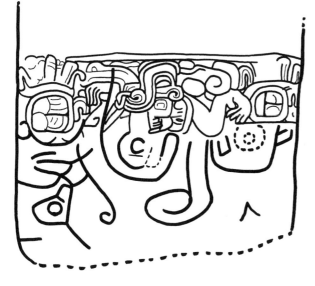

8.5. Basal panel of Yaxhá Stela 6, with stylistically early carving below (drawn from photograph in Hellmuth 1976:88).

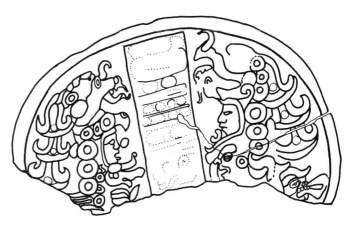

8.6. Polol Altar 1 (drawn from Pahl 1982:fig. 1a).

periods were erected to celebrate important events in rulers' lives and in the histories of their domains, and the stelae themselves might have had a degree of personification (Stuart 1996). Fields (1989:88) concludes from this that the Long Count system of dating was invented because the "emerging elite class" needed to calculate "genealogical descent, both mythological and historical," in order to document its legitimate right to rule.

However, the appearance of Long Count dates on monuments that also depicted rulers' portraits reveals that these early paramounts publicly proclaimed their power as deriving from control of the temporal cycles of history (see Freidel and Schele 1988a:549). A large corpus of monuments of the Classic stela-altar cult played a signal role in commemorating Maya rulers' roles in celebrations of time's passage, which is to say, their role as "lords of time." Among the lowland Maya in the Early Classic period, for example, it became a common practice to erect stelae to commemorate period endings. This is revealed in the values of the sign *tun*: "stone" and "year" (of 360 days). The meaning "stone" seems to be very ancient, going back to Proto-Mayan, while the "year" meaning exists only in colonial Yukatekan and in the Classic inscriptions (Justeson and Mathews 1983:587). This dual meaning, as stone and year (ending), and the stela cult to which the word *tun* relates, must have existed "by the middle of the Late Preclassic at the latest" (ibid.:591), suggesting long-standing connections between the endings/beginnings of periods of time and the ritual placement of stones. The earliest dated stelae erected to commemorate a period ending, in this case a *k'atun* ending, are Uaxactún Stelae 18 and 19, which were erected in that site's E-Group and date to 8.16.0.0.0 (A.D. 357). The presence of plain stelae in E-Groups (e.g., at El Mirador in Petén, and also at Monte Alto in the Pacific piedmont) suggests that they could have had painted calendrical information on them.

While the stelae at Uaxactún support a date of A.D. 357 for the end of the sixteenth and beginning of the seventeenth *k'atun* in B'ak'tun 8, an earlier *k'atun*-ending celebration might be registered on a portable object: the Dumbarton Oaks celt, clearly Early Classic in its style of carving, marks a period ending at either 8.4.0.0.0 (June 15, A.D. 150) or 9.4.0.0.0 (A.D. 514). Schele and Miller (1986:82–83)

believe the latter date is too late for the style of the piece, thus suggesting that the celt may date to the middle of the second century A.D. This would be one of the earliest records of period-ending commemoration and underscores the widely held notion that celts were early, miniature stelae.[3] It also raises the possibility that early *k'atun* celebrations were commemorated on personal objects of wealth and power before being registered on carved public monuments.

The Long Count as a *K'atun* Count

The Long Count, a dating system used by the Epi-Olmec and the lowland Maya, allowed users to set the events of any specific day in the 260-, 360-, and 365-day calendars into the greater cycles of time by counting elapsed days from a calculated zero date. This zero point is the origin of time in the current Great Cycle, beginning with cosmic creation on a day 0.0.0.0.0 or 13.0.0.0.0 4 Ajaw 8 Kumk'u, which corresponds to August 11, 3114 B.C. The date of invention of the Long Count is not known (see Table 8.1), but as discussed in Chapter 3, it is traditionally thought to have been in the early Late Preclassic, and the earliest known Long Count dates come from the last part of Cycle (or B'ak'tun) 7, in the last decades before the Common Era.

Maya Long Count dates begin with the large, elaborate Initial Series Introducing Glyph, or ISIG, which usually occupies the space of two to four glyphs and spans two columns. It consists of an ornamented head atop a *tun* sign (Fig. 8.7). The *tun* sign (T548) means "hollow drum" as well as "year" (and "stone"), and a similar "year/drum" signifier appears on Long Count dates on La Mojarra Stela 1. Kaufman and Justeson (2001:2.31) suggest that this sign was borrowed into Epi-Olmec script from the Maya, implying an early date for it. The ornamented head is the only variable part of the Maya ISIG, as it is always the head of the patron god of the *ja'ab'* month of the date being recorded. It is topped by a triple scroll sign *tzik*, perhaps meaning "count," and is flanked by combs or "fish fins" (*ma* or *ka/kay*). The ISIG is basically an embellished *tun* or *k'atun* sign.

In Classic Maya inscriptions, the calendrical information that follows the ISIG in Long Count

TABLE 8.1. *Important proposed dates (Gregorian) in the development of Mesoamerican and Maya calendars and writing*

DATE B.C.	CALENDAR DEVELOPMENT	SOURCE
3114	Long Count starting date	
3000–1500	Spread and diversification of major Mesoamerican	
	language families: Uto-Aztecan, Otomanguean,	
	Mixe-Zoquean, and Mayan (as proto-languages)	
2200	Beginning of breakup of Proto-Mayan	
2060	Seasonal alignment of solar calendar month names?	Bricker 1982:103
1650	Calendar Round already in use?	Clark 2004
1400–1000	Yukatekan Mayan separation from Proto-Mayan	
1358	Beginning of use of 260-day calendar?	Malmström 1978
1281	Beginning of use of Long Count?	Rice, herein
1243	Beginning of use of Long Count?	Rice, herein
1000	Separation of Greater Tzeltalan from Greater Kanjobalan begins	
900?	Humboldt Celt	
739	Invention of Calendar Round?	Edmonson 1988:117
594	Monte Albán Stela 12, Calendar Round date	
563	Monte Albán Stela 13, text	
550	Seasonal alignment of solar calendar month names?	Bricker 1982:103
600–500	Internal differentiation of highland Mayan languages	
600–300	Development of Isthmian script traditions	Justeson 1986:451
500–400	Monte Albán; use of 365- and 260-day calendars	Marcus 1992a:38–41
433	Accurate estimate of tropical year?	Edmonson 1988:117
400?	El Portón Monument 1	
	La Venta Stela 3	Sharer 1989b:173
355	(Olmec) initiation of Long Count?	Edmonson 1988:194
300–200	San Bartolo text on stone	Saturno, Stuart, and Beltrán 2006
256	Initiation of Long Count?	Thompson 1932:370
255–235	System of positional notation?	Justeson 1986:447
250	Differentiation of Lowland Mayan script tradition	Justeson 1986:451
235/236	Initiation of Maya Long Count; initiation of Tikal calendar	Malmström 1978; Teeple 1926; Edmonson 1986b:86
36	Chiapa de Corzo Stela 2	
32	Tres Zapotes Stela C	

DATE A.D.		
1	Adoption of Mixean script by Ch'olan-Tzeltalan speakers	Justeson 1986:447
37	El Baúl Stela 1, Maya LC date	
84	Inauguration of Tikal calendar	Edmonson 1988
100	Adoption of Ch'olan-Tzeltalan script; plain stela at Cuello, Belize	Justeson 1986:447; Hammond 1982
143–157	Dates on La Mojarra Stela 1	
162	First use of ISIG, Tuxtla Statuette	
199	Maya LC and text on Hauberg Stela	
292	Tikal Stela 29, first Maya use of Long Count on an in situ monument	
357	Earliest period-ending stelae, Stelae 18 and 19, Uaxactún; uniform system of recording lunar eclipses	Justeson 1989:87–88
400	Development of simple phonetic spelling	Justeson 1986:452
934	Venus calendar formally instituted	Aveni 2002:205
937	Invention of Mayapán calendar	Edmonson 1988
1000	Differentiation of Yukatekan languages	Hofling n.d.
1539	Promulgation of Mayapán calendar	Edmonson 1988

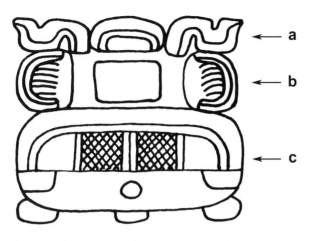

8.7. The Classic Maya Initial Series Introducing Glyph:
(a) triple scrolls; *tzi* or *tzik* 'count'?; (b) head of the patron
month in the *ja'ab'* flanked by "fish fins" or combs (*ka*);
(c) *tun* sign.

dates is referred to collectively as the Initial Series
and consists of five signs representing the "bundles" of multiple days known among Mayanists as
the *b'ak'tun, k'atun, tun, winal,* and *k'in* (Fig. 8.8;
also Fig. 3.3). Each sign is preceded by a numerical
prefix indicating how many of each unit of days
have elapsed. This system had several variants,
however, as the temporal units can be identified by
glyphs or personified into "head variants" or full-
figure glyphs (Table 8.2) of avians or toads, revealing deep roots in mythology. In the full-figure
glyphs for *k'atun* and *b'ak'tun,* the avian is shown
struggling with or dominating an anthropomorphic god of the number of units, or being carried in
a tumpline by the god. Glyphic signs for *k'atun* are
typically read as "twenty *tun* endings" or "closing
stone." Following these specifications of elapsed
time is the day number and name in the 260-day
calendar.

Next come as many as ten glyphs known
together as the Supplementary Series, which
include reference to the patron among the Nine
Lords of the Night and the "lunar series" giving
information on the placement of the day within
lunar cycles, or lunations. The lunar series consists of three components: Glyph D/E; Glyphs C,
B, and X; and Glyph A (Harris and Stearns
1997:16–17; Teeple 2001[1928]). The first of these,
Glyph D/E, gives the "age" of the moon, that is,
the number of elapsed days since its first appearance after conjunction (invisibility); Glyph E is a

U-shaped "moon sign" with the value 20. Glyphs
C, X, and B record the number and names of completed lunations (out of six); there are at least thirteen forms of Glyph X, which may relate to
Macri's (2005) observation of the thirteen days of
the waxing moon. One depicts crossed human
legs, which might represent "seating" of the moon
as it begins its waxing phase. Glyph A, another
"moon sign," states the length of the lunation as
either 29 or 30 days. From A.D. 350 to A.D. 687, at
least five systems of counting lunations were used
(Justeson 1989, cited in Milbrath 1999:107; Teeple
2001) until the so-called Period of Uniformity.[4]
On a few inscriptions the Supplementary Series
may be followed by dates in the poorly known 819-
day calendar (Harris and Stearns 1997:17). The
inscribed date ends with the day number and
month in the 365-day calendar. All in all, complete
dates in the Maya Long Count might incorporate
fifteen to twenty glyphs to record an event—a
king's inauguration or the celebration of completion of a *k'atun* ending, for example—by its precise
intersection in the many flows of time.

As discussed in Chapter 3, there have been
numerous theories about how and when the Long
Count was developed. One necessary element of
knowledge was counting and numeracy: the creation of a theoretical hierarchy of ever-larger units
of time into which days, or *k'ins,* could be grouped
and nested for easier arithmetic manipulation.
K'ins, winals (twenty-day units), and *tuns* (360-day
units) were obviously part of existing calendrical
systems, but the Long Count added still larger
units via vigesimal multipliers. If Clark's (2004:59)
calculations about structural dimensions at Paso
de la Amada are correct—that is, that they were
built on standard units in multiples of 52, ~260,
and 365—this suggests that both calendars as well
as the 52-year Calendar Round were developed perhaps as early as 1650 cal. B.C. This corroborates
my proposal that ancient historical memories,
preserved in oral traditions by daykeepers since
Late Archaic times, were long a part of the
Mesoamerican worldview and calendrical traditions. The Long Count could have been developed
simultaneously, or any time thereafter.

Several lines of argument suggest that the
Long Count developed from recording *k'atuns,* or
twenty *tuns* of 360 days equaling 7,200 days
(Edmonson 1988:119). One comes from the ISIG:

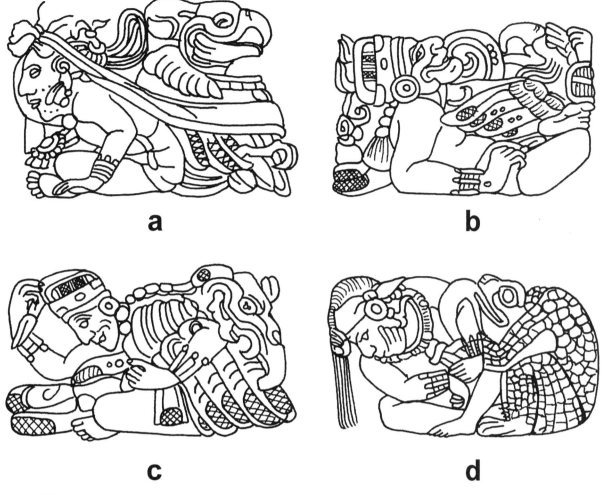

8.8. Full-figure glyphs for periods of time from Copán Stela D, in which gods interact with the zoomorphic representation of the periods (drawn from Thompson 1960:figs. 28, 29): (a) 9 *b'ak'tuns*; the god of number 9 carries the *b'ak'tun*, represented as an avian, by tumpline on his back; (b) 15 *k'atuns*; the god of number 15 rests with the *k'atun*, another avian; (c) 5 *tuns*; the god of number 5 supports a long-beaked avian on his shoulder; (d) 0 *winals*; the god of null or 0 rests with the winal frog. Note that the gods bearing the *tun* and the *k'atun* wear the *tun* sign as their headdress.

TABLE 8.2. *Glyph variants for periods in the Maya Long Count*

PERIOD	GLYPH	HEAD VARIANT	FULL-FIGURE FORM
K'in	Four-petaled flower (plumeria)	Sun god; dog or jaguar head	Monkey
Winal	Uncertain	*Wo* frog; *Bufo marinus**	*Wo* frog; *Bufo marinus**
Tun	Jade; *kawak*	Screech owl or *muwan* bird; long-nosed head with missing or skeletal jaw	Long-nosed composite creature
K'atun	*Tun* sign under a small *kawak* sign flanked by combs	Avian with hand at lower jaw (may be topped by *kawak* sign and combs)	Bird of prey (eagle, hawk, vulture?)
B'ak'tun	Two *kawak* signs	Avian with hand at lower jaw	Avian

Source: Thompson 1966:142–147.

*Thompson (1966:143) says this is a *wo* frog, but the three dots above the earplug are symbols of the pores of the paratoid glands of the *Bufo marinus* toad (Kennedy 1982:277).

as noted, this singularly important glyph is basically an elaborated *tun* or *k'atun* sign, suggesting that the Long Count originated as a count of *k'atuns* or as a means of facilitating such counts. In addition, Justeson and colleagues (1985:76) note that the "head-variant signs for the baktun and tun are modifications of a more basic head-variant sign for the katun." Even earlier, Linton Satterthwaite (1965:627) commented that the Long Count might have been built on "a more ancient Short Count of 13 *k'atuns*" (see also Farriss 1987:578n22). As I suggest in Chapter 9, the *k'atun* itself might have been compounded from smaller units of five years, later known as a *jotun*.

Edmonson's (1988:120) proposal that the Long Count starting date was based on terminating the current creation on a winter solstice is attractive because it skirts the puzzlement of why the Long Count began on a late summer day in 3114 B.C.: that date was merely derivative from, or an artifact of, the intended *ending* date. However, this suggestion also opens the door to facile conclusions that Mesoamerican calendrical accomplishments were simply retrodictive calculations by later "civilized" people, ignoring the possibility that they could be accumulations of centuries and millennia of increasingly precise sky-watching knowledge begun by "primitive" hunters and gatherers.

Justeson and colleagues (1985:76) adumbrate several lines of evidence to determine when the Long Count might have originated. First, they note that a date 4 Ajaw 8 Kumk'u is not an inaugural date for either the 260-day calendar or the 365-day one, nor does it end another *k'atun* for more than 18,700 years. This day-month combination does, however, end a *tun* three times prior to the Late Classic period: at 2.7.9.0.0 (2179 B.C.), 4.14.18.0.0 (1243 B.C.), and 7.2.7.0.0 (308 B.C.). These scholars prefer the last of these dates, specifying a slightly later interval during the K'atun 11 Ajaw ending at 7.6.0.0.0 B.C. (or 255–235 B.C.) for the start of the Long Count.[5] As indicated in the *Chilam Balam of Chumayel*, "Katun 11 Ahau was the beginning of the katun-count, the first katun" (Roys 1967:54, 146), and this *k'atun* would have begun on 7.5.0.0.1 on a day 1 Imix, which is always the first day of a *k'atun*. Justeson and colleagues (1985:76) dismiss the earlier occurrence of a 4 Ajaw 8 Kumk'u *tun*-ending date in 4.14.18.0.0 (May 15, 1243 B.C.), which roughly corresponds to the beginning of the

early Olmec florescence, as "not a serious contender," presumably because it is so early.

However, a 1 Imix starting day for a *k'atun* would have occurred fewer than forty years beforehand, following the end of a K'atun 13 Ajaw in B'ak'tun 4: this date would be 4.13.0.0.0 13 Ajaw 13 Ch'en (November 30, 1281 B.C.). This date—completing thirteen *k'atuns* on a 13 Ajaw day and a 13 Ch'en day—surely would have been of supreme significance to early daykeepers. I therefore favor a date near the end of the third quarter of B'ak'tun 4, or during our thirteenth century B.C., for the beginning of the Long Count dating system.

But why did the inventors of the Long Count settle on 13 *b'ak'tuns* as the appropriate period of a Great Cycle? Why not 20, as a continuation of the vigesimal system of units (cf. Edmonson 1988:119, who notes this use in the Dresden Codex, 61, 69)? As we have seen, 13 is a significant number for the Maya, beginning with 13 days of the waxing moon and appearing in other contexts involving multipliers of 20 and units of 260, such as 13 numbers used with 20 day-names in the 260-day calendar. If, as I hypothesize, the Long Count and Great Cycles developed out of *k'atuns*, then it is a matter of creating larger bundles of 7,200 days, the number of days in a *k'atun*. For example, multiplying 7,200 (days in a *k'atun*) by the sacred numbers 20 and 13, to create larger units of days, we get the following:

7,200 days x 20 = 144,000 days x 13 = 1,872,000 days

and

7,200 days x 13 = 93,600 days x 20 = 1,872,000 days

Obviously, 1,872,000 days, the total in a Great Cycle, was a singularly symbolic number of days for early daykeepers to reckon with. And the intermediate totals, above, are also significant: 144,000 days is a *b'ak'tun*, of which there are thirteen in a Great Cycle; and 93,600 days is a period of thirteen *k'atuns*, or a *may* cycle, with twenty in a Great Cycle. The Great Cycle and the Long Count, in other words, seem to have been created to accommodate the highest multiples of days by the numbers thirteen (*b'ak'tuns*) and twenty (*mays*). This, plus the evident importance of *k'atuns*, suggests that the *may* system was an early and integral part of the Long Count from its very initiation.[6]

A key question to ask here is who (in an eth-nolinguistic sense) erected the earliest monuments in the Maya lowlands? Proto-Mixe-Zoquean speakers? Proto-Yukatekan speakers? Greater Tzeltalan/(Pre)-Ch'olan speakers? Given the few and widely separated early monuments in the lowlands, combined with their apparent repositioning, it may be impossible in the near future to determine the identity of the earliest monument carvers. The practice of erecting plain monuments and carved, dated stelae and altars might have been carried by separate in-migrating groups, borrowed and adopted after travels to external regions, or independently invented.

Early Stelae Locations and K'atun-ending Celebrations

Additional evidence for development of the Long Count through k'atun record-keeping comes from the locations and dates of early lowland Maya stelae. That is, some of the earliest carved and dated monuments in the lowlands (Table 8.1) were recovered in the commemorative solstitial-sunrise architectural assemblages known as E-Groups. For example, thirteen stelae at Late Preclassic El Mirador, one carved and twelve plain, were found in that site's E-Group. Although they cannot be precisely dated, the presence of thirteen of them suggests that they might have been erected every twenty tuns to celebrate the completion of k'atuns within a may cycle. A Middle or Late Preclassic lowland "cultic" practice of erecting plain stelae—perhaps focused on E-Groups—might represent a formalization of the practice which in succeeding generations became the familiar Classic carved stela-altar pairs.

Uaxactún Stelae 18 and 19, which mark the period-ending 8.16.0.0.0 in A.D. 357, were found in front of the east building of the site's E-Group, and Stela 5 celebrates the half-k'atun, or lajuntun, ten years later, in 8.16.10.0.0 (A.D. 366). Tikal Stela 29, although not dated to a period ending, is thought to have been placed originally in the Mundo Perdido E-Group (Laporte and Fialko 1990:40–41). An early k'atun ending is referred to on Tikal Stela 31, believed to date to A.D. 445, which states that Lady Ix Une' B'alam celebrated the k'atun ending of 8.14.0.0.0 (A.D. 317) (Martin and Grube 2000:34), but no monument has been found bearing this date. Three monuments, at Tikal, Uaxactún, and Xultún, might have been erected to celebrate the 8.15.0.0.0 period ending, but this surmise is based solely on style dating. The 8.17.0.0.0 k'atun ending was celebrated by Tikal Stela 39, believed to have been erected in Mundo Perdido. Period endings continued to be celebrated with monuments in the Tikal area, as the 8.18.0.0.0 date was commemorated by the erection of stelae at Tikal, El Zapote, and Uaxactún; the lajuntun of 8.18.10.0.0 at Balakbal (near Calakmul); 8.19.0.0.0 at Uaxactún and Waka (El Perú); and 9.0.0.0.0 (also a b'ak'tun ending) at El Zapote and to the west at Piedras Negras.

On the one hand, it might seem curious that early-period endings were so distinctively celebrated in north-central Petén. But Aveni (2002a:211) notes a peculiar phenomenon of day counting that occurs only around the latitude of Tikal (17°13′ N): the year can be "perfectly segmented into multiples of 20 days, with each segment ending on a highly visible pivot of the annual solar cycle": zeniths, solstices, and equinoxes. North-central Petén was thus an ideal place for formally commemorating such temporal cycling through an ambitious building program, such as the construction of E-Group assemblages. These assemblages would celebrate these sites' sacred charters as exemplary centers and cosmic fulcrums where time's passage conformed to the ideal: even multiples of twenty days (see B. Tedlock 1992c:33) separate points of the sun's annual movement. It is in these distinctive groups that the earliest k'atun-ending stelae are found.

Details of celebrations at the endings of k'atuns and other calendrical periods are not available for the Classic period, but they can be cautiously retrodicted on the basis of the Late Postclassic and Colonial-period ceremonies (Edmonson 1986a:21–23, 82–99; P. Rice 2004:79–83). In these later events, endings/beginnings of the may and the b'ak'tun, and presumably also the k'atun, were celebrated by grand festivals featuring processions, feasts and drinking, speeches, confirmation of land titles and officerships, and sacrifices, and also by the erection of a stone or a wooden cross to commemorate the ancestors. This is clearly paralleled by the Classic-period erection of stone stelae recording dates that end k'atuns, lajuntuns, and so on. Some of these ceremonies occurring on period endings are known by terms or activities that also might have been significant in the Preclassic period: proclaiming "the word" (*mut*, a prophecy for the upcoming *k'atun*); seating of the *k'atun* on the mat of the *k'atun*; and "dawn" (the ranking of the mats, or seats of authority).

TIES TO THE ISTHMUS

For a long time it was believed that there were no clear relations between the Gulf coast Olmec and the lowland Maya, a lack of ties that was perplexing, given their proximity and ease of contact via riverine and coastal travel. Several decades ago, however, it was judged that the Olmec contributed concepts of kingship and authority to the Maya, as well as ideas and symbols manifest in art and architecture. For example, Schele and Miller (1986:104–105) noted that lowland Maya

> political symbolism did not evolve in a vacuum. It arose within a complex network of cultural systems spread across all of Mesoamerica. As early as 1100 B.C., the Olmec of the Gulf Coast had built large centers with massive programs of art and architecture designed to support their political system. This was the symbol system that spread throughout Mesoamerica. . . . The Maya took systems of cultural symbols that the Olmec had already tried, and adapted them to their situation. They neither invented the idea of state art nor did they have to experiment with different approaches to political art.

It is increasingly evident that the Olmec and Middle Formative occupants of the Maya lowlands had some direct contact with each other, and relations seem to be particularly indicated between the northern lowlands and the Gulf coast. E. Wyllys Andrews V (1986:30), for example, notes similarities between the pottery of the northern lowlands (e.g., Komchen) and that of the Isthmian region. And at Yaxuná, Middle Formative whitewares appear to include imports from the Gulf coast (Stanton and Ardren 2005:224).

But while analyses of art and iconography are typically interpreted as Olmec influences on the Maya, Andrews (1986:40) discusses the possibility of goods and influences moving in the other direction, from the Maya lowlands to the Gulf coast. Pottery is one example: most of the red-slipped pottery at La Venta, about 2 percent of the entire collection, is typologically identical to Maya Joventud Red of northern Yucatán (ibid.), and the excavators of San Lorenzo identified a sherd of Mars Orange ware (known from western Belize) in their excavations (Coe and Diehl 1980, 1:202).

Architecture is another example. Arthur Demarest (1976:100–102) suggests that large-scale Maya intrusions into Tabasco and Veracruz might have been responsible for the introduction of monumental mound-building, and possibly the construction of La Venta Mound C. Richard Hansen (Clark and Hansen 2001:23) thinks that E-Groups originated in the Maya lowlands and were adopted by peoples in the Isthmian region, a suggestion that accords nicely with Aveni's observation about day counting at Tikal's latitude. And it has already been mentioned that the "hollow drum" *tun* sign (glyph T548) of the ISIG, which came to have the sense of "year," appears in the Initial Series on Epi-Olmec monuments in the Isthmian region but originated in Mayan language (Justeson and Mathews 1983:592).

Some general themes of Olmec art appear in Late and Terminal Classic Maya art, particularly at Tikal and in the surrounding region. For example, the theme of down-gazing heads (i.e., ancestors) is prominent on Late and Terminal Classic period-ending stelae in central Petén, and it also appears at La Venta. La Venta Stela 3 (Fig. 5.5; ca. 400 B.C.?; also Stela 2), inside the Ceremonial Court basalt-walled enclosure, shows two facing individuals with smaller human figures in the "sky" above. Similarly, Terminal Classic *k'atun*-ending stelae at Tikal with "sky riders" (Paddler Gods) overhead, are set in walled enclosures in Tikal's bilaterally symmetrical twin-pyramid complexes (see P. Rice 2004:152–153). Downward-gazing heads also appear on earlier Tikal monuments, including Stelae 29 (A.D. 292) and 31 (A.D. 445).

A recurrent theme on many early monuments consists of seated figures gesturing and conversing, sometimes with incense burners between them.

This theme appears on some Izapa monuments—Monuments 5 (multiple pairs), 12, 14, 18, 24, and 27 (in sky panel)—and is common on Terminal Classic monuments in Petén (Fig. 8.9; P. Rice 2004:205, 238–239, 242). References to the earlier Olmec theme of contact with foreigners, however, are oblique (but see Chase, Grube, and Chase 1991).

The portrayal of captives is another theme on both Olmec monuments and those of the Late Classic Maya. La Venta Throne ("Altar") 4 (Fig. 5.6), which was found on the east centerline of Structure D-8, the E-Group long mound, shows an individual seated in a cave or in the mouth of a large jaguar creature, holding a rope that is attached to several smaller figures around the sides of the stone. These can be interpreted as captives bound by a continuous rope around the stone's sides, although Grove (1981b:66) calls it a "rope of kinship." A similar scene appears on San Lorenzo Monument 14. At Tikal, the faces and sides of altars accompanying stelae in the stela enclosure of Late Classic twin-pyramid groups often show seated captives bound to each other by ropes and/or mat motifs, and a mat or braid motif surrounds the scene on the Kaminaljuyú altar known as Stela 10 (Fig. 6.19).

LEADERSHIP, POLITICS, AND GOVERNMENT

The origin of leadership positions in society—and the evolution of such positions from temporary decision-making roles (in divination, curing, conflict resolution, hunting parties) into permanent chieftainships and then complex, hierarchical decision-making bureaucracies headed by kings, frequently sacred or divine—has been a matter of endless debate among anthropologists and social historians. It is within these processes that concepts of power and authority are realized and take on material expression, allowing archaeologists to discern not only "haves" from "have-nots," but gradations between these extremes. Discussions emanating from such debates expand into multiple realms, but the realm of interest here concerns the basis of power and authority. Attention to these affairs, in turn, frequently focuses on prime movers involving food production (hydraulic agriculture), environmental circumscription, warfare,

and ideology. Here I consider the last of these: the complex, interrelated roles of ideas about worldview, cosmology, and, specifically, time and calendrics, this last having played a surprisingly minor role in studies of the evolution of political organization among the Maya (P. Rice N.d.b).

A major and exceedingly difficult question to answer concerns when the institution of divine kingship emerged and why. It is generally thought that divine kingship began around 100 B.C. (Freidel and Schele 1988a)—relatively late in Mesoamerican prehistory, given the precocious developments occurring earlier in central Mexico, Oaxaca, and the Isthmian region. McAnany (2004b:151) argues that among the Late Preclassic Maya the lack of temples as royal mortuary shrines, the large iconographic programs focusing on supernaturals rather than rulers, and the absence of palace structures indicate that the "royal court . . . [was] not fully constituted" and the "tradition of divine rulers had not yet crystallized." Somewhat similarly, Rosemary Joyce (2000) follows Freidel and Schele (1988a, 1988b) in seeing a suppression of social-status distinctions among the Maya until the Late Formative, although they had long been present elsewhere as evidenced in burial goods. The Maya, she feels, were merely late

8.9. Terminal Classic Maya altar with conversation scene (drawing by Paulino Morales; from P. Rice 2004:166).

borrowers of indicators of complexity, such as jade regalia and the stela-altar complex, and by "adopting these traditional Mesoamerican media of state formation, Maya elites *opted into* Mesoamerica" (Joyce 2000:75, emphasis added). It is likely, however, that the apparent "lag" in Formative Maya adoption of the ideological underpinnings of order, legitimacy, and wealth as manifest in the trappings of kingship is equally if not more a consequence of such indicators being buried under centuries of subsequent construction, as attested by the findings at San Bartolo, Petén.

Clark's (1997:212) analysis of the "arts" of early "government" in the Isthmian region of Mesoamerica calls attention to the role of ideology, particularly as it can be addressed by public art: "Public art legitimated privileged access to supernatural forces and powers by marking a leader's exclusive access to revered ancestors, supernatural spirits, or deities." He (ibid.:217) goes on to note the power of drama and oratory—the spoken word—to emphasize the "naturalness of class differences and of the superiority of nobles and their rights to rule" as a basis for asserting rights to royal power in order to govern commoners. This is precisely the position I am arguing here, but mine is based not so much on public art as on control of time and temporal cycles, which I consider the basis of much early public art in the Isthmian and lowland Maya areas of Mesoamerica. Early expressions of elite authority were based on or supported by two major pillars. One was materialization of an ideology(~ies) of time via construction of public, civic-ceremonial architecture that established the setting for community ritual (e.g., ballgames, observations of solar solstitial zeniths and sunrise/sunset). The second was the adoption of symbol systems and vocabulary for asserting the legitimacy of authority figures who, as a consequence of their increasingly critical role in maintaining order by counting and recording the passage of days and their auguries, were also early daykeepers or calendar priests.

Xook and Shark

A relationship can be discerned between the Maya word *xok*—most commonly translated (e.g., in the Yukatekan *Diccionario maya-español*) as "count, number, sum, read"—and the responsibilities of early daykeepers. Daykeepers not only counted the days but also, aided by developing script systems, kept the calendars and their auguries, recorded the dates of significant events, and generally oversaw time's journeys. These duties, I contend, were fundamental to the development of later Maya (and also perhaps general Mesoamerican) leadership positions that English-speaking social scientists call "chief," "ruler," or "king."

For a long time it was thought that, in a bit of wordplay characteristic of the Maya, Classic hieroglyphic signs depicting fish were to be read not only as the verb "to count" but also as a noun referring to a fish, probably a shark, *xook* (C. Jones 1991; Thompson 2001). This reading is no longer accepted, although I wonder if it once might have had that meaning but it was long ago lost. *Xok* has been assigned many other meanings: verbs "to obey," "to respect," and noun "obedience" (*Diccionario maya-español*), and Barthel (1968b: 136) indicates that it means "tied cloth, noose" and also "to put in office" in Colonial Yukatekan (cited in Justeson, Norman, and Hammond 1988:137). Justeson, Norman, and Hammond (ibid.:138) also note that a reconstructed "root verb *xó.k*'" also may be used in accession statements to mean "emerge, appear," and this sense includes the rising of the sun.

The words *xok/xook* and their possible associations with sharks or other fish are important because fish are portrayed in Middle and Late Formative iconography (Fig. 5.12; C. Jones 1991; Joyce et al. 1991). Simon Martin (2003:38n3) notes that "the common appearance of shark motifs in Preclassic iconography, especially as earflare emblems, suggests that sharks had a special role within royal and mythic identity and may evoke ancestral creation myths." This comment, appearing only as a footnote and mentioning solely earflares, minimizes what is actually a rather prominent role of this imagery, particularly in headdresses. In the Late Preclassic, the individual on the Epi-Olmec La Mojarra Stela 1 (Figs. 5.18, 8.10a) wears a headdress that is a "maize plant depicted as—or transformed into—a shark, with a curved blade for a fin and a twin maize ear for a tail" (Stross 1994:9; for fish and maize, see also Taube 1986:52–58). This somewhat bizarre conflation reflects what Stross (1994:16) has reported as a near homophony between words for "fish" and "maize" in Proto-Mixe-Zoquean. A shark or fish headdress also appears on the Dumbarton Oaks pectoral (Fig. 8.10b),[7] late La Venta Stela 3 (Fig. 8.10c), Kaminaljuyú Stela 11 (Fig. 8.10d), and a Late Classic panel at El Tajín. Given these primarily early Late Preclassic depictions of sharks in the headdresses of apparently important and powerful individuals, it is also worth noting that the dynastic founder of Tikal is named Yax Eb' Xok,[8] or First Step Shark (Fig. 8.10e), who is believed to have ruled late in the first century A.D. (Martin and Grube 2000:26).

Earlier iconographic depictions show a creature described as a "fish-dragon": a long-lipped zoomorph with an underslung mouth (Stross 1994:12), which is a concise description of a shark's face. On the La Mojarra stela, three months are named Longlip. A shark motif appears on decorated Middle Preclassic mortuary pottery at Copán (Fig. 7.13), which also features the common Olmec paw-wing and flame-eyebrow motifs (Fash 1991:69; Schele and Miller 1986:119). The significance of fish in early iconography might be related to a myth about an earlier creation of humans who became "fish-men" after a flood and may be alluded to in the *Popol Vuh*, when the Hero Twins emerge as fish after self-immolation. The idea of humans of one creation turning into fish-men and then those of a subsequent creation being formed of maize dough is an allegory for human subsistence transformations in the Archaic through Formative periods, certainly in aquatic environments: "you are what you eat."

Piscine creatures or their attributes continued to be represented in Classic Maya iconography. In the Early Classic period, a common image has come to be known as the "Quadripartite Badge" as part of the insignia of a quadripartite cosmic monster. The "badge" consists of a bowl with an infixed *k'in* sign holding three elements (Fig. 8.11): a shell, a crossed-bands sign, and a perforator typically described as a stingray spine (see Freidel and Schele 1988b:75; Hellmuth 1988:166–167), which appears equally if not more like a stylized shark's tooth. This motif often appears in headdresses (Fig. 8.11b, c, d) and continues into the Late Classic period (Fig. 8.11d, e).

In Classic Maya script, the fish sign (Fig. 8.12a) is read as either *ka* or *kay* 'fish', or *u*, the third-person-dependent pronoun, although one sign (T204)

pictures a shark without a lower jaw (Macri and Looper 2003:52–53). Regardless of whether or not the fish sign represents a shark, fish appear in a number of Classic Maya hieroglyphs with little ostensible connection to fish or bodies of water: a fish head or body appears in glyphs for cacao (Fig. 8.12b; Montgomery 2002:132); the "hand-grasping fish" glyph (Fig. 8.12c) is read *tzak* 'conjure';[9] and the name and glyph of the month Sotz' are that of a leaf-nosed bat but the "patron" of the month is a fish (Macri and Looper 2003:52–53).

References to fish or fishing also appear in kingly titles, such as the collocation in the badly eroded upper text on Late Preclassic Kaminaljuyú Stela 10, which may read "fish-lord" (Mora-Marín 2005:78). They continue to be found in the Classic period,[10] including *Ah kaya* (he/she/it of fish?) on the Copán Structure 10L-26 Hieroglyphic Stairway; *ka nal* (fish? place) on the façade of Copán Temple 22a (see also Fig. 8.11d); and *kayoma* (fisherman) in the phrase "he is day fisherman night fisherman" on the Palenque Palace Tower Court Creation Stone. This role might be reflected in the incised drawing on one of the bones in Tikal Burial 116, which shows an anthropomorphic deity, with a fishing basket on his back, brandishing a large fish (Fig. 8.13; also Izapa Stela 1).

Selachian attributes are frequently associated with supernaturals. Maize deities are typically identified by their netlike overskirt of jade beads worn with a belt-ornament mask probably based on a shark (Miller and Martin 2004:97). This "Xok Shell girdle" bears a *Spondylus* shell and has been suggested to be a symbol of the womb from which the Maize God was born (Freidel, Reese-Taylor, and Mora-Marín 2002:67). At Palenque, the Temple of the Sun depicts God L holding a zoomorphic bar with shark monster heads at either end, which Milbrath (1999:272, 281, 295) associates with a "fish-snake" in the constellation we know as Sagittarius. GI of the Palenque Triad is depicted with fish barbels on his face, which have been interpreted as those of either a nurse shark or a catfish (ibid.:205), and the Stingray Paddler wears a fish headdress (ibid.:129, 205). This pairing of a fish-shark creature with a jaguar (the Jaguar Paddler), Tom Jones (1991:250–252) suggests, continued into the early Colonial period as recorded in a prophecy in the *Chilam Balam of Kaua*: "Muluc: Ah Xoc, El-tiburón, y Ah Balam, El-jaguar, son su anuncio." A fish-shark deity also continued to be recognized and was known as Chak Wayeb' Xok among the Yucatán Maya and Chak Xok among the Lacandon (ibid.).

Many kinds of fish (along with shellfish, reptiles, amphibians, and waterfowl) would have played a key role in early subsistence in Mesoamerica from Archaic times onward, particularly in the complex lowland wetland environments

that yielded early evidence for agriculture. Surprisingly, perhaps, the long history of Mesoamerican exploitation of sharks has received relatively little attention. Ethnographic evidence (see Borhegyi 1961; T. Jones 1985) suggests that sharks were regularly hunted in the Gulf of Mexico and the Caribbean Sea by fishermen venturing out in canoes or small boats. The animals were caught most frequently after they swallowed a large

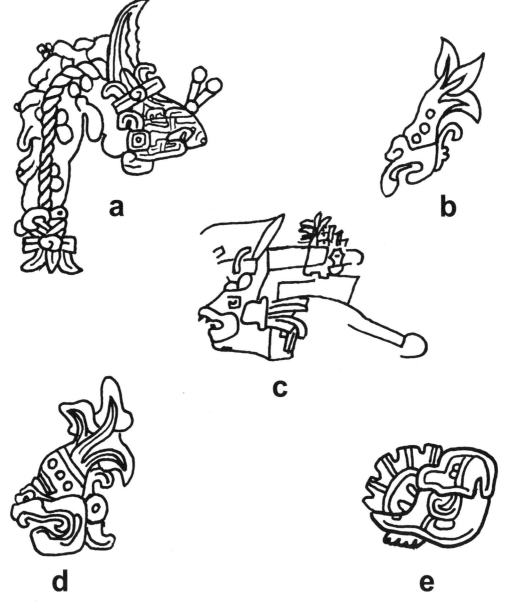

8.10. Fish in Mesoamerican headdresses: (a) La Mojarra Stela 1 (detail drawn from drawing by George Stuart); (b) Dumbarton Oaks pectoral (drawn from Schele and Miller 1986:fig. 32a); (c) La Venta Stela 3 (drawn from Drucker, Heizer, and Squier 1959:fig. 67); (d) Kaminaljuyú Stela 11 (drawing by Linda Schele, © David Schele, courtesy Foundation for the Advancement of Mesoamerican Studies, Inc., www.famsi.org); (e) Yax Eb' Xok's name glyph (drawn from Martin and Grube 2000:26).

baited hook and then swam to exhaustion trying to eject it, after which the fishermen clubbed them to death. It is assumed that sharks were fished primarily for food (one tiger shark can supply more than 450 kilograms of edible meat), but they can have a variety of other uses (Kozuch 1993:2, 3, 35): their livers are valuable sources of oil rich in vitamin A; their fins can be boiled to produce a gelatinous substance useful as glue; their skin has a sandpapery texture useful for smoothing wood;[11] and, once the tiny scales (dermal denticles, placoid scales) are removed, the skin makes a fine-quality leather known today as shagreen. Their serrated teeth would have been useful for shredding, scraping, and drilling, or as dart points; they also might have been used in bloodletting (Flannery 1976:344).[12]

Shark teeth and vertebrae, sometimes with drilled holes and sometimes unmodified, have been recovered archaeologically throughout Mesoamerica: in both domestic and ritual contexts (burials, caches); at sites both along the coasts, where the fish very likely were butchered, and in the interiors, suggesting an active trade in these materials; and in the Preclassic through Postclassic periods (Borhegyi 1961; Carr 1985; Hamblin 1984:24–30; idem 1985; Pohl 1985; Woodbury and Trik 1953). Numerous species are represented in these remains, including *Carcharhinus maculipinnis* (black-tipped or spinner), *Carcharhinus* sp. (requiem), *Sphyrna* sp. (hammerhead), *Ginglymostoma cirratum* (nurse), *Galeocerdo cuvier* (tiger) (Hamblin 1984:24–30), and great white (*C. carcharias*), as well as an

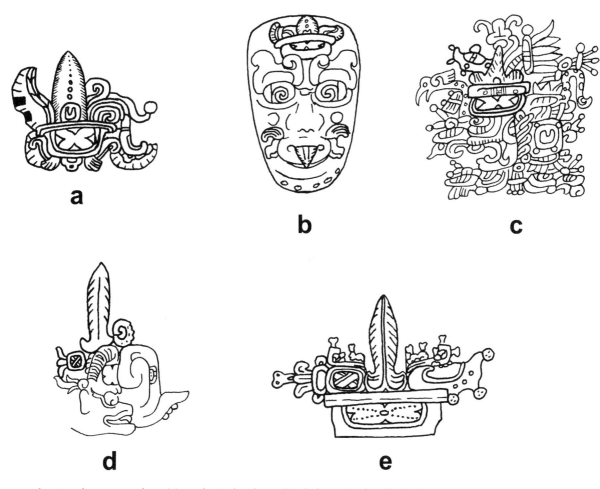

8.11. The "Quadripartite Badge": (a) on the Early Classic (Tzakol 2–3?) Delataille blackware cylinder tripod (drawn from Hellmuth 1988:fig. 4.20); (b) a fuchsite mask from Río Azul (drawn from Jones 1985:fig. 9g); (c) on an unprovenienced Early Classic (Tzakol) vessel (drawn from Hellmuth 1988:fig. 4.11c); (d) from façade of Structure 22, Copán; (e) on Tablet of the Temple of the Cross, Palenque (drawn from Schele and Freidel 1990:fig. 6.12).

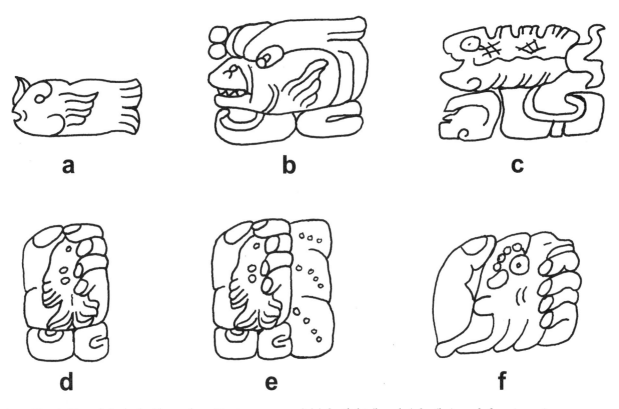

8.12. Classic Maya fish glyphs (drawn from Montgomery 2002): (a) *ka* 'fish'; (b and c) *ka-(ka)-wa*, *kakaw* 'cacao'; (d–f) *tzak* 'conjure'.

extinct species, *C. megalodon* (Borhegyi 1961; note that genus and species names have been modified since his publication).

In sum, the Yukatekan word *xok/xook* has various meanings, including "count," "read," "obey," "install in office," and "emerge" or "appear"; in Mixe-Zoquean there are near homonyms between words for "fish" and "maize." In the Late Formative, and perhaps earlier, certain personages of sufficient importance to be commemorated on stelae wore costume elements, particularly headdresses, displaying fish, perhaps sharks. Some of the early depictions of fish/sharks relate to bloodletting (Joyce et al. 1991), while among the Classic Maya piscine creatures appear in several glyphs that represent important ritual actions, for example, the fish-in-hand glyph meaning "conjure." All of these meanings and portrayals are congruent with the interpretation—based on observations of temporal/calendrical phenomena, including the sun's journey, and involving counting, enumerating, record keeping, and reading—of *xok* as indicating a high leadership role.

The headdresses and bodily ornamentation featuring sharks on Maya monuments illustrate Clark's (1997:212) point about public art, that it demonstrated rulers' access to supernaturals. All these representations appear to reflect some ancient and early invocations of power with sharks/fish, perhaps through the considerable feat of killing these giant, highly dangerous creatures of the seas and particularly by capturing the power of their mouths/teeth. These associations were subsequently diminished, apparently as the early kings took on the mantle of divinity or sacredness and became identified with maize, the Sun God, and the jaguar of the terrestrial and Underworld realms, but among the Classic Maya these meanings did not completely vanish.

The *May*

As I have argued elsewhere (Rice 2004), Classic lowland Maya geopolitico-ritual organization can best be understood with reference to such organization in the Late Postclassic and Colonial periods;

8.13. Anthropomorphic "fisherman deity" (?) on an incised bone from Tikal Burial 116, believed to be that of Late Classic ruler Jasaw Kan K'awil (A.D. 682–734) (drawn from Schele and Miller 1986:fig. 32).

this was based on the cycling of political capitals corresponding to the cycling of calendrical intervals of the *k'atun* (twenty *tuns*) and the *may* (thirteen *k'atuns*, or approximately 256 years). Evidence for celebration of these cycles can be seen, I believe, in sculpted monuments and architectural programs in central Petén and elsewhere in the Maya lowlands. The present review of archaeological, sculptural, and linguistic data of the Formative period leads me to propose that the origins of such Maya geopolitico-ritual organization were shared with the Isthmian area of Mesoamerica during the Middle and Late Formative periods (Table 8.3).

The possibility of Formative *may* seats in the Isthmian region was first mentioned by Edmonson (1979:14) along with his initial suggestions of the operation of the *may* among the Classic Maya. Nearly simultaneously, a closely related idea of movable regional "capital centers" was proposed for the Preclassic Isthmus by Izapa's excavators (Lowe, Lee, and Martínez Espinosa 1982:320):

> On the basis of massive earthworks and massed stone sculpture that was mutilated and moved about or buried in some chronological order, it has been suggested or implied by several authors that the Gulf Coast San Lorenzo (and possibly Laguna de los Cerros), La Venta, and Tres Zapotes sites were each in turn successive capitals of the Isthmian Olmecs during approximately the first thousand years B.C. . . . Cerro de las Mesas then appears to have become the regional Gulf Coast capital in the Early Classic. . . . Izapa would seem, in this sequence, to be a southern contemporary to part of later Tres Zapotes. . . . Abaj Takalik in the Guatemalan Pacific Coast piedmont . . . conceivably could have at one time preceded and then later succeeded Izapa.

A similar idea of movable capitals has been proposed for the El Mirador–Calakmul region. Richard Hansen and Stanley Guenter (2005:61) suggest that a Snake Kingdom, identified hieroglyphically by a snake (*kaan, chaan*)-head Emblem Glyph, existed in northern Petén/southern Quintana Roo, but the political center of this kingdom moved through time. The kingdom was first centered in the Mirador Basin in the Preclassic, then moved to Dzibanche in the Early Classic, and to Calakmul in the Late Classic. Although the authors do not connect these transformations to *may* cycling, that model of movable geopolitical capitals is a good fit.

Edmonson's arguments are based specifically on K'atuns 8 Ajaw (*k'atuns* being named for their last day) as marking the endings of *may* cycles. Following his reasoning, I propose that *k'atun* and *may* cycles had begun to be celebrated in the Petén area by 334 B.C., and perhaps as early as 590 B.C. (as perhaps some kind of a "proto-*may*") (Rice 2004:90). These dates are K'atun 8 Ajaw dates and correspond well to the ceramic sequence-dating of Tikal's early Mundo Perdido complex, where an E-Group began to be constructed in the Middle Formative period (Laporte and Fialko 1990, 1995).

It is not yet clear how or why K'atuns 8 Ajaw specifically came to have such critical importance in the history of the lowland Maya,[13] although they seem to have been recognized by the Middle Preclassic. The roughly 250- to 260-year periods of florescence and decline of the two important Olmec sites of San Lorenzo and La Venta are suggestive in terms of the *may* model (see Chap. 5),

TABLE 8.3. *Proposed Preclassic* may *seats in the Isthmian region and Maya lowlands*

MAY CYCLE	MAY SEAT		
	Gulf Coast	Pacific Region	Maya Lowlands
1102–846 B.C.	San Lorenzo, Laguna de los Cerros	Paso de la Amada?	
846–590 B.C.	La Venta I, II	La Blanca Chalchuapa	Seibal, El Mirador?, Cuello?
590–334 B.C.	La Venta III, IV	Tak'alik Ab'aj? Izapa Mound 30A El Baúl?	Tikal, Nakbe, Komchen
334–79 B.C.	????	Izapa Tak'alik Ab'aj?	Tikal, El Mirador, Cerros, Uaxactún, etc.
79 B.C.–A.D. 177	Tres Zapotes	Tak'alik Ab'aj? Kaminaljuyú Izapa	Tikal and ????
A.D. 177–435	Cerro de las Mesas	Kaminaljuyú Chalchuapa	Tikal, Copán, Calakmul
A.D. 435–692	????	Kaminaljuyú Chalchuapa	Tikal, Copán, Calakmul, Palenque, Caracol, etc.

Note: See also P. Rice 2004.

the transitions being marked by changes in artifact assemblages (particularly in exotics such as jade and greenstone), the conspicuous mutilation of monuments at San Lorenzo, and apparent demographic shifts. The Gulf coastal Olmec florescence began around 1150 B.C., some 130 years (half a *may*) after my hypothesized date of 1281 B.C. (4.13.0.0.0 13 Ajaw 13 Ch'en) for the beginning of the Long Count system of dating. During these 130 years, several generations of daykeepers would have had time to master the Long Count, expand its emphasis on *k'atuns* and *may* cycles, and rationalize the role of K'atuns 8 Ajaw as the starting/ending point.

As for cultural histories at this time, it bears recalling that in Pacific coastal Chiapas, Paso de la Amada was the seat of a populous chiefdom by 1350 B.C., and around 250 years later (1100–1050 B.C.) the region is said to have experienced an "aggressive takeover" by the Olmec (Clark 1997:228). The Isthmian region, in other words, was an area of population growth, trade, and competition in the late Early Formative, involving not only intraregional interactions but also contacts with peoples in Oaxaca to the west and the Maya region to the east. This was fertile ground for a variety of intellectual enterprises, including calendrical developments.

The Materialization and Politicization of Time

9 It has been proposed that the analytical concepts of order (social and cosmic), political legitimacy, and wealth (OLW) and their interrelations are key factors for understanding ancient civilizations, both how they overcame ever-present politico-economic instability and how their variable bases of political and economic power operated (Baines and Yoffee 1998, 2000; Richards and Van Buren 2000). Ideology, its negotiation and manipulation, underlies both OLW and political stability, and this facilitates application of another analytical concept, the "materialization of ideology": the expression of ideas in physical form in art, artifacts, monuments, architecture, ritual, and performance (DeMarrais, Castillo, and Earle 1996). Such physical and visual manifestations frequently appear in nonlocal materials, thereby representing wealth and value for elites through their connections to, and the imported knowledge from, distant lands and exotic crafts at the boundaries of the known, ordered world (Helms 1988, 1993).

The ideology of interest here is that pertaining to time, calendrics, and cosmology. Cyclical time was and is sacred in Mesoamerica; early paramounts owed their legitimacy and secular powers to "control" of sacred time—that is, their apparent manipulation of earthly and cosmic order—and regularly displayed that control through public ritual. I argue that the earliest "political" leaders in much of Formative Mesoamerica were skywatchers or daykeepers: individuals who possessed a body of recondite knowledge of the movements of the sun, moon, Venus, and other celestial phenomena and who used that special knowledge to guide quotidian and ritual events, thereby maintaining order. Such an individual can be considered a kind of shaman or augurer, or, in Helms's (1993) broad construal, a "skilled craftsman" whose craft is manipulating knowledge of the cosmos. Over generations and centuries and millennia, as the body of knowledge about celestial and terrestrial cycles expanded, so too did the sociopolitico-ritual role of these individuals. Time and control of time—also manifest in the development of systems for counting days and grouping them into units of months, years, and multiples of years—became a legitimizing basis for power in its own right.

Personal-wealth ornaments and objects made of exotic materials—Early Formative sun-reflecting mirrors of iron ores worn on

The key . . . to the Mesoamericans' conception of time and to their entire cosmology is their preoccupation with order and above all with cosmic order. . . . For the Maya and the rest of Mesoamerica, time is cosmic order, its cyclical patterning the counterforce to the randomness of evil.

—Nancy M. Farriss, "Remembering the Future, Anticipating the Past" headdresses or as pectorals, and Middle Formative jade earflares, celts, and pectorals with inscribed calendrical names—are early attestations of the materialization of time and its role in legitimizing early Mesoamerican elites. As early leadership positions became more formalized in connection with temporal control, so too did the material means of commemorating the beginning and ending of cycles of time, which involved massive deployments of local laborers to create architectural complexes, waterworks, and carved monuments. Classic Lowland Maya rulers are the epitome of this millennium-long process, materializing their control of time and its rituals in carefully carved and dated stones portraying divine kings in a "perpetual state of ritual action," as "embodiments of time and its passage" (Stuart 1996: 165–167). The rituals memorialized on stelae celebrating cyclical completions are dedicated to their kingly responsibility for renewing the grand cycles of cosmic time.

Poised at the fulcrum of the cosmos, Classic Maya dynasts bedecked with resplendent solar symbolism not only flaunted extravagant wealth but also revealed explicit identification as maize and/or sun gods. As Maize God, they symbolize the role of maize as the foundation of personal and communal wealth and well-being. More metaphorically, they embody Stross's (1994) observations concerning the Tzeltal Maya sequence of thirteen months corresponding to thirteen stages of growing maize during the agrarian year (and the thirteen day names in the 260-day calendar). In their role as Sun God, the kings not only are exemplars of cosmic order, they also represent the culmination of a process beginning, perhaps, by the late Early Formative, of development of a "solar cult" of sorts. Rulers wore sun-related adornments and tools like mirrors; at the same time, architectural complexes—materializations of this ideology on a grand scale—increasingly focused on the east. These developments reflect accelerating emphasis on the movements of the sun, dramatically illustrated in the *Popol Vuh* myth as the appearance of dawn and its four yearbearers.

DEVELOPMENT OF THE CALENDARS

Fundamental principles of order, legitimacy, and wealth underlay elite power and, ultimately, Classic Maya politico-ritual organization. These principles were based in an ideology of time—calendars, calendrical cycles of the *k'atun* and *may*, and rotation of divinely sanctioned "capitals" legitimized by these cycles—and they were born in the Early Formative period and greatly elaborated in the Middle Formative. Creation of the Mesoamerican calendars demanded focused intellectual effort in at least six areas: observing seasonal and celestial phenomena; developing a counting and tallying system; invention of the 260-day calendar; refining the solar calendar to 365 days; coordinating the two calendars (the Calendar Round); and innovating a system of signs, precursor to a script, to represent the days and months in each calendar. These developments likely occurred in the order given.

I propose that the foundations of what eventually became these calendars—observations of celestial and seasonal changes—were established during the fourth and third millennia B.C., when critical transformations also were occurring in subsistence, settlement, and social systems. In many areas of Mesoamerica, including the Isthmian region (but apparently slightly later in the Maya lowlands), by the mid-second millennium B.C., domesticated crops and food production had largely displaced hunting and gathering; permanently settled villages with monumental art and architecture had replaced temporary encampments; language groups were differentiating, social statuses were beginning to be manifest, and chiefly political organization was in place. The calendars developed in this milieu.

Knowledge of some of the regularities of the natural world that underlie the Mesoamerican calendars likely developed tens of millennia ago in the Paleolithic period and were brought to the New World by its earliest settlers. The earliest recorded observations of celestial cyclicity, dating back into Paleolithic times in Europe (as evidenced by scratched marks on bone; see Marshack 1972), appear to be lunar. The regularly recurring changes in the moon's appearance and disappearance and in its size, shape, and position in the sky over intervals of twenty-nine days or so would have been readily visible even to the most uninterested observers of the night sky. Similar lunar and solar observations would have been of increasing importance to groups moving from foraging to collecting subsistence strategies during the early Archaic, as a means of coping with the seasonal differences in food supply that accompanied environmental changes at the close of the Pleistocene. Early efforts to track the size and shape of the moon, the tides, and the movements of the sun along the horizon and the shadows the sun cast were pragmatic strategies for predicting the locations and times of availability of different kinds of food and scheduling activities such as communal hunting drives. Observations of cyclical natural phenomena relate to what E. E. Evans-Pritchard (1939) calls "eco-time."

My reconstruction of the developmental sequence of the two main Mesoamerican calendars, 260- and 365-day, proposes that they were created in conjunction with seasonal settlement aggregations (macrobands) in the Late Archaic period. Such large encampments would have occurred during the mid-to-late rainy season in tropical regions (late summer/early fall in northern-hemisphere temperate climes), when seeds and pods ripen and vegetal foods are relatively abundant. By analogy with hunter-gatherer bands in the southwestern United States, activities and rituals fostering group solidarity, such as dances, games, performances, feasts, "marriages," mourning, gambling, curing, exchange (of goods and information), and so on, were carried out in these expanded encampments. Important to this reconstruction, the late-summer solar zenith (one of two in Mesoamerica) fell in early August during settlement aggregation in various regions, and this solar event would have been a useful baseline for early timekeeping. I suggest that, as part of the ceremonies and information exchange of these events, early daykeepers also would have conferred about celestial phenomena and reckoned zenith passage.

Among Mesoamericans, counts of the passage of days likely began with the days of the moon's cycle, beginning with the first appearance of the new moon and leading to a register of thirteen waxing days and seven waning days (for a total of twenty, equal to the number of fingers and toes), followed by another nine or so days of relative darkness with the moon in the Underworld (see Macri 2005). These early lunar observations led to four important concepts and three symbolically important numbers among the Maya: thirteen levels of the heavens; gods of the numbers 1 through 13;

nine Lords of the Underworld; and twenty days of the *veintena*, or "month," in the 260-day calendar.

The twenty days of primary lunar visibility were assigned names of animals and other natural phenomena, most of which—and even their sequence—are shared by virtually all Mesoamerican calendars, not just the Mayan. It cannot be determined if the early 260-day calendar began at a particular time (e.g., during the late-summer zenith) and ended 260 days later, at spring zenith, or if it was counted continuously as a series of cycles of 260 days. Human gestation must have figured into these correlations from earliest times, particularly given the physiological and symbolic connection with cycles of moons/months/menses. If the August–September expanded settlements led to pairing of mates, the anticipatable outcome of childbirth nine months (ca. 260 days) later would fall around May, the beginning of the rainy season. In this light, Stewart's (1981) argument about an early "luni-solar calendar" holds considerable merit, as it accommodates the possibility that such a calendar was also the original basis of the 260-day calendar. This notion also can be reconciled with Stross's (1994) proposal that a sequence of thirteen of the twenty day names of the 260-day calendar served as mnemonics with reference to the maize-planting sequence. And it is consonant with Mathews's (2001) suggestion that the 260-day calendar emphasized nighttime ritual and thus may have begun at sunset.

Solar positional changes, like the annual north-south oscillation of the rising and setting sun along the horizons, also would have been obvious but initially complex to track and record because of the sun's longer time scales. Moreover, regular observation of the sun's movements by wandering bands would have been precluded because the people's own peregrinations would negate viewing solar positions from a single vantage point, unless they returned regularly to some designated place for observations (A. Aveni, pers. com., October 2005). Such a practice might correlate with the later and lengthening process of seasonal semisedentariness. Equinoxes—the two times of the year in which day and night are of equal length—would not have been easily measured by early Mesoamericans. These Archaic folk would, however, have been able to observe the solar zeniths by measuring the length of their own shadows or the shadows of sticks or staffs and maintaining a tally of the days between. The symbolism of such measuring devices for confirming seasonal changes might be seen on later Classic Maya monuments that portray kings holding large staffs. In any case, I propose that, because the second, or late-summer, zenith in August occurred during late Archaic settlement aggregations, this would have been a baseline for early timekeeping and developing a solar calendar.

At some point, and for reasons that can be readily guessed (e.g., the increasing importance of agriculture in the subsistence system) but not testably formulated, early Mesoamerican daykeepers desired or needed a calendar more closely matching the solar year. Such a calendar for "structural time" could have been developed in several ways:

1. Lunar observations: calculating the solar year as a count of repetitive events of the moon's cycle, or lunations, of twenty-nine days. A lunar year normally consists of twelve months of twenty-nine days, and the mean length of a lunation is 29.5306 days (Whitrow 1988:31). Counting a lunar year as twelve units of twenty-nine days leads to a 348-day year; twelve units of thirty days results in a much more accurate 360-day estimate of the solar year. Thirteen units of twenty-nine days overestimates the year at 377 days. Perhaps the solution was to alternate twenty-nine- and thirty-day counts (A. Aveni, pers. com., October 2005).

2. Solar observations, such as solstices, equinoxes, or zeniths: at some point, likely after agriculture began to be established, Mesoamericans realized the importance of a 260-day interval, such as a growing season, still recognized today in some areas as an "agricultural year," from February to October. Perhaps maize or another important food ripened in an average of 260 days. But many additional days had to pass before the growing season recurred.

3. A 400-day calendar, created as twenty "months" of twenty days each: evidence comes from the Kaqchikel language, in which *may* refers to a cycle of twenty "years" of 400 days (Lounsbury 1978:762; Lowe 1982b:281; Recinos and Goetz 1953:31). This overestimate of the solar year would have been whittled down to a closer approximation by omitting two months, resulting in a 360-day calendar.

4. Expanding the thirteen day names of the 260-day calendar into a series of twenty-day months and doubling certain months (see Chap. 4): many Mesoamerican calendars have doubled month names, and these are primarily found in the rainy season (see, e.g., Edmonson 1988:216–217). In so doing, calendar specialists kept late-summer zenith (later shifting to the winter solstice) as the starting point of the calendar because the months corresponding to the autumn and winter seasons in the present 260-day calendars are generally the same throughout Mesoamerica.

It is not clear which of these (or any other) methods might have been used by early Mesoamerican calendrical specialists, and several methods were likely employed as a check against each other. The real problem in creating an accurate solar calendar would have been determining the need for extra days beyond 360, how many of them were necessary, and how to keep the calendar in line with the agricultural seasons. In ancient Babylonia, calendar specialists periodically inserted a thirteenth month into the calendar to keep it in line with the agricultural seasons, "but there was no regular system for the intercalation of this additional month until the fifth century B.C., when seven of these months began to be inserted at fixed intervals in a cycle of nineteen years" (Whitrow 1988:31–32). The names of the months of the 365-day calendar in Mesoamerica may reflect origins in an agricultural cycle, but the increasing asynchrony of the calendar and the agricultural year apparently was not a matter of theoretical or empirical concern.

When did these calendrical developments occur? Calendars and chiefly political organization developed in Mesoamerica during the period from ca. 2000 to 1500 B.C., as part of the Archaic-to-Formative transition. If the 260-day calendar was created first, by 2500–2000 B.C., as I think can be argued, the calendar of 360 + 5 days was relatively quickly developed thereafter. Indirect evidence—the appearance of measurement units of 52, 260, and 365 at Paso de la Amada—suggests that by 1650–1500 B.C. or so the two calendars had been intermeshed into the 52-year Calendar Round. Solid evidence for the Mesoamerican calendars—dates inscribed in stone—do not occur until a millennium later, with Calendar Round dates in Oaxaca dating to the sixth century B.C. These dates, of course, provide only a terminus a quo for the earliest survivals of a sign system for representing dates in these calendars in permanent media. They do not indicate the date of development of the calendars themselves, and early records might have been kept on perishable materials for many centuries.

The existence of the Calendar Round is a baseline requisite for the later developments on which the distinctive pattern of Maya geopolitico-ritual cycling is premised. The Maya continued to maintain a ritually significant 360-day calendar as the *tun* in the Long Count; it was used only by them and by the Epi-Olmec. The invention of the Long Count, traditionally thought to date to the mid-fourth century B.C., involves coordinating the calendars and projecting those coordinates back to the creation of the present era in 3114 B.C. I propose that the Long Count system of dating was invented far earlier, during the thirteenth century B.C.; the Long Count is based on the ritually critical *k'atuns*, which are the focal intervals of rotational geopolitical cycling.

Additional evidence pertaining to calendrical origins can be drawn from historical linguistics.

Although the many Mesoamerican calendars shared numerous components, particularly day names in the 260-day calendar (some of which are very old), the calendars were and still are ethnolinguistically specific (see Edmonson 1988:216–217; Marcus 1992a:118), and their differentiation might be related to the Early Formative differentiation of Mesoamerican languages. Unfortunately, glottochronological evidence for the diversification of major Mesoamerican language families is imprecise and provides conservative ("not later than") dates in the range of 3000–1500 B.C. With respect to Mayan languages, Proto-Mayan is believed to have emerged by 2200 B.C.; it may be related to Proto-Mixe-Zoquean, ancestral to the languages spoken in the Isthmian region. Yukatekan separated from the major highland Maya languages around 1400 to 1000 B.C., followed by Greater Tzeltalan around the latter date; highland Mayan languages underwent internal differentiation beginning around 600 B.C. (Kaufman 1976:108). Although one cannot formulate satisfying conclusions on the basis of such a generalized historical outline, the sharing of day names in the 260-day calendar throughout Mesoamerica underscores the likelihood that the earliest developments toward calendar creation, involving "Proto"-Mayan, -Mixean, -Zoquean, and -Otomanguean (in Oaxaca) speakers, were well elaborated by 1500 B.C.

I argue that these calendrical advances might have taken place a millennium earlier than conservative estimates would suggest. More specifically, I think it not unlikely that the precursors to what eventually became the Mesoamerican calendars—fundamental observations of celestial and seasonal changes—were being noted by the end of the third millennium B.C. These precursors include lunar observations, an emphasis on the second solar zenith, and creation of the 260-day calendar, all of which probably existed in rudimentary form by 2000 B.C. They coincided with the end of an Archaic/macroband lifeway and the beginnings of food-producing, sedentary settlements. I maintain that early leaders were daykeepers (among other duties) with a heritage of knowledge going back to the time of Archaic hunter-gatherers, and they earned and legitimized their status by invoking order: tracking days/suns and other celestial phenomena; using calendrics to augur the future; and thereby manifesting their unique comprehension of and oneness with the cosmos. With increasing emphasis on food production, the need for and creation of a solar calendar (including observation of solstices) would have been realized and synchronized with the 260-day calendar, probably during the first half of the second millennium B.C.

By the end of the second millennium B.C., villages in the Isthmian region displayed monumental architecture, ballcourts, extensive trade networks, ranking systems, and a whole host of phenomena that bespeak complex chiefdom political organization, as well as the components of order, legitimacy, wealth, and materialization of ideology by which complex societies can be usefully characterized. Shortly thereafter, the complex symbol systems characterizing Mesoamerican literacy and numeracy—counts and concepts, such as calendrical dates—began to be recorded on permanent media. With the current recognition of much greater Early Formative societal complexity than heretofore known, it is not unreasonable to propose that observation of temporal cycles, "control" of time, and development of calendars, including the Long Count, occurred much earlier than supposed and significantly influenced this complexity.

In this context, cultural patterns in eastern and western Mesoamerica began to differentiate by the second millennium (Fig. 8.2). Flannery and Marcus (2000:9–11; see also Clark 1991), comparing Oaxaca and central Mexico vis-à-vis the Isthmian, Olmec, and Maya areas, note differences in material culture variations apparent by 1400–1150 B.C. Similarly, major early language family differences can be identified: Proto-Otomanguean and Proto-Uto-Aztecan in the west and Proto-Mixe-Zoquean and Proto-Mayan in the east (Schele 1992). Major differences in script traditions developed in the late Middle Formative (600–300 B.C.), with "Oaxacan" in the west and "Southeastern" script in the east (Justeson 1986). Within the eastern part of this region—that is, the Isthmus proper and the Maya area—early stylistic differences also can be seen in Middle Formative pottery (Lowe 1989a:364–365) and script development (Justeson 1986:451). These differences appear to be language related: Mixe-Zoquean speakers in the Veracruz-Tabasco-Chiapas area (*tecomate* forms of pottery; Isthmian script tradition) and Mayan speakers farther to the east (jars with handles; lowland Mayan script). Clearly,

however, the east-west style zones were not impermeable boundaries, as it has long been documented that trade goods and vocabulary passed between Mixe-Zoque and Maya, particularly from the former to the latter, and even between Maya and Zapotec. Such early stylistic differences also can be seen within ceramic spheres in the Maya lowlands (E. Andrews V 1990; Ball and Taschek 2003), perhaps relating to Proto-Mixe-Zoquean, Proto-Yukatekan, and Proto-Greater Tzeltalan speakers.

THE *POPOL VUH* AND CALENDARS

Myths, writes Susan Gillespie (1989:209), reach "far beyond astral allegories and folk legends or the garbled mythicization of actual historical events" to constitute sacred history, relating how the world came to be and establishing the foundation for human behavior and institutions. Sacred histories are passed down orally through the generations and are performed on important occasions because they are "part of the ceremonial calendar that mapped social relations in space and time" (ibid.:211; see also Lamb 2002:342–343). It is not surprising, then, given my position that the *Popol Vuh* encodes the history of the origin and development of the Mesoamerican calendars, to find that "Aztec, Mixtec, Zapotec, and especially Maya cosmological beliefs were grounded in some version of the Popol Vuh" (Diehl 2004:98). Myths are key components of the ideological foundations of a society, and their recitation, performance, and recording in stone or writing constitute critical examples of materialization. The role of the *Popol Vuh* has been elucidated with regard to many aspects of Classic lowland Maya art, architecture, and culture history, but its relation to the major calendars has not been recognized previously (cf. D. Tedlock 1996:205–209, for discussion of Venus).

I hypothesize that the Mesoamerican calendars began with timekeeping by lunar cycles, and solar record-keeping began slightly later. This is reflected in the *Popol Vuh* by the story's beginning in darkness (night) with the major early events occurring before sunrise, that is, before the ancient Mesoamericans had achieved "control" of time by recording solar movements, memorialized in the myth by the arrival of dawn. The role of the grandmother as the moon heightens the ancient importance of that celestial body in early

Maya mythology, a role that continues today among the Cubulco Achi (Neuenswander 1981).

The gods created the world by their words and thoughts, and they undertook several efforts to populate the world with creatures that would "keep the days." What the gods wanted, according to Dennis Tedlock (1996:32, emphasis added), was beings who would "walk, work, and talk . . . visiting shrines, giving offerings, and calling upon their makers by name, *all according to the rhythms of a calendar*." They were unsuccessful in their first three tries; although the creatures of wood on the third attempt resembled humans in the way they looked and talked, they failed to "time their actions in an orderly way" (ibid.).

The *Popol Vuh* relates the killing of the Four Hundred Boys, who rise into the heavens and become the star cluster known to us as the Pleiades. I suggest that their death is an allegory for the abandonment of an early 400-day calendar. Reference to the "death" of 400 individuals can be found in both Aztec and Maya myth, hinting that this calendrical abandonment must have occurred very early, probably antedating the east-west cultural and stylistic boundaries referred to above.

Three sets of twins are in the *Popol Vuh*, the most important being the youngest set, the Hero Twins Hunahpu and Xbalanque. Twins can be understood as part of the broader cultural construction of dualities, widely celebrated worldwide. However, it is of no little interest that, among the Maya, twins and maize have a shared referent, and the various generations of twins in the *Popol Vuh*, especially First Father (GI'), have been identified with the Maya Maize God (Schele and Mathews 1998). Twins and maize play pivotal roles in the creation and re-creation of the Maya world. I suggest that the conceptual equation of twins and maize is a consequence of early Mesoamericans' increasing reliance on the ancestor of maize, teosinte (variously known as *Zea mexicana*, *Zea mays* spp. *mexicana*, or *parviglumis*), and maize itself for food during the Archaic period. As is well known, modern hybridized varieties of corn (maize) grow as tall single stalks with several large ears bearing numerous rows of starchy, nutritious kernels, each held to the cob by a small cupule and the entire cob enclosed by a husk. Teosinte, on the other hand, is a smaller, wild, multistalked and multibranched grass with both annual and perennial varieties. Its small "ears," two to three centimeters in length, commonly occur in pairs (i.e., as twins), hidden by a protective leaf on the grass stalk.[1] I suggest that the mythic emphasis on twins, and the relation between Hunahpu and maize, reflects an early regard for teosinte/maize as a preferred and perhaps ritual food.

Ears of teosinte bear only a single row of five to ten small kernels, each enclosed in a hard fruit case. The earliest archaeological examples of maize, dating around 4000 B.C., appear to have been modified by selection and cross-fertilization such that during domestication the hard fruit case disappeared. Kernels of teosinte or maize could be consumed by chewing them raw or after soaking, or they could be popped in a fire; the grains also could be dried and ground into a flour and then toasted or cooked as a gruel. The *Popol Vuh*'s stories of the Hero Twins jumping into a fire and their bones being ground into a flour could be oblique references to these maize preparations—popping and grinding. Stross (1994:33) concludes that maize symbolism and elite ritual were more closely intertwined in Preclassic times than commonly acknowledged, an observation dramatically illustrated by the newly discovered paintings at San Bartolo, and Taube's (see, e.g., 1996) interpretations emphasize such continuities through the Classic period. The association between twin grains of teosinte and Hero Twin as Maize God are doubtless part of the explanation.

The *Popol Vuh* is frequently consulted when interpreting Classic iconography, particularly that of the ballgame, because of its important role in that myth. Numerous exegeses of the Maya ballgame relate it to Classic politics, particularly warfare, sacrifice, and accession, and also as a reenactment of creation ritual, a role that may go back to Preclassic times (Hill and Clark 2001). In an extended discussion of the imagery of sculpture and murals at the Great Ballcourt at Chich'en Itza with respect to the *Popol Vuh*, Schele and Mathews (1998:206–255) interpret the court as a crevice in the earth's surface, providing access to the Otherworld, and suggest that ball play reenacts the end of the third creation and beginning of the fourth. They believe the Jaguar Throne in the ballcourt's Lower Temple of the Jaguar is the Jaguar Throne Stone at First Five-Sky, referred to in the

Maya creation myth at Palenque. The carved panels in the alley of the ballcourt show multiple figures costumed as ballplayers and a decapitated player with blood spurting from his neck; in front of the latter figure is a ball with a skull in it, mimicking the Hero Twins' play.

PILGRIMAGES AND *TOLLANS*

Sites in the Isthmian region such as La Venta and Izapa may have been *"tollans"* (see also Schele and Mathews 1998:39–40), long held sacred by Mesoamerican peoples, including the Maya, as "cradles of civilization" at least with respect to the origins of shared cosmology, creation myth, calendrics, and the calendrical basis of political power. The lowland Maya and others could have maintained ties with the Isthmian region through pilgrimages long after the Formative/Preclassic calendrical and political developments discussed here, allowing the sojourners access to the ancestral and heroic past (Helms 1988). In discussing Postclassic and Colonial-period Mesoamerican pilgrimages, George Kubler (1985) notes that they differed significantly from those of the Old World, which were usually journeys of individuals seeking some personal favor. Mesoamerican pilgrimages, in contrast, were generally collective journeys to places associated with particular gods or oracles, typically undertaken in behalf of a group, often timed to calendrical cycles, and sometimes involving sacrifices. Kubler (1985:314) refers to eighteen known (and late) destinations in Mesoamerica: fifteen in central and south-central Mexico and three in Yucatán. The Maya destinations, known from the Late Postclassic period, include the cenote at Chich'en Itza, which was dedicated to the rain gods; the "talking idol" of Ixchel on Cozumel Island; and an oracle at a shrine at Izamal. Kubler also relates pilgrimages to ballgame activity and trade (see also Helms 1988).

In addition to formal pilgrimages, Mesoamerican culture histories, particularly in the Postclassic period, are replete with themes of population movements and migrations: "An origin from some removed locale, a journey with stops along the way, the arrival at the new settlement where order is established and the world renewed" (Stuart 2000:501–502). The "stops along the way" were visits to sacred cities, or *tollans*, revered in social memory, where dynastic legitimacy and the right to rule were conferred. Such cities also may have been pilgrimage destinations for people from already settled populations. Variously seen as *tule*, Tula, *tulan*, and Tollan—all translated as "place of reeds" (or cattails)—the term is a metaphorical toponym used by the Aztecs to designate an exemplary metropolis or a place of civilization (Schele and Guernsey Kappelman 2001:37). For the Aztecs, Tollan was inhabited by the Toltecs, "great sages who had invented the calendar, divination, astronomy, the arts, writing, medicine, monumental architecture, the institutions of government, agriculture, money, and all things civilized. They discovered jade," obsidian, and turquoise; they were pious, rich, and "ancestors of all the people who spoke properly" (Schele and Mathews 1998:38).

There have been many arguments about what site constituted Tula for the Aztecs, the suggestions being principally Teotihuacan or the later Toltec site nearby known today by the name Tula. Michel Davoust (1981:180) proposes three *tollans*—Teotihuacan, Tikal (in the east), and Palenque—noting that Thomas Barthel (1979) associates them with GI, GII, and GIII, respectively. It is now widely agreed that there was no single Tula in Mesoamerica; rather, the term *tula* or *tollan* could refer to the capital of any polity (Schele and Mathews 1998:330n23). The Maya had a parallel term, *puh* 'place of reeds', suggesting that the *tollan* concept had a long existence, and Stuart (2000:502–506) explicitly associates *puh* with Teotihuacan.

In the K'iche' history portion of the *Popol Vuh*, the four men that Xmucane modeled from corn dough went to a "citadel" named Tulan Zuyua, Seven Caves, Seven Canyons, before dawn. Tedlock, in his 1985 edition of the *Popol Vuh*, comments that this particular *tulan* was probably near the Gulf coast in Tabasco or Campeche (1985:48), but in his later edition he suggests that the city was specifically Kaminaljuyú, "the eastern twin" of Teotihuacan (1996:45). Regardless of the specific location of the Tulan Zuyua of *Popol Vuh* fame, it is also likely that Formative sites in the Isthmian region, and perhaps the region as a whole, constituted what Mesoamericans called a *"tollan."* As Schele and Mathews (1998:40) observe, the topography and vegetation of the Gulf coast closely correspond to Aztec myth about the sacred place of creation, Snake Mountain and Place of Reeds, and its inhabitants, the Olmec, surely can be called "great sages" for their role in formalizing many core institutions and symbols of Mesoamerican political authority. The sacred landscape of La Venta has been interpreted as representing an earthly model of the place of creation and the site of the activities related in Classic creation myth (Reilly 1999).

What might constitute evidence for the Isthmian region as a *tollan* and destination of pilgrimages? Some data come from La Venta (e.g., Monuments 19 and 13, Stela 3, and Offering 4), which appear to show Olmec individuals interacting with personages presumed to be non-Olmec on the basis of their costuming or raw material. A similar situation may obtain for Laguna de los Cerros, where Late Classic pottery was found beneath Olmec sculpture. Diehl (2004:47) suggests that the "Late Classic inhabitants probably moved and perhaps even venerated the Formative-period monuments." Izapa also is a likely pilgrimage destination, with the inferences about the lack of texts situating the site outside historical time (Newsome 2001:18) resonating strongly. Most compelling is the astonishing preservation of so many of Izapa's monuments (Lowe, Lee, and Martínez 1982), although the monuments in Group F might have been destroyed by Late Classic occupants. This preservation suggests that the sacred landscapes of Izapa and its monuments were protected and revered—and perhaps visited by pilgrims in processionals—over the centuries following the site's Late Preclassic florescence. Stela 90, with a polished patch on the principal figure's leg, might represent a sacred monumental talisman that pilgrims touched in veneration, and an Early Postclassic cache was found at the base of Mound 60 in Plaza G-a (ibid.:249). All of this supports the notion that, as in other parts of the early world, ancient Mesoamericans were very conscious of the past. Time and social memory were couched in sites such as La Venta and Izapa and other features of the landscape, such as volcanoes and caves. Not only did they become part of mythical history, they can also be considered "engines for the creation of time, through the repetition at them of ritual acts" (Gosden and Lock 1998:6).

It is interesting to note similarities between some Terminal Classic Maya iconography and the iconography of the Gulf coast and Izapa: ancestors "floating" overhead; pairs of seated individuals conversing and gesturing; and, at Chich'en Itza, Atlantean figures supporting benches and similar ballplayer scenes. Such Late and Terminal Classic lowland Maya icons might have been prompted by pilgrimages to the Isthmian region on or in connection with calendrical (or other) events, such as the turning of the *b'ak'tun*, or on particular *k'atuns*.

An example of such a calendrical pilgrimage comes from an account by Fernando de Alva Ixtlilxochitl in the early Colonial-period Toltec *Relaciones*. He mentions two early "calendrical congresses" convened in 37 B.C. and A.D. 129, in which calendar priests adjusted the solar calendar to the equinoxes (Aveni and Calnek 1999:91–92, quoting Jiménez-Moreno 1954–1955:225). During the latter meeting on the fall equinox (a day 1 Flint in the Aztec calendar) in A.D. 129, "Toltec sages, astrologers, and [masters of] all other arts, assembled in their capital city, Huehuetlapallan, where they examined the happenings, calamities and movements of the sky since the creation of the world, and [accomplished] many other things . . . among which was the adding of a leap year in order to adjust the solar [i.e., calendar] year to the equinox . . . [and] it had been one hundred and sixty-six years since they had adjusted their years and times with the equinox" (ibid.). The location of Huehuetlapallan has been tentatively identified as the Olmec region near Coatzacoalcos in southern Veracruz (ibid.).

Obviously, this was not a gathering of archaeologico-culturally specific "Toltecs" but, rather, of many Mesoamerican sages and astrologers (i.e., daykeepers), who apparently met semiregularly on calendrical matters. It is likely that this was not a one-day affair, but the day 1 Flint, an equinox and first day of the Aztec calendar, was the canonical date for convening the group. For the Maya the conference might have been connected, symbolically or actually, to the half-*k'atun* (*lajuntun*) celebration eight months later, on 8.4.10.0.0 13 Ajaw 3 K'ayab' (May 22, A.D. 130). In the Gulf coastal region, several monuments were erected after this congress,[2] including La Mojarra Stela 1 with Long Count dates between A.D. 143 and 157 (Kaufman and Justeson 2001:2.74). The Tuxtla Statuette has a Long Count and *k'atun*-ending date of A.D. 179.

The La Mojarra stela suggests that reeds (*tule; puh*) already had importance, as some of the glyphs, not yet deciphered, show a human face with a bundle of reeds at the rear part of the head and various signs on the front. Kaufman and Justeson (2001:2.11) conclude that the signs atop the head indicate titles or offices, the bundle of reeds at the back being, in effect, a semantic determiner indicating a title, while the varying element at the front gives the specific title.

CYCLING: CHIEFLY AND CALENDRICAL

The kinds and sources of social and political powers by which acephalous, or egalitarian, societies are transformed into the complex societies known as chiefdoms and states have long been a topic of scholarly inquiry. Although the vast literature and arguments surpass the scope of the present work, the positions presented in the preceding chapters contribute to these discussions.

Certain themes lie at the nexus of debates about the origins of political and economic power, social ranking, and later stratification. Around the 1960s, researchers advanced various "prime-mover," monocausal, theories and explanations: warfare, environmental circumscription (Carneiro 1970), ideology, population pressure, agricultural intensification (Boserup 1965), agricultural hydraulics (Wittfogel 1957), harnessed energy (White 1959), and so on. Related studies focused on definitions and typologies: band, tribe, chiefdom, and state societies based on social organization (Service 1966), and egalitarian, rank, stratified, and state societies via political organization (Fried 1967). Subsequent exchanges, including a synthetic theory involving multiple causes (Robert Adams 1966), modified these concepts substantially, and the bases of the definitions have been altered by new data (Haas 2001b). Prime-mover theories were subdivided into managerial versus conflict theories (Wright 1978:50), and also formulations based on balancing opposing processes, such as centrifugal versus centripetal tendencies, cooperation versus competition, or fission-fusion.

These latter concerns demand attention to instability in early political systems, whether simple or complex. My explorations herein have been conducted with reference to a model in which similarities and differences among civilizations can be understood by the interrelations of three constructs—order, legitimacy, and wealth—as they act, through ideology, to overcome such instability (Baines and Yoffee 1998, 2000). For my purposes, the OLW model is not completely satisfactory because it is descriptive (by intent) and does not address the ways differing individual expressions and interrelations among these concerns came about. The underlying role of ideology (and, especially for Mesoamerica, cosmology), however, admits the process of its "materialization" (DeMarrais, Castillo, and Earle 1996) as a basis for inquiry into origins. In addition, discussions about the development of societal complexity in smaller-scale polities, including band-level hunter-gatherer units (Crothers 2004; Sassaman 2004), are informative.

These last two points are of interest because they permit archaeological study of the inception of leadership positions and power bases in small-scale societies with emerging sociopolitical roles. Most discussions of prehistoric and ethnographically known chiefdoms and their developmental processes (e.g., Earle 1991; Fried 1967; Gregg 1991; Service 1966; Upham 1990) highlight instability (also present in the OLW model), that is, the role of competition for prestige and power among rivals—be they big men, aggrandizers (Hayden 1990; Hayden and Gargett 1990), or (emergent) chiefs—and problems of succession. Such analyses also emphasize that the primary source of power in these generally small, kin-based societies is people: relatives and commoners who can be counted on to support decisions and perform labor as producers of agricultural products and craft goods. But these early leaders could not reliably count on others for permanent, unwavering support because they lacked the authority structure to enforce their decisions. Potential successors, whether relatives or others, always lurked in the wings.

Chiefdom political formations tend to be unstable cross-culturally, moving through relatively long-term cycles of greater or lesser complexity in decision-making administrative levels (Anderson 1994). Part of the explanation for this instability may be the fact that chiefly leadership is largely based on genealogical claims (descent from an important ancestor). Different descent lines or elite lineages may compete for advantage by attracting followers, for example, through competitive feasting (Hayden 1990) or factional jousting (Brumfiel and Fox 1994). The creation of large groups of allied elites over time tends to result in more complex chiefdoms. Complex chiefdoms encounter more information-management and decision-making problems and possess more levels to deal with them, but the paramounts have little coercive power to enforce their decisions. Challenges to leadership and succession were regularly stared down by the paramount. The responses to these challenges—the survival or failure to survive of the chief and his retinue—culminate in the seeming cycles of different levels of political complexity.

Chiefdom-level societies developed in many parts of Mesoamerica by the end of the second millennium B.C. (ca. 1150 B.C.; see Flannery and Marcus 2000:3), and it is not unlikely that political instability and cycling of the sort that Anderson (1994) described in the southeastern United States also played out among these early Mesoamerican chiefdoms. One example comes from Paso de la Amada in Chiapas (Lesure 1997:232–233, citing the work of Blake [1991] and Clark [1991]). The early Locona-phase (1400–1250 B.C.) village settlement pattern of dispersed platforms indicates a "segmental organization [that was] highly unstable," but by the late Locona and Ocós phases (1250–1100 B.C.), organizational activities were concentrated around a single large mound, perhaps representing the emergence of a simple chiefdom. This system collapsed at the end of the Ocós phase with the return to segmental organization. Richard Lesure (1997:233) concludes that "sociopolitical organization at Paso de la Amada from 1400–1000 B.C. is not, therefore, characterized by a simple trend to ever-more-complex organizational forms, but rather by a more complicated—perhaps cyclical—dynamic."[3]

I suggest that early Isthmian and Mayan societies developed a mechanism that managed these perturbing issues of succession and chiefly cycling. This mechanism was the *institutionalization* of such cycling through an ideologically and calendrically based rotation of leadership roles and power (see also Farriss 1987:578). Such cosmically sanctioned rotations established and sustained social and natural order by dictating conditions of legitimacy: transitions of both individual power (i.e., chiefly succession) and the geopolitical power of sites and polities were by means of units of sacred time, *k'atun* seats and the *may*. I propose that this calendrically based program began considerably earlier than the Late Preclassic and was in place no later than the Early Formative–Middle Formative transition (Table 9.1).

How might such a program of calendrically based rotating leadership have begun? Forty years ago, Marshall Sahlins (1968:12, emphasis added) elucidated the function of ritual in "tribal" societies, albeit with an essentializing that is unfashionable today: "Public, communal rituals . . . impose at the minimum a ceremonial peace, and by the implication of common dependence on supernatural powers instill a sense of the collectivity and of the dependence of every man upon every man. The latter effect may be heightened by *a ceremonial division of labor among kin groups, each charged with a special ritual function or performance, such that collaboration becomes necessary to secure supernatural benefits*." The kind of program I envision would have been based on these elements: communal ritual and ceremonial divisions of labor. It would have developed in a sociopolitical environment in which competition was discouraged, suppressed, or unrewarded; instead, collaboration and the need for order entailed greater advantage. And it would have been funded by the creation and growth of a "ceremonial fund" based on resources accumulated through surplus production, as outlined by Eric Wolf (1966:7–9). This "fund," as Wolf describes it, is a symbolic depository into which householders must contribute, above and beyond the "replacement fund" of grain and seed for continued agricultural productivity. As part of ordered society, and in order to accommodate the increasing economic differentiation of members of the community, members' contributions to this fund increasingly subsidize the growth of elites.

The role of cooperation in the evolution of societal complexity and also in chiefly cycling can be illuminated through simulation models

TABLE 9.I. B'ak'tun-*ending and* may *seating dates in the current Great Cycle*

LONG COUNT DATE	GREGORIAN DATE	*B'AK'TUN* ENDING AND *MAY* SEATING
0.0.0.0.0 4 Ajaw	3114 B.C.	Beginning of current Great Cycle and calendar
1.0.0.0.0 3 Ajaw	2720, Nov. 13	End B'aktun 13 or 0 (first *b'ak'tun* of cycle), begin B'ak'tun 1 (second *b'ak'tun*)
2.0.0.0.0 2 Ajaw	2325, Feb. 16	End B'ak'tun 1, begin B'ak'tun 2
3.0.0.0.0 1 Ajaw	1931, May 21	End B'ak'tun 2, begin B'ak'tun 3
4.0.0.0.0 13 Ajaw	1537, Aug. 23	End B'ak'tun 3, begin B'ak'tun 4
5.0.0.0.0 12 Ajaw	1143, Nov. 26	End B'ak'tun 4, begin B'ak'tun 5
5.2.0.0.0 8 Ajaw	1103, Apr. 30	*May* seating?
5.15.0.0.0 8 Ajaw	847, Aug. 7	*May* seating?
6.0.0.0.0 11 Ajaw	748, Feb. 28	End B'ak'tun 5, begin B'ak'tun 6
6.8.0.0.0 8 Ajaw	591, Nov. 13	*May* seating?
7.0.0.0.0 10 Ajaw	354, June 3	End B'ak'tun 6, begin B'ak'tun 7
7.1.0.0.0 8 Ajaw	334, Feb. 18	*May* seating
7.14.0.0.0 8 Ajaw	78, May 28	*May* seating
8.0.0.0.0 9 Ajaw	A.D. 41, Sept. 5	End B'ak'tun 7, begin B'ak'tun 8
8.7.0.0.0 8 Ajaw	179, Sept. 2	*May* seating
9.0.0.0.0 8 Ajaw	435, Dec. 6	End B'ak'tun 8, begin B'ak'tun 9 *May* seating
9.13.0.0.0 8 Ajaw	692, Mar. 16	*May* seating
10.0.0.0.0 7 Ajaw	830, Mar. 13	End B'ak'tun 9, begin B'ak'tun 10
10.6.0.0.0 8 Ajaw	948, June 22	*May* seating
10.19.0.0.0 8 Ajaw	1204, Sept. 28	*May* seating
11.0.0.0.0 6 Ajaw	1224, June 15	End B'ak'tun 10, begin B'ak'tun 11
11.12.0.0.0 8 Ajaw	1461, Jan. 4	*May* seating
12.0.0.0.0 5 Ajaw	1618, Sept. 18	End B'aktun 11, begin B'ak'tun 12
13.0.0.0.0 4 Ajaw	2012, Dec. 21	End B'ak'tun 12 and Great Cycle

Note: Based on K'atun 8 Ajaw cycling.

of so-called public-goods problems in mathematics and in game and evolutionary theory, which have investigated behavior in human and non-human biological systems (Doebeli, Hauert, and Killingback 2004; Gürek, Irlenbusch, and Rockenbach 2006; Panchanathan and Boyd 2004; also Henrich 2006). Cooperation involves costly investments (in time, effort, resources), and the simulation models are based on calculations of such costs versus benefits of investments by participants that aid the self, the other, or all. At a simple level, the simulations and experiments involve two-party games or scenarios in which each actor can make choices to act altruistically to benefit both parties or only himself or herself. More complex simulations use cost-benefit assumptions to elicit variations and assess the long-term stability or equilibrium of systems resulting from different levels of investment in cooperation or altruism among groups, as opposed to individuals, and may build in factors of "reputation" (actors' histories of contributions). It has been found repeatedly in such studies that *groups* of cooperators are more successful (in a long-term, evolutionary sense) than *individuals*, who are more successful by not cooperating or by competing.

With regard to humans and the evolution of cooperative sociopolitical behaviors, several findings from these simulations, particularly those employing reputations or historical sequences, are relevant. One model takes into consideration various types of what the investigators call "assortment" or nonrandom interactions, such as between relatives. Over long periods of time they find "a powerful synergy between small amounts of assortment and long periods of interaction, making increasing amounts of reciprocity the probable evolutionary outcome" (Panchanathan and Boyd 2004:500). But cooperative systems eventually collapse because of the "free rider" problem: cooperators and reciprocators contribute less and less out of frustration with those who do not contribute to the overall good but enjoy a free ride, a phenomenon known as the "paradox of altruism" or the "tragedy of the commons" (Doebeli, Hauert, and Killingback 2004:860). How, then, did the "evolutionary conundrum" (ibid.:859) of cooperative group behavior actually evolve?

One important element appears to have been an element of sanctions, or "punishment," for noncooperators. In an experiment with live participants asked to make choices in a "social dilemma situation," actors were initially asked to choose to play in a "sanctioning institution," which allowed them to punish a lack of reciprocal behavior by other participants, or in a "sanction-free institution," and then they were allowed to move between them (Gürek, Irlenbusch, and Rockenbach 2006). The investigators (ibid.:108) found that that the opportunity to deliver negative sanctions to noncooperators was highly popular and, although the sanctioning institution was not initially an attractive choice, by the end of the experiment all subjects had moved into the sanctioning institution and cooperated strongly. The researchers conclude (ibid.:110) that "the initial establishment of the 'norm to cooperate and punish free-riders' is mainly driven by the steadfastness of the strong reciprocators to punish noncooperative subjects, despite severe individual losses. Although strong reciprocators are a minority, they manage to establish and enforce a cooperative culture that attracts even previously noncooperative individuals."

In anthropological and archaeological discussions of the emergence of social ranking and complexity, the role of cooperation usually has been underplayed vis-à-vis that of competition or coercion, although in some of his early writings William Sanders emphasizes the role of cooperation: "Cooperation and competition are frequently seen as polar processes but . . . competition may be the major stimulus to cooperation—and in fact almost demand cooperation as a solution to particularly acute problems of competition" (Sanders and Price 1968:96). This discussion is situated in the context of the cultural ecology of the development of civilization in Mesoamerica, specifically,

the role of cooperation in maintaining irrigation systems. This has led Sanders and Barbara Price (1968:230) to note that "there is in some circumstances strong selective pressure in favor of cooperation as a response to competition."

I suggest that the situation of developing early, sedentary, agricultural settlements in the Isthmian and Mayan regions represents such a circumstance favoring cooperation and generous contributions toward the public good as, for example, in feasts (see also Clark and Blake 1994:21, whose economic model places emphasis on the role of aggrandizers, generosity, and reciprocity). It is easy to conjecture that from very early times there also would have been an advantage to cooperation, rather than competition, in sharing observations of celestial and seasonal phenomena, as these would have contributed to the material security and welfare of Archaic-period hunter-gatherers. Daykeeper-shamans were likely viewed as repositories of knowledge in their bands, their words gaining greater authoritativeness as they moved to elder status. Their words especially held weight in situations of conflict (Helms 1993:26), which was likely to increase as settlements were extended in size and duration. Moreover, as large seasonal groupings grew, whether in arid highland or lowland aquatic environments, multiple daykeeper-shamans from the assembled bands would have been able to compare observations relating to the second solar zenith and later equinox and to share information on a host of related matters. In such settings, information exchange would have been advantageous for discussing times and locations of food availability, planning the next year's gathering, noting the position of the stars, evaluating unusual events such as eclipses and meteors, assessing favorable and unfavorable omens, and so on. At some point, following archaeologists' scenarios of macroband settlement's lengthening, over centuries and millennia, into permanent year-round settlement, so too the role of daykeeper-sky-watcher-shaman devolved permanently onto a single individual or group of individuals, perhaps a family or descent line (à la Sahlins; also Panchanathan and Boyd's [2004] "assortment").

A formal system of rotational leadership would have to be grounded in the emergence of permanent leadership positions—chiefs—and little evidence supports their existence much before

1200–1000 B.C. Lesure (1997) raises the possibility of some kind of political cycling in the late second millennium B.C., which seems to immediately precede the development of a complex chiefly type of political organization in the Mazatán area. Alternatively, a powerful chief already existed among the Olmec and engineered a takeover of the area around 1100–1050 B.C., consolidating it into one complex chiefdom (Clark 1997:228–229).

In addition, a formal system of rotational leadership of the kind I propose implies strong cooperative relations and mutual support—strong reciprocation, in the simulations' terms—among early chiefs, leaders, or elites within what is typically characterized as a highly charged atmosphere of material competition. As Anderson (1994:51–52) remarks with respect to elite cooperation in complex chiefdoms (an outcome of the developmental processes I am discussing here),

> Elite support was fragile, however, since the elites living within the constituent parts of a complex chiefdom were fully capable of operating on their own. Obtaining the cooperation of fellow elites was thus an essential prerequisite and primary means by which paramount elites emerged and retained their positions as leaders/rulers of complex chiefdoms. . . . Because of these legitimate successors to power, challenges to chiefly leadership were inevitable, given human ambition and opportunity. The outcome of these leadership struggles in complex chiefdoms, as noted, almost invariably took one of three courses. Either the office of the paramount chief and its associated rank echelon continued at the original center, or it rotated or relocated to a new center, or it disappeared altogether, as the paramount chiefdom fragmented back into a series of simple chiefdoms and the process began anew.

If early leaders or big-men or "proto-chiefs" in early Mesoamerican simple chiefdoms were actors in a similar kind of environment, they somehow managed to turn competition into cooperation and

foster the first or second outcomes, rather than the third. To do so, they would have had to agree to cede some degree of prestige and power to other would-be leaders. Why would they do something so altruistic? Probably because such cooperation was already built into the system through tradition, and also because they received something equally important in return. This might have begun, as Sahlins (1968:12) suggests, with a "ceremonial division of labor among kin groups" having differing but complementary and reciprocal ritual obligations that were all essential to pleasing the supernaturals. I propose that early leaders conceded (albeit perhaps very reluctantly) that their terms of power would be neither lifelong nor indefinite, but, rather, limited to a finite period; after this period ended, another individual or kin group would assume leadership. In exchange, the system gave them some assurance—assuming everybody followed the rules—that during this specific interval they would not face challengers or usurpers. Cooperation assured cosmic continuity; noncooperation could bring about undesirable cosmic sanctions.

It is not possible to determine, at this remove, what the earliest periods of rotating leadership might have been. It seems likely, however, that any program of rotating positions began with fairly small intervals of time—ritual time—probably initially less than the twenty-year *k'atun*, and certainly not as long as the 256-year *may*. The origin of the *k'atun* itself is unknown,[4] but if these early terms of rotating authority were of five years' duration, for example, they could have been combined with the principle of quadripartition to yield the ritually important number of twenty years or *tuns*. Or, they could have lasted ten years/*tuns*. As I suggest elsewhere (Rice 2004:111–114), the rule of Classic *k'atun* seats was comparable to that of Colonial-period *k'atun* "idols" in Yucatán: incoming "guest" for ten years; sole power for the next ten years; then diminishing and shared power in the final decade.[5]

I propose that *k'atuns* were counted earlier than the Long Count and that the Long Count originated as a count of *k'atuns*, as early as the late second millennium B.C. The *may* totals thirteen *k'atuns*, combining the ritually important numbers 13 and 20 such that the Long Count consisted of thirteen *b'ak'tuns* and twenty *mays*. How and when this unit developed is difficult to hypothesize. Nonetheless, I suggest that it was in existence by the Middle Preclassic period. The evidence for this is admittedly weaker than I would wish, consisting of the timing of florescence and decline of the major early Isthmian and Maya centers, the existence of at least thirteen sites with the early E-Group "observatory complex" in Chiapas, and the presence of thirteen stelae in the E-Group at the site of El Mirador in Petén. Carved stelae erected for calendrical commemorations were outgrowths of stones or wooden posts originally placed on the early long mounds of E-Groups for observational purposes and of uncarved stelae set in north-south rows in plazas. The presence of many early E-Groups in central Petén is of interest and may relate to Aveni's (2002a:211) observation that sites there are, "by a curious quirk of astronomy and geography, situated at that 'magic latitude' in which the year can be perfectly segmented into multiples of 20 days . . . the ideal place to develop a year cycle based upon the principle of tying solstice and equinox to zenith passage in neat 20-day bundles."

I have argued that the development of the 260-day calendar with its twenty-day "bundles" occurred in the Early Formative or the Archaic-to-Formative Transition, as early as 2500–2000 B.C. Unfortunately, we know little about the early occupation of the Maya lowlands during this time. However, the latitude of Tikal (17°13′) is nearly identical to that of the Etla valley north of Oaxaca City,[6] and in this latter arid, highland region Archaic microband-macroband patterns and Early Formative settlement and culture are better known. Moreover, the Oaxaca valley is a place of early calendrical developments (Marcus 1992a), equivalent to the eastern Isthmian region discussed here. Although Tikal and the central Petén region might have been "ideal" to develop the twenty-day units of the 260-day calendar, the region was certainly also ideal for elaborating these calendrical achievements by materializing time in stelae and commemorative architecture. It is highly conjectural, but perhaps a need to find an optimal place for perfecting calendrical observations was a part of what fueled early migrations of Maya speakers into the lowlands and the appearance of early E-Group assemblages in central Petén.

MAYA CALENDARS: ORDER, LEGITIMACY, AND WEALTH

The lowland Maya, perhaps alone among the world's ancient civilizations, maintained an almost unfathomable obsession with precision in recording time. The Maya were literate and "numerate," as were many ancient civilizations, but unlike most of them, the Maya knew the concept of zero as well as the fact that the solar year was slightly longer than 365 days, and they made adjustments accordingly. The evolutionary steps toward this precision and these concepts do not, at least at this point in our understanding, seem to be unique to the Maya; instead, they were shared among several Formative cultures in the greater Isthmian region. There and elsewhere in Mesoamerica, calculations of the passage of time since creation, registered in the intricate Long Count, were lost after the Epi-Olmec florescence in the Gulf coast, but the lowland Maya to the east retained and perfected such knowledge. Why? Why did these distinctive flourishes of mathematical and calendrical precocity develop in Mesoamerica, and why were they so emphatically sustained and proclaimed by the Maya specifically, as opposed to other cultures?

The Baines and Yoffee (1998, 2000) model specifies order, legitimacy, and wealth—along with ideology, political instability, and high culture, and the interrelations among all of them—as the critical elements for characterizing early civilizations. For the Maya, as suggested in the chapter epigraph, the greatest of these was order. Order is the fundamental theme of the K'iche' Maya myth of cosmogenesis, the *Popol Vuh*, in which the gods' early attempts at creating humans were met with chaos and disorder because the creatures could not speak the gods' names or "keep the days" (D. Tedlock 1996:67). Thus speech, veneration of supernaturals, and maintenance of the calendar were fundamental duties of humans to maintain order in the cosmos and in the natural world. Indeed, if I am correct in my hypothesis about the *Popol Vuh's* recapitulating the history of creation of the calendars, then this myth is actually the sacred charter underwriting that order.

I suggest that the Maya obsession with "control of Time" had deep roots in the late Archaic and early Formative periods. Of all the important elements in the Baines-Yoffee OLW model, the keystone in early Mesoamerica was order, and the other elements were submerged in and outgrowths of this central focus. Why was there such an early focus on order among early Mesoamericans? A history of environmental unpredictability and violence is one easy and obvious answer, particularly for those predisposed to ecological explanations: the region is one of volcanoes, earthquakes, and hurricanes. Life in marginal environments, such as that of highland Mexico, would engender deep concerns about the availability of water (and the coming of the rains) and food, and put a premium (i.e., social and political "capital") on the ability of individuals to solve such problems. What about life in high-energy (i.e., nutritionally rich) environments, such as coastal, riverine, or lacustrine regions? Some evidence suggests that important developments of calendrics, numeracy, and literacy occurred in such areas. The question, then, is why would "order"—cosmic, natural, or social—be an imperative in such a setting? Perhaps there would be some concerns about variability in rainfall vis-à-vis sustaining maize agriculture, not an unlikely proposition, given the three hundred to four hundred centimeters of rain in parts of the Gulf coast, but a mere five centimeters in northwestern Yucatán, only six hundred kilometers distant. Interpretations of an angry sky/lightning/storm/rain god in many areas of the isthmus (including Oaxaca) and the importance of rulers as maize gods throughout the Classic period among the Maya might provide some support for this speculation: order was manifest by the regular arrival of the rains and the growth of maize. The early importance of sharks/fish is not easy to explain in this context, but seems most clearly related to concepts of order in a lowland coastal setting.

Order confers legitimacy. The ability to create and sustain social, natural, and cosmic order was the most fundamental requisite of establishing early rulers' legitimacy, expressing their unique partnership with the supernatural forces of the cosmos. How did early paramounts demonstrate this capability? The *Popol Vuh* indicates that what the early gods sought of early humans (and, more specifically, of early elites and leaders) was beings who would speak their names, praise them, and keep the days. I suggest that, with respect to maintaining social order, another critical factor was their pragmatic ability to participate in a network of collaborative relations ensuring that "government" would consist of orderly transitions of power rotating among social units. These collaborative relations were founded on a version of what might be called shared governance based on sequential periods of rule that maintained the order of time through the correlation of calendars, and the successive rule of *k'atuns* or their subdivisions. Time itself was the sacred ruler; humans were merely its mortal and temporal custodians.

The tertiary element of the OLW model, at least in early Mesoamerica, is wealth. Wealth and the legitimacy of elites are intimately tied in the model, and wealth is particularly determined by access to and accumulation and display of exotic goods in ancient civilizations. In Formative Mesoamerica different kinds of elite goods were widely distributed (by unclear exchange mechanisms): iron-ore mirrors, jade and greenstone, and marine shell were sequentially favored as elite goods in the Early, Middle, and Late Formative periods, respectively, throughout the Isthmian region. I suggest that such goods were, at least in Formative Mesoamerica, not simply vehicles for elites to flaunt their legitimacy but, more important, they constituted the armature of order. That is, sumptuous displays of exotic wealth goods demonstrated in part that rulers had the responsibility, authority, and sanction to uphold social/earthly order: their access to exotic goods constituted recognition of their legitimate skills and powers to interact positively with, and be regarded as legitimate by, rulers of the communities or regions that controlled those goods. But in addition, these goods also revealed that cosmic order was upholding *the elites*: the supernaturals representing the powers of sky, earth, rain, and so on, were satisfied with the elites' rule, their offerings, their words, and their calendrical rituals. Thus elites' conspicuous regalia and wealth on monuments and in burials were not "mere" displays of personal material wealth; they were materializations of supernatural approbation of the social/earthly and cosmic order they oversaw by "keeping the days."

Ideology (here incorporating cosmology and worldview) was obviously an underpinning of the focus on order, and materializations of time (in monuments and architecture, and in its personification in gods and units of time) are the mechanical and measurable manifestations of the ideology(~ies) of Time that lies at the core of Mesoamerican order. In the OLW model applied to Formative Mesoamerica, ideology is fundamental: the pragmatic utility of ideology was to overcome the political instability of early chiefdoms and specify the necessary components of order. I propose that, as part of this constitution, there also came to be an ideology of cooperation/partnership vested in sustaining cycles of time to maintain social and cosmic order; the political agendas of individuals or individual kin lines were submerged in recognition of the benefits of adherence to a wider corporate agenda. The outcome of these developments was the rotational model of geopolitico-ritual cycling of *k'atun* and *may* seats.

In bringing my thoughts to a close, I note that I have examined the origins of the Maya calendars primarily from the perspective of the better-known data and sites of the Isthmian region in the Early and Middle Formative periods. It is unfortunate that the heavily overbuilt Preclassic settlements in the Maya lowlands rarely (although increasingly) allow similar evidence to come to light. Many components of the general worldview and the calendrical ideology discussed herein, such as quadripartition, lunar observations, color symbolism, and creation myths, are not unique to the Maya but are widely shared throughout Mesoamerica and have deep and ancient roots possibly antedating the Archaic period (Coe 1981a:161–162; Grove 1993:91; Lathrap 1974; Marcus, Flannery, and Spores 1983:38–39; Schele 1992:2). And more and more data are accumulating from the early Maya lowlands to suggest that Maya developments in calendrical and related matters are contemporaneous with, and might even precede, those of the Isthmian region and reveal more wide-ranging contacts. For example, it has already been mentioned that

- ceramic evidence suggests close and direct relations: La Venta might have imported Maya red-slipped Joventud Red pottery from the lowlands (E. Andrews V 1986:40; Green and Lowe 1967:66); a sherd of Mars Orange ware of the Belize valley was found at San Lorenzo (Coe and Diehl 1980, 1:202); and Gulf coastal white slipped pottery was found at Middle Formative Yaxuná (Stanton and Ardren 2005);
- monumental mound-building might have been introduced into the eastern Gulf coastal area from the Maya lowlands (Demarest 1976:100–102);
- the so-called observatory E-Group complexes might have originated in the Maya area (Clark and Hansen 2001:23);
- the cruciform cache of jades at Seibal is dated ca. 830–780 B.C. and could slightly predate similar caches at La Venta;
- the hollow drum sign of the Long Count ISIG is the Maya *tun*, or year, and represents the influence of lowland Mayan speakers in the Isthmian region (Justeson and Mathews 1983:592); and
- the newly discovered writing at San Bartolo in Petén appears to date around 300 B.C., earlier than known examples of Epi-Olmec script.

Currently available data are unclear as to the temporal primacy of the Maya lowlands versus the Isthmian region in these developments. Future research with new and carefully calibrated radiocarbon dates is necessary to clarify these issues of origins and directionality of influence.

I close with the words of Barbara Tedlock (1992b:224, emphasis added), and her comments on the role of contemporary Maya calendrics for understanding the past:

> It appears that Maya peoples have, and had in their Precolumbian past, differing systems of timekeeping that they used in the separate provinces of their biological, astronomical, psychological, religious, and social realities, and that these various systems underwent a process of totalization within the

overlapping, intermeshing cycles of their calendars. Given the complexity of this cosmology, which is ritually reenacted, shared, and thus maintained by contemporary Maya, their knowledge ought not be dismissed as the degenerate remains of Classic Maya glory. Rather, *current cosmological theory and practice ought to be respected as a precious resource providing the conceptual tools for reconstructing the meaning of the material objects that happened to have survived from the Classic period.*

I would extend this respect also to cover material objects that happened to have survived from the Preclassic or Formative period and push it even earlier into the Archaic, as suggested by Flannery (1976:344–345).

Today we know something about the endpoint of the development of the Mesoamerican calendars and their use, thanks to inscriptions, codices, and other indigenous writings, and to the Spanish chronicles. But we understand virtually nothing about—nor do we seem to have much contemplated—their origins several millennia ago. To say it is unfortunate that we have no physical traces of the accomplishments of these millennia is a gross understatement. I do not believe, however, that we are therefore forced to remove such developments from discussion. Rather, we can work iteratively back from what we do know—about early/simple and later/complex chiefdoms, subsistence patterns, linguistic changes, iconography, calendars, monumental architecture, and so on—to retrodict calendrical origins in an "if-then" manner: if, at T_3, we know C was present, then what must have happened earlier, at point T_2, in order for it to occur? And if at T_2, B was also present, then what would have occurred even earlier, at T_1, to allow it to exist? Similarly, if calendars and control of time were the basis of early leadership positions, then this should be manifest in calendrical expressions or observational aids as personal items of wealth and legitimacy. This is the procedure I used here to illuminate the still-clouded origins of Mesoamerican calendars and the expansion of calendrically based rotating geopolitical organization and ritual by the Maya.

Notes

CHAPTER 1

1. In a related vein, Esther Pasztory (1993:135) notes that, "for southern Mesoamerica in the Classic period, the Olmec and Izapan traditions fulfill the role that Classical antiquity plays in Europe."

2. One problem in the *Popol Vuh* is determining how many gods of creation there were and who they were, in part because of its lack of punctuation and its couplet structure. The text begins with a long list of deities, identified in pairs: "the Framer and the Shaper, She Who Has Borne Children and He Who Has Begotten Sons . . . Hunahpu Possum and Hunahpu Coyote, Great White Peccary and Coati, Sovereign and Quetzal Serpent, Heart of Lake and Heart of Sea, [and] Creator of the Green Earth and Creator of the Blue Sky . . . the Midwife and the Patriarch whose names are Xpiyacoc and Xmucane, the Protector and the Shelterer, Twice Midwife and Twice Patriarch" (Christenson 2003:60–62). Dennis Tedlock (1996:63) translates the first two pairs, Tz'aqol, B'itol, Alom, K'ajolom as "Maker, Modeler, named Bearer, Begetter." Regardless of the translations, Christenson (2003:61n11) concludes that there were only three pairs of gods at creation: the Framer and the Shaper; Sovereign and Quetzal Serpent (the latter, Q'ukumatz, being equivalent to Quetzalcoatl/Kukulcan); and Xmucane and Xpiyacoc.

There also appears to be a superior deity, Heart of Sky, or Huracan, who is "the only deity to appear in every phase of the creation, as well as throughout the mythological and historical portions of the text." Further, he "combines the powers of life and creativity, which are believed to exist in the midst of the heavens. During each creative period, Heart of Sky is the deity who first conceives the idea of what is to be formed. Other deities then carry out his will by giving it material expression" (Christenson 2003:67n56). The name Huracan, or Juraqan, is difficult to translate, but is often seen as *hun raqan* 'one leg', and indeed a one-legged deity known as K'awil (God II of the lowland Maya Palenque Triad) was typically portrayed on a "Manikin Scepter" carried by Classic kings. This heritage may offset the concept of Heart of Sky as a trinity (D. Tedlock 1996:222n65, 225n65) and an introduced Christian concept of a god in heaven.

3. Xpiyacoc and Xmucane are creator gods, especially in the sense of giving birth to humans. They are given various paired titles such as Hunahpu Possum and Hunahpu Coyote (Christenson 2003:61n15), Creator of the Green Earth and Creator of the Blue Sky, Midwife and Patriarch, and Protector and Shelterer (ibid.:62–63). According to Christenson (ibid.:63n27, 153n361), Xpiyacoc, the male deity, is represented as a grandfather in the story, and his name may relate to a textile design featuring a turtle (*kok*), while the name of the female deity and grandmother, Xmucane, may be derived from *muqik* (to bury, cover, plant in the ground) plus *x-*, a female

or diminutive marker. She may be a version of the aged female goddess, Goddess O (also Ix Chel), in the Maya lowlands (ibid.:63n27, 153n361). Dennis Tedlock (1996:216–217n63) refers to them as "Midwife, Matchmaker" and suggests that the name Xpiyacoc is related to a verb, "to put in order," while Xmucane is derived from "to do a favor."

4. The meaning or translation of the name Hunahpu is problematic. It is usually thought to relate to *hun ah pu(b')* 'One Lord Blowgun' or 'One Blowgunner.' Christenson (2003:94n163) notes that the authors of the *Popol Vuh* wrote *ub'* rather than *pu* to mean "blowgun." In the lowlands Hunahpu is Hun Ajaw; Yukatekan *p'uh* is a verb meaning "to hunt," with *ahp'uh* meaning "hunter" (D. Tedlock 1996:238n7). Although Christenson raises the possibility that there is some association with the famous "place of reeds" (*tollan*; Maya *puh*), he thinks the nominal is simply a proper name and, like Tedlock, eschews a specific translation.

5. This name may be *x-baqui-ya'-lo*, or "Lady Bone Water" (Christenson 2003:113n226); Dennis Tedlock (1996:250n91) translates it as "Egret Woman," from *bak ha'*, referring to a white egret or heron.

6. The falcon is the laughing falcon (*Herpetotheres cachinnans*), with the onomatopoetic name of *wak* (Nawatl *wactli*?), from its call, which is an indication of the start of the rainy season (Christenson 2003: 156n366). The falcon is also "a common symbol of the reborn sun at dawn" (ibid.:156n367).

7. The meaning of the name of Hunahpu's twin brother, Xbalanque, has been translated as "sun's hidden aspect" (D. Tedlock 1996:361), although *balan* is usually read *b'alam* 'jaguar'. Dennis Tedlock (ibid.:239–240n77) notes that Xbalanque has a "specifically underworld character" in that he takes the lead in action over Hunahpu only in Xib'alb'a, whereas the reverse is true when they are on the earth's surface. The *x-* prefix is usually a feminine indicator or a diminutive, while the *-ke* suffix might indicate either deer (*kej*) or sun/day (*q'ij*), suggesting a translation of "Young Hidden/Jaguar Sun" (Christenson 2003:95), which could be the later Maya jaguar night sun, or the moon. The Classic or Yukatekan hieroglyphic version of Xbalanque is Yax B'alam 'First/New Jaguar' (D. Tedlock 1996:239).

8. Dennis Tedlock (1996:211n35, 240n77) notes that Zipacna and Cabracan/Earthquake probably represent the K'iche' version of a two-headed dragon or celestial monster of Classic Maya iconography. A similar representation may exist among the Olmec and can be seen in Izapan art.

9. I am grateful to David Freidel for reminding me of the critical importance of numeracy as well as literacy in developing my arguments.

10. The interval from roughly 1600 B.C. to A.D. 200 is referred to either as the Formative stage, particularly in western Mesoamerica, where the term is associated with evolutionary stages of a civilization (see Powis 2005b:1–3; also Chap. 2, note 1 here) or, primarily in the Maya area, as the Preclassic period, where it is a chronological designation. I use the two terms interchangeably here.

11. The very word *wealth* and related considerations make it evident that the materialization of ideology is also a critical economic process, involving the circulation of agricultural surpluses and the creation of what Eric Wolf (1966:7–9) has called a "ceremonial fund." I do not pursue these economic implications here for reasons of space.

CHAPTER 2

1. A stage is a division of a historical sequence characterized by a particular technological-economic pattern, as distinct from a dated period (Willey and Phillips 1958:68–69).

2. David R. Harris (2002:35), summarizing the most recent dating of Mesoamerica's key cultigens, identifies the earliest dates and locations of domesticated remains: pepo squash, Guilá Naquitz cave (Oaxaca), ca. 10,000 cal. B.P.; maize, Guilá Naquitz cave (Oaxaca), ca. 6300 cal. B.P.; common beans, Coxcatlán cave (Tehuacán valley), ca. 2300 cal. B.P.

3. Societies at this level may be called tribal. Clark and Cheetham (2002:288) refer to a "tribal era" in "proto-Mesoamerica" during the Late Archaic period, from roughly 5000 b.c. to 1200 b.c., reaching its "heyday" between ca. 2500 and 1600 b.c. with the spread of swidden agriculture.

4. This achievement may relate to the yields of prehistoric maize in the Oaxaca highlands, estimated from cob lengths. This suggests that it was not until around 2000–1500 B.C. that yields reached a satisfactory 200–250 kilograms per hectare (Flannery 1973:298–299).

5. In this context, it is of interest that the Epi-Olmec vocabulary includes words for "hand span," "hand-span-measuring device," and "ground jointly measured by hand-spans" (Kaufman and Justeson 2004). It is not known if or how these would fit into Clark's units, although I find that eight of my own hand spans are roughly equal to my arm span.

6. These early domesticates circulated widely throughout Mesoamerica before or during the Formative period, along with cashew, originally domesticated in the Amazon basin (Lentz, Pohl, and Pope 2005), and sunflower (ca. 2700 cal. B.C.).

7. These broad east-west differences in pottery forms and decoration seem to correlate with language

distributions, but they can also be noted in proximate areas such as the Oaxaca and Tehuacán valleys. Explanations likely result from intervening variables—function and use of the pottery, including settlements' proximity to water, motor patterns in carrying water, different foods, food-preparation techniques, serving patterns, ritual or domestic contexts, and the like—and the degree to which these are isomorphic with ethnolinguistic identities.

8. The reconstructed Proto-Uto-Aztecan word for mat', *peta', was borrowed from Proto-Zoquean *pata, and ultimately (through Nawa) became the Spanish *petate* (W. Miller 1967:46; Wichmann 1995:576).

CHAPTER 3

1. Analysis of the glyphs and iconography on the newly discovered murals at San Bartolo, Petén, appears to indicate the yearbearers of the Classic or Tikal calendar as they reference the day 3 Ik', which Stuart (2005:6) believes may correlate with the first day, or "seating," of the first month, Pop. Stuart goes on to suggest that this date might correspond to the years 131 B.C., 79 B.C., or 27 B.C., indicating that the yearbearer concept existed by the Late Preclassic in the Maya lowlands.

2. The movement of the sun on the horizon appears to change velocity at different times of year. Around the equinoxes, it moves approximately thirty minutes of arc, that is, a distance equal to its own diameter, per day, whereas at the solstices it appears to stand still, moving one diameter in about ten days (Aveni 2001:65; Aveni and Hartung 1989:459).

3. In the Gulf coast region, as many as four maize crops can be grown per year, each planted at specified times and typically in certain kinds of soils, although no farmer plants all four (Coe and Diehl 1980, 2:69, 71).

4. An interesting but little-known point is that some celestial phenomena have unusual, but not repeating, intervals of 260 days between them. For example, the inferior conjunctions of Venus (that is, its position between the earth and the sun) occur on an average of 584 days and repeat on an eight-year cycle. On extremely rare occasions, these inferior conjunctions result in a "transit" of Venus, in which its path can be seen across the sun (Peeler and Winter 1992:43). At 1000 B.C., a transit would have occurred about November 11, the same date as the closest match between the setting of the star Alnilam, the middle star in Orion's Belt, at the 262° azimuth (or 8° west of north) architectural association (ibid.; see also Chap. 5 here). Some 260 (+/- 1) days before this setting azimuth of Alnilam, Venus set at this same point, a coincidence that lasted for one thousand to maybe as many as fourteen hundred years (ibid.:44). Peeler and Winter

(ibid.:56) conclude that this 260-day coincidence in the affairs of Venus might be related to the origin of the 260-day calendar, noting that "any two dates separated by 260 days would bear the same number name combination. If Venus set along the 262 degree architectural alignment, on, say, the day 8 Rabbit, then the expected day of a possible transit would also be 8 Rabbit."

5. This nineteen-year (or 6,940-day) Metonic calendrical cycle is named for the Greek astronomer Meton, who introduced it on the summer solstice in 432 B.C. It depends on the recognition that nineteen solar years (spring equinox to spring equinox) are very nearly equal to 235 lunations (Whitrow 1988:189). The cycle actually overestimates the length of the year and was corrected a century later.

6. Gordon Brotherston (1982, 1983), however, has proposed that "Mixtec-Aztec" texts, for example, the Codex Vindobonensis, also reference a late-fourth-millennium starting date, in this case, a year 13 Reed in 3113 B.C. instead of 3114 B.C. (the one-year difference is an artifact of his not counting a year "0" for the B.C./A.D. transition, as do historians). In these densely written articles, he claims that counts of time are tallied by a Flag for twenty years, a "Round" of fifty-two years, and a "Head" (or *tzontli*, 'feather') of four hundred years. He acknowledges close correspondences with Maya calendars: a Flag is commensurate with a *k'atun*; five Calendar Rounds of fifty-two years equal the Maya 260-*tun may* cycle; and four hundred years are close to the Maya *b'ak'tun* of 400 *tuns*. The difference, which he does not articulate clearly, is that the Aztec years are solar years of 365 days, while Maya *tuns* are of 360 days.

7. The term *may* has many meanings (P. Rice 2004:76–77), and its linguistic origins are unclear. It occurs widely in Mesoamerica, suggesting considerable antiquity, and might have entered Maya languages from Mixe-Zoquean (Justeson and Campbell 1997:49–52), in which it meant 'count, divine'. In modern highland languages, *may* refers to a cycle of twenty "years" of four hundred days (Lounsbury 1978:762; Recinos and Goetz 1953:31), and it is also a unit of measure for counting years (Justeson and Campbell 1997:51). Other meanings include references to dust, deer hoof (*Diccionario maya-español*), and four-sided or -cornered things (Lowe, Lee, and Martínez 1982:321). The ceremonial importance of four-sided and four-cornered things is apparent at the beginning of the *Popol Vuh*, in which the creation of the world is described as the gods' establishment of the four corners of the sky and earth, an act that Maya farmers regularly repeat in setting out their maize fields, houses, and divinatory altars for shamans.

8. It is also possible that people living in coastal areas might have noticed the relationship between the moon and the tides, particularly the higher high tides

(neap tides) and lower low tides (spring tides) at new moon.

9. Flannery (1976c:344–345) points out that the ritual paraphernalia recovered in excavations at the Formative site of San José Mogote in Oaxaca includes numerous items having lowland or coastal origins, such as conch shells (trumpets), turtle shells (drums), stingray spines (bloodletters), and shark teeth (bloodletters). He relates this to the probable lowland source of Mesoamerican origin myths, which, he notes, might go back to Preceramic or Archaic times.

10. One month of the Mazatec (north of Oaxaca) calendar, Huaje, is the name of a leguminous tree, the guaje (*Leucaena esculenta*), which produces pods with edible seeds in late summer and early fall. These have been identified in archaeological remains as a component of Archaic subsistence in Oaxaca (Flannery 1986c).

11. Sprajc (2005:211) goes on to suggest that the "correspondence between the most frequently recorded dates [of the structural alignments in central Mexico] and the crucial moments of the cultivation cycle suggests that the reconstructed observational schemes facilitated a proper scheduling of agricultural and associated ritual activities." But it is difficult to imagine that, during the Late Preclassic and Classic periods, leaders (not to mention farmers) in central Mexico relied on such alignments to schedule agricultural activities. It is more likely that these alignments were historical artifacts and commemorations of earlier observations, in much the same way that Maya E-Groups (Aimers and Rice 2006) commemorated sunrise points rather than being accurate, functional, observational devices.

12. Malmström (1997:96, 103–104) cites the five-sided Building J at Monte Albán, in Oaxaca, and the Pyramid of the Moon, at the north end of the Street of the Dead at Teotihuacan, as examples of this phenomenon. In addition, he (ibid.:91–103) claims that a number of structures in the Mexican highlands—including the Pyramid of the Sun at Teotihuacan—display an orientation of 285.5°, the position of the setting sun on August 13. August 13 is the alternative to August 11, depending on the correlation used (see Note on Orthography and Dates), as the starting day of the Long Count, which is not known to have been used at Teotihuacan. It is also the date of the second solar zenith at lower latitudes in Mesoamerica.

13. J. Eric S. Thompson (2001) notes that the etymology of the English word *shark* is thought to be the anglicized *xok* with an introduced "r."

14. Similar distinctions are noted by Bradley (1991:209–211; see also Bailey 1983), who refers to Shanks and Tilley's (1987) differentiation of "human" or "substantial" time from "chronological" or "abstract" time, Braudel's (1969) ideas of the *longue*

durée versus *évennements*, and Bloch's (1977) notions of "ritual" versus mundane time. Helms (1988:33–49) associates geographical distance with distance in time.

CHAPTER 4

1. Gossen (1974b:238–239) suggests that four month names have the root *winik*, which the Chamulas interpret as "men" or "companions." They believe these are the four bearers of the earth at the intercardinal directions.

2. The Zuni of the American Southwest name some months, but others, although officially nameless, are known by colors—Yellow, Blue, Red, White, Variegated, Black—which are "derived from the colours of the prayer-sticks offered up at every full moon to the gods of the north, west, south, east, zenith, and nadir, who are represented by these colours" (Nilsson 1920:195).

3. Glyph numbers preceded by "T" indicate reference to glyphs in the J. Eric S. Thompson (1962) numbering system.

4. With reference to the month of Kej, Dennis Tedlock (1996:229–230n67) notes a ritual in Momostenango: when a woman gets pregnant, the head of her patrilineage selects a low-numbered ("gentle") day in the month of Kej on which to visit other lineage shrines to announce the pregnancy and to pray for the unborn child. This ritual is called a "sowing." In addition, among the Colonial Maya of Yucatán, Kej was associated with New Fire rituals (Sharer 1994:538).

5. These correspondences of Kank'in/Imix as "yellow; fruitfulness" in the lowland Maya calendar call to mind the similar senses of the day Q'anil in the K'iche' calendar (see note 16 below), which means "the yellow of ripe maize; it is sometimes used as a metaphor for the fruitfulness of the earth in general" (Christenson 2003:138n312). Alternatively, Dennis Tedlock (1996:265n103) emphasizes *toj* as a day of payment in the K'iche' calendar, reminding us that cacao pods once served as currency. Likewise, Q'anil is a day for harvesting maize.

6. The identity of the *muwan*, or *moan* bird, whether owl or hawk, has long been a matter of disagreement. Taube (1992:85) asserts that the *muwan* owl is a screech owl or a horned owl, as distinct from the *kuy* owl of ill omen and warfare. Grube and Schele (1994:10–12) say the *kuy* owl of war is a ferruginous pygmy-owl (*Glaucidium brasilianum*) and that this is also the owl associated with God L and Tlaloc-Venus warfare. They believe the *muwan* bird is a hawk. Dennis Tedlock (1985:154, 347, 361) says that in the *Popol Vuh* Mercury is an owl that is quadripartite (see also Milbrath 1999:214–215). The macaw owl is the

messenger of Xib'alb'a and perhaps the *muwan* bird of the Classic Maya. The *muwan* bird appears in full-figure and head variants of the *b'ak'tun*, *k'atun*, and *tun* glyphs; the *tun* has a skeletal lower jaw (referring to the *Popol Vuh* episode of Seven Macaw having his jaw shot?), while the others have a human hand replacing the lower jaw.

7. At the start of the myth the Earth was extremely dry, "dry with the desperate dryness of the Dry season . . . before the sun in his strength rises into the sky and falls in the riches of all his forms: life giving sky-water" (Tarn and Prechtel 1981:106). Dry was also a metaphor for pre-sun times, for Xib'alb'a, and for the wooden proto-humans. But "everything valuable arises out of water and goes back to water," as illustrated in the sun's daily journey: it rises from the sea in the east and sets in the western sea. The authors see in this pattern the "establishment of a Wet/Dry season-system as the condition for the accomplishment of *normal*, life-giving and life-enhancing work" (ibid.:107; original emphasis). This paradigm is associated with agriculture, the ballgame, and the structural oppositions of youth and maturity and relative strengths of equinoctial versus solstitial suns (ibid.:110–111). The sun, once it emerges, controls dryness in its own way while the moon, particularly its shape as an indicator of rainfall, equates with water.

8. Ajaw is the last of the twenty named days in the 260-day calendar of the lowland Maya. The equivalent in the K'iche' calendar, Hunahpu, is associated with revering the memory of ancestors, the Underworld, and rebirth. "When there is a death within the family, the patrilineage priest goes to the family shrine on a Hunahpu day that falls after the day of death to pray for the person's soul," and these days are also the time to leave offerings at graves (Christenson 2003:94n163; see also ibid. 191n449). Furthermore, the number of the Hunahpu day that is chosen for the visit is based on the age and importance of the deceased, with a low number chosen for a young child and a high one for an elder who held office (D. Tedlock 1996:286n141; see also B. Tedlock 1992a:107–108).

9. Deer and birds are frequently mentioned together in couplet form, perhaps an example of merismus ("the expression of a broad concept by a pair of complementary elements that are narrower in scope" [Christenson 2003:73n71]) indicating all the animals of the earth and the sky. Christenson (ibid.:75n81) also notes that, of all the animals named in this section, the gods explicitly describe the homes and sleeping places of only the deer and the birds.

10. The parallels to creation in the Book of Genesis are striking but are not pursued here.

11. Reference to reeds is not common in Parts 1 through 3 of the *Popol Vuh*, and I initially missed it in the Tedlock translation, which refers to rushes. Christenson (2003:121, 122n125), however, notes that the body of the woman was created from "the type of reed commonly used for weaving mats in Guatemala (*Typha angustifolia*)." References to Cane and Reed are more common in the K'iche'-specific Parts 4 and 5 as Rotten Cane, a citadel built by the K'iche' lords, and through mention of Tulan (Tollan), the origin of civilization, as "place of reeds or cattails" (*puh*). Christenson (ibid.:94n163) suggests the possibility that the *pu* (reed) in the name Hunahpu might refer to this legendary place, thus identifying this Twin as having origins in the Place of Cattails.

12. J. Eric S. Thompson (1966:144) notes that three full-figure glyphs for the *tun* on monuments at Quiriguá may show a crab rather than an avian or saurian, and he also comments that El Baúl, in the Guatemalan Pacific piedmont, had a "strong cult of the crab god" associated with earth and fertility.

13. Central Mexican origin myths (Chavero 1952, 2:11–15, 19) have some general parallels with Parts 1 and 2 of the *Popol Vuh*. There are multiple creations, the first of which is destroyed by a flood. The second creation, or *sol* (sun), is an era of giants destroyed by an earthquake, great rains, and hurricanes. After the third creation attempt, men were converted into monkeys. Schele (1992:2), noting that the creation story in the beginning of the Codex Vindobonensis is "exactly structurally parallel" to the Maya creation story, suspects that this myth "is so ancient in the Americas that it was there and available as a part of the cultural structures that all of the Meso-American peoples carry; it was essentially in place when the Long Count was set."

14. This "yellow tree," generally identified as *k'ante'*—*k'an* 'yellow' plus *te* 'tree'—is *Gliricidia sepium*, widely known in Spanish as *madre de cacao* (mother of cacao): the tall trees planted in orchards to give shade to the crop-bearing cacao trees (*Theobroma cacao*) (Christenson 2003:143n329; D. Tedlock 1996:266n105). The relationship between the marooned stepbrothers and the trees sheltering the cacao crop may explain why, in Classic iconography, monkeys are frequently depicted with cacao pods.

15. The young toad is named Tamazul, a name that Christenson (2003:155n364) attributes to Nawatl *tamasolli* 'toad'.

16. A perplexing reference exists to four days of various highland calendars: the sequence Toj, Q'anil, Tz'i', and B'atz' (although in some calendars Q'anil and Toj are reversed; see Christenson 2003:138–139nn311–315; Edmonson 1988:174–177). The meanings or senses of the K'iche' day names correspond to the same sequence of lowland Maya day names, and they occur in the same place in both

calendars (Edmonson 1988:174–177; see Table 3.1 here);
they also occur in sequence in Part 1 of the *Popol Vuh*:

- K'iche' Q'anil ('yellow, fruitfulness; rabbit');
  Yukateko Lamat ('rabbit')
- K'iche' Toj ('sickness; rain/storm; payment');
  Yukateko Muluk ('rain/water')
- K'iche' Tz'i' ('dog'); Yukateko Ok ('dog')
- K'iche' B'atz' ('howler monkey'); Yukateko
  Chuwen ('spider monkey')

Only two of these day names/senses are part of the
widely shared eleven: rain and monkey. Otherwise, the
significance of this particular sequence in calendrical
development is unclear, although it might suggest
a specifically Maya (as opposed to more generally
Mesoamerican) set of circumstances. In one translation
of the *Popol Vuh*, Blood Woman invokes these four
as female "guardians of food" (Christenson 2003:137)
to assist her in her task, while in another (D. Tedlock
1996:103, 265n103) there is emphasis on the maiden's
having, in essence, to pay tribute (to Xmucane), and
she may be invoking lunar patrons. I am unable to
relate this to calendrical development.

17. Christenson (2003:136n304) comments that
"the net is a significant symbol for the divine order of
the universe. Its fixed pattern represents the regularity
of the seasons in the fabric of time." The patterns of
Maya woven mats probably represent the same sense
of cosmic and social order.

18. The lowland Maya *wo* frogs are *Rhynophrynus
dorsalis* [Thompson 1970:258], the Mexican burrowing
toad, about which Stuart (1964:331) aptly comments,
"These bloated creatures are well known to Maya
experts whose nights during the rainy season have been
rendered miserable by the brute's call which resembles
nothing quite so much as the retchings of hundreds of
very ill humans." The Classic Maya head variant glyph
for the twenty-day *winal* is the *wo* frog.

CHAPTER 5

1. This pattern, described as a "basic template or
layout" with a large mound facing a plaza defined by
"one or two long, linear mounds," can be seen by 700
b.c. (900 cal. B.C.; Clark 2004:64) in Pacific coastal and
highland Chiapas; in the Olmec area at San Lorenzo,
La Venta, and Laguna de los Cerros; and in highland
Mexico at Chalcatzingo (Grove and Gillespie
1992:32–33). Clark (2001:189) says ten sites in
Chiapas share the site plan of La Venta, which
he and Richard Hansen (Clark and Hansen 2001)
refer to as the "Middle Formative Chiapas" plan.

2. Clark (2000:50–51; Clark and Pye 2005) notes
that many of these Chiapan sites—La Libertad, Finca

Acapulco, Ocozocuautla, Mirador, Vistahermosa,
San Isidro—lay on a major trade route along the Río
Grijalva (and tributaries) for bringing goods such as
obsidian and jade from highland Guatemala to the
Olmec lowlands.

3. Grove and Gillespie (1992:31) note that a similar
paw-and-claws motif appeared on La Venta Colossal
Head 1, which later may have been positioned next
to Stela 2 (with a similar headdress motif) in order
to reinforce connections to that apparent ancestor.

4. Disarticulated *Bufo marinus* toad bones were
found at San Lorenzo under sealed floors (Kennedy
1982:274). Bones also have been found in sealed burial
contexts at a variety of later sites in eastern
Mesoamerica (ibid.:285).

5. Carolyn Tate (2000, 2001) links figures in Olmec
iconography to two dyadic deities among the contemporary Mixe beliefs. One is a male/female pair, 'Ene,
associated with rain and wind, whose ancestor is the
"anthropomorphic, almond-eyed Olmec supernatural"
appearing on four stelae at the southern foot of Mound
C and wearing the four-seed (earth-power) headband.
The other is a female terrestrial dyad, Naswin, which
represents the earth's surface and Mother Earth, and
which Tate relates to the dots-and-bar motif in the
form of mosaic masks of serpentine blocks and colored
sands of the buried Olmec mosaic pavements.

6. In the upper portion of the scene as many as
six anthropomorphic figures (supernaturals? ancestors?)
appear, at least two of which carry batons, but these
are held upraised at the shoulder. Taube (1986) raises
the possibility that such objects held by early figures
might represent lightning, suggesting connections to
an early rain/storm god or spirit. I wonder if there
might also be some connection to one version of the
later Maya glyph *kalomte'* (T1030), which shows a
Chaak head with an upraised arm holding an axe.

7. This could be related to the male/female dyadic
supernaturals in contemporary Mixe belief systems
(Tate 2000, 2001). Concerning the first set of twins
in the *Popol Vuh*, One Hunahpu has a wife and two
children, but his brother, Seven Hunahpu, "has no wife.
He's just a partner and just secondary; he just remains
a boy" (D. Tedlock 1996:91). Christenson (2003:113)
translates this last phrase as "he was like a servant."

8. A parallel to the mother of twins occurs among
the Maya, as Dennis Tedlock (1996:250n91) notes that
the "crested head of a snowy egret (*Egretta thula*) is
featured in the name glyph for Egret Woman's Classic
Maya counterpart at Palenque, where the tablet in the
Temple of the Cross describes her as the mother of
twins and possibly triplets."

9. Anthropological insights into how one non-
Mesoamerican culture conceptualizes twins come from
the Nuer of Africa (Evans-Pritchard 1967:134–136).

Among the Nuer, twins are considered a manifestation of "the Spirit" in earthly affairs and, although they are acknowledged as two physical beings, they are nonetheless regarded as one person with a single personality and soul. In marriage, "when the senior of male twins marries, the junior acts with him in the ritual acts he has to perform; female twins ought to be married on the same day" (ibid.:134). At death, "no mortuary ceremonies are held for twins because, for one reason, one of them cannot be cut off from the living without the other" (ibid.). Nuer twins are also identified with birds . . . not "like" birds, they *are* birds. Apparently, multiple births—whether of human twins or multiple hatchings of birds or other animals—place creatures in a single ethnotaxonomic category. Twins who die in infancy are not buried but, rather, are "covered in a reed basket or winnowing-tray and placed in the fork of a tree, because birds rest in trees" (ibid.:135). Birds will not bother the bodies, because they would see the twins as "kinsmen." In another extension of this analogy, all Nuer consider it "shameful" to eat any avian or its eggs, but for a twin to do so would be a "grave sin" (ibid.).

Twins may have held a special status as far back as the Late Paleolithic: a burial of two newborn infants accompanied by grave goods and red ochre has been found in Austria and dates around twenty-seven thousand years ago (Holden 2005). It has not yet been determined through DNA or other analyses whether they were actually twins. In Mesoamerica, the name of a month of the Matlazinca calendar has the sense "twins" (Edmonson 1988:216).

10. This date may commemorate an annular or ringlike solar eclipse at dawn (Malmström 1997:140–142).

11. The closest relative of Epi-Olmec writing is Mayan (Kaufman and Justeson 2004:1075), and the Epi-Olmec word /nup/, meaning "counterpart; the other member of a pair," or, in other words, a twin, was borrowed from Greater Lowland Mayan *nuhp* (ibid.:1099), rather than the more common pattern of being derived from Mixe-Zoquean.

12. Houston and Coe (2003) have issued a strong critique of Kaufman and Justeson's decipherment efforts, arguing that application of the system to a newfound text on the back of an unprovenienced jade mask produced gibberish. This mask is similar to Teotihuacan masks, except that it has a hollowed rather than a flat back, and it may have been carved in the Gulf coast region (ibid.:156). They suggest (ibid.:157, 158) that the mask might date fairly late, perhaps after A.D. 500. It is likely that significant changes in or branches of the Isthmian script developed during the ~350-year gap between the La Mojarra stela and the mask, which would explain the unsatisfactory reading of the latter.

13. Hummingbirds continue to appear in Classic Maya kingly iconography, for example, at Quiriguá and Tikal (Looper 2003:164).

14. Heyden (1981:6) notes that in central Mexico the sky and earth "are said to be square and arranged in folds or tiers."

CHAPTER 6

1. I consider Izapa to be the center of its own polity in the Late Preclassic, but Michael Love (1999:137) considers it a secondary center in La Blanca polity, thirty kilometers to the south, in the early Middle Preclassic. La Blanca, with an apparently due north–south orientation, has some enormous mounds but has been substantially damaged by modern road construction.

2. Alternatively, this might relate to a myth that persisted until modern times in some parts of Mesoamerica, particularly central Mexico: the previous "sun," or creation of the cosmos, included humans who, when the world was destroyed by a flood, became "fish-men" (Taube 1986:52). Fish thus may represent ancestors or creatures left from the previous creation (ibid.:53, 56).

3. Another category of Late or Terminal Preclassic monuments could have acted as gnomons: tall stone shafts surmounted by small sculptures. One is Izapa Monument 4, topped by a kneeling human, found in its original position in the center of Mound 113 in Group F, a "monument platform" off the northeast corner of the ceremonial group (Lowe, Lee, and Martínez 1982:226). Similar sculptures are known from Kaminaljuyú, El Portón (Baja Verapaz), and Tecpan (Chimaltenango), in Guatemala (L. Parsons 1986:figs. 38–41).

4. In Group A, some Early Classic material was found at Mound 58 (Lowe, Lee, and Martínez 1982:167); Group B, Mound 47 has Late Classic material (ibid.:167, 200); and an Early Postclassic intrusive cache of chert points and bifaces and a Tojil Plumbate effigy vessel were found at the eastern base of Mound 60 in Group G (ibid.:249, 251).

5. Four monuments in the Group B plaza, Stelae 24, 11, 12, and 50, appear to portray late episodes in the *Popol Vuh*, suggesting that the procession through the site's plazas might have been clockwise rather than counterclockwise. In particular, Stela 11 depicts the arrival of dawn, while Stela 12, marking the abandonment of a possible four hundred–day calendar, can be read as commemorating the achievement of the calculation of the true length of the solar year. Its message is "year (*ja'ab'*) = sun = dawn." Finally, Stela 50 marks the end of Dennis Tedlock's (1996) Part 3 of the *Popol Vuh*, with death and apotheosis beginning a new round of cycles.

6. This same ca. 20–21° east-of-north azimuth was also found at Izapa, Tak'alik Ab'aj, Chiapa de Corzo, and other Pacific-region sites. Thousands of years earlier, the mirror orientation, 20° west of north, was noted for the alignment of the Gheo-Shih dance ground/ballcourt (see Chap. 2). Both orientations, whether east or west of north, bracket by a few days or weeks the extreme positions of the sun at summer-solstice rise and set.

7. These references to "Mountain Lord" likely are not to the same individual but, rather, to a title. The Maya identified the temple mounds at their cities as artificial mountains, using the same term, *witz*, that refers to natural hills or mountains. Perhaps Preclassic rulers of important places distinguished by tall temple mounds were given the title "Mountain Lord." If so, the titles might be predecessors of Emblem Glyphs.

8. Distinctive zoomorphic altars occur at Late Classic Quiriguá and Copán. At Quiriguá, four were *hotun* (five-year divisions of a *k'atun*) markers between A.D. 775 and 795; only Monument 7 (Zoomorph G, the earliest) seems to be a toad, as indicated by paratoid glands.

CHAPTER 7

1. Roys interprets the references to "grace" as kernels of corn; in contrast, Edmonson (1986a:227) comments that the Colonial-period Maya were "mightily impressed with the Spanish seven-day week, which they interpreted as a set of yearbearers" associated with the sun, the moon, the planets, and so on.

2. The Paddler Gods are but one among several sets of twins among Classic Maya deities, besides those of the *Popol Vuh*. These include GI and GIII of the Palenque Triad, the "Headband Twins" (virtually identical to the Hero Twins), the Monkey Scribe twins, and the "Twins of the Sacrificial Dance" (Schele and Miller 1986:51–52). Schele and Freidel (1990:115–117) refer to the Hero Twins of the *Popol Vuh* as the "Ancestral Twins," prototypes of later Classic rulers known as *ajaws*, and suggest that they were represented on the Preclassic masks on Structure 5C-2nd at Cerros (Fig. 7.8).

3. Clark and Cheetham (2002:296, 298) consider the Maya lowlands to represent a case of "prolonged tribalism," lasting from the earliest Archaic habitation until around 850 B.C.

4. Pollen is a standard proxy datum for human disturbance associated with cutting high forest for agriculture and replacement of tropical-forest trees with species characteristic of open areas.

5. It is of interest that pollen data from sediment cores in the central Petén lakes do not indicate

deforestation until around 2000–1500 B.C. (Brenner et al. 2002:150, 151; Leyden 2002:94). This relatively late date could be a consequence of comparatively late settlement by agriculturalists in this area, or a consequence of pollen preservation in the sediments themselves.

6. The various languages of the lowlands are referred to in terms of a "Greater Lowland Maya diffusion area," and some parts of the lowlands, particularly the central area, may have been, in effect, bilingual in Yukatekan and Ch'olan from the end of the Late Preclassic onward. Ch'olan differentiated internally around A.D. 600, with one division (Ch'ol and Chontal) continuing to be spoken in the lowlands through the contact period. Yukatekan (or, technically, Proto-Yukatekan) did not further differentiate until around A.D. 1000, as part of the events and population movements accompanying the so-called Maya collapse of the Terminal Classic period (see Hofling N.d.). Some thirty individual languages, including a few that are now extinct, are known within the Mayan language family.

7. There are iconographic ties between Izapa and the Maya region (Laughton 1997:79–90). Early motifs on the basal panels of some Classic stelae at the site of Yaxhá may be Izapan style (Fig. 8.5; Hellmuth 1976:52; Lowe 1982a:29), and iconography on the façades of Structure G-103 at Río Azul resembles that of Izapa (Reese-Taylor and Walker 2002:89). A Maya variant of the Izapa skyband threshold may appear on Structure 5D–Sub 10-1st in Tikal's North Acropolis (Laughton 1997:79).

8. Ties to the Olmec area are seen at Seibal in a cache of jade and ceramics including six celts, a perforator, and five black jars, all arranged in a cruciform pattern reminiscent of caches from La Venta (Willey 1978:figs. 90, 91, 104, 105). This cache dates ca. 830–780 B.C., perhaps slightly older than the earliest ones at La Venta.

9. These sites include Altar de Sacrificios, Seibal, central Tikal, peripheral Tikal, Tikal/Yaxhá, Macanché/Salpetén, Quexil/Petenxil, Yaxhá/Sacnab, Tayasal/Paxcaman, the Belize River area, Barton Ramie, Pulltrouser Swamp, Santa Rita Corozal, Komchen, and Dzibilchaltun. Note that at Dzibilchaltun the Middle Preclassic and Late Preclassic are in a single complex. The Rice and Culbert volume was compiled before much of the more recent work in Belize and the Mirador basin revealed substantial Middle Preclassic settlement in these areas.

10. Ashmore (1989, 1991, 1992) stresses north/up versus south/down as the primary axis for Maya site layouts in the Classic period. She and Sabloff (2002:203, 209) refer to a shift from Preclassic east-west axial dominance (e.g., at Nakbe and El Mirador) to later

Classic emphasis on north-south. I tend to read most of these sites and structural complexes (e.g., Tikal's twin-pyramid groups) as emphasizing an east-west axis and the sun's journey (see also M. Smith 2003). That emphasis, I believe, begins with the Middle Preclassic lowland Maya (particularly evident in E-Groups) and is distinct from late Early through Late Preclassic site layouts in the Isthmian region.

11. That Seven Macaw, the first of his mythological "family" to die, was enshrined in the north reflects a primary emphasis on that direction for ancestors. However, the Seven Macaw of the Big Dipper is empirically in the north, while ancestors—especially royal ancestors—occupy north as symbolically "up," or solar zenith. At death, their corporeal remains are buried in the earth—symbolically south—but their spirit or soul stuff resides above ("north") with the sun and the gods.

12. Juan Pío Pérez of Yucatán (2001:215), penning his observations in the nineteenth century, believed that the ancient Maya knew the use of the gnomon, and this site appears to bear out his thoughts.

13. This interpretation (Hansen 1991a:14) identifies the figures as ballgame players largely on the basis of their belts, which look like the belt on the figure at Loltún cave. Xbalanque is on the left pointing to God E, the Maize God; the figure on the right is Hunahpu, judging from his belt with the vulture head *ajaw* (T747) and the number 6. His decapitated father, Hun Hunahpu, is in front of Hunahpu's headdress. Laughton (1997:167), based in part on the figures' belts, sees ties between this stela and Izapa but does not specifically name the Hero Twins.

14. In the Pacific coastal region, Tajumulco obsidian was most common from the Late Archaic period through about 1150 B.C. (Clark, Lee, and Salcedo 1989). At Early Formative sites, obsidian was primarily from El Chayal and San Martín Jilotepeque as well as Tajumulco (E. Andrews V 1990:12; Aoyama 2004; Bove 1989:4; Clark, Lee, and Salcedo 1989). In the Olmec region El Chayal obsidian was common at Early Formative San Lorenzo, while Middle Formative La Venta primarily used San Martín Jilotepeque material. In the central depression of Chiapas, both El Chayal and San Martín Jilotepeque were common sources in the Early Formative, but in later periods San Martín Jilotepeque dominated and El Chayal was rare. In the Maya lowlands, San Martín Jilotepeque was most common in the Middle Preclassic in the Pasión region (E. Andrews V 1990:12), in central Petén (Rice et al. 1985), and at Colha, Belize (Brown, Dreiss, and Hughes 2004), where Ixtepeque material (eastern Guatemala, near Copán) was also present but in small quantities. Relatively little obsidian was found at K'axob, the three sourced blades from Middle Formative contexts being

from the San Martín Jilotepeque source (McAnany 2004c:table 12.2). Aoyama's (2004) use-wear analyses of Early Formative obsidian from Grajeda, in Pacific coastal Guatemala, demonstrates an increase in use for wood crafts.

The sourcing data indicate that obsidian from both El Chayal and San Martín Jilotepeque sources was moved widely in the Early Formative, but by the Middle Formative the San Martín Jilotepeque source was most commonly represented in the lowlands, circulated by way of macrocores (Clark, Lee, and Salcedo 1989:280). Interestingly, San Martín Jilotepeque obsidian is of relatively poor quality, bearing crystalline inclusions that can interrupt clean fracturing during flake removal (ibid.). The mechanisms of its trade are unclear, in part because there are no signs of settlement hierarchies or specialized manufacturing in the vicinity: exchange could have been dyadic down-the-line, open access, or controlled by a chiefdom some distance away (Braswell 2002:301–302).

If access to obsidian was not under the control of any specific highland site but, rather, open to any and all, then residents of the Isthmus and lowlands might have depended on preexisting kin ties or other relationships to furnish their supplies. This kind of down-the-line or partner exchange seems to be characteristic of the Early Preclassic (Braswell 2002; Clark, Lee, and Salcedo 1989:281). Later, however, it seems that one or more important Middle and Late Preclassic sources, especially El Chayal, were controlled by Kaminaljuyú, the nearest major center, with the result that production and distribution decisions might have been made by powerful individuals or groups at that site. Clark, Lee, and Salcedo (1989:280) suggest that these elites ordered the production of only enough blades to satisfy their minimum demand for foreign, that is, lowland, goods.

CHAPTER 8

1. The numerologically inclined Mesoamericans and Maya were fond of all their numbers, but the number 3 seems to have held special significance with respect to origins/creation and the Preclassic period: three stones of creation, three stars of Orion's Belt, three stones marking the major sunrise points, three buildings in triadic groups, three eastern structures of E-Groups, triadic dot clusters, three lineages or gods of the Palenque Triad, three "jewels" of the Jester God's diadem, three pairs of gods at creation and three sets of twins in the *Popol Vuh*, three main Mixe deities, "three" as part of the ancient names of sites (Oxmal 'thrice built' [Uxmal]; Oxte'tun 'three stones' [Calakmul]; Oxwitza' 'three hills water' [Caracol]).

2. A similar possibility of a script's being created by a single scribe has been noted in China (see Baines and Yoffee 1998:215).

3. If stelae can be considered supersized jade celts—which in turn are often seen as representations of maize cobs—one wonders if the Olmec and other Middle Formative caches of upright jade and greenstone could be related to calendrical celebrations, particularly relating to the maize agricultural cycle. These "planted" celts might also relate to the ears of corn that Hunahpu and Xbalanque dedicated and "planted" in the center of their grandmother's house before they left for Xib'alb'a. A similar practice was recorded among the contemporary K'iche' Maya in connection with planting and harvesting corn (D. Tedlock 1996:284–286).

4. Teeple (2001:243) identifies three periods of Maya calendrical notation with respect to lunar positions: (1) "Independence," up to A.D. 682, when each city was "trying to coordinate its lunar calendar to its solar calendar" by its own methods; (2) "Unity," from 687 to 756 A.D., when "the lunar calendar under the leadership possibly of Palenque was standardized into a lunar year of exactly 12 moons" and the count began with the appearance of the new moon; and (3) "Revolt," after A.D. 756, when "Copán abandoned the standard lunar year and adopted instead a lunar year to coincide approximately with the eclipse periods." Teeple (ibid.:253) sees Palenque as an important player in the move to standardize the lunar calendar but is not sure if the site was an innovator, a convert, or an opponent.

5. The Maya always named their *k'atuns* for a day Ajaw (Lord), the last of the twenty day names in the *tzolk'in*. In this sense, the day Ajaw represented the "face" or "lord" of the period ending (Stuart 1996:166), and thus it was "his" authoritative words or pronouncements that can be considered to have constituted or inspired the *k'atun* prophecies. The Maya day name Ajaw was also present in the Olmec calendar, while other Mesoamerican calendars had Flower as the name of the last day of the 260-day calendar. "Flower" may be the plumeria flower represented schematically by the Maya *k'in* sign (Thompson 1966:142).

6. In working with days of the *may* cycle and the 365-day *ja'ab'*, rather than the 360-day *tun*, we find that 93,600 divided by 365 yields an uneven number, 256.44, or 256 solar years plus 160 days (compared with 260 *tuns*). We know today, as did the ancient Maya and apparently other early daykeepers, that the true length of the solar year is a little more than 365 days, which is accommodated in modern calendars with an extra day every four years. Early daykeepers, putatively unable to work with fractions, nonetheless apparently realized this discrepancy between their *ja'ab'* and the true solar year, which is one day every 1,508 days (ca. four years, not a significant unit of Maya timekeeping), or a total of 62 days in a *may* cycle (31 days every 128 *ja'ab'*s or 130 *tuns*). While I do not believe that the *may* was created specifically to accommodate what we know as leap year calculations, they might have been facilitated by these intervals. And this might explain the perplexing number of 128 tesserae in the Las Bocas pyrite plaque: the tracking of extra days in the *ja'ab'* 365-day calendar.

7. Fish, usually nibbling water lilies, also appear in the headdresses of some Late Classic kings and on some Late Classic polychromes, where they may represent the Hero Twins' death and resurrection as catfish (Kerr N.d.).

8. The nominal Eb' Xok also appears on a jade earring, probably an heirloom, from Kaminaljuyú (Mora-Marín 2005:75, 77).

9. A folktale reported by Alfonso Caso includes a fish that reports the "location of the treasure in a tomb. A fish that could impart information of this nature would certainly qualify as a supernatural creature" (Thurber and Thurber 1961:225).

10. I am grateful to Bethany Myers for pointing this out to me (pers. com., April 29, 2005).

11. Juan Pío Pérez (2001:212) notes that the Yukatekan day name Ix (also Gix, Hix) may have at its root *iixcay*, which means "sandpaper, fish skin."

12. There is a resemblance between triangular sharks' teeth—a long, pointed center element flanked by shorter rounded elements—and male genitalia. This resemblance might account for the use of sharks' teeth in ritual bloodletting as well as their depiction in ritual contexts, including headdresses. The latter, of course, calls to mind the various "penis titles" in use in the Maya Classic and Postclassic periods.

13. A possible explanation might be that the number 8 follows 7, which, as I propose, appears to represent weakness or death in some Formative symbolism. Eight might then be construed as representing rebirth and strength.

CHAPTER 9

1. A traditional planting ceremony among the Tz'utujil Maya in Santiago Atitlán, Guatemala, involves placement of a special ear of corn in the center of a square with candles at the four corners. This maize ear is called *yo'x*, or twins, and it "splits at the end to form extra little cobs" (Christenson 2003:189n445), which are burned and the ashes buried. Christenson (ibid.) draws a parallel with the Hero Twins in the *Popol Vuh*, who were burned to ashes but returned to a new life.

2. One might wonder as well if there was any connection between the earlier convocation, occurring in 37 B.C., and Stela 2 at Chiapa de Corzo, in Chiapas, which displays what might be the earliest known Long Count date (7.16.3.2.13 6 Cane [or 6 B'en 16 Xul in the Tikal calendar], December 6, 36 B.C.; see Edmonson 1988:27).

3. Clark (1997:228–229) poses a different scenario, suggesting that by 1350 B.C. Paso de la Amada was the "seat of the largest chiefdom that had a population of 3000 to 5000 people." Some 250–300 years later, ca. 1100–1050 B.C., the Mazatán region experienced "an aggressive takeover" by the Olmec, in which all the small simple chiefdoms were abandoned and absorbed into a single complex chiefdom with a regional center and new villages nearby. Given the

date, it would seem that this operation might have been led by San Lorenzo.

4. It might be relevant that a twenty-year *k'atun* is close to what demographers calculate as a generation in prehistory, generally, the average number of years between parents and their children, or twenty to twenty-two years (A. Swedlund, pers. com. to D. Rice, October 20, 2005).

5. Support for this interpretation comes from a study of the Classic Maya "half-period glyph," referring to completion of half a period of time, such as half (ten years) of a *k'atun*. The new reading of this glyph is as a verb, to "half-diminish" (Wichmann 2004), reflecting the decline in power at the midpoint of a calendrical period.

6. Indeed, this latitude establishes a nearly precise bisecting axis over the entire Isthmus.

References Cited

Adams, Richard E. W.

1971   *The Ceramics of Altar de Sacrificios.* Papers of the Peabody
        Museum of Archaeology and Ethnology, vol. 63, no. 1. Cambridge,
        Mass.: Peabody Museum.

1991   *Prehistoric Mesoamerica* (rev. ed.). Norman: University of
        Oklahoma Press.

1995   Early Classic Maya Civilization: A View from Río Azul. In *The
        Emergence of Lowland Maya Civilization: The Transition from
        the Preclassic to the Early Classic,* ed. Nikolai Grube, pp. 35–48.
        Acta Mesoamericana 8. Mockmuhl: Verlag Anton Saurwein.

Adams, Robert McCormick

1966   *The Evolution of Urban Society.* Chicago: Aldine.

Aimers, James John

1993   Messages from the Gods: An Hermeneutic Analysis of the Maya
        E-Group Complex. M.A. thesis, Trent University.

Aimers, James J., and Prudence M. Rice

2006   Astronomy, Ritual, and the Interpretation of Maya "E-Group"
        Architectural Assemblages. *Ancient Mesoamerica* 17(1):79–96.

Anderson, David G.

1994   *The Savannah River Chiefdoms: Political Change in the Late
        Prehistoric Southeast.* Tuscaloosa: University of Alabama Press.

Anderson, David G., and J. Christopher Gillam

2000   Paleoindian Colonization of the Americas: Implications from an
        Examination of Physiography, Demography, and Artifact
        Distribution. *American Antiquity* 65(1):43–66.

Andrews, E. Wyllys, V

1986   Olmec Jades from Chacsinkin, Yucatan, and Maya Ceramics from
        La Venta, Tabasco. In *Research and Reflections in Archaeology
        and History: Essays in Honor of Doris Stone,* ed. E. Wyllys
        Andrews V, pp. 11–49. Middle American Research Institute Pub.
        57. New Orleans, La.: Tulane University.

1990   Early Ceramic History of the Lowland Maya. In *Vision and
        Revision in Maya Studies,* ed. Flora S. Clancy and Peter D.
        Harrison, pp. 1–19. Albuquerque: University of New Mexico
        Press.

Andrews, E. Wyllys, IV, and E. Wyllys Andrews V

1980   *Excavations at Dzibilchaltun, Yucatan, Mexico.* Middle American
        Research Institute Pub. 48. New Orleans, La.: Tulane University.

Andrews, E. Wyllys, V, and Norman Hammond

1990   Redefinition of the Swasey Phase at Cuello, Belize. *American
        Antiquity* 55(3):570–584.

Aoyama, Kazuo

2004 El intercambio, producción y función de los artefactos de obsidiana del período Formativo Temprano en la costa del Pacífico de Guatemala: un estudio diacrónico y análisis de las microhuellas de uso sobre la lítica de obsidiana del complejo San Jerónimo, Escuintla, Guatemala. *Utz'ib* 3(7):14–34.

Apenes, Ola

1936 Possible Derivation of the 260-day Period of the Maya Calendar. *Ethnos* 1(1):5–8.

Arnold, Phillip J.

2003 Early Formative Pottery from the Tuxtla Mountains and Implications for Gulf Olmec Origins. *Latin American Antiquity* 14(1):29–46.

Ashmore, Wendy

1989 Construction and Cosmology: Politics and Ideology in Lowland Maya Settlement Patterns. In *Word and Image in Maya Culture: Explorations in Language, Writing, and Representation*, ed. William F. Hanks and Don S. Rice, pp. 272–286. Salt Lake City: University of Utah Press.

1991 Site-planning Principles and Concepts of Directionality among the Ancient Maya. *Latin American Antiquity* 2(3):199–226.

1992 Deciphering Maya Architectural Plans. In *New Theories on the Ancient Maya*, ed. Elin C. Danien and Robert J. Sharer, pp. 173–184. University Museum Symposium Series, vol. 3, University Museum Monograph 77. Philadelphia: The University Museum, University of Pennsylvania.

Ashmore, Wendy, and Jeremy A. Sabloff

2002 Spatial Orders in Maya Civic Plans. *Latin American Antiquity* 13(2):201–215.

Aveni, Anthony F.

1980 Mathematical and Astronomical Content of the Mesoamerican Inscriptions. In *Skywatchers of Ancient Mexico*, ed. Anthony F. Aveni, pp. 133–217. Austin: University of Texas Press.

1991 The Real Venus-Kukulcan in the Maya Inscriptions and Alignments. In *Sixth Palenque Round Table, 1986*, ed. Merle Greene Robertson and Virginia M. Fields, pp. 309–321. Norman: University of Oklahoma Press.

2000 Out of Teotihuacan: Origins of the Celestial Canon in Mesoamerica. In *Mesoamerica's Classic Heritage, from Teotihuacan to the Aztecs*, ed. David Carrasco, Lindsay Jones, and Scott Sessions, pp. 253–268. Boulder: University Press of Colorado.

2001 *Skywatchers*. Austin: University of Texas Press.

2002a *Empires of Time: Calendars, Clocks, and Cultures* (rev. ed.). Boulder: University Press of Colorado.

2002b *Conversing with the Planets: How Science and Myth Invented the Cosmos* (rev. ed.). Boulder: University Press of Colorado.

Aveni, Anthony F., and Edward E. Calnek

1999 Astronomical Considerations in the Aztec Expression of History: Eclipse Data. *Ancient Mesoamerica* 10(1):87–98.

Aveni, Anthony F., Anne Dowd, and Benjamin Vining

2003 Maya Calendar Reform? Evidence from Orientations of Specialized Architectural Assemblages. *Latin American Antiquity* 14(2):159–178.

Aveni, Anthony F., and Horst Hartung

1986 Maya City Planning and the Calendar. *Transactions of the American Philosophical Society* 76(Pt. 7):1–87.

1989 Uaxactun, Guatemala, Group E and Similar Assemblages: An Archaeoastronomical Reconsideration. In *World Archaeoastronomy*, ed. Anthony Aveni, pp. 441–460. Cambridge: Cambridge University Press.

2000 Water, Mountain, Sky: The Evolution of Site Orientations in Southeastern Mesoamerica. In *In Chalchihuitl in Quetzalli: Precious Greenstone Precious Quetzal Feather: Mesoamerican Studies in Honor of Doris Heyden*, ed. Eloise Quiñones Keber. Culver City, Calif.: Labyrinthos.

Aveni, Anthony F., Horst Hartung, and Beth Buckingham

1978 The Pecked Cross Symbol in Ancient Mesoamerica. *Science* 202(4365):267–279.

Bailey, G.

1983 Concepts of Time in Quaternary Prehistory. *Annual Review of Anthropology* 12:165–192.

Baines, John, and Norman Yoffee

1998 Order, Legitimacy, and Wealth in Ancient Egypt and Mesopotamia. In *Archaic States*, ed. Gary M. Feinman and Joyce Marcus, pp. 199–260. Santa Fe, N.M.: School of American Research.

2000 Order, Legitimacy, and Wealth: Setting the Terms. In *Order, Legitimacy, and Wealth in Ancient States*, ed. Janet Richards and Mary Van Buren, pp. 13–17. Cambridge: Cambridge University Press.

Ball, Joseph W., and Jennifer T. Taschek

2003 Reconsidering the Belize Valley Preclassic: A Case for Multiethnic Interactions in the

Development of a Regional Culture Tradition. *Ancient Mesoamerica* 14(2):179–217.

Barnosky, Anthony D., Paul L. Koch, Robert S. Feranec, Scott L. Wing, and Alan B. Shabel
2004 Assessing the Causes of Late Pleistocene Extinctions on the Continents. *Science* 306:70–75.

Barthel, Thomas S.
1968a El complejo "emblema." *Estudios de Cultura Maya* 7:159–193. Mexico City: Universidad Nacional de México.
1968b Historisches in dem klassischen Mayainschriften. *Zeitschrift für Ethnologie* 93(1–2):119–156.
1979 Mourning and Consolation: Themes of the Palenque Sarcophagus. In *Tercera Mesa Redonda de Palenque, 1978*, ed. Merle Greene Robertson and Donnan Call Jeffers, pp. 81–90. Monterey, Calif.: Pre-Columbian Art Research Institute.

Bauer, Jeremy R.
2005 Between Heaven and Earth: The Cival Cache and the Creation of the Mesoamerican Cosmos. In *Lords of Creation: The Origins of Sacred Maya Kingship*, ed. Virginia M. Fields and Dorie Reents-Budet, pp. 28–29. Los Angeles, Calif.: Los Angeles County Museum of Art and Scala Publishers Ltd.

Bauer, Jeremy R., Ángel Castillo, Daniel Leonard, Mónica Antillón, Antolín Velásquez, Jennifer M. Johnson, and Joel Zovar
2005 El pasado preclásico y monumental de la región de Holmul: resultados de las temporadas de campo 2003 y 2004 en Cival, Petén. In *XVIII Simposio de Investigaciones Arqueológicas en Guatemala, 2004*, ed. Juan Pedro Laporte, Bárbara Arroyo, and Héctor E. Mejía, pp. 201–213. Guatemala City: Museo Nacional de Arqueología y Etnología, Ministerio de Cultura y Deportes, Instituto de Antropología e Historia, Asociación Tikal, and Foundation for the Advancement of Mesoamerican Studies, Inc.

Bellwood, Peter, and Colin Renfrew (eds.)
2002 *Examining the Farming/Language Dispersal Hypothesis*. McDonald Institute Monograph. Cambridge: McDonald Institute for Archaeological Research.

Benson, Elizabeth P.
1971 *An Olmec Figure at Dumbarton Oaks*. Washington, D.C.: Dumbarton Oaks.
1972 (ed.) *The Cult of the Feline*. Washington, D.C.: Dumbarton Oaks.
1996 History of Olmec Investigations. In *Olmec Art of Ancient Mexico*, ed. Elizabeth P. Benson and Beatriz de la Fuente, pp. 17–27. Washington, D.C.: National Gallery of Art.

Benson, Elizabeth P., and Beatriz de la Fuente
1996 Catalogue. In *Olmec Art of Ancient Mexico*, ed. Elizabeth P. Benson and Beatriz de la Fuente, pp. 153–273. Washington, D.C.: National Gallery of Art.

Benz, Bruce F.
2001 Archaeological Evidence of Teosinte Domestication from Guilá Naquitz, Oaxaca. *Proceedings of the National Academy of Sciences* 98(4):2104–2106

Benz, Bruce F., and Hugh H. Iltis
1990 Studies in Archaeological Maize I: The "Wild" Maize from San Marcos Cave Reexamined. *American Antiquity* 55(3):500–511.

Berlin, Heinrich
1963 The Palenque Triad. *Journal de la Société des Américanistes* (N.s.) 52:91–99.

Binford, Lewis R.
1980 Willow Smoke and Dogs' Tails: Hunter-Gatherer Settlement Systems and Archaeological Site Formation. *American Antiquity* 45(1):4–20.

Blake, Michael
1991 An Emerging Early Formative Chiefdom at Paso de la Amada, Chiapas, Mexico. In *The Formation of Complex Society in Southeastern Mesoamerica*, ed. William R. Fowler, pp. 27–46. Boca Raton, Fla.: CRC Press.

Blake, Michael, John E. Clark, Barbara Voorhies, George Michaels, Michael W. Love, Mary E. Pye, Arthur A. Demarest, and Bárbara Arroyo
1995 Radiocarbon Chronology for the Late Archaic and Formative Periods on the Pacific Coast of Southeastern Mesoamerica. *Ancient Mesoamerica* 6(2):161–183.

Blanton, Richard E., Gary M. Feinman, Stephen A. Kowalewski, and Peter N. Peregrine
1996 A Dual-Processual Theory for the Evolution of Mesoamerican Civilization. *Current Anthropology* 37(1):1–14.

Bloch, Maurice
1977 The Past and Present in the Present. *Man* 12:278–292.

Boone, Elizabeth
1991 Migration Histories as Ritual Performance. In *To Change Place: Aztec Ceremonial Landscapes*, ed. David Carrasco, pp. 121–151. Boulder: University of Colorado Press.

Boot, Erik
2003 An Overview of Classic Maya Ceramics Containing Sequences of Day Signs. *Mesoweb*: www.mesoweb.com. Accessed August 29, 2006.

Borhegyi, Stephan F. de

1961　Shark Teeth, Stingray Spines, and Shark Fishing in Ancient Mexico and Central America. *Southwestern Journal of Anthropology* 17(3):273–296.

1965　Archaeological Synthesis of the Guatemala Highlands. In *Archaeology of Southern Mesoamerica, Part 1*, vol. ed. Gordon R. Willey, pp. 3–58. Handbook of Middle American Indians, vol. 2, gen. ed., Robert Wauchope. Austin: University of Texas Press.

Boserup, Ester

1965　*The Conditions of Agricultural Growth.* Chicago: Aldine.

Bove, Frederick J.

1978　Laguna de los Cerros, an Olmec Central Place. *Journal of New World Archaeology* 2(3):1–56.

1989　Dedicated to the Costeños: Introduction and New Insights. In *New Frontiers in the Archaeology of the Pacific Coast of Southern Mesoamerica*, ed. Frederick Bove and Lynette Heller, pp. 1–13. Anthropological Research Papers, no. 39.

1999　Plain Stelae of the Guatemala Pacific Coast: An Interpretation. http://www.famsi.org/reports/98001/section03.htm. Accessed August 29, 2006.

2005　The Dichotomy of Formative Complex Societies in Pacific Guatemala: Local Developments vs. External Relationships. In *New Perspectives on Formative Mesoamerican Cultures*, ed. Terry G. Powis, pp. 95–110. B.A.R. International Series 1377. Oxford: Archaeopress.

Bowditch, Charles P.

1910　*The Numeration, Calendar System and Astronomical Knowledge of the Mayas.* Cambridge, Mass.: Peabody Museum of American Archaeology and Ethnology, Harvard University.

Bradley, Richard

1991　Ritual, Time, and History. *World Archaeology* 23(2):209–219.

Braswell, Geoffrey E.

2002　Praise the Gods and Pass the Obsidian?: The Organization of Ancient Economy in San Martín Jilotepeque, Guatemala. In *Ancient Maya Political Economies*, ed. Marilyn A. Masson and David A. Freidel, pp. 285–306. Walnut Creek, Calif.: AltaMira.

Braudel, Fernand

1969　*Écrits sur l'histoire.* Paris: Flammarion.

Bray, Warwick

1978　An Eighteenth Century Reference to a Fluted Point from Guatemala. *American Antiquity* 43:457–460.

Brenner, Mark, Michael F. Rosenmeier, David A. Hodell, and Jason H. Curtis

2001　Paleolimnology of the Maya Lowlands: Long-term Perspectives on Interactions among Climate, Environment, and Humans. *Ancient Mesoamerica* 13(1):141–157.

Bricker, Victoria R.

1982　The Origin of the Maya Solar Calendar. *Current Anthropology* 23(1):101–103.

Broda, Johanna

2000　Calendrics and Ritual Landscape at Teotihuacan: Themes of Continuity in Mesoamerican "Cosmovision." In *Mesoamerica's Classic Heritage, from Teotihuacan to the Aztecs*, ed. David Carrasco, Lindsay Jones, and Scott Sessions, pp. 397–432. Boulder: University Press of Colorado.

Brotherston, Gordon

1982　Year 13 Reed Equals 3113 BC, a Clue to Mesoamerican Chronology. *New Scholar* 8(1–2):75–84.

1983　The Year 3113 BC and the Fifth Sun of Mesoamerica: An Orthodox Reading of the Tepexic Annals (Codex Vindobonensis Obverse). In *Calendars in Mesoamerica and Peru: Native American Computations of Time*, ed. Anthony F. Aveni and Gordon Brotherston, pp. 167–220. B.A.R. International Series 174. Oxford: B.A.R.

Brown, David O., Meredith L. Dreiss, and Richard E. Hughes

2004　Preclassic Obsidian Procurement and Utilization at the Maya Site of Colha, Belize. *Latin American Antiquity* 15(2):222–240.

Brown, Kenneth L.

1975　Valley of Guatemala: A Highland Port of Trade. Ph.D. dissertation, Pennsylvania State University.

1980　A Brief Report on Paleoindian-Archaic Occupation in the Quiche Basin, Guatemala. *American Antiquity* 45(2):313–324.

Brown, Linda A.

2005　Planting the Bones: Hunting Ceremonialism at Contemporary and Nineteenth-century Shrines in the Guatemala Highlands. *Latin American Antiquity* 16(2):131–146.

Brown, M. Kathryn

1997　Investigations of Middle Preclassic Public Architecture at the Site of Blackman Eddy, Belize. www.famsi.org/reports/96052. Accessed August 29, 2006.

Brown, M. Kathryn, and James F. Garber

2003   Evidence of Conflict during the Middle
        Formative in the Maya Lowlands: A View
        from Blackman Eddy, Belize. In *Ancient
        Mesoamerican Warfare*, ed. M. Kathryn Brown
        and Travis W. Stanton, pp. 91–108. New York:
        AltaMira.

2005   Preclassic Architecture, Ritual, and the
        Emergence of Cultural Complexity: A
        Diachronic Perspective from the Belize Valley.
        In *Lords of Creation: The Origins of Sacred
        Maya Kingship*, ed. Virginia M. Fields and
        Dorie Reents-Budet, pp. 47–51. Los Angeles,
        Calif.: Los Angeles County Museum of Art
        and Scala Publishers Ltd.

Brumfiel, Elizabeth M., and John W. Fox (eds.)

1994   *Factional Competition and Political
        Development in the New World.* Cambridge:
        Cambridge University Press.

Brush, C. E.

1965   Pox Pottery: Earliest Identified Mexican
        Ceramic. *Science* 149:194–195.

Brush, Stephen G.

2005   Letter re Lipton. *Science* 308:1410.

Bullington, Jill, and Steven R. Leigh

2002   Rock Art Revisited. *Science* 296:468.

Cabrera Castro, Rubén

2000   Teotihuacan Cultural Traditions Transmitted
        into the Postclassic According to Recent
        Excavations. In *Mesoamerica's Classic
        Heritage, from Teotihuacan to the Aztecs*, ed.
        David Carrasco, Lindsay Jones, and Scott
        Sessions, pp. 195–218. Boulder: University
        Press of Colorado.

Campbell, Lyle

1997   *American Indian Languages: The Historical
        Linguistics of Native America.* Oxford: Oxford
        University Press.

2002   What Drives Linguistic Diversification and
        Language Spread? In *Examining the
        Farming/Language Dispersal Hypothesis*, ed.
        Peter Bellwood and Colin Renfrew, pp. 49–63.
        McDonald Institute Monograph. Cambridge:
        McDonald Institute for Archaeological
        Research.

Campbell, Lyle, and Terrence Kaufman

1976   A Linguistic Look at the Olmecs. *American
        Antiquity* 41(1):80–89.

**Campbell, Lyle, Terrence Kaufman, and Thomas C.
Smith-Stark**

1986   Meso-America as a Linguistic Area. *Language*
        62(3):530–570.

Carlson, John B.

1975   Lodestone Compass: Chinese or Olmec
        Primacy? *Science* 189(4205):753–760.

1981   Olmec Concave Iron-Ore Mirrors: The
        Aesthetics of a Lithic Technology and the
        Lord of the Mirror. In *The Olmec and Their
        Neighbors: Essays in Memory of Matthew W.
        Stirling*, org. Michael D. Coe and David C.
        Grove, ed. Elizabeth P. Benson, pp. 117–147.
        Washington, D.C.: Dumbarton Oaks.

Carneiro, Robert

1970   A Theory of the Origins of the State. *Science*
        169:733–738.

Carr, Helen Sorayya

1985   Subsistence and Ceremony: Faunal Utilization
        in a Late Preclassic Community at Cerros,
        Belize. In *Prehistoric Lowland Maya
        Environment and Subsistence Economy*, ed.
        Mary Pohl, pp. 115–132. Peabody Museum
        Papers, vol. 77. Cambridge, Mass.: Peabody
        Museum, Harvard University.

Caso, Alfonso

1967   *Los calendarios prehispánicos.* Mexico City:
        Universidad Nacional Autónoma de México.

Cavalli-Sforza, Luca

2002   Demic Diffusion as the Basic Process of
        Human Expansions. In *Examining the
        Farming/Language Dispersal Hypothesis*, ed.
        Peter Bellwood and Colin Renfrew, pp. 79–88.
        McDonald Institute Monograph. Cambridge:
        McDonald Institute for Archaeological
        Research.

Ceja Tenorio, Jorge Fausto

1985   *Paso de la Amada: An Early Preclassic Site in
        the Soconusco, Chiapas, Mexico.* Papers of the
        New World Archaeological Foundation, no. 49.
        Provo, Utah: New World Archaeological
        Foundation, Brigham Young University.

Chambers, Mary Elizabeth, and Richard D. Hansen

1996   Monumento 18 de El Mirador: el contexto
        arqueológico y la iconografía. In *IX Simposio
        de Investigaciones Arqueológicas en
        Guatemala, 1995*, ed. Juan Pedro Laporte and
        Héctor Escobedo, pp. 313–329. Guatemala
        City: Museo Nacional de Arqueología y
        Etnología, Ministerio de Cultura y Deportes,
        Instituto de Antropología e Historia, and
        Asociación Tikal.

Chase, Arlen F.

1991   Cycles of Time: Caracol in the Maya Realm.
        In *Sixth Palenque Round Table, 1986*, gen. ed.
        Merle Greene Robertson, pp. 32–50. Norman:
        University of Oklahoma Press.

Chase, Arlen F., Nikolai Grube, and Diane Z. Chase

1991   Three Terminal Classic Monuments from
        Caracol, Belize. *Research Reports on Ancient
        Maya Writing*, no. 36. Washington, D.C.:
        Center for Maya Research.

Chase, Diane Z.

1990   The Invisible Maya: Population History and Archaeology at Santa Rita Corozal. In *Precolumbian Population History in the Maya Lowlands*, ed. T. Patrick Culbert and Don S. Rice, pp. 199–213. Albuquerque: University of New Mexico Press.

Chavero, Alfredo (ed. and ann.)

1952   *Obras históricas de don Fernando de Alva Ixtlilxochitl*, 2 vols. Mexico City: Editora Nacional.

Cheetham, David

2005   Cunil: A Pre-Mamom Horizon in the Southern Maya Lowlands. In *New Perspectives on Formative Mesoamerican Cultures*, ed. Terry G. Powis, pp. 27–38. B.A.R. International Series 1377. Oxford: Archaeopress.

Christie, Jessica Joyce

1995   Maya Period Ending Ceremonies: Restarting Time and Rebuilding the Cosmos to Assure Survival of the Maya World. Ph.D. dissertation, University of Texas at Austin.

Christenson, Allen J.

2003   *Popol Vuh: The Sacred Book of the Maya.* New York: O Books.

Clancy, Flora S.

1990   A Genealogy for Freestanding Maya Monuments. In *Vision and Revision in Maya Studies*, ed. Flora S. Clancy and Peter D. Harrison, pp. 21–32. Albuquerque: University of New Mexico Press.

1999   *Sculpture in the Ancient Maya Plaza: The Early Classic Period.* Albuquerque: University of New Mexico Press.

Clark, John E.

1987   Politics, Prismatic Blades, and Mesoamerican Civilization. In *The Organization of Core Technology*, ed. Jay K. Johnson and Carol A. Morrow, pp. 259–284. Boulder, Colo.: Westview Press.

1991   The Beginnings of Mesoamerica: Apologia for the Soconusco Early Formative. In *The Formation of Complex Society in Southeastern Mesoamerica*, ed. William R. Fowler, pp. 13–26. Boca Raton, Fla.: CRC Press.

1997   The Arts of Government in Early Mesoamerica. *Annual Review of Anthropology* 21:211–234.

2000   Los pueblos de Chiapas en el Formativo. In *Las culturas de Chiapas en el período prehispánico*, ed. Durdica Segota, pp. 37–57. Tuxtla Gutiérrez, Chiapas, Mexico: Conaculta.

2001   Ciudades tempranas olmecas. In *Reconstruyendo la ciudad maya: el urbanismo en las sociedades antiguas*, ed. Andrés Ciudad Ruiz, María Josefa Iglesias Ponce de León, and María del Carmen Martínez Martínez, pp. 183–210. Pub. no. 6. Madrid: Sociedad Española de Estudios Mayas.

2004   Mesoamerica Goes Public: Early Ceremonial Centers, Leaders, and Communities. In *Mesoamerican Archaeology, Theory and Practice*, ed. Julia A. Hendon and Rosemary A. Joyce, pp. 43–72. London: Blackwell.

Clark, John E., and Michael Blake

1994   The Power of Prestige: Competitive Generosity and the Emergence of Rank Societies in Lowland Mesoamerica. In *Factional Competition and Political Development in the New World*, ed. Elizabeth M. Brumfiel and John W. Fox, pp. 17–30. Cambridge: Cambridge University Press.

Clark, John E., and David Cheetham

2002   Mesoamerica's Tribal Foundation. In *The Archaeology of Tribal Societies*, ed. William A. Parkinson, pp. 278–339. International Monographs in Prehistory, Archaeological Series 15. Ann Arbor, Mich.: International Monographs in Prehistory.

Clark, John E., Jon L. Gibson, and James A. Zeidler

2004   First Towns in the Americas: Searching for Agriculture and Other Enabling Conditions. MS.

Clark, John E., and Dennis Gosser

1995   Reinventing Mesoamerica's First Pottery. In *The Emergence of Pottery: Technology and Innovation in Ancient Societies*, ed. William K. Barnett and John W. Hoopes, pp. 209–221. Washington, D.C.: Smithsonian Institution.

Clark, John E., and Richard D. Hansen

2001   The Architecture of Early Kingship: Comparative Perspectives on the Origins of the Maya Royal Court. In *Royal Courts of the Ancient Maya*, vol. 2: *Data and Case Studies*, ed. Takeshi Inomata and Stephen D. Houston, pp. 1–45. Boulder, Colo.: Westview Press.

Clark, John E., Richard D. Hansen, and T. Pérez S.

2000   La zona maya en el Preclásico. In *Historia de México*, vol. 1: *El México antiguo, sus áreas culturales, los orígenes y el horizonte preclásico*, ed. Linda Manzanilla and Leonardo López Luján, pp. 437–510. Mexico City: Instituto Nacional de Antropología e Historia.

Clark, John E., Thomas A. Lee Jr., and Tamara Salcedo

1989   The Distribution of Obsidian. In *Ancient Trade and Tribute: Economies of the Soconusco Region of Mesoamerica*, ed. Barbara

Voorhies, pp. 268–284. Salt Lake City: University of Utah Press.

Clark, John E., and Mary E. Pye

2005   Re-Visiting the Mixe-Zoque: Slighted Neighbors and Predecessors of the Early Lowland Maya. In *Anuario, 2004.* Tuxtla Gutiérrez, Chiapas, Mexico: Centro de Estudios Superiores México y Centroamérica, Universidad de Ciencias y Artes de Chiapas.

Clark, John E., and Tamara Salcedo Romero

1989   Ocós Obsidian Distribution in Chiapas, Mexico. In *New Frontiers in the Archaeology of the Pacific Coast of Southern Mesoamerica,* ed. Frederick Bove and Lynette Heller, pp. 15–24. Anthropological Research Papers, no. 39. Tempe: Arizona State University.

Coe, Michael D.

1957   Cycle 7 Monuments in Middle America: A Reconsideration. *American Anthropologist* 59(4):597–611.

1962   *Mexico: Ancient Peoples and Places.* New York: Frederick Praeger.

1965a   Archaeological Synthesis of Southern Veracruz and Tabasco. In *Archaeology of Southern Mesoamerica, Part Two,* vol. ed., Gordon R. Willey, pp. 679–715. Handbook of Middle American Indians, vol. 3, gen. ed., Robert Wauchope. Austin: University of Texas Press.

1965b   The Olmec Style and Its Distributions. In *Archaeology of Southern Mesoamerica, Part Two,* vol. ed., Gordon R. Willey, pp. 739–775. Handbook of Middle American Indians, vol. 3, gen. ed., Robert Wauchope. Austin: University of Texas Press.

1965c   *The Jaguar's Children.* New York: Museum of Primitive Art.

1967   Solving a Monumental Mystery. *Discovery* 3(1):21–26.

1968a   San Lorenzo and the Olmec Civilization. In *Dumbarton Oaks Conference on the Olmec,* ed. Elizabeth P. Benson, pp. 41–71. Washington, D.C.: Dumbarton Oaks.

1968b   *America's First Civilization: Discovering the Olmec.* New York: American Heritage Publishing.

1973   *The Maya Scribe and His World.* New York: Grolier Club.

1978   *Lords of the Underworld: Masterpieces of Classic Maya Ceramics.* Princeton, N.J.: The Art Museum, Princeton University.

1981a   Religion and the Rise of Mesoamerican States. In *The Transition to Statehood in the New World,* ed. Grant D. Jones and Robert R. Kautz, pp. 157–171. Cambridge: Cambridge University Press.

1981b   Gift of the River: Ecology of the San Lorenzo Olmec. In *The Olmec and Their Neighbors: Essays in Memory of Matthew W. Stirling,* org. Michael D. Coe and David C. Grove, ed. Elizabeth P. Benson, pp. 15–19. Washington, D.C.: Dumbarton Oaks.

1981c   San Lorenzo Tenochtitlan. In *Archaeology,* Supplement to the Handbook of Middle American Indians, vol. 1, gen. ed., Victoria Reifler Bricker; vol. ed., Jeremy A. Sabloff, pp. 117–146. Austin: University of Texas Press.

1989a   The Olmec Heartland: Evolution of Ideology. In *Regional Perspectives on the Olmec,* ed. Robert J. Sharer and David C. Grove, pp. 68–82. Cambridge: Cambridge University Press and School of American Research.

1989b   The Hero Twins: Myth and Image. In *The Maya Vase Book: A Corpus of Rollout Photographs of Maya Vases,* vol. 1, by Justin Kerr, pp. 161–184. New York: Kerr and Associates.

1994   *Mexico, from the Olmecs to the Aztecs* (4th ed.). London: Thames and Hudson.

Coe, Michael D., and Richard A. Diehl

1980   *In the Land of the Olmec.* 2 vols. Austin: University of Texas Press.

Coe, Michael D., and David C. Grove (orgs.)

1981   *The Olmec and Their Neighbors: Essays in Memory of Matthew W. Stirling,* ed. Elizabeth P. Benson. Washington, D.C.: Dumbarton Oaks.

Coe, Michael D., and Mark Van Stone

2001   *Reading the Maya Glyphs.* London: Thames and Hudson.

Coggins, Clemency C.

1979   A New Order and the Role of the Calendar: Some Characteristics of the Middle Classic Period at Tikal. In *Maya Archaeology and Ethnohistory,* ed. Norman Hammond and Gordon R. Willey, pp. 38–50. Austin: University of Texas Press.

1980   The Shape of Time: Some Political Implications of a Four-part Figure. *American Antiquity* 45(4):727–739.

1996   Creation Religion and the Numbers at Teotihuacan and Izapa. *RES* 29–30:17–38.

Cohen, Ronald, and Elman R. Service

1978   *Origins of the State: The Anthropology of Political Evolution.* Philadelphia, Pa.: Institute for the Study of Human Issues, Inc.

Cohodas, Marvin

1975   The Symbolism and Ritual Function of the Middle Classic Ball Game in Mesoamerica. *American Indian Quarterly* 11(2):99–130.

1980   Radial Pyramids and Radial Associated
        Assemblages of the Central Maya Area.
        *Journal of the Society of Architectural
        Historians* 39(3):208–223.

Cortez, Constance

2005   The Principal Bird Deity in Preclassic and
        Early Classic Art. In *Lords of Creation: The
        Origins of Sacred Maya Kingship*, ed. Virginia
        M. Fields and Dorie Reents-Budet, pp. 44–45.
        Los Angeles, Calif.: Los Angeles County
        Museum of Art and Scala Publishers Ltd.

Covarrubias, Miguel

1946   El arte olmeca o de La Venta. *Cuadernos
        Americanos* 4:154–179.

1966   *Indian Art of Mexico and Central America.*
        New York: Alfred A. Knopf.

Cowgill, George

1997   State and Society at Teotihuacan, Mexico.
        Annual Review of Anthropology 26:129–161.

Cowgill, Ursula M., and G. Evelyn Hutchinson

1966   The Chemical History of Laguna de Petenxil.
        *Memoirs of the Connecticut Academy of Arts
        and Sciences* 17:121–126.

Crothers, George M. (ed.)

2004   *Hunters and Gatherers in Theory and
        Archaeology.* Occasional Paper, no. 31.
        Carbondale: Center for Archaeological
        Investigations, Southern Illinois University.

Cyphers, Ann

1995   Las cabezas colosales. In *Arqueología
        Mexicana* 2(12):43–47.

1996   Reconstructing Olmec Life at San Lorenzo. In
        Olmec Art of Ancient Mexico, ed. Elizabeth P.
        Benson and Beatriz de la Fuente, pp. 61–71.
        Washington, D.C.: National Gallery of Art.

1997   Olmec Architecture at San Lorenzo. In *Olmec
        to Aztec: Settlement Patterns in the Ancient
        Gulf Lowlands*, ed. Barbara L. Stark and Philip
        J. Arnold III, pp. 96–114. Tucson: University of
        Arizona Press.

1999   From Stone to Symbols: Olmec Art in Social
        Context at San Lorenzo Tenochtitlán. In *Social
        Patterns in Pre-Classic Mesoamerica*, ed.
        David C. Grove and Rosemary A. Joyce, pp.
        155–181. Washington, D.C.: Dumbarton Oaks.

Davoust, Michel

1981   Étude des glyphes locatifs dans l'épigraphie
        maya. *Estudios de Cultura Maya* 13:165–185.

**Dehaene, Stanislas, Véronique Izard, Pierre Pica, and
Elizabeth Spelke**

2006   Core Knowledge of Geometry in an Amazonian
        Indigene Group. *Science* 311:381–384.

de la Fuente, Beatriz

1985   El arte olmeca. *Arqueología Mexicana*
        2(12):18–25.

1996   Homocentrism in Olmec Monumental Art. In
        Olmec Art of Ancient Mexico, ed. Elizabeth P.
        Benson and Beatriz de la Fuente, pp. 41–49.
        Washington, D.C.: National Gallery of Art.

**DeMarrais, Elizabeth, Luis Jaime Castillo, and
Timothy Earle**

1996   Ideology, Materialization, and Power
        Strategies. *Current Anthropology* 37(1):15–31.

Demarest, Arthur A.

1976   A Re-evaluation of the Archaeological
        Sequences of Preclassic Chiapas. In *Studies in
        Middle American Anthropology*, pp. 75–107.
        Middle American Research Institute Pub. 22.
        New Orleans, La.: Tulane University.

2004   *Ancient Maya: The Rise and Fall of a
        Rainforest Civilization.* Cambridge:
        Cambridge University Press.

Diamond, Jared, and Peter Bellwood

2003   Farmers and Their Languages: The First
        Expansions. *Science* 300:597–603.

Diehl, Richard A.

1981   Olmec Architecture: A Comparison of San
        Lorenzo and La Venta. In *The Olmec and
        Their Neighbors: Essays in Memory of
        Matthew W. Stirling*, org. Michael D. Coe and
        David C. Grove, ed. Elizabeth P. Benson, pp.
        69–81. Washington, D.C.: Dumbarton Oaks.

2004   *The Olmecs, America's First Civilization.*
        London: Thames and Hudson.

Digby, Adrian

1974   Crossed Trapezes: A Pre-Columbian
        Astronomical Instrument. In *Mesoamerican
        Archaeology, New Approaches*, ed. Norman
        Hammond, pp. 271–283. Austin: University of
        Texas Press.

Dillehay, Thomas D.

1989   *Monte Verde: A Late Pleistocene Settlement
        in Chile*, vol. 1. Washington, D.C.:
        Smithsonian Institution.

1997   *Monte Verde: A Late Pleistocene Settlement
        in Chile*, vol. 2. Washington, D.C.:
        Smithsonian Institution.

Diringer, David

1962   *Writing.* New York: Praeger.

Dixon, James

1999   *Bones, Boats, and Bison: Archaeology and the
        First Colonization of Western North America.*
        Albuquerque: University of New Mexico Press.

**Doebeli, Michael, Christoph Hauert, and Timothy
Killingback**

2004   The Evolutionary Origin of Cooperators and
        Defectors. *Science* 306:859–862.

Doebley, John, Adrian Stec, and Lauren Hubbard

1997   The Evolution of Apical Dominance in Maize.
        Nature 386:485–488.

Drennan, Robert D.

1976   Religion and Social Evolution in Formative Mesoamerica. In *The Early Mesoamerican Village*, ed. Kent V. Flannery, pp. 345–368. New York: Academic Press.

1983a   Ritual and Ceremonial Development at the Hunter-Gatherer Level. In *The Cloud People: Divergent Evolution of the Zapotec and Mixtec Civilizations*, ed. Kent V. Flannery and Joyce Marcus, pp. 30–32. New York: Academic Press.

1983b   Ritual and Ceremonial Development at the Early Village Level. In *The Cloud People: Divergent Evolution of the Zapotec and Mixtec Civilizations*, ed. Kent V. Flannery and Joyce Marcus, pp. 46–50. New York: Academic Press.

Drucker, Philip

1952   *La Venta, Tabasco: A Study of Olmec Ceramics and Art*. Bureau of American Ethnology Bulletin 153. Washington, D.C.: Smithsonian Institution.

1981   On the Nature of Olmec Polity. In *The Olmec and Their Neighbors: Essays in Memory of Matthew W. Stirling*, org. Michael D. Coe and David C. Grove, ed. Elizabeth P. Benson, pp. 29–47. Washington, D.C.: Dumbarton Oaks.

Drucker, Philip, Robert F. Heizer, and Robert J. Squier

1959   *Excavations at La Venta, Tabasco, 1955*. Bureau of American Ethnology, Bulletin 170. Washington, D.C.: Smithsonian Institution.

Duncan, William N.

2005   The Bioarchaeology of Ritual Violence in Postclassic El Petén, Guatemala (AD 950–1524). Ph.D. dissertation, Southern Illinois University Carbondale.

Earle, Duncan M.

1986   The Metaphor of the Day in Quiche: Notes on the Nature of Everyday Life. In *Symbol and Meaning Beyond the Closed Community: Essays in Mesoamerican Ideas*, ed. Gary H. Gossen, pp 155–172. Studies on Culture and Society, vol. 1. Institute for Mesoamerican Studies. Albany: State University of New York at Albany.

Earle, Duncan M., and Dean R. Snow

1985   The Origin of the 260-day Calendar: The Gestation Hypothesis Reconsidered in Light of Its Use among the Quiche People. In *Fifth Palenque Round Table, 1983*, ed. Virginia M. Fields, gen. ed. Merle Greene Robertson, pp. 241–244. San Francisco: Pre-Columbian Art Research Institute.

Earle, Timothy (ed.)

1991   *Chiefdoms: Power, Economy, and Ideology*. Cambridge: Cambridge University Press.

Edmonson, Munro S.

1971   *The Book of Counsel: The Popol Vuh of the Quiche Maya of Guatemala*. New Orleans, La.: Middle American Research Institute, Tulane University.

1979   Some Postclassic Questions about the Classic Maya. In *Tercera Mesa Redonda de Palenque*, vol. 4, ed. Merle Greene Robertson and Donnan Call Jeffers, pp. 9–18. Palenque, Chiapas, Mexico: Pre-Columbian Art Research Center. (Reprinted in *Ancient Mesoamerica, Selected Readings* [2nd ed., 1981], ed. John A. Graham, pp. 221–228. Palo Alto, Calif.: Peek Publications.)

1982   (trans. and ann.) *The Ancient Future of the Itza: The Book of Chilam Balam of Tizimin*. Austin: University of Texas Press.

1985   The Baktun Ceremonial of 1618. In *Fourth Palenque Round Table, 1980*, vol. 6, ed. Merle Greene Robertson and Elizabeth P. Benson, pp. 261–265. San Francisco, Calif.: Pre-Columbian Art Research Institute.

1986a   *Heaven Born Merida and Its Destiny: The Book of Chilam Balam of Chumayel*. Austin: University of Texas Press.

1986b   The Olmec Calendar Round. In *Research and Reflections in Archaeology and History: Essays in Honor of Doris Stone*, ed. E. Wyllys Andrews V, pp. 81–86. Middle American Research Institute Pub. 57. New Orleans, La.: Tulane University.

1988   *The Book of the Year: Middle American Calendrical Systems*. Salt Lake City: University of Utah Press.

Ekholm, Susanna M.

1969   *Mound 30a and the Early Preclassic Ceramic Sequence of Izapa, Chiapas, Mexico*. Papers of the New World Archaeological Foundation, no. 25. Provo, Utah: New World Archaeological Foundation, Brigham Young University.

Estrada-Belli, Francisco

2004   Archaeological Investigations in the Holmul Region, Petén, Guatemala: Results of the Fourth Season, 2003. http://www.famsi.org/reports/02093/index.html. Accessed August 29, 2006.

Evans-Pritchard, E. E.

1939   Nuer Time Reckoning. *Africa* 12:189–216.

1967 [1954] A Problem of Nuer Religious Thought. In *Myth and Cosmos: Readings in Mythology and Symbolism*, ed. John Middleton, pp.

127–148. Garden City, N.Y.: Natural
History Press.

Fagan, Brian M.

1987   *The Great Journey: The Peopling of Ancient America.* London: Thames and Hudson.

Fahsen, Federico, and Nikolai Grube

1999   La celebración de los trece tunes en Tikal en el final del clásico temprano. *Utz'ib* 2(7):1–20.

2005   The Origins of Maya Writing. In *Lords of Creation: The Origins of Sacred Maya Kingship*, ed. Virginia M. Fields and Dorie Reents-Budet, pp. 74–79. Los Angeles, Calif.: Los Angeles County Museum of Art and Scala Publishers Ltd.

Farriss, Nancy M.

1987   Remembering the Future, Anticipating the Past: History, Time and Cosmology among the Maya of Yucatan. *Comparative Studies in Society and History* 29(3):566–593.

Fash, William L.

1991   *Scribes, Warriors and Kings: The City of Copán and the Ancient Maya.* London: Thames and Hudson.

Feder, Kenneth L.

1990   *Frauds, Myths, and Mysteries: Science and Pseudoscience in Archaeology.* Mountain View, Calif.: Mayfield.

Fedoroff, Nina V.

2003   Prehistoric GM Corn. *Science* 302:1158–1159.

Feinman, Gary M., and Joyce Marcus (eds.)

1998   *Archaic States.* Santa Fe, N.M.: School of American Research.

Fialko, Vilma

2005   Diez años de investigaciones arqueológicas en la cuenca del Río Holmul, región noreste de Petén. In *XVIII Simposio de Investigaciones Arqueológicas en Guatemala, 2004,* ed. Juan Pedro Laporte, Bárbara Arroyo, and Héctor E. Mejía, pp. 253–268. Guatemala City: Museo Nacional de Arqueología y Etnología, Ministerio de Cultura y Deportes, Instituto de Antropología e Historia, Asociación Tikal, and Foundation for the Advancement of Mesoamerican Studies, Inc.

Fields, Virginia M.

1989   The Origins of Divine Kingship among the Lowland Classic Maya. Ph.D. dissertation, University of Texas at Austin.

Fields, Virginia M., and Dorie Reents-Budet (eds.)

2005a   *Lords of Creation: The Origins of Sacred Maya Kingship.* Los Angeles, Calif.: Los Angeles County Museum of Art and Scala Publishers Ltd.

2005b   Introduction: The First Sacred Kings of Mesoamerica. In *Lords of Creation: The Origins of Sacred Maya Kingship,* ed. Virginia M. Fields and Dorie Reents-Budet, pp. 21–26. Los Angeles, Calif.: Los Angeles County Museum of Art and Scala Publishers Ltd.

Fitchett, Arthur G.

1974   Origin of the 260-day Cycle in Mesoamerica. *Science* 185:542–543.

Fladmark, Knut

1979   Routes: Alternate Migration Corridors for Early Man in North America. *American Antiquity* 44(1):55–69.

Flannery, Kent V.

1966   Postglacial Readaptation as Viewed from Mesoamerica. *American Antiquity* 31(6):800–805.

1973   The Origins of Agriculture. *Annual Review of Anthropology* 2:271–310.

1976a   (ed.) *The Early Mesoamerican Village.* New York: Academic Press.

1976b   Sampling by Intensive Surface Collection. In *The Early Mesoamerican Village,* ed. Kent V. Flannery, pp. 51–62. New York: Academic Press.

1976c   Contextual Analysis of Ritual Paraphernalia from Formative Oaxaca. In *The Early Mesoamerican Village,* ed. Kent V. Flannery, pp. 333–345. New York: Academic Press.

1976d   Evolution of Complex Settlement Systems. In *The Early Mesoamerican Village,* ed. Kent V. Flannery, pp. 162–173. New York: Academic Press.

1986a   (ed.) *Guilá Naquitz: Archaic Foraging and Early Agriculture in Oaxaca, Mexico.* Orlando, Fla.: Academic Press.

1986b   Ecosystem Models and Information Flow in the Tehuacán-Oaxaca Region. In *Guilá Naquitz: Archaic Foraging and Early Agriculture in Oaxaca, Mexico,* ed. Kent V. Flannery, pp. 19–28. Orlando, Fla.: Academic Press.

1986c   Food Procurement Area and Preceramic Diet at Guilá Naquitz. In *Guilá Naquitz: Archaic Foraging and Early Agriculture in Oaxaca, Mexico,* ed. Kent V. Flannery, pp. 303–317. Orlando, Fla.: Academic Press.

Flannery, Kent V., Andrew K. Balkansky, Gary M. Feinman, David C. Grove, Joyce Marcus, Elsa M. Redmond, Robert G. Reynolds, Robert J. Sharer, Charles S. Spencer, and Jason Yaeger

2005   Implications of New Petrographic Analysis for the Olmec "Mother Culture" Model. *Proceedings of the National Academy of Science* 102(32):11219–11223.

Flannery, Kent V., and Joyce Marcus

1976   Evolution of the Public Building in Formative Oaxaca. In *Cultural Change and Continuity:*

Essays in Honor of James Bennett Griffin, ed. Charles Cleland, pp. 205–221. New York: Academic Press.

1983   (eds.) *The Cloud People: Divergent Evolution of the Zapotec and Mixtec Civilizations.* New York: Academic Press.

1994   *Early Formative Pottery of the Valley of Oaxaca.* Memoirs, no. 27. Ann Arbor: Museum of Anthropology, University of Michigan.

2000   Formative Mexican Chiefdoms and the Myth of the "Mother Culture." *Journal of Anthropological Archaeology* 19(1):1–37.

2003   The Origin of War: New 14C Dates from Ancient Mexico. *Proceedings of the National Academy of Sciences* 100(20):11801–11805.

2005   *Excavations at San José Mogote 1: The Household Archaeology.* Prehistory and Human Ecology of the Valley of Oaxaca, vol. 13. Memoirs of the Museum of Anthropology, no. 40. Ann Arbor: University of Michigan.

Flannery, Kent V., and Ronald Spores

1983   Excavated Sites of the Oaxaca Preceramic. In *The Cloud People: Divergent Evolution of the Zapotec and Mixtec Civilizations*, ed. Kent V. Flannery and Joyce Marcus, pp. 20–26. New York: Academic Press.

Florescano, Enrique

2005   Preface: Images of the Ruler in Mesoamerica. In *Lords of Creation: The Origins of Sacred Maya Kingship*, ed. Virginia M. Fields and Dorie Reents-Budet, pp. 17–19. Los Angeles, Calif.: Los Angeles County Museum of Art and Scala Publishers Ltd.

Folan, William J., Joyce Marcus, and Sophia Pincemin et al.

1995   Calakmul: New Data from an Ancient Maya Capital in Campeche, Mexico. *Latin American Antiquity* 6(4):310–334.

Forsyth, Donald W.

1993   Ceramic Sequence at Nakbé, Guatemala. *Ancient Mesoamerica* 4(1):31–53.

Foundation for the Advancement of Mesoamerican Studies, Inc.

2006   Copyrighted drawings by Linda Schele and John Montgomery. www.famsi.org. Accessed August 29, 2006.

Freidel, David A.

1982   Maya City of Cerros. *Archaeology* 35(4):12–21.

1992   *Ahau* as Idea and Artifact in Classic Lowland Maya Civilization. In *Ideology and Pre-Columbian Civilizations*, ed. Arthur A. Demarest and Geoffrey W. Conrad, pp. 115–133. Santa Fe, N.M.: School of American Research Press.

2001a   Foreword: Landscape and Power in Ancient Mesoamerica. In *Landscape and Power in Ancient Mesoamerica*, ed. Rex Koontz, Kathryn Reese-Taylor, and Annabeth Headrick, pp. xvii–xxi. Boulder, Colo.: Westview Press.

2001b   Cerros (Corozal, Belize). In *Archaeology of Ancient Mexico and Central America: An Encyclopedia*, ed. Susan T. Evans and David L. Webster, pp. 115–116. New York: Garland.

2005   The Creation Mountains: Structure 5C-2nd and Late Preclassic Kingship. In *Lords of Creation: The Origins of Sacred Maya Kingship*, ed. Virginia M. Fields and Dorie Reents-Budet, pp. 52–53. Los Angeles, Calif.: Los Angeles County Museum of Art and Scala Publishers Ltd.

Freidel, David A., Kathryn Reese-Taylor, and David Mora-Marín

2002   The Origins of Maya Civilization: The Old Shell Game, Commodity, Treasure, and Kingship. In *Ancient Maya Political Economies*, ed. Marilyn A. Masson and David A. Freidel, pp. 41–86. Walnut Creek, Calif.: AltaMira Press.

Freidel, David A., and Linda Schele

1988a   Kingship in the Late Preclassic Maya Lowlands. *American Anthropologist* 90(3):547–567.

1988b   Symbol and Power: A History of the Lowland Maya Cosmogram. In *Maya Iconography*, ed. Elizabeth P. Benson and Gillett G. Griffin, pp. 44–93. Princeton, N.J.: Princeton University Press.

Freidel, David A., Linda Schele, and Joy Parker

1993   *Maya Cosmos: Three Thousand Years on the Shaman's Path.* New York: William Morrow.

Freidel, David A., Charles K. Suhler, and Rafael Cobos P.

1998   Termination Ritual Deposits at Yaxuna: Detecting the Historical in Archaeological Contexts. In *The Sowing and the Dawning: Termination, Dedication, and Transformation in the Archaeological and Ethnographic Record of Mesoamerica*, ed. Shirley B. Mock, pp. 135–144. Albuquerque: University of New Mexico Press.

Fried, Morton H.

1967   *The Evolution of Political Society: An Essay in Political Anthropology.* New York: Random House.

Furst, Peter T.

1968   The Olmec Were-Jaguar Motif in the Light of Ethnographic Reality. In *Dumbarton Oaks Conference on the Olmec, October 28th and*

29th, 1967, ed. Elizabeth P. Benson, pp. 143–174. Washington, D.C.: Dumbarton Oaks.

1981 Jaguar Baby or Toad Mother: A New Look at an Old Problem in Olmec Iconography. In *The Olmec and Their Neighbors: Essays in Honor of Matthew W. Stirling*, ed. Elizabeth P. Benson, pp. 149–162. Washington, D.C.: Dumbarton Oaks.

1986 Human Biology and the Origin of the 260-day Sacred Almanac: The Contribution of Leonhard Schultze Jena (1872–1955). In *Symbol and Meaning Beyond the Closed Community: Essays in Mesoamerican Ideas*, ed. Gary H. Gossen, pp. 69–76. Studies on Culture and Society, vol. 1. Institute for Mesoamerican Studies. Albany: State University of New York at Albany.

Fuson, Robert H.

1969 The Orientation of Mayan Ceremonial Centers. *Annals of the Association of American Geographers* 59(3):494–511.

Garber, James F., M. Kathryn Brown, and Christopher J. Hartman

2002 The Early/Middle Formative Kanocha Phase (1200–850 B.C.) at Blackman Eddy, Belize. http://www.famsi.org/reports/00090/index.html. Accessed August 29, 2006.

García Cook, Ángel

1981 The Historical Importance of Tlaxcala in the Cultural Development of the Central Highlands. In *Archaeology*, ed. Jeremy A. Sabloff; gen. ed., Victoria R. Bricker, pp. 244–276. Handbook of Middle American Indians, Supp. 1. Austin: University of Texas Press.

Garfinkel, Yosef

2003 *Dancing at the Dawn of Agriculture*. Austin: University of Texas Press.

Garza, Sergio, James E. Brady, and Christian Christensen

2002 Balam Na Cave 4: Implications for Understanding Preclassic Cave Mortuary Practices. *California Anthropologist* 28(1):15–22.

Gifford, James C.

1976 *Prehistoric Pottery Analysis and the Ceramics of Barton Ramie in the Belize Valley*. Memoirs of the Peabody Museum of Archaeology and Ethnology, vol. 18. Cambridge, Mass.: Harvard University.

Gillespie, Susan

1989 *The Aztec Kings: The Construction of Rulership in Mexica History*. Tucson: University of Arizona Press.

1999 Olmec Thrones as Ancestral Altars: The Two Sides of Power. In *Material Symbols: Culture and Economy in Prehistory*, ed. John E. Robb, pp. 224–253. Occasional Paper, no. 26. Carbondale: Center for Archaeological Investigations, Southern Illinois University.

Girard, Rafael

1962 *Los mayas eternos*. Mexico City: Antigua Librería Robredo.

Godelier, Maurice

1978 Infrastructures, Societies, and History. *Current Anthropology* 19(4):763–771.

Gómez Rueda, Hernando, and Liwy Grazioso Sierra

1997 Nuevos elementos de la iconografía de Izapa: la Estela 90. In *X Simposio de Investigaciones Arqueológicas en Guatemala*, vol. 1, ed. Juan Pedro Laporte and Héctor L. Escobedo, pp. 223–235. Guatemala City: Museo Nacional de Arqueología y Etnología, Ministerio de Cultura y Deportes, Instituto de Antropología e Historia, and Asociación Tikal.

González Lauck, Rebecca B.

1989 Recientes investigaciones en La Venta, Tabasco. In *El Preclásico o Formativo: avances y perspectivas*, coord. Martha Carmona Macías, pp. 81–89. Mexico City: Instituto Nacional de Antropología e Historia.

1996 La Venta: An Olmec Capital. In *Olmec Art of Ancient Mexico*, ed. Elizabeth P. Benson and Beatriz de la Fuente, pp. 61–81. Washington, D.C.: National Gallery of Art.

Gosden, Chris, and Gary Lock

1998 Prehistoric Histories. *World Archaeology* 39(1):2–12.

Gossen, Gary H.

1974a *Chamulas in the World of the Sun: Time and Space in a Maya Oral Tradition*. Cambridge, Mass.: Harvard University Press.

1974b A Chamula Solar Calendar Board from Chiapas, Mexico. In *Mesoamerican Archaeology, New Approaches*, ed. Norman Hammond, pp. 217–253. Austin: University of Texas Press.

1986 Mesoamerican Ideas as a Foundation for Regional Synthesis. In *Symbol and Meaning Beyond the Closed Community: Essays in Mesoamerican Ideas*, ed. Gary H. Gossen, pp. 1–8. Studies on Culture and Society, vol. 1. Albany: Institute for Mesoamerican Studies, State University of New York at Albany.

2002 (ed. and trans.) *Four Creations: An Epic Story of the Chiapas Mayas*. Norman: University of Oklahoma Press.

Gossen, Gary H., and Richard M. Leventhal

1993 The Topography of Ancient Maya Religious Pluralism: A Dialogue with the Present. In

Lowland Maya Civilization in the Eighth Century A.D., ed. Jeremy A. Sabloff and John S. Henderson, pp. 185–217. Washington, D.C.: Dumbarton Oaks.

Graulich, Michel
1981   The Metaphor of the Day in Ancient Mexican Myth and Ritual. *Current Anthropology* 22(1):45–60.

Green, Dee F., and Gareth W. Lowe
1967   *Altamira and Padre Piedra: Early Preclassic Sites in Chiapas, Mexico.* Papers of the New World Archaeological Foundation, no. 20. Provo, Utah: New World Archaeological Foundation, Brigham Young University.

Greenberg, Joseph H.
1987   *Language in the Americas.* Stanford, Calif.: Stanford University Press.

Gregg, Susan A. (ed.)
1991   *Between Bands and States.* Occasional Paper, no. 9. Carbondale: Center for Archaeological Investigations, Southern Illinois University.

Grove, David C.
1973   Olmec Altars and Myths. *Archaeology* 26(2):128–135.
1981a   The Formative Period and the Evolution of Complex Culture. In *Archaeology, Supplement to the Handbook of Middle American Indians*, vol. 1, gen. ed., Victoria Reifler Bricker; vol. ed., Jeremy A. Sabloff, pp. 373–391. Austin: University of Texas Press.
1981b   Olmec Monuments: Mutilation as a Clue to Meaning. In *The Olmec and Their Neighbors: Essays in Memory of Matthew W. Stirling*, org. Michael D. Coe and David C. Grove, ed. Elizabeth P. Benson, pp. 49–68. Washington, D.C.: Dumbarton Oaks.
1989   Olmec: What's In a Name? In *Regional Perspectives on the Olmec*, ed. Robert J. Sharer and David C. Grove, pp. 8–14. New York: Cambridge University Press and School for American Research.
1993   "Olmec" Horizons in Formative Period Mesoamerica: Diffusion or Social Evolution? In *Latin American Horizons*, ed. Don Stephen Rice, pp. 83–111. Washington, D.C.: Dumbarton Oaks.
1995   Los olmecas. *Arqueología Mexicana* 2(12):26–33.
1997   Olmec Archaeology: A Half Century of Research and Its Accomplishments. *Journal of World Prehistory* 11(1):51–101.
1999   Public Monuments and Sacred Mountains: Observations on Three Formative Period Sacred Landscapes. In *Social Patterns in Pre-Classic Mesoamerica*, ed. David C. Grove and Rosemary A. Joyce, pp. 255–299. Washington, D.C.: Dumbarton Oaks.

Grove, David C., and Susan D. Gillespie
1992   Ideology and Evolution at the Pre-State Level: Formative Period Mesoamerica. In *Ideology and Pre-Columbian Civilizations*, ed. Arthur A. Demarest and Geoffrey W. Conrad, p. 15–36. Santa Fe, N.M.: School of American Research Press.

Grove, David C., and Rosemary A. Joyce (eds.)
1999   *Social Patterns in Pre-Classic Mesoamerica.* Washington, D.C.: Dumbarton Oaks.

Grube, Nikolai, and Linda Schele
1994   Kuy, the Owl of Omen and War. *Méxicon* 16(1):10–17.

Gruhn, Ruth
1988   Linguistic Evidence in Support of the Coastal Route of Earliest Entry into the New World. *Man* 23:77–100.

Gruhn, Ruth, and Alan L. Bryan
1977   Los Tapiales: A Paleo-Indian Campsite in the Guatemalan Highlands. *Proceedings of the American Philosophical Society* 121:235–273.

Gürek, Özgür, Bernd Irlenbusch, and Bettina Rockenbach
2006   The Competitive Advantage of Sanctioning Institutions. *Science* 312:108–110.

Guernsey Kappelman, Julia
2001   Sacred Geography at Izapa and the Performance of Rulership. In *Landscape and Power in Ancient Mesoamerica*, ed. Rex Koontz, Kathryn Reese-Taylor, and Annabeth Headrick, pp. 81–111. Boulder, Colo.: Westview Press.
2002   Carved in Stone: The Cosmological Narratives of Late Preclassic Izapan-Style Monuments from the Pacific Slope. In *Heart of Creation. The Mesoamerican World and the Legacy of Linda Schele*, ed. Andrea Stone, pp. 66–82. Tuscaloosa: University of Alabama Press.
2003   Demystifying the Late Preclassic Izapan-Style Stela-Altar "Cult." *RES* 45:99–122.

Guernsey, Julia, and Michael Love
2005   Late Preclassic Expressions of Authority on the Pacific Slope. In *Lords of Creation: The Origins of Sacred Maya Kingship*, ed. Virginia M. Fields and Dorie Reents-Budet, pp. 37–43. Los Angeles, Calif.: Los Angeles County Museum of Art and Scala Publishers Ltd.

Haas, Jonathan
1982   *The Evolution of the Prehistoric State.* New York: Columbia University Press.
2001a   (ed.) *From Leaders to Rulers.* New York: Kluwer Academic/Plenum Publishers.

2001b   Cultural Evolution and Political Centralization. In *From Leaders to Rulers*, ed. Jonathan Haas, pp. 3–18. New York: Kluwer Academic/Plenum Publishers.

Hall, Jay, and René Viel

2004   The Early Classic Copan Landscape: A View from the Preclassic. In *Understanding Early Classic Copán*, ed. Ellen E. Bell, Marcello A. Canuto, and Robert J. Sharer, pp. 17–28. Philadelphia: The University Museum, University of Pennsylvania.

Hamblin, Nancy L.

1984   *Animal Use by the Cozumel Maya*. Tucson: University of Arizona Press.

1985   The Role of Marine Resources in the Maya Economy: A Case Study from Cozumel, Mexico. In *Prehistoric Lowland Maya Environment and Subsistence Economy*, ed. Mary Pohl, pp. 159–173. Peabody Museum Papers, vol. 77. Cambridge, Mass.: Peabody Museum of Archaeology and Ethnology, Harvard University.

Hammond, Norman

1982   A Late Formative Period Stela in the Maya Lowlands. *American Antiquity* 47:396–403.

1986   The Emergence of Maya Civilization. *Scientific American* 255:106–115.

1987   The Sun Also Rises: Iconographic Syntax of the Pomona Flare. *Research Reports on Ancient Maya Writing*, no. 7. Washington, D.C.: Center for Maya Research.

1992   Preclassic Maya Civilization. In *New Theories on the Ancient Maya*, ed. Elin C. Danien and Robert J. Sharer, pp. 137–144. University Museum Symposium Series, vol. 3, University Museum Monograph 77. Philadelphia: The University Museum, University of Pennsylvania.

1995   Ceremony and Society at Cuello: Preclassic Ritual Behavior and Social Differentiation. In *The Emergence of Lowland Maya Civilization: The Transition from the Preclassic to the Early Classic*, ed. Nikolai Grube, pp. 49–59. Acta Mesoamericana 8. Mockmuhl: Verlag Anton Saurwein.

1999   The Genesis of Hierarchy: Mortuary and Offertory Ritual in the Pre-Classic at Cuello, Belize. In *Social Patterns in Pre-Classic Mesoamerica*, ed. David C. Grove and Rosemary A. Joyce, pp. 49–66. Washington, D.C.: Dumbarton Oaks.

Hammond, Norman, Amanda Clarke, and Sara Donaghey

1995   The Long Goodbye: Middle Preclassic Maya Archaeology at Cuello, Belize. *Latin American Antiquity* 6(2):120–128.

Hammond, Norman, Duncan Pring, Richard Wilk, Sara Donaghey, Frank P. Saul, Elizabeth S. Wing, Arlene V. Miller, and Lawrence H. Feldman

1979   The Earliest Lowland Maya? Definition of the Swasey Phase. *American Antiquity* 44(1):92–110.

Hansen, Richard D.

1990   *Excavations in the Tigre Complex, El Mirador, Petén, Guatemala*. El Mirador Series, pt. 3. Papers of the New World Archaeological Foundation, no. 62. Provo, Utah: New World Archaeological Foundation, Brigham Young University.

1991a   The Road to Nakbe. *Natural History* (May 1991):8–14.

1991b   Resultados preliminares de las investigaciones arqueológicas en el sitio Nakbé, Petén, Guatemala. In *II Simposio de Investigaciones Arqueológicas en Guatemala, 1988*, ed. Juan Pedro Laporte, pp. 160–174. Guatemala City: Museo Nacional de Arqueología y Etnología, Ministerio de Cultura y Deportes, Instituto de Antropología e Historia, and Asociación Tikal.

1998   Continuity and Disjunction: The Pre-Classic Antecedents of Classic Maya Architecture. In *Function and Meaning in Classic Maya Architecture*, ed. Stephen D. Houston, pp. 49–122. Washington, D.C.: Dumbarton Oaks.

2000   The First Cities: The Beginnings of Urbanization and State Formation in the Maya Lowlands. In *Maya: Divine Kings of the Rain Forest*, ed. Nikolai Grube, pp. 51–65. Cologne: Könemann.

2005   Perspectives on Olmec-Maya Interaction in the Middle Formative Period. In *New Perspectives on Formative Mesoamerican Cultures*, ed. Terry G. Powis, pp. 51–72. B.A.R. International Series 1377. Oxford: Archaeopress.

Hansen, Richard D., Ronald L. Bishop, and Federico Fahsen

1991   Notes on Maya Codex-style Ceramics from Nakbe, Petén, Guatemala. *Ancient Mesoamerica* 2(2):225–243.

Hansen, Richard D., Steven Bozarth, John Jacob, David Wahl, and Thomas Schreiner

2002   Climatic and Environmental Variability in the Rise of Maya Civilization: A Preliminary Perspective from Northern Peten. *Ancient Mesoamerica* 13(2):273–296.

Hansen, Richard D., and Stanley P. Guenter

2005   Early Social Complexity and Kingship in the Mirador Basin. In *Lords of Creation: The Origins of Sacred Maya Kingship*, ed. Virginia M. Fields and Dorie Reents-Budet, pp. 60–61.

Los Angeles, Calif.: Los Angeles County Museum of Art and Scala Publishers Ltd.

Harris, David R.

2002   The Expansion Capacity of Early Agricultural Systems: A Comparative Perspective on the Spread of Agriculture. In *Examining the Farming/Language Dispersal Hypothesis*, ed. Peter Bellwood and Colin Renfrew, pp. 31–39. McDonald Institute Monograph. Cambridge: McDonald Institute for Archaeological Research.

Harris, John F., and Stephen K. Stearns

1997   *Understanding Maya Inscriptions: A Hieroglyph Handbook* (2nd rev. ed.). Philadelphia: The University Museum, University of Pennsylvania.

Hassig, Ross

2001   *Time, History, and Belief in Aztec and Colonial Mexico*. Austin: University of Texas Press.

Hatch, Marion Popenoe de

1971   An Hypothesis on Olmec Astronomy, with Special Reference to the La Venta Site. *Contributions of the University of California Archaeological Research Facility* 13:1–64.

1991   Kaminaljuyú: un resumen general hasta 1991. *Utz'ib* 1(1):2–6.

Hatch, Marion Popenoe de, Erick Ponciano, Tomás Barrientos Q., Mark Brenner, and Charles Ortloff

2001   Climate and Technological Innovation at Kaminaljuyu, Guatemala. *Ancient Mesoamerica* 13(1):103–114.

Hayden, Brian

1990   Nimrods, Piscators, Pluckers, and Planters: The Emergence of Food Production. *Journal of Anthropological Archaeology* 9:31–69.

1998   Practical and Prestige Technologies: The Evolution of Material Systems. *Journal of Archaeological Method and Theory* 5:1–55.

Hayden, Brian, and Rob Gargett

1990   Big Man, Big Heart? A Mesoamerican View of the Emergence of Complex Society. *Ancient Mesoamerica* 1:3–20.

Headrick, Annabeth

2004   The Quadripartite Motif and the Centralization of Power. In *K'axob: Ritual, Work, and Family in an Ancient Maya Village*, ed. Patricia A. McAnany, pp. 367–378. Monumenta Archaeologica 22. Los Angeles: Cotsen Institute of Archaeology, University of California, Los Angeles.

Heizer, Robert F., and Jonas E. Gullberg

1981   Concave Mirrors from the Site of La Venta, Tabasco: Their Occurrence, Mineralogy, Optical Description, and Function. In *The Olmec and Their Neighbors: Essays in Memory of Matthew W. Stirling*, org. Michael D. Coe and David C. Grove, ed. Elizabeth P. Benson, pp. 109–116. Washington, D.C.: Dumbarton Oaks.

Hellmuth, Nicholas M.

1976   *Tikal Copan Travel Guide: A General Introduction to Maya Art, Architecture, and Archaeology*. St. Louis, Mo.: Foundation for Latin American Archaeological Research.

1987   *Monster und Menschen in der Maya-Kunst*. Graz: Akademische Druck u. Verlagsanstalt.

1988   Early Maya Iconography on an Incised Cylindrical Tripod. In *Maya Iconography*, ed. Elizabeth P. Benson and Gillett G. Griffin, pp. 152–174. Princeton, N.J.: Princeton University Press.

Helms, Mary W.

1988   *Ulysses' Sail: An Ethnographic Odyssey of Power, Knowledge, and Geographical Distance*. Princeton, N.J.: Princeton University Press.

1993   *Craft and the Kingly Ideal: Art, Trade, and Power*. Austin: University of Texas Press.

Henrich, Joseph

2006   Cooperation, Punishment, and the Evolution of Human Institutions. *Science* 312:60–61.

Henshilwood, C. S., F. D'Errico, R. Yates, and Z. Jacobs et al.

2002   Emergence of Modern Human Behavior: Middle Stone Age Engravings from South Africa. *Science* 295:1278–1280.

Hester, Thomas R., Harry J. Shafer, Thomas C. Kelly, and Giancarlo Ligabue

1982   Observations on the Patination Process and the Context of Antiquity: A Fluted Projectile Point from Belize, Central America. *Lithic Technology* 11(2):29–34.

Heyden, Doris

1981   Caves, Gods, and Myths: World-View and Planning in Teotihuacan. In *Mesoamerican Sites and World-Views*, ed. Elizabeth P. Benson, pp. 1–35. Washington, D.C.: Dumbarton Oaks.

Hill, Jane H.

2001   Proto-Uto-Aztecan: A Community of Cultivators in Central Mexico? *American Anthropologist* 103(4):913–934.

Hill, Warren D., Michael Blake, and John E. Clark

1998   Ball Court Design Dates Back 3,400 Years. *Nature* 392:878.

Hill, Warren D., and John E. Clark

2001   Sports, Gambling, and Government: America's First Social Compact? *American Anthropologist* 103(2):331–345.

Hofling, C. Andrew

N.d.   The Linguistic Context of the Kowoj: Historical
Linguistics of the Central Petén from the Late
Late Classic Period through the 18th Century.
In *The Kowoj: Identity, Migration, and Politics
in Late Postclassic Petén, Guatemala*, ed.
Prudence M. Rice and Don S. Rice. Boulder:
University Press of Colorado.

Hofling, Charles A., and Thomas O'Neil

1992   Eclipse Cycles in the Moon Goddess
Almanacs in the Dresden Codex. In *The Sky
in Mayan Literature*, ed. Anthony F. Aveni, pp.
102–132. Oxford: Oxford University Press.

Holden, Constance (ed.)

2005   Buried with Care. *Science* 310(1):46.

Houston, Stephen D.

1989   *Maya Glyphs*. Berkeley and Los Angeles:
University of California.

2000   Into the Minds of Ancients. *Journal of World
Prehistory* 14(2):121–201.

2006   An Example of Preclassic Mayan Writing?
Science 311:1249–1250.

Houston, Stephen D., and Michael D. Coe

2003   Has Isthmian Writing Been Deciphered?
Mexicon 15(6):151–161.

**Houston, Stephen D., John Robertson,
and David Stuart**

2000   The Language of Classic Maya Inscriptions.
Current Anthropology 41(3):321–356.

**Hovers, Erella, Shimon Ilani, Ofer Bar-Yosef, and
Bernard Vandermeersch**

2003   An Early Case of Color Symbolism: Ochre Use
by Modern Humans in Qafzeh Cave. *Current
Anthropology* 44(4):491–522.

Iceland, Harry B.

2005   The Preceramic to Early Middle Formative
Transition in Northern Belize: Evidence for
the Ethnic Identity of the Preceramic
Inhabitants. In *New Perspectives on Formative
Mesoamerican Cultures*, ed. Terry G. Powis,
pp. 15–26. B.A.R. International Series 1377.
Oxford: Archaeopress.

Iltis, Hugh H.

1983   From Teosinte to Maize: The Catastrophic
Sexual Transmutation. *Science* 222:886–894.

Jackson, Sarah, and David Stuart

2001   The *Aj K'uhun* Title: Deciphering a Classic
Maya Term of Rank. *Ancient Mesoamerica*
12(2):217–218.

**Jaenicke-Després, Viviane, Ed S. Buckler, Bruce D.
Smith, M. Thomas P. Gilbert, John Doebley, and
Svante Pääbo**

2003   Early Allelic Selection in Maize as Revealed
by Ancient DNA. *Science*
302(5648):1206–1208.

Jiménez-Moreno, Wigberto

1954–1955 Síntesis de la historia precolonial del valle
de México. *Revista de Estudios
Antropológicos* 14:219–236.

Joesink-Mandeville, Leroy

1973   The Importance of Gourd Prototypes in the
Analysis of Mesoamerican Ceramics. *Katunob*
8:47–33.

Jones, Christopher

1969   The Twin-Pyramid Group Pattern: A Classic
Maya Architectural Assemblage at Tikal,
Guatemala. Ph.D. dissertation, University of
Pennsylvania.

1991   Cycles of Growth at Tikal. In *Classic Maya
Political History: Hieroglyphic and
Archaeological Evidence*, ed. T. Patrick
Culbert, pp. 102–127. Cambridge: Cambridge
University Press and School of American
Research.

Jones, Grant D., and Robert R. Kautz (eds.)

1981   *The Transition to Statehood in the New
World*. Cambridge: Cambridge University
Press.

Jones, John G.

1994   Pollen Evidence for Early Settlement and
Agriculture in Northern Belize. *Palynology*
18:205–211.

Jones, Tom

1985   The Xoc, the Sharke, and the Sea Dogs: An
Historical Encounter. In *Fifth Palenque Round
Table, 1983*, ed. Virginia M. Fields, gen. ed.
Merle Greene Robertson, pp. 211–222. San
Francisco, Calif.: Pre-Columbian Art Research
Institute.

1991   Jaws II: Return of the *Xoc*. In *Sixth Palenque
Round Table, 1986*, gen. ed. Merle Greene
Robertson, pp. 246–254. Norman: University
of Oklahoma Press.

Joralemon, Peter D.

1971   A Study of Olmec Iconography. Studies in Pre-
Columbian Art and Archaeology, 7.
Washington, D.C.: Dumbarton Oaks.

1976   The Olmec Dragon: A Study in Precolumbian
Iconography. In *Origins of Religious Art and
Iconography in Preclassic Mesoamerica*, ed. H.
B. Nicholson, pp. 27–72. Los Angeles:
University of California, Los Angeles Latin
American Center.

1981   Old Woman and the Child: Themes in the
Iconography of Pre-classic Mesoamerica. In
*The Olmec and Their Neighbors: Essays in
Memory of Matthew W. Stirling*, org. Michael
D. Coe and David C. Grove, ed. Elizabeth P.
Benson, pp. 163–180. Washington, D.C.:
Dumbarton Oaks.

1996   Comments on individual catalog items. In *Olmec Art of Ancient Mexico*, ed. Elizabeth P. Benson and Beatriz de la Fuente. Washington, D.C.: National Gallery of Art.

Joyce, Rosemary

1999   Social Dimensions of Pre-Classic Burials. In *Social Patterns in Pre-Classic Mesoamerica*, ed. David C. Grove and Rosemary A. Joyce, pp. 15–47. Washington, D.C.: Dumbarton Oaks.

2000   High Culture, Mesoamerican Civilization, and the Classic Maya Tradition. In *Order, Legitimacy, and Wealth in Ancient States*, ed. Janet Richards and Mary Van Buren, pp. 64–76. Cambridge: Cambridge University Press.

2003   Unintended Consequences? Monumentality as a Novel Experience in Formative Mesoamerica. *Journal of Archaeological Method and Theory* 11(1):5–29.

2004   Mesoamerica: A Working Model for Archaeology. In *Mesoamerican Archaeology*, ed. Julia A. Hendon and Rosemary A. Joyce, pp. 1–42. Malden, Mass: Blackwell Publishing.

Joyce, Rosemary, Richard Edging, Karl Lorenz, and Susan D. Gillespie

1991   Olmec Bloodletting: An Iconographic Study. In *Sixth Palenque Round Table, 1986*, gen. ed. Merle Greene Robertson, pp. 143–150. Norman: University of Oklahoma Press.

Joyce, Rosemary A., and David C. Grove

1999   Asking New Questions about the Mesoamerican Pre-Classic. In *Social Patterns in Pre-Classic Mesoamerica*, ed. David C. Grove and Rosemary A. Joyce, pp. 1–14. Washington, D.C.: Dumbarton Oaks.

Justeson, John S.

1986   The Origin of Writing Systems: Preclassic Mesoamerica. *World Archaeology* 17(3): 437–457.

1989   Ancient Maya Ethnoastronomy: An Overview of Hieroglyphic Sources. In *World Archaeoastronomy*, ed. Anthony Aveni, pp. 76–129. Cambridge: Cambridge University Press.

Justeson, John S., and Lyle Campbell

1997   The Linguistic Background of Maya Hieroglyphic Writing: Arguments about a "Highland Mayan" Role. In *The Language of Maya Hieroglyphs*, ed. Martha J. Macri and Anabel Ford, pp. 41–67. San Francisco, Calif.: Pre-Columbian Art Research Institute.

Justeson, John S., and Terrence Kaufman

1993   A Decipherment of Epi-Olmec Hieroglyphic Writing. *Science* 259:1703–1711.

1997   Newly Discovered Column in the Hieroglyphic Text on La Mojarra Stela 1: A Test of the Epi-Olmec Decipherment. *Science* 277:207–210

Justeson, John S., and Peter Mathews

1983   The Seating of the *Tun*: Further Evidence Concerning a Late Preclassic Lowland Maya Stela Cult. *American Antiquity* 48(3):586–593.

Justeson, John S., William M. Norman, Lyle Campbell, and Terrence Kaufman

1985   *The Foreign Impact on Lowland Mayan Language and Script*. Middle American Research Institute Pub. 53. New Orleans, La.: Tulane University.

Justeson, John S., William M. Norman, and Norman Hammond

1988   The Pomona Flare: A Preclassic Maya Hieroglyphic Text. In *Maya Iconography*, ed. Elizabeth P. Benson and Gillett Griffin, pp. 94–151. Princeton, N.J.: Princeton University Press.

Kaplan, Hillard S.

2001   Evolution and Our Reproductive Physiology. *Science* 293:809–810.

Kaplan, Jonathan

1995   The Incienso Throne and Other Thrones from Kaminaljuyu, Guatemala. *Ancient Mesoamerica* 6(2):185–196.

1996   El Monumento 65 de Kaminaljuyu y su ilustración de ritos dinásticos de gobierno del Preclásico Tardío. In *IX Simposio de Investigaciones Arqueológicas en Guatemala, 1995*, vol. 2, ed. Juan Pedro Laporte and Héctor Escobedo, pp. 451–459. Guatemala City: Museo Nacional de Arqueología y Etnología, Ministerio de Cultura y Deportes, Instituto de Antropología e Historia, and Asociación Tikal.

Kaufman, Terrence

1976   Archaeological and Linguistic Correlations in Mayaland and Associated Areas of Mesoamerica. *World Archaeology* 8:101–118.

Kaufman, Terrence, and John Justeson

2001   Epi-Olmec Hieroglyphic Writing and Texts. Mesoamerican Languages Documentation Project. http://www.albany.edu/anthro/maldp. Accessed August 29, 2006.

2004   Epi-Olmec. In *The Cambridge Encyclopedia of the World's Ancient Languages*, pp. 1071–1111. Cambridge: Cambridge University Press.

Kelley, David H.

1965   The Birth of the Gods at Palenque. *Estudios de Cultura Maya* 5:93–134.

1974   Eurasian Evidence and the Mayan Calendar Correlation Problem. In *Mesoamerican Archaeology: New Approaches*, ed. Norman Hammond, pp. 135–143. Austin: University of Texas Press.

Kelly, Thomas C.

1993   Preceramic Projectile-Point Typology in Belize. *Ancient Mesoamerica* 4(2):204–227.

Kennedy, Alison Bailey

1982   *Ecce Bufo*: The Toad in Nature and in Olmec Iconography. *Current Anthropology* 23(3):273–290.

Kennett, Douglas J., and Barbara Voorhies

1996   Oxygen Isotopic Analysis of Archaeological Shells to Detect Seasonal Use of Wetlands on the Southern Pacific Coast of Mexico. *Journal of Archaeological Science* 24:1051–1059.

Kerr, Justin

1992   The Myth of the Popol Vuh as an Instrument of Power. In *New Theories on the Ancient Maya*, ed. Elin C. Danien and Robert J. Sharer, pp. 109–121. University Museum Symposium Series, vol. 3, University Museum Monograph 77. Philadelphia: The University Museum, University of Pennsylvania.

N.d.   A Fishy Story. http://www.mayavase.com/fishy.html. Accessed August 29, 2006.

Kirchoff, Paul

1943   Mesoamerica. *Acta Americana* 1:92–107.

Kirkby, Michael J., Anne V. Whyte, and Kent V. Flannery

1986   The Physical Environment of the Guilá Naquitz Cave Group. In *Guilá Naquitz: Archaic Foraging and Early Agriculture in Oaxaca, Mexico*, ed. Kent V. Flannery, pp. 43–61. Orlando, Fla.: Academic Press.

Knapp, A. Bernard

1988   Ideology, Archaeology and Polity. *Man* (N.s.) 23:133–163.

Kosakowsky, Laura J., and Duncan C. Pring

1998   The Ceramics of Cuello, Belize: A New Evaluation. *Ancient Mesoamerica* 9:55–66.

Kozuch, Laura

1993   *Sharks and Shark Products in Prehistoric South Florida*. Monograph, no. 2. Gainesville: Institute of Archaeology and Paleoenvironmental Studies, University of Florida.

Kroeber, Alfred

1939   *Cultural and Natural Areas of Native North America*. University of California Publications in American Archaeology and Ethnology, vol. 38.

Kubler, George

1985   Pre-Columbian Pilgrimages in Mesoamerica. In *Fourth Palenque Round Table, 1980*, ed. Elizabeth P. Benson, pp. 313–316. San Francisco, Calif.: Pre-Columbian Archaeological Research Institute.

Lamb, Weldon W.

2002   The Maya Month Names. Ph.D. dissertation, Tulane University.

Laporte, Juan Pedro

2004   Terminal Classic Settlement and Polity in the Mopan Valley, Petén, Guatemala. In *The Terminal Classic in the Maya Lowlands: Collapse, Transition, and Transformation*, ed. Arthur A. Demarest, Prudence M. Rice, and Don S. Rice, pp. 195–230. Boulder: University Press of Colorado.

Laporte, Juan Pedro, and Vilma Fialko C.

1990   New Perspectives on Old Problems: Dynastic References for the Early Classic at Tikal. In *Vision and Revision in Maya Studies*, ed. Flora S. Clancy and Peter D. Harrison, pp. 33–66. Albuquerque: University of New Mexico Press.

1995   Un reëncuentro con Mundo Perdido, Tikal, Guatemala. *Ancient Mesoamerica* 6:41–94.

Lathrap, Donald W.

1974   The Moist Tropics, the Arid Lands, and the Appearance of Great Art Styles in the New World. In *Art and Environment in Native America*, ed. M. King and I. Traylor. Special Pub. 77. Lubbock: Texas Tech University Museum.

Laughton, Timothy B.

1997   Sculpture on the Threshold: The Iconography of Izapa and Its Relationship to That of the Maya. Ph.D. dissertation, University of Essex.

Lee, Thomas A., Jr.

1989   Chiapas and the Olmec. In *Regional Perspectives on the Olmec*, ed. Robert J. Sharer and David C. Grove, pp. 198–226. Cambridge: Cambridge University Press and School of American Research.

Lentz, David L., Mary E. D. Pohl, and Kevin O. Pope

2005   Domesticated Plants and Cultural Connections in Early Mesoamerica: Formative Period Paleoethnobotanical Evidence from Belize, Mexico, and Honduras. In *New Perspectives on Formative Mesoamerican Cultures*, ed. Terry G. Powis, pp. 121–126. B.A.R. International Series 1377. Oxford: Archaeopress.

León-Portilla, Miguel

1988   *Time and Reality in the Thought of the Maya* (2nd ed.). Norman: University of Oklahoma Press.

Leopold, A. Starker

1959   The Range of the Jaguar in Mexico. App. 5 in *Excavations at La Venta, Tabasco, 1955*, by Philip Drucker, Robert F. Heizer, and Robert J.

Squier, pp. 290–291. Bureau of American Ethnology Bulletin 170. Washington, D.C.: Smithsonian Institution.

Lesure, Richard G.

1997 Early Formative Platforms at Paso de la Amada, Chiapas, Mexico. *Latin American Antiquity* 8(3):217–235.

1998 Refining an Early Formative Ceramic Sequence from the Chiapas Coast of Mexico. *Ancient Mesoamerica* 9(1):67–81.

2004 Shared Art Styles and Long-distance Contact in Early Mesoamerica. In *Mesoamerican Archaeology*, ed. Julia A. Hendon and Rosemary A. Joyce, pp. 73–96. Oxford: Blackwell Publishing.

Leyden, Barbara W.

2002 Pollen Evidence for Climatic Variability and Cultural Disturbance in the Maya Lowlands. *Ancient Mesoamerica* 13(1):85–101.

Lipton, Peter

2005 Testing Hypotheses: Prediction and Prejudice. *Science* 307:219–221.

Looper, Matthew G.

2003 *Lightning Warrior: Maya Art and Kingship at Quirigua.* Austin: University of Texas Press.

López-Varela, Sandra L.

2004 Ceramic History of K'axob: The Early Years. In *K'axob: Ritual, Work and Family in an Ancient Maya Village*, ed. Patricia A. McAnany, pp. 169–191. Monumenta Archaeologica 22. Los Angeles: Cotsen Institute of Archaeology, University of California, Los Angeles.

Lounsbury, Floyd G.

1978 Maya Numeration, Computation, and Calendrical Astronomy. *Dictionary of Scientific Biography*, vol. 15, supp. 1, ed. Charles Coulston-Gillispie, pp. 757–818. New York: Charles Scribner's Sons.

1983 The Base of the Venus Table of the Dresden Codex and Its Significance for the Calendar Correlation. In *Calendars in Mesoamerica and Peru: Native Computations of Time*, pp. 1–26. British Archaeological Reports, International Series S174, Oxford.

1985 The Identities of the Mythological Figures in the Cross Group Inscriptions of Palenque. *Fourth Palenque Round Table, 1980*, ed. Elizabeth P. Benson, pp. 45–58. San Francisco, Calif.: Pre-Columbian Art Research Institute.

Love, Michael

1999 Ideology, Material Culture, and Daily Practice in Pre-Classic Mesoamerica: A Pacific Coast Perspective. In *Social Patterns in Pre-Classic Mesoamerica*, ed. David C. Grove and Rosemary A. Joyce, pp. 127–153. Washington, D.C.: Dumbarton Oaks.

Lowe, Gareth W.

1965 Desarrollo y función del incensario en Izapa. *Estudios de Cultura Maya* 5:53–63.

1977 The Mixe-Zoque as Competing Neighbors of the Early Lowland Maya. In *The Origins of Maya Civilization*, ed. Richard E. W. Adams, pp. 197–248. Albuquerque: University of New Mexico Press.

1981 Olmec Horizons Defined in Mound 20, San Isidro, Chiapas. In *The Olmec and Their Neighbors: Essays in Memory of Matthew W. Stirling*, org. Michael D. Coe and David C. Grove, ed. Elizabeth P. Benson, pp. 231–255. Washington, D.C.: Dumbarton Oaks.

1982a The Izapa Sculpture Horizon. In *Izapa: An Introduction to the Ruins and Monuments*, ed. Gareth W. Lowe, Thomas A. Lee Jr., and Eduardo Martínez E., pp. 17–41. Papers of the New World Archaeological Foundation, no. 31. Provo, Utah: New World Archaeological Foundation, Brigham Young University.

1982b Izapa Religion, Cosmology, and Ritual. In *Izapa: An Introduction to the Ruins and Monuments*, ed. Gareth W. Lowe, Thomas A. Lee, Jr., and Eduardo Martínez E., pp. 269–305. Papers of the New World Archaeological Foundation, no. 31. Provo, Utah: New World Archaeological Foundation, Brigham Young University.

1989a Algunas aclaraciones sobre la presencia olmeca y maya en el Preclásico de Chiapas. In *El Preclásico o Formativo: Avances y perspectivas*, coord. Martha Carmona Macías, pp. 363–384. Mexico City: Instituto Nacional de Antropología e Historia.

1989b The Heartland Olmec: Evolution of Material Culture. In *Regional Perspectives on the Olmec*, ed. Robert J. Sharer and David C. Grove, pp. 33–67. Cambridge: Cambridge University Press and School of American Research.

1998 *Los olmecas de San Isidro en Malpaso, Chiapas.* Serie Arqueología. Mexico City: Instituto Nacional de Antropología e Historia and Universidad Nacional Autónoma de México.

Lowe, Gareth W., Thomas A. Lee Jr., and Eduardo Martínez E. (eds.)

1982 *Izapa: An Introduction to the Ruins and Monuments.* Papers of the New World Archaeological Foundation, no. 31. Provo, Utah: New World Archaeological Foundation, Brigham Young University.

MacNeish, Richard S.

1961   *Restos precerámicos de la cueva de Coxcatlán en el sur de Puebla.* Dirección de Prehistoria, Pub. 10. Mexico City: Instituto Nacional de Antropología e Historia.

1964   The Food-gathering and Incipient Agriculture Stage of Prehistoric Middle America. In *Natural Environment and Early Cultures,* Handbook of Middle American Indians, vol. 1, vol. ed., Robert C. West; gen. ed., Robert Wauchope, pp. 413–436. Austin: University of Texas Press.

1967   A Summary of the Subsistence. In *The Prehistory of the Tehuacan Valley,* vol. 1: *Environment and Subsistence,* ed. Douglas S. Byers, pp. 290–309. Austin: University of Texas Press.

1972   Summary of the Cultural Sequence and Its Implications in the Tehuacan Valley. In *The Prehistory of the Tehuacan Valley,* vol. 5: *Excavations and Reconnaissance,* ed. Douglas S. Byers, pp. 496–504. Austin: University of Texas Press.

1981   Tehuacan's Accomplishments. In *Archaeology,* ed. Jeremy A. Sabloff; gen. ed., Victoria C. Bricker, pp. 31–47. Handbook of Middle American Indians, Supp. 1. Austin: University of Texas Press.

MacNeish, Richard S., and Antoinette Nelken-Terner

1983   Preceramic of Mesoamerica. *Journal of Field Archaeology* 10(1):71–84.

Macri, Martha J.

2000   *Mutal,* a Possible Mixe-Zoque Toponym. *Glyph Dwellers,* Rep. 12. Davis: University of California.

2005   A Lunar Origin for the Mesoamerican Calendars of 20, 13, 9, and 7 Days. In *Current Studies in Archaeoastronomy: Conversations Across Time and Space,* ed. John W. Fountain and Rolf M. Sinclair, pp. 275–288. Durham, N.C.: Carolina Academic Press.

Macri, Martha J., and Matthew G. Looper

2003   *The New Catalog of Maya Hieroglyphs,* vol. 1, *The Classic Period Inscriptions.* Norman: University of Oklahoma Press.

Macri, Martha J., and Laura Stark

1993   *A Sign Catalog of the La Mojarra Script.* Monograph 5. San Francisco, Calif.: Pre-Columbian Art Research Institute.

Malinowski, Bronislaw

1927   Lunar and Seasonal Calendar in the Trobriands. *Journal of the Royal Anthropological Institute* 57:203–215.

Malmström, Vincent H.

1973   Origins of the Mesoamerican 260-day Calendar. *Science* 181:939–941.

1978   A Reconstruction of the Chronology of Mesoamerican Calendrical Systems. *Journal for the History of Astronomy,* ed. M. A. Hoskin, 9:105–116.

1997   *Cycles of the Sun, Mysteries of the Moon: The Calendar in Mesoamerican Civilization.* Austin: University of Texas Press.

Manzanilla, Linda

2000   The Construction of the Underworld in Central Mexico: Transformations from the Classic to the Postclassic. In *Mesoamerica's Classic Heritage: From Teotihuacan to the Aztecs,* ed. David Carrasco, Lindsay Jones, and Scott Sessions, pp. 87–116. Boulder: University Press of Colorado.

Marcus, Joyce

1976   The Origins of Mesoamerican Writing. *Annual Review of Anthropology* 5:35–67.

1983a   The Genetic Model and the Linguistic Divergence of the Otomangueans. In *The Cloud People: Divergent Evolution of the Zapotec and Mixtec Civilizations,* ed. Kent V. Flannery and Joyce Marcus, pp. 4–9. New York: Academic Press.

1983b   The Espiridión Complex and the Origins of the Oaxacan Formative. In *The Cloud People: Divergent Evolution of the Zapotec and Mixtec Civilizations,* ed. Kent V. Flannery and Joyce Marcus, pp. 42–43. New York: Academic Press.

1989   Zapotec Chiefdoms and the Nature of Formative Religions. In *Regional Perspectives on the Olmec,* ed. Robert J. Sharer and David C. Grove, pp. 148–197. Cambridge: Cambridge University Press and School of American Research.

1992a   *Mesoamerican Writing Systems: Propaganda, Myth, and History in Four Ancient Civilizations.* Princeton, N.J.: Princeton University Press.

1992b   Political Fluctuations in Mesoamerica. *National Geographic Research and Exploration* 8(4):392–411.

1993   Ancient Maya Political Organization. In *Lowland Maya Civilization in the Eighth Century A.D.,* ed. Jeremy A. Sabloff and John S. Henderson, pp. 111–183. Washington, D.C.: Dumbarton Oaks.

1999   Men's and Women's Ritual in Formative Oaxaca. In *Social Patterns in Pre-Classic Mesoamerica,* ed. David C. Grove and Rosemary A. Joyce, pp. 67–96. Washington, D.C.: Dumbarton Oaks.

2004   Primary and Secondary State Formation in Southern Mesoamerica. In *Understanding Early Classic Copan*, ed. Ellen E. Bell, Marcello A. Canuto, and Robert J. Sharer, pp. 357–373. Philadelphia: University of Pennsylvania Museum of Archaeology and Anthropology.

Marcus, Joyce, and Kent V. Flannery

1996   *Zapotec Civilization: How Urban Society Evolved in Mexico's Oaxaca Valley.* London: Thames and Hudson.

2000   Ancient Zapotec Ritual and Religion: An Application of the Direct Historical Approach. In *The Ancient Civilizations of Mesoamerica: A Reader*, ed. Michael E. Smith and Marilyn A. Masson, pp. 400–421. Malden, Mass.: Blackwell Publishers. (Originally appeared in *The Ancient Mind: Elements of Cognitive Archaeology*, ed. Colin Renfrew and Ezra B. W. Zubrow, pp. 55–74. New York: Cambridge University Press.)

Marcus, Joyce, Kent V. Flannery, and Ronald Spores

1983   The Cultural Legacy of the Oaxacan Preceramic. In *The Cloud People: Divergent Evolution of the Zapotec and Mixtec Civilizations*, ed. Kent V. Flannery and Joyce Marcus, pp. 36–39. New York: Academic Press.

Marshack, Alexander

1972   Upper Paleolithic Notation and Symbol. *Science* 1978:817–828.

1974   The Chamula Calendar Board: An Internal and Comparative Analysis. In *Mesoamerican Archaeology: New Approaches*, ed. Norman Hammond, pp. 255–270. Austin: University of Texas Press.

1977   Olmec Mosaic Pendant. In *Archaeoastronomy in Pre-Columbian America*, ed. Anthony F. Aveni, pp. 341–377. Austin: University of Texas Press.

1985   A Lunar-Solar Year Calendar Stick from North America. *American Antiquity* 50(1):27–51.

Martin, Simon

2003   In Line of the Founder: A View of Dynastic Politics at Tikal. In *Tikal: Dynasties, Foreigners, and Affairs of State: Advancing Maya Archaeology*, ed. Jeremy A. Sabloff, pp. 3–45. Santa Fe, N.M.: School of American Research Press.

Martin, Simon, and Nikolai Grube

2000   *Chronicle of the Maya Kings and Queens: Deciphering the Dynasties of the Ancient Maya.* London: Thames and Hudson.

Martínez Hidalgo, Gustavo, and Richard D. Hansen

1992   Excavaciones en el Complejo 59, Grupo 66 y Grupo 18, Nakbé, Petén. In *III Simposio de Investigaciones Arqueológicas en Guatemala, 1989*, ed. Juan Pedro Laporte, pp. 73–85. Guatemala City: Museo Nacional de Arqueología y Etnología, Ministerio de Cultura y Deportes, Instituto de Antropología e Historia, and Asociación Tikal.

Masson, Marilyn A., and Shirley Boteler Mock

2004   Ceramics and Settlement Patterns at Terminal Classic-Period Lagoon Sites in Northeastern Belize. In *The Terminal Classic in the Maya Lowlands: Collapse, Transition, and Transformation*, ed. Arthur A. Demarest, Prudence M. Rice, and Don S. Rice, pp. 367–401. Boulder: University Press of Colorado.

Matheny, Ray T.

1986   Investigations at El Mirador, Petén, Guatemala. *National Geographic Research* 2(3):332–353.

2001   Mirador, El (Petén, Guatemala). In *Archaeology of Ancient Mexico and Central America: An Encyclopedia*, ed. Susan Toby Evans and David L. Webster, pp. 472–473. New York: Garland Publishing.

Mathews, Peter

2001   The Inscription on the Back of Stela 8, Dos Pilas, Guatemala. In *The Decipherment of Maya Hieroglyphic Writing*, ed. Stephen D. Houston, David Stuart, and Oswaldo Chinchilla Mazariegos, pp. 394–415. Norman: University of Oklahoma Press.

Mathews, Peter, and John S. Justeson.

1984 [1977]   Patterns of Sign Substitution in Mayan Hieroglyphic Writing: The Affix Cluster. In *Phoneticism in Mayan Hieroglyphic Writing*, ed. John S. Justeson and Lyle Campbell, pp. 185–231. Institute for Mesoamerican Studies, Pub. 9. Albany: State University of New York at Albany.

McAnany, Patricia A.

2001   Cosmology and the Institutionalization of Hierarchy in the Maya Region. In *From Leaders to Rulers*, ed. Jonathan Haas, pp. 125–148. New York: Kluwer Academic/Plenum Publishers.

2004a   (ed.) *K'axob: Ritual, Work and Family in an Ancient Maya Village.* Monumenta Archaeologica 22. Los Angeles: Cotsen Institute of Archaeology, University of California, Los Angeles.

2004b   Appropriative Economies: Labor Obligations and Luxury Goods in Ancient Maya Societies. In *Archaeological Perspectives on Political Economies*, ed. Gary M. Feinman and Linda M. Nicholas, pp. 145–165. Salt Lake City: University of Utah Press.

2004c   Obsidian Blades and Source Areas. In *K'axob: Ritual, Work and Family in an Ancient Maya Village*, ed. Patricia A. McAnany, pp. 307–315. Monumenta Archaeologica 22. Los Angeles: Cotsen Institute of Archaeology, University of California, Los Angeles.

McAnany, Patricia, Rebecca Storey, and Angela K. Lockard
1999   Mortuary Ritual and Family Politics at Formative and Early Classic K'axob, Belize. *Ancient Mesoamerica* 10(1):129–146.

McDonald, Andrew J.
1977   Two Middle Preclassic Engraved Monuments at Tzutzuculi on the Chiapas Coast of Mexico. *American Antiquity*: 42(4):560–566.

Meltzer, David J.
1997   On the Pleistocene Antiquity of Monte Verde, Southern Chile. *American Antiquity* 62(4):659–663.

Merrill, R. H.
1945   Maya Sun Calendar Dictum Disproved. *American Antiquity* 10:307–311.

Michels, Joseph W.
1979   *The Kaminaljuyu Chiefdom*. Monograph Series on Kaminaljuyu. State College: Pennsylvania State University Press.

Milbrath, Susan
1999   *Star Gods of the Maya: Astronomy in Art, Folklore, and Calendars*. Austin: University of Texas Press.

Miles, Suzanne W.
1965   Sculpture of the Guatemala-Chiapas Highlands and Pacific Slopes and Associated Hieroglyphs. In *Handbook of Middle American Indians, vol. 2*, ed. Gordon R. Willey; gen. ed., Robert C. Wauchope, pp. 237–275. Austin: University of Texas Press.

Miller, Arthur G.
1974   The Iconography of the Painting in the Temple of the Diving God, Tulum, Quintana Roo: The Twisted Cords. In *Mesoamerican Archaeology: New Approaches*, ed. Norman Hammond, pp. 167–186. Austin: University of Texas Press.

Miller, Mary Ellen, and Stephen D. Houston
1987   Stairways and Ballcourt Glyphs: New Perspectives on the Classic Maya Ballgame. *RES* 14:47–66.

Miller, Mary Ellen, and Simon Martin
2004   *Courtly Art of the Ancient Maya*. New York: Thames and Hudson and Fine Arts Museum of San Francisco.

Miller, Mary Ellen, and Karl Taube
1993   *The Gods and Symbols of Ancient Mexico and the Maya: An Illustrated Dictionary of Mesoamerican Religion*. New York: Thames and Hudson.

Miller, Wick R.
1967   *Uto-Aztecan Cognate Sets*. Publications in Linguistics, vol. 48. Berkeley and Los Angeles: University of California Press.

Mirambell, Lorena
1994   Los primeros pobladores del actual territorio mexicano. In *Historia antigua de México, vol. 1: El México antiguo: sus áreas culturales, los orígenes y el horizonte preclásico*, ed. Linda Manzanilla and Leonardo López Luján, pp. 177–208. Mexico City: Instituto Nacional de Antropología e Historia and Universidad Nacional Autónoma de México.

Mock, Shirley Boteler (ed.)
1998   *The Sowing and the Dawning: Termination, Dedication, and Transformation in the Archaeological and Ethnographic Record of Mesoamerica*. Albuquerque: University of New Mexico Press.

Montgomery, John
2001a   *Tikal: An Illustrated History of the Ancient Maya Capital*. New York: Hippocrene Books.
2001b   *How to Read Maya Hieroglyphs*. New York: Hippocrene Books.
2002   *Dictionary of Maya Hieroglyphs*. New York: Hippocrene Books.

Mora-Marín, David F.
2005   Kaminaljuyu Stela 10: Script Classification and Linguistic Affiliation. *Ancient Mesoamerica* 16(1):63–87.

Moyes, Holley
2004   Changes and Continuities in Ritual Practice at Chechem Ha Cave, Belize: Report on Excavations Conducted in the 2003 Field Season. www.famsi.org/reports/02086. Accessed August 29, 2006.

Munn, Nancy D.
1992   The Cultural Anthropology of Time: A Critical Essay. *Annual Review of Anthropology* 21:93–123.

Murdy, Carson N.
1981   Congenital Deformities and the Olmec Were-Jaguar Motif. *American Antiquity* 46(4):861–871.

Neff, Hector, Deborah M. Pearsall, John G. Jones, Bárbara Arroyo, Shawn K. Collins, and Dorothy E. Freidel
2006   Early Maya Adaptive Patterns: Mid-Late Holocene Paleoenvironmental Evidence from Pacific Guatemala. *Latin American Antiquity* 17(3):287–315.

Neuenswander, Helen

1981   Vestiges of Early Maya Time Concepts in a Contemporary Maya (Cubulco Achi) Community: Implications for Epigraphy. *Estudios de Cultura Maya* 13:125–163.

Newsome, Elizabeth A.

2001   *Trees of Paradise and Pillars of the World: The Serial Stela Cycle of "18-Rabbit-God K," King of Copan.* Austin: University of Texas Press.

Niederberger, Christine

1979   Early Sedentary Economy in the Basin of Mexico. *Science* 203:131–142.

1996   The Basin of Mexico: A Multimillennial Development toward Cultural Complexity. In *Olmec Art of Ancient Mexico*, ed. Elizabeth P. Benson and Beatriz de la Fuente, pp. 83–93. Washington, D.C.: National Gallery of Art.

Nilsson, Martin P.

1920   *Primitive Time-Reckoning: A Study in the Origins and First Development of the Art of Counting Time among the Primitive and Early Culture Peoples.* Lund: C. W. K. Gleerup.

Norman, V. Garth

1973   *Izapa Sculpture*, pt. 1: *Album*. Papers of the New World Archaeological Foundation, no. 30, pt. 1. Provo, Utah: New World Archaeological Foundation, Brigham Young University.

1976   *Izapa Sculpture*, pt. 2: *Text*. Papers of the New World Archaeological Foundation, no. 30, pt. 2. Provo, Utah: New World Archaeological Foundation, Brigham Young University.

Nuttall, Zelia

1928   Novelles lumières sur les civilizations américaines et le système du calendrier. In *Proceedings of the 22nd International Congress of Americanists*, pp. 119–148. Rome.

Orrego Corzo, Miguel

1992   Costa sur de Guatemala: importante evidencia sobre la presencia de la cultura maya, para los períodos Preclásico Tardío y Clásico Temprano. In *The Emergence of Lowland Maya Civilization: The Transition from the Preclassic to the Early Classic*, ed. Nikolai Grube, pp. 7–15. Acta Mesoamericana 8. Mockmuhl: Verlag Anton Saurwein.

Ortiz C., Ponciano, and María del Carmen Rodríguez

1999   Olmec Ritual Behavior at El Manatí: A Sacred Space. In *Social Patterns in Pre-Classic Mesoamerica*, ed. David C. Grove and Rosemary A. Joyce, pp. 225–254. Washington, D.C.: Dumbarton Oaks.

Pagliaro, Jonathan B., James F. Garber, and Travis W. Stanton

2003   Evaluating the Archaeological Signatures of Maya Ritual and Conflict. In *Ancient Mesoamerican Warfare*, ed. M. Kathryn Brown and Travis W. Stanton, pp. 75–89. New York: AltaMira Press.

Pahl, Gary W.

1982   A Possible Cycle 7 Monument from Polol, El Petén, Guatemala. In *Pre-Columbian Art History: Selected Readings*, ed. Alana Cordy-Collins, pp. 23–31. Palo Alto, Calif.: Peek Publications.

Panchanathan, Karthik, and Robert Boyd

2004   Indirect Reciprocity Can Stabilize Cooperation without the Second-order Free Rider Problem. *Nature* 432:499–502.

Parker Pearson, Michael, and Colin Richards

1994a   (eds.) *Architecture and Order: Approaches to Social Space.* London: Routledge.

1994b   Ordering the World: Perceptions of Architecture, Space and Time. In *Architecture and Order: Approaches to Social Space*, ed. Michael Parker Pearson and Colin Richards, pp. 1–37. London: Routledge.

Parsons, Jeffrey R.

1974   Development of a Prehistoric Complex Society: A Regional Perspective from the Valley of Mexico. *Journal of Field Archaeology* 9(1–2):81–108.

Parsons, Lee Allen

    The Origins of Maya Art: Monumental Stone Sculpture of Kaminaljuyu, Guatemala, and the Southern Pacific Coast. Studies in Pre-Columbian Art and Archaeology, no. 28. Washington, D.C.: Dumbarton Oaks.

Pasztory, Esther

1972   The Historical and Religious Significance of the Middle Classic Ballgame. In *Religión en Mesoamérica: XII Mesa Redonda de la Sociedad Mexicana de Antropología*, ed. Jaime Litvak King and Noemí Castillo Tejero, pp. 441–455. Mexico City: Sociedad Mexicana de Antropología.

1993   An Image Is Worth a Thousand Words: Teotihuacan and the Meanings of Style in Classic Mesoamerica. In *Latin American Horizons*, ed. Don S. Rice, pp. 113–145. Washington, D.C.: Dumbarton Oaks.

Paxton, Merideth

2001   *The Cosmos of the Yucatec Maya: Cycles and Steps from the Madrid Codex.* Albuquerque: University of New Mexico Press.

Peeler, Damon E., and Marcus C. Winter

1992   Mesoamerican Site Orientations and Their Relationship to the 260-day Ritual Period. *Notas Mesoamericanas* 11:37–62.

Pío Pérez, Juan

2001 [1846]   Antigua cronología yucateca. In *The Decipherment of Ancient Maya Writing*, ed. Stephen Houston, Oswaldo Chinchilla Mazariegos, and David Stuart, pp. 210–223. Norman: University of Oklahoma Press.

Pohl, Mary D.

1985   The Privileges of Maya Elites: Prehistoric Vertebrate Fauna from Seibal. In *Prehistoric Lowland Maya Environment and Subsistence Economy*, ed. Mary Pohl, pp. 133–145. Peabody Museum Papers, vol. 77. Cambridge, Mass.: Peabody Museum, Harvard University.

2001   Economic Foundations of Olmec Civilization in the Gulf Coast Lowlands of México. http://www.famsi.org/reports/99069/. Accessed August 29, 2006.

Pohl, Mary D., Kevin O. Pope, John G. Jones, John S. Jacob, Dolores R. Piperno, Susan D. deFrance, David L. Lentz, John A. Gifford, Marie E. Danforth, and J. Kathryn Josserand

1996   Early Agriculture in the Maya Lowlands. *Latin American Antiquity* 7(4):355–372.

Pohl, Mary D., Kevin O. Pope, and Christopher von Nagy

2002   Olmec Origins of Mesoamerican Writing. *Science* 298:1984–1987.

Pohorilenko, Anatole

1996   Portable Carvings in the Olmec Style. In *Olmec Art of Ancient Mexico*, ed. Elizabeth P. Benson and Beatriz de la Fuente, pp. 119–131. Washington, D.C.: National Gallery of Art.

Pool, Christopher A.

1997   The Spatial Structure of Formative Houselots at Bezuapan. In *Olmec to Aztec: Settlement Patterns in the Ancient Gulf Lowlands*, ed. Barbara L. Stark and Philip J. Arnold III, pp. 40–67. Tucson: University of Arizona Press.

2000   From Olmec to Epi-Olmec at Tres Zapotes, Veracruz, Mexico. In *Olmec Art and Archaeology in Mesoamerica*, ed. John E. Clark and Mary E. Pye, 137–153. Washington, D.C.: National Gallery of Art.

2003   (ed.) *Settlement Archaeology and Political Economy at Tres Zapotes, Veracruz, Mexico*. Monograph 50. Los Angeles: Cotsen Institute of Archaeology, University of California, Los Angeles.

Porter, James B.

1989   Olmec Colossal Heads as Recarved Thrones: "Mutilation," Revolution, and Recarving. *RES* 1718:23–29.

1990   Las cabezas colosales olmecas como altares reesculpidos: "mutilación," revolución y reesculpido. *Arqueología* 3:91–97.

1996   Celtiform Stelae. In *Beyond Indigenous Voices: LAILA/ALILA 11th International Symposium on Latin American Indian Literatures*, ed. Mary Preuss, pp. 65–72. Lancaster, Calif.: Labyrinthos.

Powis, Terry G. (ed.)

2005a   *New Perspectives on Formative Mesoamerican Cultures*. B.A.R. International Series 1377. Oxford: Archaeopress.

2005b   Formative Mesoamerican Cultures: An Introduction. In *New Perspectives on Formative Mesoamerican Cultures*, ed. Terry G. Powis, pp. 1–14. B.A.R. International Series 1377. Oxford: Archaeopress.

Prater, Ariadne

1989   Kaminaljuyú and Izapan Style Art. In *New Frontiers in the Archaeology of the Pacific Coast of Southern Mesoamerica*, ed. Frederick Bove and Lynette Heller, pp. 125–133. Anthropological Research Papers, no. 39. Tempe: Arizona State University.

Puleston, Dennis

1979   An Epistemological Pathology and the Collapse, or Why the Maya Kept the Short Count. In *Maya Archaeology and Ethnohistory*, ed. Norman Hammond and Gordon R. Willey, pp. 63–74. Austin: University of Texas Press.

Puleston, Dennis, and Olga Puleston

1971   An Ecological Approach to the Origins of Maya Civilization. *Archaeology* 24(4):330–337.

Pyne, Nanette M.

1976   The Fire-Serpent and Were-Jaguar in Formative Oaxaca: A Contingency Table Analysis. In *The Early Mesoamerican Village*, ed. Kent V. Flannery, pp. 272–282. New York: Academic Press.

Quirarte, Jacinto

1977   Early Art Styles of Mesoamerica and Early Classic Maya Art. In *Origins of Maya Civilization*, ed. Richard E. W. Adams, pp. 249–283. Albuquerque: University of New Mexico Press.

1979   Sculptural Documents on the Origins of Maya Civilization. *Actes du XLII Congrès International des Américanistes*, vol. 8, pp. 189–196. Paris.

1981   Tricephalic Units in Olmec, Izapan-style, and Maya Art. In *The Olmec and Their Neighbors: Essays in Memory of Matthew W. Stirling*, org. Michael D. Coe and David C. Grove, ed. Elizabeth P. Benson, pp. 289–308. Washington, D.C.: Dumbarton Oaks.

Recinos, Adrián, and Delia Goetz (trans.)

1953   *The Annals of the Cakchiquels*. Norman: University of Oklahoma Press.

Redfield, Robert, and Alfonso Villa Rojas

1962 [1934]   *Chan Kom: A Maya Village.* Chicago: University of Chicago Press.

Reents-Budet, Dorie

1994   *Painting the Maya Universe: Royal Ceramics of the Classic Period.* Durham, N.C.: Duke University Press.

Reese-Taylor, Kathryn, and Debra S. Walker

2002   The Passage of the Late Preclassic into the Early Classic. In *Ancient Maya Political Economies*, ed. Marilyn A. Masson and David A. Freidel, pp. 87–122. Walnut Creek, Calif.: AltaMira Press.

Reilly, F. Kent, III

1991   Olmec Iconographic Influences on the Symbols of Maya Rulership: An Examination of Possible Sources. In *Sixth Palenque Round Table, 1986*, gen. ed. Merle Greene Robertson, pp. 151–166. Norman: University of Oklahoma Press.

1994   Visions to Another World: Art, Shamanism, and Political Power in Middle Formative Mesoamerica. Ph.D. dissertation, University of Texas at Austin.

1999   Mountains of Creation and Underworld Portals: The Ritual Function of Olmec Architecture at La Venta, Tabasco. In *Mesoamerican Architecture as a Cultural Symbol*, ed. Jeff Karl Kowalski, pp. 14–39. New York: Oxford University Press.

2000   Art, Ritual, and Rulership in the Olmec World. In *The Ancient Civilizations of Mesoamerica: A Reader*, ed. Michael E. Smith and Marilyn A. Masson, pp. 369–399. Malden, Mass.: Blackwell Publishers. (Originally published in 1995 in *The Olmec World: Ritual and Rulership*, pp. 27–45. Princeton, N.J.: The Art Museum, Princeton University.)

2005   Olmec Ideological, Ritual, and Symbolic Contributions to the Institution of Classic Maya Kingship. In *Lords of Creation: The Origins of Sacred Maya Kingship*, ed. Virginia M. Fields and Dorie Reents-Budet, pp. 30–36. Los Angeles, Calif.: Los Angeles County Museum of Art and Scala Publishers Ltd.

Reilly, F. Kent, III, and James F. Garber

2003   The Symbolic Representation of Warfare in Formative Period Mesoamerica. In *Ancient Mesoamerican Warfare*, ed. M. Kathryn Brown and Travis W. Stanton, pp. 127–148. Walnut Creek, Calif.: AltaMira Press.

Rice, Don S., and T. Patrick Culbert

1990   Historical Contexts for Population Reconstruction in the Maya Lowlands. In *Precolumbian Population History in the Maya Lowlands*, ed. T. Patrick Culbert and Don S. Rice, pp. 1–36. Albuquerque: University of New Mexico Press.

Rice, Prudence M.

1999   On the Origins of Pottery. *Journal of Archaeological Method and Theory* 6(1):1–54.

2004   *Maya Political Science: Time, Astronomy, and the Cosmos.* Austin: University of Texas Press.

2007   The Classic Maya "Collapse" and Its Causes: The Role of Warfare? In *Gordon R. Willey's Contributions to American Archaeology: A Contemporary Perspective*, ed. William Fash and Jeremy A. Sabloff, pp. 141–186. Norman: University of Oklahoma Press.

N.d.a.   The Las Bocas Mirror. Manuscript in possession of the author.

N.d.b.   Time, Power, and the Maya. *Late American Antiquity* (accepted for publication).

Rice, Prudence M., Helen V. Michel, Frank Asaro, and Fred Stross

1985   Provenience Analysis of Obsidians from the Central Peten Lakes Region, Guatemala. *American Antiquity* 50(3):591–604.

Richards, Janet, and Mary Van Buren (eds.)

2000   *Order, Legitimacy, and Wealth in Ancient States.* Cambridge: Cambridge University Press.

Ricketson, Oliver G.

1928   Notes on Two Maya Astronomic Observatories. *American Anthropologist* 30:434–444.

Rissolo, Dominique

2005   Beneath the Yalahau: Emerging Patterns of Ancient Maya Ritual Cave Use from Northern Quintana Roo, Mexico. In *In the Maw of the Earth Monster: Mesoamerican Ritual Cave Use*, ed. James E. Brady and Keith M. Prufer, pp. 342–372. Austin: University of Texas Press.

Roach, John

2006   Oldest Dentistry in Americas Found—Fang Dentures? *National Geographic News* (June 14, 2006). http://news.nationalgeographic.com/news/2006/06/060614-oldest-teeth.html. Accessed August 30, 2006.

Rodríguez, María del Carmen, and Ponciano Ortiz Ceballos

1997   Olmec Ritual and Sacred Geography at Manatí. In *Olmec to Aztec: Settlement Patterns in the Ancient Gulf Lowlands*, ed. Barbara L. Stark and Philip J. Arnold III, pp. 68–95. Tucson: University of Arizona Press.

Rosenswig, Robert M., and Marilyn A. Masson

2001   Seven New Preceramic Sites Documented in Northern Belize. *Mexicon* 23:138–140.

Rothchild, Irving

2006   Induction, Deduction, and the Scientific Method: An Eclectic Overview of the Practice of Science. http://www.ssr.org/induction.html. Accessed August 30, 2006.

Roys, Ralph L.

1967 [1933] *The Book of Chilam Balam of Chumayel.* Norman: University of Oklahoma Press.

Rust, William F., III

1992   New Ceremonial and Settlement Evidence at La Venta, and Its Relation to Preclassic Maya Cultures. In *New Theories on the Ancient Maya*, ed. Elin C. Danien and Robert J. Sharer, pp. 123–129. University Museum Symposium Series, vol. 3, University Museum Monograph 77. Philadelphia: The University Museum, University of Pennsylvania.

Rust, William F., III, and Barbara W. Leyden

1994   Evidence of Maize Use at Early and Middle Preclassic La Venta Olmec Sites. In *Corn and Culture in the Prehistoric New World*, ed. Sissel Johannessen and Christine A. Hastorf, pp. 181–201. Boulder, Colo.: Westview Press.

Rust, William F., and Robert J. Sharer

1988   Olmec Settlement Data from La Venta, Tabasco, Mexico. *Science* 242:102–104.

Sabloff, Jeremy A.

1975   Ceramics. In *Excavations at Seibal, Department of Peten, Guatemala.* Peabody Museum of Archaeology and Ethnology, Memoirs, vol. 13, no. 2. Cambridge, Mass.: Harvard University.

Sahlins, Marshall

1968   *Tribesmen.* Englewood Cliffs, N.J.: Prentice-Hall.

Sanders, William T., and Barbara Price

1968   *Mesoamerica: The Evolution of a Civilization.* New York: Random House.

Santley, Robert S., Philip J. Arnold III, and Thomas P. Barrett

1997   Formative Period Settlement Patterns in the Tuxtla Mountains. In *Olmec to Aztec: Settlement Patterns in the Ancient Gulf Lowlands*, ed. Barbara L. Stark and Philip J. Arnold III, pp. 174–205. Tucson: University of Arizona Press.

Santos Granero, Fernando

1986   Power, Ideology and the Ritual of Production in Lowland South America. *Man* (N.s.) 21:657–679.

Sassaman, Kenneth E.

2004   Complex Hunter-Gatherers in Evolution and History: A North American Perspective. *Journal of Archaeological Research* 12(3):227–280.

Satterthwaite, Linton

1965   Calendrics of the Maya Lowlands. In *Archaeology of Southern Mesoamerica, Part 2*, vol. ed. Gordon R. Willey, pp. 603–631. *Handbook of Middle American Indians, vol. 3*, gen. ed. Robert Wauchope. Austin: University of Texas Press.

Saturno, William

2006   The Dawn of Maya Gods and Kings. *National Geographic* 209(1):68–77.

Saturno, William A., David Stuart, and Boris Beltrán

2006   Early Maya Writing at San Bartolo, Guatemala. *Science* 311:1281–1283 *http://www.science mag.org/cgi/content/short/311/5765/1281. Accessed August 30, 2006.*

Saturno, William A., Karl A. Taube, and David Stuart

2005   The Murals of San Bartolo, El Petén, Guatemala. Part 1: The North Wall. *Ancient America*, vol. 7. Barnardsville, N.C.: Center for Ancient American Studies.

Scarborough, Vernon L., and David Wilcox (eds.)

1991   *The Mesoamerican Ballgame.* Tucson: University of Arizona Press.

Scheffler, Timothy E.

2002   El Gigante Rock Shelter: Archaic Mesoamerica and Transitions to Settled Life. www.famsi.org /reports/00071/index.html. Accessed August 30, 2006.

Schele, Linda

1992   *The Proceedings of the Maya Hieroglyphic Workshop, March 14–15, 1992*, trans. and ed. Phil Wanyerka. Austin: Department of Art History, University of Texas at Austin.

Schele, Linda, and David Freidel

1990   *A Forest of Kings: The Untold Story of the Ancient Maya.* New York: William Morrow.

Schele, Linda, Nikolai Grube, and Erik Boot

1995   Some Suggestions on the K'atun Prophecies in the Books of Chilam Balam in Light of Classic-Period History. *Texas Notes on Precolumbian Art, Writing, and Culture*, no. 72. Austin: Center of the History and Art of Ancient American Culture, Art Department, University of Texas at Austin.

Schele, Linda, and Julia Guernsey Kappelman

2001   What the Heck's Coatépec? The Formative Roots of an Enduring Mythology. In *Landscape and Power in Ancient Mesoamerica*, ed. Rex Koontz, Kathryn Reese-Taylor, and Annabeth Headrick, pp. 29–53. Boulder, Colo.: Westview Press.

Schele, Linda, and Peter Mathews

1998   *The Code of Kings: The Language of Seven Sacred Maya Temples and Tombs.* New York: Simon and Schuster.

Schele, Linda, and Mary Ellen Miller

1986 *The Blood of Kings: Dynasty and Ritual in Maya Art*. Dallas, Tex.: Kimbell Art Museum.

Schieber de Lavarreda, Christa

1994 Abaj Takalik: hallazgo de un juego de pelota del preclásico medio. In *Simposio de investigaciones arqueológicas en Guatemala, 1993*, ed. Juan Pedro Laporte, pp. 95–111. Guatemala City: Museo Nacional de Arqueología y Etnología, Ministerio de Cultura y Deportes, Instituto de Antropología e Historia, and Asociación Tikal.

Schultze Jena, Leonhard

1986 [1933] The Numerical Foundations of the Indian Calendar. In *Symbol and Meaning Beyond the Closed Community: Essays in Mesoamerican Ideas*, ed. Gary H. Gossen, pp. 69–76. Studies on Culture and Society, vol. 1. Albany: Institute for Mesoamerican Studies, State University of New York at Albany. (Translated from *Indiana* 1:32–38 by Peter T. Furst and published as pp. 72–75 in *Human Biology and the Origin of the 260-day Sacred Almanac: The Contribution of Leonhard Schultze Jena [1872–1955]*.)

Scott, Ann M., and James E. Brady

2005 Formative Cave Utilization: An Examination of Mesoamerican Ritual Foundations. In *New Perspectives on Formative Mesoamerican Cultures*, ed. Terry G. Powis, pp. 147–157. B.A.R. International Series 1377. Oxford: Archaeopress.

Sedat, David W.

1992 Preclassic Notation and the Development of Maya Writing. In *New Theories on the Ancient Maya*, ed. Elin C. Danien and Robert J. Sharer, pp. 81–90. University Museum Symposium Series, vol. 3. Philadelphia: The University Museum, University of Pennsylvania.

Service, Elman R.

1966 *Primitive Social Organization: An Evolutionary Perspective*. New York: Random House.

1975 *Origins of the State and Civilization: The Process of Cultural Evolution*. New York: W. W. Norton.

Shanks, Michael, and Christopher Tilley

1987 *Social Theory and Archaeology*. Oxford: Polity Press.

Sharer, Robert J.

1989a In the Land of Olmec Archaeology. *Journal of Field Archaeology* 9(2):254–267.

1989b The Preclassic Origins of Maya Writing: A Highland Perspective. In *Word and Image in Maya Culture: Explorations in Language, Writing, and Representation*, ed. William F. Hanks and Don S. Rice, pp. 165–175. Salt Lake City: University of Utah Press.

1994 *The Ancient Maya* (5th ed.). Stanford, Calif.: Stanford University Press.

2003 Tikal and the Copan Dynastic Founding. In *Tikal: Dynasties, Foreigners, and Affairs of State: Advancing Maya Archaeology*, ed. Jeremy A. Sabloff, pp. 319–353. Santa Fe, N.M.: School of American Research Press.

Sharer, Robert J., and David C. Grove (eds.)

1989 *Regional Perspectives on the Olmec*. Cambridge: Cambridge University Press and School of American Research.

Sharer, Robert J., with Loa P. Traxler

2006 *The Ancient Maya* (6th ed.). Stanford, Calif.: Stanford University Press.

Smalley, John, and Michael Blake

2003 Sweet Beginnings: Stalk Sugar and the Domestication of Maize. *Current Anthropology* 44(5):675–703.

Smith, A. Ledyard

1950 *Uaxactun, Guatemala: Excavations of 1931–1937*. Pub. 588. Washington, D.C.: Carnegie Institution of Washington.

Smith, Michael E.

2003 Can We Read Cosmology in Ancient Maya City Plans? Comment on Ashmore and Sabloff. *Latin American Antiquity* 14(2):221–228.

Smith, Virginia G.

1984 *Izapa Relief Carving: Form, Content, Rules for Design, and Role in Mesoamerican Art History and Archaeology*. Studies in Pre-Columbian Art and Archaeology, no. 27. Washington, D.C.: Dumbarton Oaks.

Solís, Felipe

2004 Introduction. In *The Aztec Empire*, curated by Felipe Solís, pp. 26–35. New York: The Guggenheim Museum.

Spence, Michael W., Christine E. White, Fred J. Longstaffe, and Kimberly R. Law

2004 Victims of the Victims: Human Trophies Worn by Sacrificed Soldiers from the Feathered Serpent Pyramid, Teotihuacan. *Ancient Mesoamerica* 15(1):1–15.

Spinden, Herbert

1946 *Ancient Civilizations of Mexico and Central America*. Handbook Series No. 3. New York: American Museum.

Sprajc, Ivan

1996 Venus, lluvia y maíz: simbolismo y astronomía en la cosmovisión mesoamericana.

Colección Científica, vol. 318. Mexico City: Instituto Nacional de Antropología e Historia.

2000   Astronomical Alignments at Teotihuacan. *Latin American Antiquity* 11(4):403–415.

2005   More on Mesoamerican Cosmology and City Plans. *Latin American Antiquity* 16(2):209–216.

Stanger-Hall, Kathrin

2005   Letter re Lipton. *Science* 308:1409.

Stanton, Travis W., and Traci Ardren

2005   The Middle Formative of Yucatan in Context: The View from Yaxuna. *Ancient Mesoamerica* 16(1):213–228.

Stark, Barbara L. (ed.)

1991   *Settlement Archaeology of Cerro de las Mesas, Veracruz, Mexico.* Monograph 34. Los Angeles: University of California, Los Angeles Institute of Archaeology.

Stark, Barbara L., and Philip J. Arnold III (eds.)

1997   *Olmec to Aztec: Settlement Patterns in the Ancient Gulf Lowlands.* Tucson: University of Arizona Press.

Steward, Julian

1938   *Basin-Plateau Aboriginal Sociopolitical Groups.* Bureau of American Ethnology Bulletin 120. Washington, D.C.: Smithsonian Institution.

Stewart, J. D.

1981   Comment on Graulich. *Current Anthropology* 22(1):54.

Stirling, Matthew W.

1955   *Stone Monuments of the Río Chiquito, Veracruz, Mexico.* Bureau of American Ethnology Bulletin 157. Anthropological Papers 43:1–23. Washington, D.C.: Smithsonian Institution.

Stone, Andrea

1989   The Painted Walls of Xibalba: Maya Cave Painting as Evidence of Cave Ritual. In *Word and Image in Maya Culture: Explorations in Language, Writing, and Representation*, ed. William F. Hanks and Don S. Rice, pp. 319–335. Salt Lake City: University of Utah Press.

Stross, Brian

1994   Maize and Fish: The Iconography of Power in Late Formative Mesoamerica. *RES* 25:9–35.

Stuart, David

1995   A Study of Maya Inscriptions. Ph.D. dissertation, Vanderbilt University.

1996   Kings of Stone: A Consideration of Stelae in Ancient Maya Ritual and Representations. *RES* 29/30:148–171.

2000   "The Arrival of Strangers": Teotihuacan and Tollan in Classic Maya History. In *Mesoamerica's Classic Heritage: From Teotihuacan to the Aztecs*, ed. David Carrasco, Lindsay Jones, and Scott Sessions, pp. 465–513. Boulder: University Press of Colorado.

2004   The Entering of the Day: An Unusual Date from Northern Campeche. www.mesoweb.com/stuart/notes/EnteringDay.pdf. Accessed August 30, 2006.

2005   New Year Records in Classic Maya Inscriptions. *PARI Journal* 5(2):1–6. http://www.mesoweb.com/pari/publications/journal/502/NewYear.html. Accessed August 30, 2006.

Stuart, David, and Stephen Houston

1994   *Classic Maya Place Names.* Studies in Pre-Columbian Art and Archaeology, no. 33. Washington, D.C.: Dumbarton Oaks.

Stuart, L. C.

1964   Fauna of Middle America. In *Natural Environment and Early Cultures*, Robert C. West, vol. ed., pp. 316–362. Handbook of Middle American Indians, vol. 1, Robert Wauchope, gen. ed. Austin: University of Texas Press.

Sugiyama, Saburo

2004   Governance and Polity at Classic Teotihuacan. In *Mesoamerican Archaeology*, ed. Julia A. Hendon and Rosemary A. Joyce, pp. 97–123. Malden, Mass.: Blackwell Publishing.

Sullivan, Thelma D.

1986   A Scattering of Jades: The Words of the Aztec Elders. In *Symbol and Meaning Beyond the Closed Community: Essays in Mesoamerican Ideas*, ed. Gary H. Gossen, pp. 9–17. Studies on Culture and Society, vol. 1. Albany: Institute for Mesoamerican Studies, State University of New York at Albany.

Suyuc, Edgar, Beatriz Balcárcel, Francisco López, and Silvia Alvarado

2005   Excavaciones en el sitio La Muerta, cuenca Mirador, Petén. In *XVIII Simposio de Investigaciones Arqueológicas en Guatemala, 2004*, ed. Juan Pedro Laporte, Bárbara Arroyo, and Héctor E. Mejía, pp. 75–90. Guatemala City: Museo Nacional de Arqueología y Etnología, Ministerio de Cultura y Deportes, Instituto de Antropología e Historia, Asociación Tikal, and Foundation for the Advancement of Mesoamerican Studies, Inc.

Swadesh, Maurice

1967   Lexicostatistic Classification. In *Linguistics*, Handbook of Middle American Indians, vol. 5, vol. ed., Norman A. McQuown, pp. 79–115. Austin: University of Texas Press.

Symonds, Stacey Clover

1995   Settlement Distribution and the Development of Cultural Complexity in the Lower Coatzacoalcos Drainage, Veracruz, Mexico: An Archaeological Survey at San Lorenzo Tenochtitlan. Ph.D. dissertation, Vanderbilt University.

Symonds, Stacy C., and Roberto Lunagómez

1997   Settlement System and Population Development at San Lorenzo. In *Olmec to Aztec: Settlement Patterns in the Ancient Gulf Lowlands*, ed. Barbara L. Stark and Philip J. Arnold III, pp. 144–173. Tucson: University of Arizona Press.

Tarn, Nathaniel, and Martin Prechtel

1981   Metaphors of Relative Elevation, Position, and Ranking in Popol Vuh. *Estudios de Cultura Maya* 18:105–123.

Tate, Carolyn E.

2000   Patrons of Shamanic Power: La Venta's Supernatural Entities in Light of Mixe Beliefs. *Ancient Mesoamerica* 10(2):169–188.

2001   The Poetics of Power and Knowledge at La Venta. In *Landscape and Power in Ancient Mesoamerica*, ed. Rex Koontz, Kathryn Reese-Taylor, and Annabeth Headrick, pp. 137–168. Boulder, Colo.: Westview Press.

Tate, Carolyn, and Gordon Bendersky

1999   Olmec Sculptures of the Human Fetus. *P.A.R.I. Online Publications: Newsletter* 30:1–11. http://www.mesoweb.com/pari/publications/news_archive/30/olmec_sculpture.html. Accessed August 30, 2006.

Taube, Karl

1986   The Teotihuacan Cave of Origin: The Iconography and Architecture of Emergence Mythology in Mesoamerica and the American Southwest. *RES* 12:51–82.

1992   *The Major Gods of Ancient Yucatan.* Studies in Pre-Columbian Art & Archaeology, no. 32. Washington, D.C.: Dumbarton Oaks.

1993   *Aztec and Maya Myths.* Austin: University of Texas Press.

1996   The Olmec Maize God. *RES* 29/30:39–81.

1998   The Jade Hearth: Centrality, Rulership, and the Classic Maya Temple. In *Function and Meaning in Classic Maya Architecture*, ed. Stephen D. Houston, pp. 427–478. Washington, D.C.: Dumbarton Oaks.

2001   The Breath of Life: The Symbolism of Wind in Mesoamerica and the American Southwest. In *The Road to Aztlan: Art from a Mythic Homeland*, ed. Virginia M. Fields and Victor Zamudio-Taylor, pp. 102–123. Los Angeles, Calif.: Los Angeles County Museum of Art.

Tedlock, Barbara

1992a   *Time and the Highland Maya.* Albuquerque: University of New Mexico Press.

1992b   Mayan Calendars, Cosmology, and Astronomical Commensuration. In *New Theories on the Ancient Maya*, ed. Elin C. Danien and Robert J. Sharer, pp. 217–227. University Museum Symposium Series, vol. 3, University Museum Monograph 77. Philadelphia: The University Museum, University of Pennsylvania.

1992c   The Road of Light: Theory and Practice of Mayan Skywatching. In *The Sky in Mayan Literature*, ed. Anthony F. Aveni, pp. 18–42. Oxford: Oxford University Press.

Tedlock, Dennis

1985   (trans.) *Popol Vuh: The Definitive Edition of the Mayan Book of the Dawn of Life and the Glories of Gods and Kings.* New York: Simon and Schuster.

1992   The Popol Vuh as a Hieroglyphic Book. In *New Theories on the Ancient Maya*, ed. Elin C. Danien and Robert J. Sharer, pp. 229–240. University Museum Symposium Series vol. 3, University Museum Monograph 77. Philadelphia: The University Museum, University of Pennsylvania.

1996   (trans.) *Popol Vuh: The Definitive Edition of the Mayan Book of the Dawn of Life and the Glories of Gods and Kings* (rev. ed.). New York: Simon and Schuster.

Teeple, John D.

1926   Maya Inscription: The Venus Calendar and Another Correlation. *American Anthropologist* 28:108–115.

2001 [1928] Maya Inscriptions, VI: The Lunar Calendar and Its Relation to Maya History. In *The Decipherment of Ancient Maya Writing*, ed. Stephen Houston, Oswaldo Chinchilla Mazariegos, and David Stuart, pp. 241–254. Norman: University of Oklahoma Press.

Thomas, Cyrus

1885   Who Were the Moundbuilders? *American Antiquarian and Oriental Journal* 2:65–74.

Thompson, J. Eric S.

1930   *Ethnology of the Mayas of Southern and Central British Honduras.* Anthropological Series 2. Chicago: Field Museum of Natural History.

1932   The Solar Year of the Mayas at Quirigua, Guatemala. *Field Museum of Natural History, Anthropological Series* 17(4).

1962   *A Catalog of Maya Hieroglyphs.* Norman: University of Oklahoma Press.

1965a   Maya Hieroglyphic Writing. In *Archaeology of Southern Mesoamerica*, pt. 2, Gordon R. Willey, vol. ed., pp. 632–658. Handbook of Middle American Indians, vol. 3, Robert Wauchope, gen. ed. Austin: University of Texas Press.

1965b   Maya Creation Myths. *Estudios de Cultura Maya* 5:13–32.

1966   *Maya Hieroglyphic Writing*. Norman: University of Oklahoma Press.

1970   *Maya History and Religion*. Norman: University of Oklahoma Press.

2001 [1944]   The Fish as a Maya Symbol for Counting and Further Discussion of Directional Glyphs. In *The Decipherment of Ancient Maya Writing*, ed. Stephen Houston, Oswaldo Chinchilla Mazariegos, and David Stuart, pp. 127–143. Norman: University of Oklahoma Press.

Thurber, Floyd, and Valerie Thurber

1961   A Comparative Analysis of Maya Hieroglyphs Muluk and Mol. *Estudios de Cultura Maya* 1:221–235.

Tichy, Franz

1981   Order and Relationship of Space and Time in Mesoamerica: Myth or Reality? In *Mesoamerican Sites and World-Views*, ed. Elizabeth P. Benson, pp. 217–245. Washington, D.C.: Dumbarton Oaks.

Tokovinine, Alexandre

N.d.   The Royal Ball Game of the Ancient Maya: An Epigrapher's View. http://www.mayavase.com /alex/alexballgame.html. Accessed October 22, 2006.

Tolstoy, Paul

1989   Coapexco and Tlatilco: Sites with Olmec Materials in the Basin of Mexico. In *Regional Perspectives on the Olmec*, ed. Robert J. Sharer and David C. Grove, pp. 85–121. Cambridge: Cambridge University Press and School of American Research.

Torroni, A., T. G. Schurr, C. C. Yang, E. J. Szathmary, R. C. Williams, M. S. Schanfield, G. A. Troup, W. C. Knowler, D. N. Lawrence, and K. M. Weiss

1992   Native American Mitochondrial DNA Analysis Indicates that the Amerind and the Nadene Populations Were Founded by Two Independent Migrations. *Genetics* 130(1):153–162. http://www.ncbi.nlm.nih.gov /entrez/query.fcgi?db=PubMed&cmd=Retrieve &dopt=Citation&list_uids=92120512. Accessed August 30, 2006.

Tozzer, Alfred M. (ed.)

1941 [1966]   *Landa's Relación de las cosas de Yucatán: A Translation*. Papers of the Peabody Museum of Archaeology and Ethnology, no. 28. Cambridge, Mass.: Peabody Museum, Harvard University.

Traxler, Loa P.

2004   Redesigning Copan: Early Architecture of the Polity Center. In *Understanding Early Classic Copan*, ed. Ellen E. Bell, Marcello A. Canuto, and Robert J. Sharer, pp. 53–64. Philadelphia: University of Pennsylvania Museum of Archaeology and Anthropology.

Turner, Christy

1984   Advances in the Dental Search for Native American Origins. *Acta Anthropogenetica* 8(1 and 2):23–78.

Upham, Steadman (ed.)

1990   *The Evolution of Political Systems: Sociopolitics in Small-scale Sedentary Societies*. Cambridge: Cambridge University Press and School of American Research.

Urton, Gary

2003   *Signs of the Inka Khipu: Binary Coding in the Andean Knotted-String Records*. Austin: University of Texas Press.

2005   Khipu Archives: Duplicate Accounts and Identity Labels in the Inka Knotted String Records. *Latin American Antiquity* 16(2):147–167.

Valdés, Juan Antonio

1992   Desarrollo cultural y señales de alarma entre los mayas: el Preclásico Tardío y la transición hacia el Clásico Temprano. In *The Emergence of Lowland Maya Civilization: The Transition from the Preclassic to the Early Classic*, ed. Nikolai Grube, pp. 71–85. Acta Mesoamericana 8. Mockmuhl: Verlag Anton Saurwein.

1997   Proyecto Miraflores II dentro del marco pre-clásico de Kaminaljuyú. In *X Simposio de Investigaciones Arqueológicas en Guatemala*, ed. Juan Pedro Laporte and Héctor L. Escobedo, pp. 81–91. Guatemala City: Museo Nacional de Arqueología y Etnología, Ministerio de Cultura y Deportes, Instituto de Antropología e Historia, and Asociación Tikal.

Valdés, Juan Antonio, and Lori E. Wright

2004   The Early Classic and Its Antecedents at Kaminaljuyu: A Complex Society with Complex Problems. In *Understanding Early Classic Copan*, ed. Ellen E. Bell, Marcelo A. Canuto, and Robert J. Sharer, pp. 337–355. Philadelphia: The University Museum, University of Pennsylvania.

Velázquez Valdez, Ricardo

1980   Recent Discoveries in the Caves of Loltun, Yucatan, Mexico. *Mexicon* 2:53–55.

Viel, René, and Jay Hall

2000   Las relaciones entre Copan y Kaminaljuyu. In *XIII Simposio de Investigaciones Arqueológicas en Guatemala, 1999*, ed. Juan Pedro Laporte, Héctor Escobedo, and Bárbara Arroyo, pp. 127–134. Guatemala City: Museo Nacional de Arqueología y Etnología, Ministerio de Cultura y Deportes, Instituto de Antropología e Historia, and Asociación Tikal.

Villa Rojas, Alfonso

1988   The Concepts of Space and Time among the Contemporary Maya. In *Time and Reality in the Thought of the Maya* (2nd ed.), by Miguel León-Portilla, pp. 113–159. Norman: University of Oklahoma Press.

von Euw, Eric, and Ian Graham

1984   Xultun, La Honradez, and Uaxactun. *Corpus of Maya Hieroglyphic Inscriptions*, vol. 5, pt. 2. Cambridge, Mass.: Peabody Museum of Archaeology and Ethnology.

von Nagy, Christopher

1997   The Geoarchaeology of Settlement in the Grijalva Delta. In *Olmec to Aztec: Settlement Patterns in the Ancient Gulf Lowlands*, ed. Barbara L. Stark and Philip J. Arnold III, pp. 253–277. Tucson: University of Arizona Press.

Voorhies, Barbara

1976   *The Chantuto People: An Archaic Period Society of the Chiapas Littoral, Mexico.* Papers of the New World Archaeological Foundation, no. 41. Provo, Utah: New World Archaeological Foundation, Brigham Young University.

1989a   (ed.) *Ancient Trade and Tribute: Economies of the Soconusco Region of Mesoamerica.* Salt Lake City: University of Utah Press.

1989b   An Introduction to the Soconusco and Its Prehistory. In *Ancient Trade and Tribute: Economies of the Soconusco Region of Mesoamerica*, ed. Barbara Voorhies, pp. 1–18. Salt Lake City: University of Utah Press.

2004   *Coastal Collectors in the Holocene: The Chantuto People of Southwest Mexico.* Gainesville: University Press of Florida.

Voorhies, Barbara, and George H. Michaels

1989   *Final Report to the National Geographic Society, grant no. 3689–87.* Washington, D.C.: National Geographic Society.

Voorhies, Barbara, Douglas J. Kennett, John G. Jones, and Thomas A. Wake

2002   A Middle Archaic Archaeological Site on the West Coast of Mexico. *Latin American Antiquity* 13(2):179–200.

Wanyerka, Phil

1999   Pecked Cross and Patolli Petroglyphs of the Lagarto Ruins, Stann Creek District, Belize. *Mexicon* 21:108–112.

Watanabe, John M.

1983   In the World of the Sun: A Cognitive Model of Mayan Cosmology. *Man* (N.s.) 18(4):710–728.

Wauchope, Robert

1962   *Lost Tribes and Sunken Continents.* Chicago: University of Chicago Press.

Waugh, Alexander

1999   *Time: Its Origin, Its Enigma, Its History.* New York: Carroll and Graf Publishers.

Weiant, C. E.

1943   *An Introduction to the Ceramics of Tres Zapotes, Veracruz, Mexico.* Bulletin 139. Washington, D.C.: Bureau of American Ethnology

Wendt, Carl J.

2005a   Using Refuse Disposal Patterns to Infer Olmec Site Structure in the San Lorenzo Region, Veracruz, Mexico. *Latin American Antiquity* 16(4):449–466.

2005b   Excavations at El Remolino: Household Archaeology in the San Lorenzo Olmec Region. *Journal of Field Archaeology* 30:163–180.

White, Leslie

1959   *The Evolution of Culture: The Development of Civilization to the Fall of Rome.* New York: McGraw-Hill.

Whitrow, G. J.

1988   *Time in History: Views of Time from Prehistory to the Present Day.* Oxford: Oxford University Press.

Wichmann, Søren

1995   *The Relationship among the Mixe-Zoquean Languages of Mexico.* Salt Lake City: University of Utah Press.

2002   Contextualizing Proto-Languages, Homelands and Distant Genetic Relationship: Some Reflections on the Comparative Method from a Mesoamerican Perspective. In *Examining the Farming/Language Dispersal Hypothesis*, ed. Peter Bellwood and Colin Renfrew, pp. 321–329. McDonald Institute Monograph. Cambridge: McDonald Institute for Archaeological Research.

2004   The Grammar of the Half-Period Glyph. In *The Linguistics of Maya Writing*, ed. Søren Wichmann, pp. 327–337. Salt Lake City: University of Utah Press.

Wilkerson, S. Jeffrey K.

1981   The Northern Olmec and Pre-Olmec Frontier on the Gulf Coast. In *The Olmec and Their*

Neighbors: Essays in Memory of Matthew W. Stirling, org. Michael D. Coe and David C. Grove, ed. Elizabeth P. Benson, pp. 181–194. Washington, D.C.: Dumbarton Oaks.

1985 Observations on the Archaic Period of the Caribbean Coast: A Summary of the 1980 Belize Archaic Archaeological Reconnaissance Project. In *Fourth Palenque Round Table, 1980*, vol. ed., Elizabeth P. Benson, gen. ed., Merle Greene Robertson, pp. 277–280. San Francisco, Calif.: Pre-Columbian Art Research Institute.

Willey, Gordon R.

1977 The Rise of Maya Civilization: A Summary View. In *The Origins of Maya Civilization*, ed. Richard E. W. Adams, pp. 383–423. Albuquerque: University of New Mexico Press and School of American Research.

1978 *Excavations at Seibal, Department of Peten, Guatemala: Artifacts*. Memoirs of the Peabody Museum of Archaeology and Ethnology, vol. 14, no. 1. Cambridge: Harvard University.

Willey, Gordon R., and Phillip Phillips

1958 *Method and Theory in American Archaeology*. Chicago: University of Chicago Press.

Willey, Gordon R., and Jeremy A. Sabloff

1980 *A History of American Archaeology* (2nd ed.). San Francisco, Calif.: W. H. Freeman and Co.

Wilson, Samuel M., Harry B. Iceland, and Thomas R. Hester

1998 Preceramic Connections between Yucatán and the Caribbean. *Latin American Antiquity* 9(4):342–352.

Winchester, Simon

2001 *The Map That Changed the World: William Smith and the Birth of Modern Geology*. New York: Harper-Collins.

Winfield Capitaine, Fernando

1988 La Estela 1 de La Mojarra, Veracruz, México. *Research Reports in Maya Hieroglyphic Writing* 16. Washington, D.C.: Center for Maya Research.

Winter, Marcus

1976 The Archaeological Household Cluster in the Valley of Oaxaca. In *The Early Mesoamerican Village*, ed. Kent V. Flannery, pp. 25–30. New York: Academic Press.

Wittfogel, Karl A.

1957 *Oriental Despotism: A Comparative Study of Total Power*. New Haven, Conn.: Yale University Press.

Wolf, Eric

1966 *Peasants*. Englewood Cliffs, N.J.: Prentice-Hall.

Woodbury, Richard B., and Aubrey S. Trik

1953 *Ruins of Zaculeu, Guatemala*. Boston: United Fruit Company.

Worthy, Morgan, and Roy S. Dickens Jr.

1983 The Mesoamerican Pecked Cross as a Calendrical Device. *American Antiquity* 48(3):573–576.

Wright, Henry T.

1978 Toward an Explanation of the Origin of the State. In *Origins of the State: The Anthropology of Political Evolution*, ed. Ronald Cohen and Elman R. Service, pp. 49–68. Philadelphia, Pa.: Institute for the Study of Human Issues.

1984 Prestate Political Formations. In *On the Evolution of Complex Societies: Essays in Honor of Harry Hoijer, 1982*, ed. Timothy Earle, pp. 41–77. Malibu, Calif.: Undena Publications.

Wright, Stephen I., Irie Vroh Bi, Steve G. Schroeder, Masanori Yamasaki, John F. Doebley, Michael D. McMullen, and Brandon S. Gaut

2005 The Effects of Artificial Selection on the Maize Genome. *Science* 308:1310–1314.

Yoffee, Norman

1993 Too Many Chiefs? (or, Safe Texts for the '90s). In *Archaeological Theory: Who Sets the Agenda?*, ed. Norman Yoffee and Andrew Sherratt, pp. 60–78. Cambridge: Cambridge University Press.

Zaro, Gregory, and Jon C. Lohse

2005 Agricultural Rhythms and Rituals: Ancient Maya Solar Observations in Hinterland Blue Creek, Northwestern Belize. *Latin American Antiquity* 16(1):81–98.

Zeitlin, Robert N.

1984 A Summary Report on Three Seasons of Field Investigations into the Archaic Period Prehistory of Lowland Belize. *American Anthropologist* 86(2):358–369.

Zeitlin, Robert N., and Judith Francis Zeitlin

2000 The Paleoindian and Archaic Cultures of Mesoamerica. In *The Cambridge History of the Native Peoples of the Americas*, ed. Richard E. W. Adams and Murdo J. MacLeod, pp. 45–121. Cambridge: Cambridge University Press.

Index